When This Cruel War Is Over

The Civil War Letters of
CHARLES HARVEY BREWSTER

Edited with an introduction by
David W. Blight

The University of Massachusetts Press
AMHERST

Copyright © 1992 by Historic Northampton

All rights reserved

Printed in the United States of America

LC 91-38861

ISBN 0-87023-773-X

Designed by Jack Harrison

Set in Adobe Caslon by Keystone Typesetting, Inc.

Printed and bound by Thomson-Shore, Inc.

Library of Congress Cataloging-in-Publication Data

Brewster, Charles Harvey, 1833–1893.

When this cruel war is over : the Civil War letters of Charles

Harvey Brewster / edited with an introduction by David W. Blight.

p.   cm.

Includes bibliographical references.

ISBN 0–87023–773–X (alk. paper)

1. Brewster, Charles Harvey, 1833–1893—Correspondence.

2. United States. Army. Massachusetts. Infantry Regiment, 10th (1861–1864)—Biography.

3. United States—History—Civil War, 1861–1865—Personal narratives.

4. Massachusetts—History—Civil War, 1861–1865—Personal narratives.

5. Soldiers—Massachusetts—Correspondence.

I. Blight, David W.   II. Title.

E513.5 10th.B74   1992

973.7′444′092—dc 20

[B]   91–38861

CIP

British Library Cataloguing in Publication data are available.

Frontispiece: Portrait of Lt. Charles Harvey Brewster, Adjutant, Tenth Massachusetts

Volunteers, c. 1864. *Courtesy of Jonathan Allured*

Maps reproduced on pages 2 and 98 from *The Civil War by Day,* by E. B. Long.

Copyright © 1971 by E. B. Long. Used by permission of Doubleday, a division of Bantam

Doubleday Dell Publishing Group, Inc.

CONTENTS

PREFACE

In the fall of 1983, while working as a volunteer at the Northampton Historical Society, I chanced upon a set of four journals containing a series of letters.* Written between 1861 and 1864, the letters recorded the Civil War experiences of Charles Harvey Brewster, a native of Northampton who had served with the Tenth Massachusetts Regiment. Yet, curiously, they were not written in Brewster's own hand. They had been copied into the journals many years after the war by one of Brewster's daughters, Mary Kate Brewster.

Interesting as the letters were, I doubt that I would have paid them much notice had I not also discovered, tucked between the pages of one volume, the original version of one of the transcriptions. A quick comparison of the two documents revealed that Miss Brewster had been a zealous editor, freely deleting or substantially altering entire passages. The changes seemed to reflect the good intentions of a daughter eager to portray her father in a favorable light, but I could not help wondering how much had been lost as a result of her editorial efforts.

Fortunately, the letter kept with the journals was not the only original to survive. More than two hundred others were in the possession of Brewster's grandson, Jonathan Allured. When I made contact with Allured at his home in Hickory, North Carolina, he invited me to visit and examine the letters first-hand. The treasure trove of Civil War memorabilia I found in his basement exceeded all expectation. In addition to his grandfather's correspondence, Jonathan Allured held more than a hundred Civil War letters from other members of the family, swords, spurs, commissions, photographs, a daily journal, and other assorted documents from the front. The two of us spent a weekend poring over the various artifacts, after which Allured graciously offered to loan the entire letter collection to the Northampton Historical Society.

Once back home, I immediately began organizing the letters. Because they

---

*In 1989 the Northampton Historical Society changed its name to Historic Northampton.

were dry and tightly folded, the first step was to humidify and flatten them. I then separated the letters by month and year, matched them with envelopes and errant pages, and prepared for the laborious task of transcription. I consulted with historian William McFeely, who advised me to transcribe the letters exactly as they were written, preserving every misspelling, punctuation error, and awkward turn of phrase. Justine Caldwell, a fellow trustee of the Northampton Historical Society, volunteered to type the letters, a job that required saintly patience and dedication. William Bernache, past president of the Boston Civil War Round Table, and Elliott Hoffman of the Quincy Historical Society carefully annotated all of the letters. The extent of their work is not fully reflected in this volume but will be of inestimable value to anyone working on the complete, unedited collection.

Since my first visit to his home nearly a decade ago, Jonathan Allured has steadfastly supported my efforts to see his grandfather's letters in print. I want to thank him and his wife, Nancy, for the hospitality and friendship they have extended to me and the generosity they have shown in formally donating the Brewster letters to Historic Northampton. I am also grateful to Ruth Wilbur, former director of the Northampton Historical Society, whose enthusiasm for the project never flagged. And, finally, I thank David Blight, whose talents as a historian will be evident to anyone who reads these remarkable letters and seeks to understand the context in which they were written more than a century ago.

James M. Parsons
Northampton, Massachusetts

EDITORIAL METHOD AND ACKNOWLEDGMENTS

Two hundred ten of Charles Harvey Brewster's Civil War letters have survived. One hundred ninety-two are original letters and eighteen others exist only as they were transcribed into journals by Brewster's daughter, Mary Kate Brewster, in 1893. Because of the sheer volume of the letters, and in the interest of clarity and to avoid repetition, I have selected 133 original letters for publication. In my selection I have attempted to represent the major themes of Brewster's thought and experience, as well as offer a chronological balance of his three and one-half years of service in the Union army. I have also included four of Mary Kate Brewster's "journal" letters in an epilogue. They represent an interesting example of the transmission of a Civil War veteran's experience into the memory of the next generation—in this case, a twenty-two-year-old daughter who in some cases recorded and in other cases re-created that experience. Brewster's spelling and grammar are preserved here intact. All letters are reprinted in full with no editorial deletions within any single letter. Only occasional paragraph breaks have been added to aid the reader. My annotation is intended as a guide not only to names, places, and some details of military movements, but also to the best examples of Brewster's values, attitudes, and emotions. In many ways, Brewster's letters stand on their own as an ordinary Yankee's self-reflective chronicle about the meaning of the Civil War. The letters are also a good source for historians, and, with that in mind, I have tried in the introductory essay to make a small contribution to the social and intellectual history of the Civil War.

In preparing this volume I have benefited from the expertise and encouragement of many people. Several years ago Jim Parsons discovered the Brewster letters. Without his dedicated detective work and his determined collection and transcriptions, publication of these letters would not have been possible. Indeed, Jim's pursuit and preservation of these letters is legendary in Northampton, and his knowledge, enthusiasm, and generosity have been indispensable to me. I am grateful to Marilyn Parsons for her kindness and hospitality during research

visits to the Parsons' basement. Jonathan Allured, Brewster's grandson, deserves everyone's gratitude for his cooperation in sharing his grandfather's treasures with the late twentieth century. Clark Dougan, my editor at the University of Massachusetts Press, first introduced this project to me; throughout the work, Clark has been an unfailing friend and adviser, as well as a superb critic. Joe Glatthaar's critical reading of my introduction was very helpful, and his work was a model in my effort to place Brewster's letters in the context of the new social history of the Civil War. Pam Wilkinson was a highly skilled copyeditor and Heidi Creamer performed several final editorial chores.

Historic Northampton, which owns the Brewster letters, offered me endless professional assistance and hospitality. Director Pamela Toma has been a wonderful guide into the vicissitudes of local history, and I am especially grateful to Terrie Korpita for all the hours she spent printing the final versions of the letters. William Bernache of Braintree, Massachusetts, and Elliott Hoffman of the Quincy, [Massachusetts] Historical Society deserve special recognition for their annotation work during earlier efforts to bring the Brewster letters to light. Hoffman has saved me from at least one glaring statistical error. At various stages, before and during my work on the project, Lynne Bassett, Justine Caldwell, Suzanne Stone-Duncan, and Ruth Wilbur have been instrumental in the transcription and preservation of these letters. Special thanks also go to the librarians at the Sophia Smith Collection, Smith College, the Forbes Library in Northampton, and the Robert Frost Library at Amherst College.

I owe an important debt to Joan Cashin for her advice on and conversations about the literature of gender and manhood in the nineteenth century. Stanley Elkins and Tom Grace offered helpful readings of the introduction as well as advice about the whole project. For their conversations and counsel about Brewster, male traditions, war in general, and Civil War memory in particular, I would like to thank Catherine Clinton, David Herbert Donald, Constance Ellis, David Glassberg, Hugh Hawkins, Norton Starr, Kevin Sweeney, Kim Townsend, and David Wills. Any errors and oversights in this book are, of course, my own.

As I first began to work on these letters in the fall of 1990, the students in my course on the Civil War and Reconstruction at Amherst College were an inspiration and a helpful sounding board. For sharing so many discussions of the impact of war on the imagination, and for her stern, critical reading of the introduction, I am, as always, grateful to Karin Beckett.

DWB
Amherst, Massachusetts
May 1991

When This
Cruel War Is Over

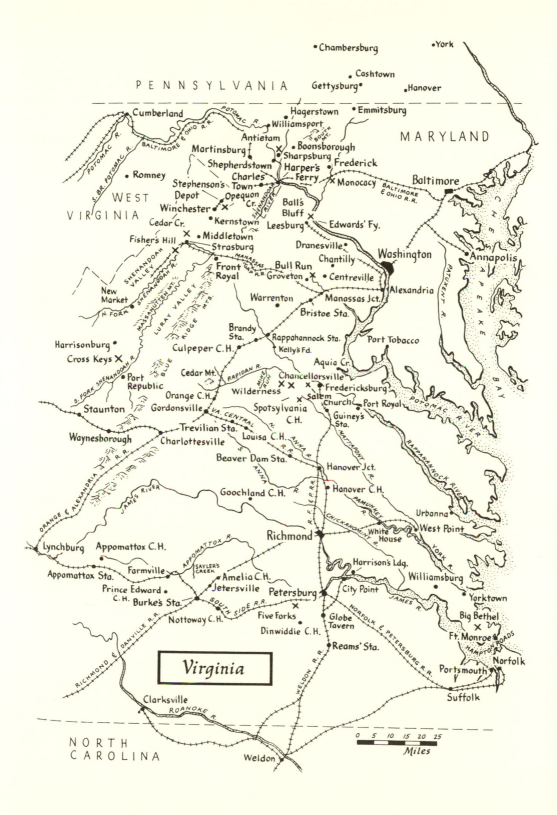

• Chambersburg   • York

PENNSYLVANIA   Gettysburg •   • Cashtown

Gettysburg •   • Hanover

• Emmitsburg

POTOMAC R.   • Hagerstown

• Cumberland   • Williamsport   MARYLAND

BALTIMORE & OHIO R.R.   Antietam

POTOMAC R.   Martinsburg •   Sharpsburg •   • Boonsborough

S. BR. POTOMAC R.   Shepherdstown   Harper's   • Frederick   Baltimore

• Romney   Charles   Ferry

WEST   Stephenson's   Town   × Monocacy   BALTIMORE & OHIO R.R.

VIRGINIA   Depot   Opequon   Cr.

Winchester   Ball's

Cedar Cr.   • Kernstown   Bluff

Leesburg •   Edwards' Fy.

Fisher's Hill   × Middletown   • Dranesville   Washington

Strasburg   Chantilly   • Annapolis

SHENANDOAH VALLEY   MANASSAS GAP R.R.   Front   Bull Run   • Centreville

New   Royal   Groveton   • Alexandria

Market   Warrenton   • Manassas Jct.

N. FORK   Bristoe Sta.

Brandy   • Port Tobacco

Harrisonburg •   Sta.   Rappahannock Sta.

Cross Keys ×   Culpeper C.H.   Kelly's Fd.

Port   Cedar Mt.   RAPIDAN R.   Aquia Cr.

Republic   MINE RUN   Chancellorsville

Orange C.H.   Wilderness   × ×   Fredericksburg

Staunton   Gordonsville   Spotsylvania   Salem   • Port Royal

VA. CENTRAL   C.H.   Church

Waynesborough   Trevilian Sta.   Guiney's

Charlottesville   Louisa C.H.   Sta.

Beaver Dam Sta.   Hanover Jct.

JAMES RIVER   Goochland C.H.   Hanover C.H.   Urbanna

ORANGE & ALEXANDRIA R.R.   PAMUNKEY   • West Point

Lynchburg •   Richmond   White   House

Appomattox C.H.   Harrison's Ldg.

Farmville   SAYLER'S   Williamsburg

Appomattox Sta.   CREEK   Amelia C.H.   City Point   • Yorktown

Prince Edward •   Jetersville   Petersburg   Big Bethel

C.H. Burke's Sta.   SOUTH SIDE R.R.   Five Forks   Globe   Ft. Monroe

Nottoway C.H.   Dinwiddie C.H.   Tavern   NORFOLK & PETERSBURG R.R.   HAMPTON ROADS

Reams' Sta.   Norfolk

RICHMOND & DANVILLE R.R.   Portsmouth

Virginia   WELDON R.R.

Clarksville   Suffolk

ROANOKE R.

0 5 10 15 20 25

NORTH   Miles

CAROLINA   Weldon

INTRODUCTION

The soil of peace is thickly sown with the seeds of war.
—AMBROSE BIERCE

With the First World War as his model, Paul Fussell wrote that "every war is ironic because every war is worse than expected." As national calamity and as individual experience, certainly this was the case with the American Civil War. That slavery could only be abolished by such wholesale slaughter, that new definitions of freedom could only be affirmed in the world's first total war, and that national unity could be preserved only through such fratricidal conflict provide some of the most tragic ironies of American history. Epic destruction of life and treasure led to epic possibilities in a new and redefined American republic in the 1860s. The freedom of the slaves and the liberties of the free were achieved or preserved at horrifying costs. The Civil War was ironic because it both violated and affirmed the nineteenth-century doctrine of progress; it would become the source of America's shame as well as its pride; and it would haunt as well as inspire the national imagination. For many Americans, the whole affair would become humankind's madness somehow converted to God's purposes. On a grand scale, such ironies are easily summarized, but as Fussell observes, all "great" wars consist of thousands of "smaller constituent" stories, which are themselves full of "ironic actions."[1] The thousands of individuals, North and South, who brought the values and aspirations of their communities to so many campgrounds, battlefields, and hospitals provide the constituent stories of this American epic. One of those stories is recorded in the remarkable Civil War letters of Charles Harvey Brewster of Northampton, Massachusetts. When viewed through the lens of social history, letters like Brewster's reveal the experience of an ordinary American man caught up not only in the sweeping events of the Civil War, but also in the values of his age and the struggle of his own self-development.

3

In a 1989 article historian Maris Vinovskis asserted that American "social historians have lost sight of the centrality of the Civil War." In recent years, responding to this and other challenges, a new social history of the Civil War era has begun to emerge, and nowhere is this more apparent than in new studies of the common soldier's experience. The questions, assumptions, and subjects of social historians have tended to make them de-emphasize, if not ignore, major political, military, or diplomatic *events*. Social historians are typically concerned with the values and life cycles of ordinary people, with social structures, community dynamics, demography, family patterns, and change as *process*. Conversely, too many Civil War historians have treated the war as almost exclusively an affair of presidents and generals, of leadership in unprecedented crises. But there is now good reason to believe that these two approaches to the Civil War era can find common ground. The magnitude of casualties suffered in the war, the social and psychological dislocation experienced by so many soldiers, women, and children, the economic growth or stagnation caused by unprecedented war production and destruction, and the emancipation of more than four million slaves demonstrate that the Civil War was an event in which profound social changes occurred. More than three million Americans, including 189,000 blacks in the Union forces, served in the armies and navies. At the end of the war, one of every six white males and one of every five blacks who served were dead. A larger proportion of the American population died in the Civil War than the British population in the First World War. Many towns and farming communities sent large percentages of their male citizenry to the war to have them replaced only by monuments on their town greens and commons in years to come. White northern widows would ultimately benefit from a pension system, but white southern widows and African-American widows in both sections would make do on their own. Some social historians now consider broad social structure, the lives of ordinary people, racial, gender, and class values, and the impact of such transforming events as the Civil War on an equal footing. That major *events* may be returning to the agenda of social historians is, indeed, a welcome occurrence.[2]

A close reading of the Brewster letters affords an intriguing window into most of the categories of inquiry mentioned above. The letters will be of interest to military historians and readers; they are an excellent source for the study of men experiencing war. But as Bell Wiley first observed in the 1940s and 1950s, the letters of Civil War soldiers are an extraordinary source for the social history of nineteenth-century America, and Brewster's letters from the front are an especially illuminating example of this phenomenon.[3] The emotions and ideas represented in these letters range from naïveté to mature realism, from romantic idealism to sheer terror, and from self-pity to enduring devotion. Most of all, Brewster seems honest with his correspondents; there are very few simple pieties in his writing and he was boldly descriptive about the immense tragedy he

witnessed. His homesickness and despair, as well as his ambition and sense of accomplishment, are quite palpable.

Born and raised in Northampton, Brewster was a relatively unsuccessful, twenty-seven-year-old store clerk and a member of the local militia when he enlisted in Company C of the Tenth Massachusetts Volunteers in April 1861. Companies of the Tenth Massachusetts were formed from towns all over the western section of the state: Springfield, Holyoke, Great Barrington, West-field, Pittsfield, Shelburne Falls, Greenfield, and Northampton. The citizens of Northampton were infected by the war fever that swept the land in the spring and summer of 1861. On April 18, only three days after the surrender of Fort Sumter, the first meeting of the Company C militia (an old unit chartered in 1801) turned into a large public rally where forty new men enlisted. By April 24, seventy-five Northampton women rallied and committed their labor to sew the uniforms of the local company. As the cloth arrived, some women worked at home and others sewed in the town hall. Local poets came to the armory to recite patriotic verses to the drilling, would-be soldiers. Yesterday farmers, clerks, and mechanics; today they were the local heroes who would "whip secesh." On May 9 Company C marched some seven miles to an overnight encampment in Haydenville, passing through the towns of Florence and Leeds on the way. In each village, a brass band, an outdoor feast, and a large crowd cheered them. War was still a local festival in this first spring of the conflict. By June 10 the seventy or so members of the company attended a farewell ball, and four days later they strode down Main Street through a throng so large that a corridor could hardly be formed. Flags waved everywhere, several brass bands competed, and Brewster and his comrades joined two other companies of the Tenth on a train for Springfield. En route the soldiers continued the joyous fervor of the day by singing "patriotic airs" to the accompaniment of a lone accordion.[4] Like most of his comrades, Brewster had enlisted for three years, never believing the war would last that long.

After a three-week encampment in Springfield, the Tenth Massachusetts again departed by train and with great ceremony. In Springfield, as in so many other American communities that summer, the "ladies" of the town formally presented the regimental colors to the commander of the regiment, in this case Col. Henry S. Briggs. It was a time, said the women's announcement, for "reverence" to flags, and they urged the men to "defend them to the death." The spokeswoman, Mrs. James Barnes, assured these young warriors that "the heart of many a wife and mother and child and sister, will beat anxiously for your *safety*, but remember, no less anxiously for your *honor*." In Palmer, on the way to Boston, several hundred women, some with bouquets of flowers, gathered at the station to bid the troops goodbye. The regiment would camp ten more days in Medford, next to Charlestown, on the banks of the Mystic River. Before

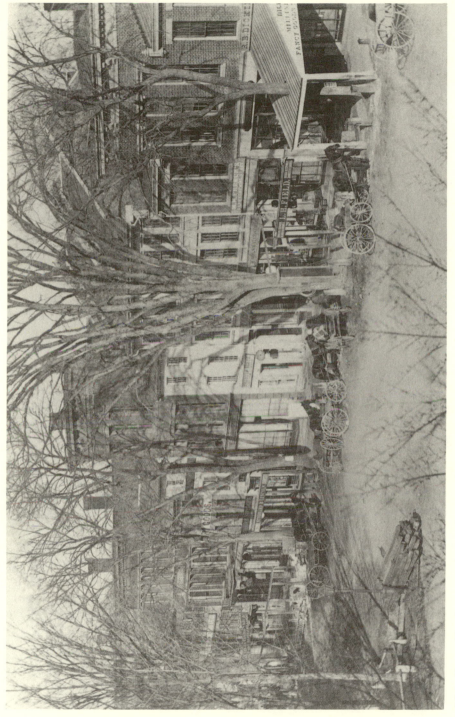

Main Street, Northampton, Massachusetts, during the Civil War. *Courtesy of Historic Northampton, Northampton, Massachusetts*

boarding transports for the voyage to Washington, D.C., the Tenth stood for one more ceremony, this time addressed by the former Massachusetts governor George N. Briggs, father of the commander. In a message fathers have passed to their sons for centuries, but rarely so explicitly, Briggs called upon farm boys and clerks to show themselves "to be *men* and *New England men.*" He urged them to be gallant and fierce, but always kind to their wounded or captured enemy. He then concluded with a flourish: "When the army of an ancient republic were going forth to battle a mother of one of the soldiers said to him: 'My son, return home *with* your shield or *on* your shield.' Adopting the sentiment of the noble mother, let me say . . . bring back those beautiful and rich colors presented you by the ladies of Springfield, the emblems of your country's power and glory, waving over your heads, unstained, or return wrapped in their gory folds."[5] One can never know how closely soldiers listened to such rhetoric in that romantic summer of 1861. The fathers' and mothers' call to war and manliness in the war their sons were soon to fight would indeed become for some men an exhilarating and ennobling challenge; others grew disillusioned by the fight that became unbearable. Brewster was to experience (and record) both the exhilaration and the disillusionment.

The Tenth Massachusetts spent the rest of 1861 and the winter of 1862 in Camp Brightwood, on the edge of the District of Columbia. There they joined the Seventh Massachusetts, the Thirty-sixth New York, and the Second Rhode Island as part of "Couch's Brigade." For three years, Brewster shared the same brigade and battle experiences as Second Rhode Island private, ultimately colonel, Elisha Hunt Rhodes, whose diary became famous as part of a 1990 PBS television documentary on the Civil War.[6] The Tenth participated in almost every major battle fought by the Army of the Potomac, beginning with the Peninsula campaign through Antietam and Fredericksburg in 1862, Chancellorsville, Gettysburg, Bristow Station, and Rappahannock Station in 1863, and the Wilderness, Spotsylvania, and Cold Harbor in 1864. When the survivors of the Tenth were mustered out at the end of their three-year enlistment and returned to Springfield in June 1864, only 220 of the nearly one thousand in the original regiment were still on active duty. They had witnessed their summer outing transform into the bloodiest war in history, seen thousands die of disease, practiced war upon civilians and the southern landscape, loyally served the cause as variously defined, and tried their best to fulfill their communities' expectations. They returned, in the words of their last commander, Col. Joseph B. Parsons, a "shattered remnant" of "mourners."[7] Brewster would probably have agreed with Parsons's characterization of the survivors; as the adjutant of the regiment it had been his duty to record constantly that shattering in casualty reports and death notices. But Brewster's letters to the women in his family record not only the ugliness and futility of war—and there is plenty of that—but

also the myriad social attitudes, values, and self-perceptions of a relatively ordinary and reflective mid-nineteenth-century white American male.

Brewster's father, Harvey Brewster, a seventh-generation *Mayflower* descendant, died in 1839 when Charles was only five years old, leaving Martha Russell Brewster a widow with three small children, including two daughters, four-year-old Martha and two-month-old Mary. Brewster's wartime letters, virtually all of which were written to his mother and two sisters, exhibit deep affection and clearly reflect a family background of financial distress. His wartime adventures and sufferings exacerbated Brewster's estimation of himself as a frustrated, if not failed, provider in his capacity as the sole male member of his family. Nevertheless, for Brewster, as has been sadly true for men throughout the ages, war gave an ordinary man the opportunity to escape from the ordinary.[8] Brewster would come to loathe war itself; after imagined and romantic warfare gave way to real battle in 1862, he would describe it in honest and realistic terms. He came to understand that in war, perhaps even more than in civilian life, fate was often indifferent to individual virtue. Educated in the Northampton public schools, sensitive and remarkably literate, Brewster was no natural warrior. He aspired to leadership and craved recognition, but in 210 surviving letters, the only time Brewster ever mentions discharging his own weapon is in describing target practice. He was under fire countless times, experienced some of the worst battles of the Virginia campaigns, frequently wished his enemies dead, and participated in the mass killing that was the Civil War. Yet, consistent with most soldiers, nowhere does he describe his own actual killing of a Confederate soldier. This silence probably reflects an emotional distancing and a soldier's natural sense of duty, as well as some consideration of his women correspondents. But the army and his incessant desire for status within its ranks became for Brewster the source of community and even vocation that he had not known before. It is tragic but true that Charles Harvey Brewster found existential meaning only when he went to war and became an officer in the cause of preserving the Union and freeing the slaves.

Brewster survived more than three years of battle, hardship, sickness, and boredom by a combination of devotion, a recognition of diminished alternatives, self-righteous ambition, and a sense of irony. He wrote letters from all kinds of places and postures, and on all kinds of stationery. As with literate soldiers in all ages, or with anyone undergoing loneliness and stress, letters became for Brewster both monologues of self-discovery and dialogues with home. Letters were a humanizing element in a dehumanizing environment, evidence that however foreign civilian life might come to appear, something called "home" still existed. Lying in a rifle pit in June 1862, having experienced his first major battle at Fair Oaks during the Peninsula campaign, Brewster scolded his mother for not writing more often: "It is the little common place incidents of everyday life at

home which we like to read," Brewster declared. "It is nothing to the inhabitants of Northampton that the beans are up in the old garden at home, or that Mary has moved her Verbena bed into the garden, but to me, way off here in the swamps, and woods, frying in the sun, or soaking in the rain, it is a very important thing indeed. You do not realize how everything that savors of home, relishes with us."[9] This is only one of many times that Brewster would contrast the pursuits of peace with the pursuits of war, partly out of self-pity and partly to remind himself that he was alive. In a letter full of volatile emotions, in which he wrote matter-of-factly about the prospect of his own death, he informed his mother that her letters were like "Angels visits." But when one was sleeping in the mud, even letters were sometimes inadequate to the task of sustaining hope and self-respect. "I think it is too bad," said Brewster from the Peninsula, "when letters are the only thing that makes existence tolerable in this God forsaken country."[10]

Letters were a soldier's means of expressing and understanding the absurdity of war, as well as a way of reaffirming commitment to the enterprise. But nothing threw this paradox into greater relief than letters to and from dead men. There are two examples of this in Brewster's letters. In the immediate aftermath of the battle of Gettysburg, Brewster lifted three letters from "a dead Rebels cartridge box, written to his mother and sisters." He sent them to his sister Mary as a souvenir. "Poor fellow," Brewster remarked, "he lay upon the field with his entrails scattered all about by a cannon shot, I cannot help pity him although as you see he expresses no very kindly intentions towards poor us. . . ." Backhandedly, Brewster expressed a sense of kinship with his dead enemy. "The mother & sisters will look in vain in the far off Florida for his return," wrote the New Englander, "or even his grave among the green hills of Penn. where his body probably lies in a pit with lots of his comrades. . . ." Brewster maintained a certain emotional distance from his unnamed foe in an unmarked grave. But the symbol of the confiscated letters to "mother & sisters" could only have made him and his family back home wonder in what "pit" beneath which "green hills" Brewster might soon find oblivion. Moreover, during the worst of the Wilderness-Spotsylvania campaign of 1864 he expressed the great "joy" with which the regiment received two large grain bags of mail. Brewster saw to the sorting of the letters, "but alas," he declared, "there was terrible sorrow connected with it which was the many letters for our dead and wounded comrades. I think I found as many as a dozen letters for poor Lt Bartlett who was killed only the day before."[11] Letters represented the continuity of life, even when they were to or from the dead.

One of the principal themes of Brewster's letters was his quest for and pride in a commission. Readers will find very little abstract discussion of patriotism here, but a great deal about Brewster's desire for a "chance" to "better" himself, for the

respect of his fellow soldiers, for the symbols and authority of rank, and for increased wages so that he could send money back home. To a significant degree Brewster's war was one man's lonely effort to compensate for prior failure and to imagine a new career within the rigid and unpredictable strictures of the army. Brewster was disappointed that he had to enter the service as a noncommissioned first sergeant and he spent the first summer and autumn of the war pining for the status a commission would bring. Put simply, Brewster had a chip on his shoulder about the hand that life had dealt him. He frequently referred to a prewar pattern of bad luck as he gossiped about those who got promotions, resented perceived slights, desperately relished compliments about his performance, and moaned to his mother that it was "hope deferred that maketh the heart sick."[12] Brewster constantly measured himself against his fellow soldiers and calculated his chances of promotion against their character and health. He could not hide his increased hope in November 1861 when he reported that the "Adjutant is very sick and to day the Doctors report that he cannot live." "Consequently," Brewster concluded, "they will have to promote a 1st Lieutenant to his place, so I am quite certain that I shall have a chance." But his desires are noteworthy for their commonality, not their venality; his relations with his comrades were a typical combination of male bonding and competition. Brewster also had a workingman's sense of practical self-interest. "A fellow can sleep very warm even in the woods," he told his mother in December 1861, "with a commission in his pocket."[13]

Brewster received his much-coveted commission and promotion to second lieutenant in December 1861. In one of the most revealing letters in the collection, he sent a detailed description of the sword, sash, belt, and cap which were purchased for him as gifts at considerable cost by members of his company. The letter reads like a description of an impending graduation or a wedding night. "My heart is full to overflowing tonight," Brewster informed his sister. All pettiness and resentment vanished as he realized the "evidence of my standing in the affections of the men." His comrades pooled more than fifty dollars to buy the officer's accoutrements, and Brewster confessed to feeling "wicked" over his good fortune while his comrades in the ranks honored him. The army in winter quarters had become a society of men living together, developing their own rituals and conventions of domestic relations. On the eve of a ceremony that would recognize his new rank, Brewster prepared for a rite of passage and new living arrangements. "I am writing in *my* tent," he told his sister. "I have not slept in it yet but am going to tonight. Lieut. Weatherill and myself have been arranging things all day." There were "new bunks" in his "future home" and he informed Mary that he would be ready to entertain her when she visited. Brewster made the most of this milestone in his life, and a certain tenderness crept into his language as he marveled at the "spontaneous outbreak of feeling" among the men.[14]

Brewster learned what war has often taught us: that men frequently find love and respect for each other more readily in warlike activities than in civilian pursuits. After first wearing his "new uniform," Brewster declared that he felt "quite like a free man once more, now that I am a commissioned Officer. it is wonderful what a difference two little straps on the shoulders make. . . ." Once again, he recognized his own aims as practical and personal. "Before I had lots of work and very little pay," he wrote, "and now I have very little work and lots of pay."[15] In other words, to Brewster promotion meant increased wages, status, and independence in controlling his own labor. But Brewster's new status also represented some ideals in the relations among men that only the army seemed to provide: loyalty, respect, and the opportunity to experience the burdens and joys of leadership. Brewster would have been deeply heartened by a September 1861 letter written by Henry W. Parsons, a twenty-two-year-old private in his company. "In reguard to Charley Brewster," Parsons wrote to his aunt, "he improves every day he is the best officer in the company that we have had with us yet you will find a large heart beneth his coat." Within a month of writing this tribute to his favorite officer, Parsons would die of disease at Camp Brightwood, but not before informing his aunt that Brewster was "a gentleman to all and will do all for the men that lays in his power—his friends may feel proud of him . . . let me tell you Aunt that this is the place to find out mens disposition one can soon tell a man from a knave or coward. . . ." Deeply affected by the loss of such a friend so early in their service, Brewster told his mother that he could not "get over Henry Parsons' death. it came so sudden and he was a particular friend of mine, and he and myself had many a confidential talk together. . . ."[16] The quest for status, the love and respect of friends, and the sheer struggle for physical survival all became part of a young officer's daily existence.

As soldiers like Brewster developed their military identities, their letters revealed what historian Reid Mitchell has called the "immense distance that grew up between the worlds of civilian and soldier." Soldiers who find themselves in a "community of the front," as Eric Leed has aptly described it, or those who experience extreme alienation because of the violence and degradation of soldiering, become acutely aware of how different they are from civilians.[17] Frequent letter writers like Brewster were readily reminded of the radical disjuncture between their precarious existence and that of the community left behind. "How I wish some of the stay at homes could enjoy one winter campaign with us," Brewster complained in 1862, "I fancy we should hear less of 'onward to Richmond.'" Once a soldier was fully initiated to war and to its psychological shocks, his misery found expression in his contempt for civilians. "People at the north do not realize at all what a soldier's life is . . . ," Brewster wrote in 1863, "a soldier has more misery in one day than occurs in a lifetime of a civilian ordinarily and their greatest comforts would be miseries to people at home." Brewster left a veteran volunteer's classic statement of the increasing estrange-

ment of soldiers from civilians in a prolonged war. "It is the general feeling among the old regiments, the real *Volunteers*," he said, "that the generality of the citizens loathe and hate them." Well into his third year of campaigning, the end of the war nowhere in sight, and about to face another winter at the front, Brewster retreated to personal and unit pride—to comradeship and fatalism—in order to give meaning to his experience.[18]

By 1864 Brewster felt estranged from his hometown and homesick at the same time. Conscription laws exacerbated such ambivalence, creating greater distance between the original volunteers—who by 1863–64 had constructed a self-image as suffering victims—and the draftees from their hometowns. As Northampton strained to fill a draft quota in February 1864, Brewster declared that he did not "believe in drafted patriotism." "I do not love the people of that delightful village as a whole," he informed his sister Martha, "and as I owe them ooo I would not lift my little finger to get a man for them." The otherness of his military experience also made him genuinely fearful of his chance of making a living in the civilian world and would prompt him, eventually, to reenlist. War defined a man's future as well as his days, and Brewster worried about what would become of him once his war was over. "This Military is a hard worrying and at the same time lazy miserable business," he wrote in April 1864, "but it pays better than anything else so I think I had better stick to it as long as I can." In words representative of Everyman's lament, Brewster declared that he had done his "share of campaigning but somebody must campaign and somebody else must have all the easy money making places and as the harder lot was always mine in civil life I suppose I must expect the same in Military."[19]

Brewster's sentiments toward civilians, as well as his fears of making a living after the war, will remind many readers of dilemmas faced by veterans of other American wars. "I don't know what I am to do for a living when I come home," Brewster wrote in his last letter from the front in June 1864. "As the end of my service grows near," he said, "I cannot but feel rather bad to leave it for all its hardships and horrors & dangers it is a fascinating kind of life, and much freer from slander jealousy & unkindness than civil life which I almost dread to come back to." Brewster groped to explain why the joy of going home should be so tarnished by fear of civilian livelihood. Suddenly, the army seemed an island of clarity, honesty, and genuineness in a laissez-faire sea of treachery. "The Veterans," he said, "wear rather long faces." He spoke for the veterans in warning that "those who will welcome them with such apparent joy," will be "ready to do them any injury for the sake of a dollar." Brewster had learned much about the terrible irony of war, about its capacity to pervert values and make organized violence seem like an ordered and strangely attractive alternative to the disorder of society.[20] Even while still in the trenches of Virginia with one week remaining in his term of service, Brewster had begun to think like a veteran of a bygone war.

His fears of civilian life and nostalgia for the comradeship of the army already made him a candidate for the cycles of selective memory that would both plague and inspire Civil War veterans. Brewster's wartime letters presaged what historian Gerald Linderman has called the "militarization of thought and the purification of memory" in postwar American society.[21]

Brewster, like most men of his generation, was deeply imbued with the Victorian American values of "manhood" and "courage." He perceived war as the test of his courage, and he constantly sought reassurance that he could meet the challenge. He aspired to the individualized and exemplary conception of bravery, by which officers especially had to exhibit their courage to the rank and file. "Courage was the cement of armies," writes Linderman, in the best study of this concept among Civil War soldiers.[22] Especially in the early stages of the war, there is no question that fear of personal dishonor, so rooted in social constructions of masculinity and in American culture, provided the motivation and much of the discipline of Civil War armies.

But the social expectations of manliness in the face of modern war and the degradation of disease almost overwhelmed Brewster, though he only guardedly admitted it. He was both a victim and a perpetrator of these values. His letters are full of observations about the endless struggle between courage and cowardice, his own and that of his comrades. Like most young men who went to war in the nineteenth century (and in our own more violent century as well), Brewster followed a destructive quest for manhood, fashioned a heroic self-image at every opportunity, and marveled at the capacity of war to subdue the environment. He also wrote of camp life and war itself as places strictly separating men from women, all the while imagining their scenes and horrors for his female correspondents. Such sentiments, of course, are not merely stored away in the nineteenth century, to be unpackaged for modern boyhood fantasies or for the mythic uses of the vast Civil War literature. Readers of great memoirs from recent wars, like William Manchester's *Goodbye Darkness: A Memoir of the Pacific War*, may find certain echoes in Brewster's letters. When Manchester, the son and grandson of soldiers, writes of his withdrawal from Massachusetts State College and enlistment in the marines in 1942, "guided by the compass that had been built into me," he represents a male tradition deeply ingrained in American society—one that common and less literary men like Brewster had helped to cultivate.[23] Brewster's own manly compass sent him irresistibly off to war, however unprepared or ill-equipped for what it would do to his body or his imagination.

In May 1862, just before the battle of Fair Oaks, Brewster wrote almost daily for a week. His letters are dramatic accounts of the impending battle, but even more they are chronicles of his desperate struggle with dysentery and "terrible exposure" while sleeping nightly in the mud. At one point he declares himself so

sick that he will have to resign and go home, but to fall back then to some makeshift hospital, he believed, would surely mean a hideous and ignoble death. He declared himself eager for battle, because it represented movement, and compared to sickness and exposure it meant a welcome "chance to live." Courage in this instance, Brewster learned, merely meant endurance and a few strokes of good luck. He could "give up" and seek a furlough, he reasoned, but he feared that the "brave ones that staid at home would call me a coward and all that so I must stay here until after the fight at any rate." In a despairing letter two months later Brewster described "burying comrads who die of disease" as the "saddest thing in the service. . . ." Wondering what he would write to a dead comrade's parents, he took heart at how well the man had performed in battle: "thank the lord I can tell them he was brave."[24]

Unable to walk and humiliated by his chronic diarrhea, Brewster spent the battle of Fredericksburg (December 1862), five miles behind the lines where he could only hear that desperate engagement. "I never felt so mean in my life . . . ," he wrote. "I lie here like a skulking coward and hear the din of battle but cannot get there it is too bad." The situation is reminiscent of the scene in Stephen Crane's *The Red Badge of Courage,* where Henry Fleming, tormented by the sounds of battle—"the crackling shots which were to him like voices"—feels "frustrated by hateful circumstances." Henry and Brewster had different burdens to bear; the latter had not run from battle. But in a letter a week later Brewster demonstrated his ambivalence about the vexing concept of courage. He hoped that the sickness would not seize him again "when there is a battle in prospect, for it lays me open to the imputation of cowardice, which I do not relish at all, although I don't claim to be very brave."[25] This final touch of honesty is an interesting contrast with all the times Brewster complained about "cowards" in his letters. In the boredom, frustration, and danger of three years at the front, sometimes Brewster could manage to assert his own manhood only by attacking that of others. But with time he became a realist about the meaning of courage. On the eve of the Wilderness campaign in April 1864, he hoped that his corps would be held in reserve in the impending fight. "I suppose you will call that a cowardly wish," he told Mary, "but although we see a great many in print, we see very few in reality, of such desperate heroes that they had rather go into the heat of battle than not, when they can do thier duty just as well by staying out. . . ." A veteran's hard-won sense of self-preservation prevailed over these sentiments, and it may help explain why Brewster survived what his regiment was about to endure. Having just lived through the worst combat of the war in late May 1864, he could write about courage without pretension. "You are mistaken about thier being nothing cowardly about me," Brewster informed Martha. "I am scared most to death every battle we have, but I don't think you need be afraid of my sneaking away unhurt."[26] When introspection overtook the need for cama-

raderie and bravado, as it frequently did in the last months of his service, Brewster found the moral courage to speak honestly about physical courage.

On the experience of battle Brewster's letters are often dramatic and revealing. Readers will find much of interest in his accounts of the Peninsula campaign of 1862, the Chancellorsville and Gettysburg campaigns of 1863, and the Wilderness-Spotsylvania-Cold Harbor battles of 1864. In these letters one can follow a young man's romantic anticipation of battle through to his experience of pitilessly realistic warfare. After landing on the Virginia peninsula in April 1862, active now in the great mobilization of McClellan's army and describing his first image of the "horrible" destruction of a town (Hampton, Va.), Brewster contrasted the "sounds of drums," the "neighing of horses," and the "hum of voices" among the multitude of troops with the quietude of a "Mass fast day" back home. Torturing his mother's emotions, he concluded the letter with the story that he had been awakened from a dream the night before by a "tremendous Thunder shower" that he mistook for the "firing of cannon."[27]

Brewster kept his women correspondents informed but probably full of tension as he encountered real war. Upon seeing the aftermath of a battlefield for the first time at Williamsburg, he described it as a "fearful, fearful sight." "The ground was strew [strewn] with dead men in every direction . . . ," he told his mother. "But language fails me and I cannot attempt to describe the scene. if ever I come home I can perhaps tell you but I cannot write it." Brewster would see much worse yet, and he would continue to write it into and out of his memory. But he was caught in that dilemma of literate soldiers in all modern wars: the gruesomeness of battlefields seemed, as Fussell put it, "an all-but-incommunicable reality" to the folks back home. Brewster's letters seem to have anticipated what Alexander Aitken wrote about his own rendering of the battle of the Somme in 1916: "I leave it to the sensitive imagination; I once wrote it all down, only to discover that horror, truthfully described, weakens to the merely clinical."[28] Brewster had a sensitive imagination, and he did try to write it all down; one wonders, though, if after the war, looking back at his letters, he might not have felt the same way Aitken did. In its own historical moment the obscenity of war, it seems, begs description; whereas, in retrospect, it often must be repressed in memory as people confront the tasks of living.

During Brewster's first major battle campaign (the Peninsula and the Seven Days, April–July 1862), he wrote a stunning series of letters where he expressed virtually every reaction or emotion that battle could evoke. At the battle of Fair Oaks, Brewster's regiment lost one of every four men engaged (killed, wounded, or missing) and, with good reason, the young officer wondered why he was still alive. He tried to describe the sounds and the stench of the battlefield, and the excitement and pulse of the fighting. He also began to demonize the enemy at every turn. In surviving such madness Brewster felt both manly exhilaration and

dehumanization. The "life" the soldiers sustained, he said, "would kill wild beasts"; and the farmers of Northampton, he maintained, "would call it cruelty to animals to keep their hogs in as bad a place as we have to live and sleep. . . ." Most of all Brewster coped with fear and loaded up on opium to command his bowels. Anticipating the great battle for Richmond, he said he could only "dread it," as he had already "seen all I want to of battle and blood."[29] But he had two more years of this to endure; his demeanor and his language would both harden and expand with the experience.

While squatting in a field or brooding in a trench, Brewster sketched battle and its aftermath from a soldier's interior perspective, rather than from the sanitized vantage point of headquarters. References to generals and grand strategy are relatively scarce in these letters; they provide an example, as John Keegan put it, of how very different the "face of battle" is from the "face of war."[30] Although he had no serious literary pretensions, Brewster's horror-struck depictions of battle scenes will remind some readers of the agonizing ironies and relentless realism of Ambrose Bierce's short stories. After Gettysburg Brewster described the countless corpses of dead men and horses as if they were macabre monuments. At Spotsylvania in 1864 the "terrors" he witnessed had become so common that he sometimes worried about his own lack of "feeling," and other times just lost himself in grim details. Describing one trench with dead and wounded Confederates piled "3 or 4 deep," he saw "one completely trodded in the mud so as to look like part of it and yet he was breathing and gasping." In the next letter came the vision of "the most terrible sight I ever saw," a breastwork fought over for twenty-four hours with the dead "piled in heaps upon heaps. . . ." As Brewster gazed over the parapet at dawn, "there was one Rebel sat up praying at the top of his voice and others were gibbering in insanity others were groaning and whining at the greatest rate. . . ." Steeling his nerves, preparing himself to continue this "terrible business," and ever the partisan, Brewster took an awkward solace that he had not, he claimed, heard any wounded Union soldiers "make any fuss."[31]

As he increasingly and self-consciously became part of a machine of total war, Brewster justified the pillaging of southern civilians, supported the execution of deserters, and in his harshest moments advocated the killing of Confederate prisoners. Yet, through nature's diversions and a healthy sense of irony, he preserved his humane sensibilities in these letters. Brewster nurtured a life-long interest in flowers, gardening, and the natural landscape. He was an astute observer of the beauty and the strangeness of the Virginia countryside. The Virginia Blue Ridge would sometimes remind the New Englander of the Berkshires or even of Vermont. Other times, especially when he was in the coastal region, he blamed slavery and a lack of proper husbandry for the misuse of land and human labor in the South. But he never ceased to describe beauty when he found it. A moonlit camp during the autumn of 1861 made him brood

that "it seems strange to see anything so beautiful and peaceful connected with 'grim visaged war.'" Ever on the watch for the contrast of peace with war, many a "beautiful morning" in Brewster's letters provided a pastoral backdrop for the dullness of camp or the terror of battle. "I wish you could see what a splendid morning this is," he said to his mother while seated on an oak log on Chickahominy Creek in the spring of 1862. "The trees are in full foliage and the Birds are singing in the trees and the water ripples and sparkles at my feet with the sun shining gloriously over all, and if it were not for the Regt I see before me each with his deadly Enfield rifle on his shoulder I could hardly imagine that there was war in the land." Brewster savored opportunities to tell his womenfolk about wild roses and a host of other flower species he observed on the march. In a field near Cold Harbor in May 1864, "magnolias in full bloom" made him reverently grateful, for "thier perfume is very refreshing," he said, "after the continual stench of the dead bodies of men and horses which we have endured for the last 19 days." Brewster confessed to some hesitation about digging a breastwork "through a farmers garden and close to his back door through peas in blossom and radishes & tomatoes. . . ." Every war brings us these contrasts of ugliness and beauty, images of life next to death, a single poppy blooming in no-man's-land, visions of nature that somehow survive the worst of human nature. Sentimentalized blossoms so often outlast and even replace the stench of the dead and the vileness of war. Brewster's expressions about beauty often came when he knew he teetered on the precarious edge of life and death. It is also worth noting that after the war Brewster would become the first successful professional florist in the upper Connecticut River valley. One can only imagine how much the old soldier reflected on his deep memories of life and death in the fields of Virginia as he nurtured the perennials in his greenhouses during the 1880s.[32]

Perhaps the most striking irony, as well as one of the most intriguing themes, in Brewster's letters is his attitudes and actions regarding race and slavery. Brewster had voted for Abraham Lincoln in 1860, and he embraced the Republican party's free labor and antislavery ideology. He had lived all his life in reform-minded Northampton and believed from the first giddy days of the war that he was fighting to save the Union and free the slaves. But Brewster was no radical abolitionist (their ranks were very small in the Union army) and he enjoyed mocking the piety and earnestness of reformers. His racial views were those of a sardonic white workingman who believed that blacks were a backward if not an inferior race. As historians Bell Wiley and Joseph Glatthaar have shown, use of such terms as "nigger" and "darkie" were very common in the letters of Union soldiers. Brewster's language was typical rather than exceptional in this regard.[33] But at the same time Brewster believed that slavery was evil, that the South was a repressive society, that a war against secession was inherently a war against racial bondage, and that out of the bloodshed a different society would emerge. Moreover, he seemed to have held these views earlier than most Union troops.

Although his estimations of black character did not change as much as one might wish, wartime experience forced an interesting evolution in Brewster's attitude toward blacks.

During the autumn and winter of 1861–62 the status of slaves who escaped into Union lines remained ambiguous. Lincoln had countermanded the order of Gen. John C. Frémont in August 1861 that would have emancipated all slaves in Missouri. Sensitive to the disposition of the four border states that remained delicately in the Union and mindful of northern racism, the president steadfastly resisted converting the war into an abolition crusade. His commanding general in the east, George B. McClellan, obliged Lincoln on this particular issue, insisting that all fugitive slaves be returned to their lawful masters. But very early in the war, at Fortress Monroe, Virginia, Gen. Benjamin F. Butler declared that slaves who entered his lines would be considered "contraband of war" and be treated as confiscated enemy property. The idea caught on, and in early August, striking a balance between legality and military necessity, Congress passed the First Confiscation Act, which allowed for seizure of all Confederate property used to aid the southern war effort. Although not technically freed by this law, the slaves of rebel masters came under its purview, and thus a process toward black freedom began. But in November, Gen. Henry W. Halleck, commanding in the west at St. Louis, issued a general order contradicting the contraband policy and requiring all Union commanders to accept no new fugitives and to eject all those currently within their lines. This contradictory policy toward fugitive slaves caused considerable controversy in the Union ranks during 1861–62, and Brewster's regiment was affected by it.[34]

All major wars tend to chart their own course of social transformation, and Halleck's exclusionary edict and Lincoln's pragmatic ambiguity were both rendered unworkable with time. Indeed, the slaves themselves were forcing a clearer settlement of this issue by their own courage and resolve. The Civil War was a conflict of such scale that its greatest lessons, collectively and individually, were being learned on the ground, where abstractions must be converted daily into pragmatic decisions. From Camp Brightwood on the outskirts of Washington, D.C., Brewster learned firsthand that many slaves were freeing themselves and converting the war's purpose. Slaves took "leg bail," Brewster wrote approvingly in November 1861; and in language that might have been fitting of a small-town, wartime abolitionist rally, he declared that "this war is playing the Dickens with slavery and if it lasts much longer will clear our Countrys name of the vile stain and enable us to live in peace hereafter."[35] In such passages Brewster represented an attitude among white Northerners that, driven by the exigencies of war against the South, prompted Lincoln to eventually commit the nation to the reality of emancipation.

By December 1861, the Lincoln administration's policy toward blacks remained limited and conflicted. The president's annual message offered little

hope to friends of the "contrabands"; he proposed only a plan to colonize escaped slaves and free blacks outside the country. From winter quarters, Brewster offered his own crude antislavery assessment of the situation. "We have got the Presidents message," he told his mother, "but I don't think it amounts to much he don't talk nigger enough, but its no use mincing the matter. Nigger has got to be talked, and thoroughly talked to and I think niggers will come out of this scrape free."[36] Written in the common coin of camp and, apparently, of Northampton as well, Brewster's letters provide an example of the way in which racist language and antislavery ideology combined in the hearts and minds of Yankee soldiers. Brewster lacked eloquence, to say the least, when it came to the question of race; but in language which that great ironist in the White House would have fully understood, he argued unequivocally that the war should be prosecuted more vigorously against slavery.

Brewster spent his first winter at war intensely interested in the "contraband" issue. In January 1862, frustrated by how "slow" the war progressed, he complained that "it seems to be a war for the preservation of slavery more than anything else." Shortly after receiving his commission and setting up his new domestic quarters, Brewster took a seventeen-year-old runaway slave named David as his personal servant. Proud and possessive, he treated his "contraband" with a gushing paternalism. Young David's former master had whipped him, according to Brewster, and forced him to run away. The young Lieutenant took pride in relieving the Confederacy of this lone asset. "He was the only slave his master had," said Brewster, "and his master never will have him again if I can help it."[37] During the long, dull winter months, the clandestine protection of his contraband from the former master's clutches became for Brewster the only war he had. He described at least two successful episodes of deception while protecting David from his pursuing master. But the contraband issue bitterly divided the Tenth Massachusetts, causing by March 1862 what Brewster called nearly "a state of mutiny" in the regiment. Brewster and his antislavery cohort (six contrabands were harbored in Company C alone) would lose this dispute to the proslavery officers in the regiment who were determined to enforce a Halleck-like policy of exclusion. Some fugitives were tearfully returned to their waiting owners; others were spirited away toward Pennsylvania to an ambiguous fate. Brewster himself believed at one point that he would be charged and court-martialed for his resistance, and at another juncture claimed he was prepared to "resign." "I should hate to have to leave now just as the Regiment is going into active service," he wrote in March, "but I will never be instrumental in returning a slave to his master in any way shape or manner, I'll die first."[38] As Brewster describes this three-month-long dispute at Camp Brightwood it has the quality of both tragic farce and high seriousness. This little war within a war reveals in microcosm the much larger social revolution American society was about to undergo, whether it was prepared to confront it or not.

Describing himself as a "free man" because he had received his commission, the recognition-starved Brewster now saw himself as a liberator of his fellow man. As a soldier he was well trained in tactical maneuvers and eager for a taste of battle. As a man he had a yearning to belong to some kind of community. In his contraband Brewster may also have found an outlet for his need to give and a form of companionship he could truly control. One can only speculate, but the letters suggest that Brewster and his contraband may have gained a mutual sense of freedom during their short relationship. The same letter that begins with Brewster appearing in his "new uniform" for the first time ends with him asking his mother to help him outfit his servant. "I wish I could get some of my old clothes to put on him," Brewster wrote, "especially my old overcoat. I do not suppose you will have any chance to send them, but if you should I wish you would . . . make a bundle of coat Pants O Coat and vest . . . send them along, and then I could rig him up so his master would hardly know him." Rejoicing in his acquisition of the contraband in another letter, Brewster described David as "quite smart for a nigger though he is quite slow." But he "is willing," Brewster continued, "and I think has improved a good deal since I got him. I have not heard anything of his master, and if I do I shan't give him up without a struggle." Out of sheer self-interest as well as moral concern, Brewster objectified and coddled his contraband. One is reminded here of the relationship between Huck and Jim in *The Adventures of Huckleberry Finn*. Like Huck, Brewster ultimately had a "sound heart" when it came to the right of a slave to his freedom, and he too decided to "go to hell" rather than return fugitive slaves to bondage. "Without the presence of blacks," Ralph Ellison aptly wrote, Mark Twain's classic "could never have been written." Without Jim, Huck's commitment to freedom could never have developed into the "moral center" of that novel. On a simpler and hidden level, without his *"right smart nigger,"* Brewster might never have developed or even understood his own commitment to freedom. Brewster's struggle to free his "contraband" has the same ironic pattern as Huck's: acts of conscience mixed with adventure, and moral revolt interrupting a life on a raft moving south. Brewster never matched Huck's revelation that "you can't pray a lie," but Brewster's experience forced him to clarify his beliefs and to understand much of what the war was about. In his own crude way, Brewster would grasp the meaning of Lincoln's haunting claim, made at the end of 1862, that "in *giving* freedom to the slave, we *assure* freedom to the free."[39] Although much of his prejudice would remain intact, the former store clerk from Northampton learned something valuable from his "contraband."

The dramatic tension that often grips Brewster's 1864 letters stems not only from the bloody Virginia campaign, but also from the calendar itself as the regiment's term of enlistment drew to a close. Many regiments in the Army of the Potomac were reaching the end of three-year enlistments that summer, and as they did so, they were sometimes slowly disengaged from the front lines

during their final weeks. The brigade that included the Tenth Massachusetts, however, remained under steady fire for the final thirty-six hours of their life at the front. What remained of the Tenth departed from City Point, on the James River, on June 21, for the return to Springfield and Northampton. But before leaving Virginia, on June 20, Sgt. Maj. George F. Polley, who was originally in Brewster's company and had just reenlisted, carved his name and the inscription "Killed June——, 1864" on a piece of board torn from a cracker box. After participating in the "goodbye" rituals with his comrades and sharing an awkward amusement with them about his carving, Polley was struck flush by an artillery shell and killed. In his diary, brigade member Elisha Hunt Rhodes recorded this incident in his matter-of-fact style. Polley "showed me a board on which he had carved his name, date of birth and had left a place for the date of his death," reported Rhodes. "I asked him if he expected to be killed and he said no, and that he had made his head board only for fun. To day he was killed by a shell from a Rebel Battery." The last act of the Tenth before boarding the mailboat for Washington, D.C., was to bury Polley.⁴⁰ Adjutant Brewster had one last death to include in a morning report.

After the Tenth returned home Brewster, anxious about civilian life, re-enlisted under the auspices of the state of Massachusetts to be a recruiter of black troops in Norfolk, Virginia. From late July to early November he worked as a recruiter, and during this final stage of his service, he wrote some of his most interesting letters. Away from the front, living in a boardinghouse, Brewster could observe the war and society from a new perspective. He was merely one among a horde of recruiters who descended upon eastern Virginia and other parts of the upper South in 1864. Brewster quipped in frustration that "there are two agents to every man who will enlist." He frequently denigrated the very blacks he sought to recruit, commenting on their alleged propensity to "lie and steal" and their "shiftless" attitude toward work. But he seemed delighted at the presence of a black cavalry regiment that made the local "secesh" furious, and, after holding back judgment, he finally praised the black troops who had "fought nobly" and filled the local hospitals with "their wounded and mangled bodies."⁴¹ For Brewster, as for most white Americans, a full recognition of the manhood of blacks only came with their battlefield sacrifices.

Unhappy and shiftless in his own way, feeling as though he were "living among strangers," and deeply ambivalent about what to do with the rest of his life, Brewster went about his business with an element of greed and very little zeal.⁴² He continually took stock of himself, as well as of the ironies and absurdities of war that surrounded him. He boarded with a southern woman named Mrs. Mitchell who had just taken the oath of allegiance to the Union. Her husband and one brother were in the Confederate army, while a second brother served in the Union navy. All the servants at the house, of course, were black and now "free." When Brewster, the Yankee conqueror and occupying

officer, was not trying to find and spirit black men into the army, he spent time playing with Mrs. Mitchell's three small children, or going to the market with his landlady's mother and a "darky girl." Such bizarre domestic tranquility in the midst of this catastrophic civil war makes an unforgettable image. Moreover, images of death and maiming frequently appear in Brewster's last letters from the war. He writes compassionately of the family of a dead New Hampshire soldier who had lived at the boardinghouse, of a former sergeant in the Tenth Massachusetts who returned from the hospital hobbling on a cane and insisting that he wanted reappointment at the front rather than in the Invalid Corps, and of street "murders" committed in Norfolk, which he contrasts with the killing in war. His only use of the concept of "courage" in these final letters was applied either to black troops or to the surgeons who volunteered to go fight a "raging" yellow fever epidemic in North Carolina.[43] Living among a subdued enemy, and quietly observing the revolution that Confederate defeat and black emancipation might bring, Brewster sat in a recruiting office reading and writing "love letters" for black women to and from their husbands at the front. This is what remained of his job and his war, and it was a remarkable vantage point. Still patronizing toward the freedpeople, he nevertheless acknowledged their humanity and their influence. "We have to read thier letters from and write letters to thier husbands and friends at the front daily," Brewster observed, "so that I expect I shall be adept in writing love letters, when I have occasion to do so on my own account, they invariably commence (the married ones) with 'my dear loving husband,' and end with 'your ever loving wife until death.'" If we can imagine Brewster sitting at a table with a lonely freedwoman, swallowing his prejudices toward blacks and women, and repeatedly writing or reciting the phrases "give my love to . . ." and "you Husband untall Death" we can glimpse in this tiny corner of the war the enormous potential of the human transformations at work in 1864. Thousands of such quiet ironies—the Northampton store clerk turned soldier, recruiter, and clerical conduit for the abiding love among black folks that slavery could not destroy—helped produce what Lincoln referred to in his Second Inaugural Address as "the result so fundamental and astounding."[44]

Brewster left the war for good in November 1864, and for a while he returned to working in a store. By 1868, he must have written some love letters of his own, for he married Anna P. Williams, the sister of one of his friends in the Tenth, Sidney Williams. Charles and Anna would eventually have six children, some of whom achieved local prominence in western Massachusetts. By the mid-1870s Brewster had reversed his prewar failures and was the owner of a steady sash, door, and paint business. By 1880, he had bought one of the most prominent houses in Northampton, built three greenhouses, and opened a successful year-round florist business. Local friends remembered him as a man "of great independence of character"; he remained an active Republican until the election of

1884 when, for reasons unknown, he supported the Democrat Grover Cleveland rather than James G. Blaine. Brewster became a financially successful, Gilded Age businessman and a prominent citizen. The disdainful, insecure, ambitious soldier of the war letters became the old veteran and family man who grew flowers, speculated in land and other property, made a comfortable living, and actively participated in the G.A.R. (the Grand Army of the Republic, the Union veterans organization). The soldier of 1864 who so feared civilian life had married well and prospered after all. His sister Mary remembered that she had always looked upon her garden for signs of Charlie's "interest in and love for us."[45] Brewster's story seems prosaically American, chronicling as it does the ups and downs of a white middle-class life and generational mobility, and that of an entrepreneur who, through pluck and luck, seems to have beaten the boom-and-bust cycles of the Gilded Age.

But the war, and those remarkable letters, became part of Brewster family lore. By the 1880s, like most veterans, Brewster was ready for reconciliation with Confederate veterans and willing to suspend competitive prospecting in favor of a misty retrospection. He seemed to love regimental reunions and other G.A.R. activities. In October 1886 he attended Blue-Gray reunions at Gettysburg and Fredericksburg, writing to his children that "papa has had the grandest time he ever had in his life." Of the Confederate veterans, he could only marvel at how they "seem as glad to see us as though we were brothers or cousins at least." The landscape of Virginia, like Brewster's own memory, was still scarred from the war. The veteran wrote that the tour of the Gettysburg battlefield "brings the fearful old days so fresh." He was reminded of all the "old miseries," but was also full of a survivor's awe and pride. The visit to the slopes where he had endured the battle of Chancellorsville was the "most glorious time," he reported, marred only by the regret that he did not get to see the "old long breastwork" at Spotsylvania. Partly as tourists, partly as icons of a refurbished martial ideal, partly just as old men searching for their more active and noble youth, and partly as "symbols of changelessness" in a rapidly industrializing age, veterans like Brewster discovered a heroic nostalgia in these reunions.[46] The former soldier who had so fervently sought a sense of community and status in the army could now truly belong in a society building monuments and rapidly forgetting the reality of combat and the deep racial and ideological roots of the war.

Brewster died in October 1893 aboard the clipper ship *Great Admiral* in New York Harbor. He had sailed from Boston down to New York to accompany his twenty-two-year-old daughter, Mary Katherine, on the initial leg of her around-the-world voyage to Australia. Brewster was the guest of the ship's captain, James Rowell, himself a Civil War veteran. During the brief journey Brewster and Rowell reminisced day and night about their war experiences. Father and daughter walked all over lower Manhattan and took care of some

"Wall St. business." On the day before the ship's departure and his planned return to Northampton, Brewster was stricken with severe head pains and died within hours. His coffin was ferried to Staten Island shortly before the ship's departure for sea. The grief-stricken daughter decided to stay on the voyage as planned. Secure in her possession and prominent in her plans for work at sea were her father's original war letters, which she intended to transcribe for publication. Mary Kate Brewster was a bright young woman with literary ambitions and considerable skill. She wrote articles for local Massachusetts newspapers while at sea, and later in life became a local author and theater critic. She cherished her father's letters which, of course, had all been written to her grandmother and aunts. To the end Brewster had an adoring female audience for his letters and his "war stories." At sea, Mary Kate and Captain Rowell spent evenings reading the letters aloud to each other. After hearing the details of Brewster's funeral, the daughter rejoiced that surviving members of the Tenth Regiment had served as pallbearers. "That pleased the capt.," she reported, "for we both have 'lived' as you might say with that regiment the past months, spending hour after hour reading those letters. . . ."[47] She transcribed most of the letters, often cleaning up her father's grammar, erasing some passages, and probably embellishing the stories with her own literary flair; a small selection of her re-creations are published in the epilogue of this volume. Fortunately, most of the originals survived this year-long journey around the world.

As we imagine Mary Kate Brewster aboard ship somewhere in the Indian Ocean on her way to Australia, vicariously reliving her father's war experiences, reading his many reflections on life and death, war and peace, physical and emotional anguish, courage and cowardice, we can also imagine American society distancing itself from and sentimentalizing the horror and the causes of the Civil War. By the 1890s, the next generation—daughters and sons—were following their parents' lead in constructing an idealized national memory of the war, rooted in a celebration of veterans' valor that rarely included Brewster's horrifying image of the screaming soldier in the trench at Spotsylvania, and instead preferred his descriptions of moonlit campgrounds and sun-drenched mornings on the march. Mary Kate was probably too young and too consumed with life to have understood fully the telling paradoxes and ironies of Charles Harvey's letters: the way he cursed and embraced war, hated and worshipped violence, condemned slavery and practiced racism. Brewster's interior struggle with his own values and with war itself, recorded in these letters, was not the one best fitted to the emerging social memory of the Civil War, nor the imagination of a young Victorian woman. But over time the letters have been lovingly preserved and today they serve as another reminder of the recurring power of war to attract and destroy individuals and to draw and repel the human imagination.

ONE

My Commission

July 1861–January 1862

During these first six months of the war, Brewster did not see real combat, but he began to witness comrades dying of disease; he began to observe and defend escaped slaves from the Maryland and Virginia countryside; he experienced the rigors and amusements of camp life; and he vigorously sought and received the rank of a commissioned officer.

1

Camp of the 10th Regt
Medford, MS
July 17th 1861

Dear Mother

I seize the first moment I have had to write you a few lines. We arrived here safe and sound after a march of some 4 or 5 miles through the streets of Boston and out to our camp where we arrived about 10 oclock PM, tired enough I can assure you our tents were all pitched and we spread our Rubber Blankets and covered ourselves up with our woolen ones and in five minutes we were all fast asleep and slept sound as pigs in clover I knew nothing till Reville this morning although those that heard it say we had a tremendous shower in the night to day I have been feeling first rate. we are encamped on the shore of some bay or inlet I don't know the name of it and it is now high tide and the water is about 30 feet from where I am writing The drummers call has sounded and I must close and go and call the roll I will write more at length when we get settled Give my love to everybody and write often and send me NHampton + Springfield Papers direct CH Brewster Company C 10th Regt Mass Volunteers Medford Mass.

Goodnight from your affectionate son

Charlie

2

Camp McClellan
July 20th 1861

Dear Mother

I wrote you day before yesterday and have received no reply but having a few leisure moments I thought I would improve them by dropping you a few lines. I think my health is improving as I feel first rate and have a good appetite though that may be owing to our feed which is much better than we had in Hampden Park as it is served out to us and we cook it ourselves. we have fresh beef, Ham + Pork alternately, together with plenty of Bread Potatoes or rice. (you know how I love the latter) we have fixed up a cooking apparatus in the bank and made gridirons +c out of some wire we picked up and we have first rate beefsteaks + have ham + Pork steaks. Miss Miranda Cook + Fannie Burt some friends of hers Joe Clark + Elizabeth Clark were over to see us yesterday I heard that Mat arrived in Boston Wednesday but she has not been over to see me yet?[1] I should try to get over to Boston to see her tomorrow but I don't know where to find her.

It is almost time for Dress Parade at 7 o'clock and I cannot write much more.

It is reported that we are going South next week. Col Briggs made us a speech last night at evening parade, and said it was very possible that we should be at the taking of Richmond so I rather think we shall have a chance at them soon. I should like to hear from home before I go as it will take a long time for a letter to follow me after we leave here. if you write as soon as you get this which I hope will be Monday and send by the first mail Tuesday morning I think I shall get it as we cannot get away before Wednesday. give my love to Aunt Lu Mary Uncle Ed and all the rest. I wonder if Mat is coming over here. I should have thought she would before this. I must close now and get the Company ready for Parade. so good by Yours with all love

Charlie.

Sunday morning July 21st

Dear Mother

Since writing the above I have seen Mat and received two letters from you one by her and one by Mrs Marsh. I received your box of goodies but as to carrying them with me to prevent seasickness or for any other purpose it is utterly impossible as I have no possible place to carry them and besides I cannot have any such things and not share it with them. I shall try to go over to Boston to dinner but I think it will be impossible as they are very strict about passes we have just passed through inspection and we have nothing to do until Dress

Parade at 7 o'clock that is the Company have not I expect to write all day So again good bye Aff yours

Charlie

3

Head Quarters 10th Regt Mass Vol
Camped near Brightwood, Aug 20th 1861

Friend Tom[2]

I have been intending to write you for some time, but what with my regular duties and my home correspondence I have not had time. we are now encamped in a much pleasanter place than when you saw us, and I wish you could come and see us now. we are very busy these day's. I have just returned from the Battery where I have been in command of a working party of one Plattoon to day, a Pick and Shovel Party the other Plattoon with Lieut Weatherill commanding started out tonight on Piquet they remain out until 10 oclock tomorrow night. I tried to get out with them but could not arrange it as all the men I could leave my duties with were already out on other duty.

Last night there were two alarms in camp one from the Piquet and one from the police Guard the latter was about 11 1/2 oclock. the sentries saw two men approaching and challenged them and fired, when they ran off they would have caught them if [they] had not been afraid, and fired too soon. The Adjutant also went out some 15 miles and arrested 4 men they are the ones mentioned in this mornings National Republican which I will send you.

Yesterday was the first pleasant day we have had for 10 or 12 days, and last night was one of the most splendid nights I ever saw. I am glad it has cleared off, for the men were getting sick, but today we have but one man seriously ill and that is Guyer but he is getting better.

So much I wrote last evening. Company C's tents are lonesome today the boys are all out on piquet + Police Guard but 14 and they are going out to work on the Battery at 3 oclock, when I shall be left in command of Co C which will consist of some half dozen indisposed men or men who are reported to stay in their quarters by the Doctor. Two of the sentries shot themselves one night last week one shattered his forefinger and had to have it taken off, the other was not so bad as the ball passed between his fingers making only a flesh wound. The same night Sam Felton in our company had his gun accidentally discharged by a man who stood near him, and the ball passed through his hat on the side when it was turned up close to his head burning his whiskers and blacking his face.

There are all sorts of rumors respecting the enemy, and every day they get up some bug bear story or other about thier coming nearer, +c +c but "I don't see it". Gen McClellan[3] visited us last week and reviewed the Regiment during a drenching rain he is a small, and not uncommon looking man, he looks rather like Tom Hayden I think.

I have just had a letter from Jim Ellsworth the first I've had since Saturday the whole company had only one letter yesterday. if you see any of my relations down in Pleasant Street (which I don't suppose you will) just say to them that they must write oftener and that I have not had any papers this week. Three companies are going by having just returned from the Battery with Picks + Shovels on their shoulders, singing Dixie loud enough to be heard a mile. Charlie Howes has just been in practicing his Bugle or Trumpet which we are to drill by when we get anybody who can sound the call. It is a simple horn with one twist and no valves. I think I might learn to sound it myself as I can already sound five notes on it, and it is capable of only seven. The Soldiery are fast spoiling the looks of this country as they are cutting down woods and orchards in every direction from the Battery, to give a fair sight at the rebels, and houses that interfere are prepared so that they can be fired and consumed in double quick time. We are expecting a call from our rebel friends at most any time, and many are getting impatient, that they do not come, but I am content to wait as no doubt it will come soon enough and enough of it, and the longer they delay the better for us and the worse for them but I think that if they should come now they would get most delightfully smashed.

I don't think of anything else of interest to write so I will close give my respects to all my friends in Haydenville and my enemies too, and believe me

Very truly your friend
CH Brewster.

PS There is a box coming to us from Ansel Wrights store. will you please tell my folks to send my Spy Glass. Please tell them at the first opportunity you have Yours +c +c

C H B

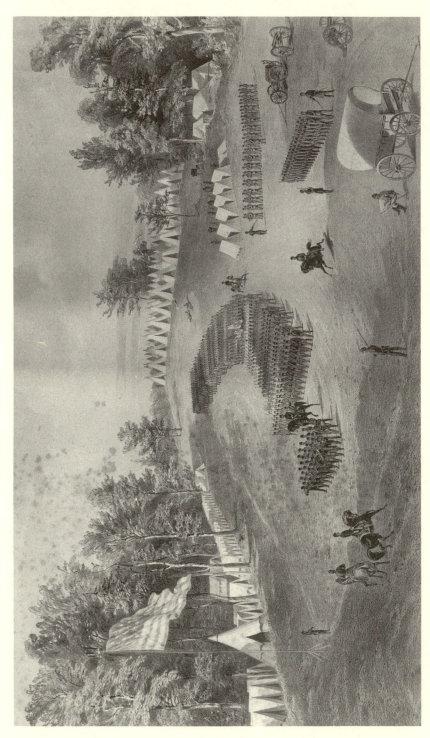

Lithograph drawing by John Donovan of Northampton, Massachusetts, showing Tenth Massachusetts Regiment during training exercises at Camp Brightwood, District of Columbia, autumn 1861. *Courtesy of Historic Northampton, Northampton, Massachusetts*

4

Head Quarters 10th Regt Mass Volunteers
Camp near Brightwood August 24th 1861

Dear Mother

I received last night a letter from Mary and was glad enough to get as I had begun to despair of hearing again as I had not for a week. you cannot imagine how letters from home are watched and waited for here. I sent one to Parthy yesterday which with this makes three written this week and I have received just one little short one from Mary.[4] I should not have written again so soon but I was so glad to hear that Aunt Lu had got a letter from home, and that Mr Campbell had begun to come to his senses that I thought I must at least begin a letter today, it seems by the letter that "sesesh" soldiers fare harder than we do, which agrees with all other accounts. we however are having very good fare now, I do wish Stuart and Brown would not join thier Company again, as sesession is certainly going to be licked, out and out there aint going to be any more bulls runs on our side, for we shall have a man for every square yard of ground, and we are furnished with good wholesome food and plenty of clothing, and are to have our pay in Uncle Sams gold once in two months, besides which we have the right, and as much enthusiasm as they and more too, and are as eager for the fight. how can Mr Campbell say they had but 250 men, when Gen McClellan took more than 1000 prisoners.[5]

Sunday August 25th

Today has been beautiful. We arose this morning at 5 oclock and got our Breakfast, had inspection at 9 oclock, after which I was ordered to take the Company down to the Creek to bathe. It is about $1/2$ or $3/4$ of a mile from here. we took our arms, which was rather useless, but tis considered best to have them on all excursions out of the lines. What an idea, going in swimming, and taking Muskets, Powder + Balls, funny, isn't it. The Regiment was paraded this afternoon at 5 oclock for divine service, and marched to a beautiful slope in the shade of a noble Grove of Oaks and chesnuts, where they had preaching, prayers and singing, from Hymn Books which have been furnished by someone. I don't know who It was a grand sight to see they were paraded in line and marched off with the band playing, and without arms, and then to see them seated on the Green Clover with the noble woods for a Back Ground. it is much better than sitting inside the church cramped up in the pew, and then the band played Old Hundred much better than any Organ I ever heard, and the singing sounds better, in fact it is better every way, and it looks as though twas for some purpose, besides showing your good clothes. We don't have to fix up much and parade before a mirror, all thats necessary is to wash our faces comb the hair, put on a

clean gray shirt and fall in, and then there is never anyone late to church to interrupt the service. I don't suppose that the worship of the congregation is any more sincere but then it seems as if Prayers would go up quicker. The inhabitants are getting to think that we are not barbarians and we now have quite a respectable show of ladies at service on Sundays, but they don't look so nice as the Northampton girls. They look dowdyish (I believe that's what you call it) they seem to have a great fancy for silk and I have seen them rigged up in old silks that I should think were Anterior to the Revolution, when they would look a great deal better in a clean Calico. I saw a woman in one house doing housework in a Black Satin skirt. You may think I have taken a new tack in observing all these things but the fact is, there is a scarcity of topics of thought in this business and anything that furnishes food for the mind we have to sieze upon however trivial.[6]

You know how much was said before we came off, and how much we were preached to about the temptation of the camp and how many fears were expressed that twould be the ruin of young men and all that sort of thing. I have yet to see one tenth of the temptations here that there are in civil life, in fact there are hardly any and there can't be as I can see, as all liquor is prohibited, and to be found gambling is to have a court martial, and punishment. The latter is a new order before it was promulgated gambling was very prevalent, but we see none of it now. The men are much more orderly and better behaved than when at home. and Sundays are more quiet. I could not but notice this to day, you know we have no work on Sundays except inspection and dress Parade, and to day I walked through the grove and the men were sitting and lying about, some writing some reading, some sleeping, and some in groups talking, but no loud or boistrous noise, and from the tents you would hear singing from the new Hymn Books, and although playing cards is a chief amusement on week day's I saw but one instance of card playing to day of which I tried to make them ashamed but did not succeed very well, and there is no law against it. They are in a hurry to get the Batteries done but all work upon it is suspended on the sabbath. it is very probable we may have to defend some Sunday though but that I suppose would be a work of necessity I think discipline and good order are on the increase every day. Col Briggs is a most excellent Col and is very much liked by all. I think Major Marsh's interest in our co never flags, and we are often indebted to him for extras in the way of vegetables and comforts for the inner man.[7] I received your welcome letter when I got back from the bathing expedition to day I have only one fault to find with it, it was not half long enough, I am sorry you could not send my Spy Glass but there is another box coming this week. Chas Rogers wife will probably know something about it. I don't know where it is to start from. Our Battery which is the especial pet just now is progressing finally I hear it is to mount 7 24 Pounders 3 10 Pound Rifle Cannon and 3 Columbiads. it is quite a

fort and will no doubt be the death of lots of rebels. There goes the Tattoo and I must close for tonight and turn the boys out for roll call I will finish tomorrow if I have anything more to say.

[There is likely a missing page for this letter.]

5

Head Quarters 10th Regt
Camp Brightwood Aug 29th /61

Dear Mother

I wrote a letter and sent to Mary yesterday morning and thinking you might still be anxious I thought I might write again this evening. Lieut Shurtleff myself and Willie Kingsley + Charlie Edwards are all of Co C there is in camp tonight except a half dozen who are not well the rest went on Piquet duty at 7 oclock last night. they will be in soon now. I went out with them and slept in a Blacksmith shop last night, that is after two oclock. I went out acting as Lieut and went out and stationed the piquets and I wish you could have seen your son, marching round through the woods in the dark and rain hunting up the stations. we relieved the Westfield Co and they should have sent a Corporal with me to the Post but they did not and I had to hunt them up as I could. I got back from that duty about ten oclock or perhaps a little after, and then Corpl Whitney and myself had to start off and go all over with them again, for the purpose of giving out new instructions, and this time we had to go a mile + a half farther to where Sergant Bishop was stationed with ten men as an advance post. he had his head Quarters in a church. it was a brown Wooden building, about half the size of Mr Kingsley's barn. the first of his men we came to were Corporal Williams, John Cook and another. we had trudged along until we concluded they had gone on to Harpers Ferry, on their own hook. we got back from that expidition about one oclock and then he and I came into camp and lunched on your cookies and Jelly, after which we went back and camped down in the aforesaid Blacksmith shop about two oclock, and at 4 oclock I woke up with an awful pain in my face and head. I came back to camp and changed my stockings, and went back and turned in again but could not sleep. I hung on until about 10 oclock am and then had to give up and come into camp and go to bed where I have staid until this evening. I feel some better.

We had a visit today from Major Longley + Frank Conkey Esq of Amherst. Yesterday there was great excitement in camp in the afternoon. we heard vollys of musketry, and cannon, and a rumor that they were having a great fight at Chain Bridge, and that they were bringing the wounded into Washington +c

+c but it turned out to be nothing but a skirmish at Balls Cross roads over somewhere in Va. to day we have seen a Balloon in the direction of Arlington Heights. it has been up at intervals all day through a glass we could see that it carried the Stars + Stripes we expect to be ordered off at any moment and when we go we shall probably go to fight we hold ourselves in readiness all the time Night before last the Major Drummer sat up all night to be in readiness to beat the long roll.

The companies have been replaced in line today and instead of the right or first Company we are now the third from the left, and are the junior company. they have arranged this from some old Militia commissions, which have nothing to do with the United States service as I can see but Capt. Miller of Shelburne Falls made a fuss about it because his old Militia Commission dated back some two or three years. it makes a great deal off fuss our not having a Capt, and tis rumored that Lieut Pierce of Greenfield will be appointed for our Captain I think that is all fudge though, but if he is then there will be a mutiny right off and you need not be surprised if we are sent to the dry Tortugas. it is Thursday and this makes the fourth letter I have written since I received any, except for a little note from Mat in the box you sent me. I think it is too bad. it looks as though my letters were considered a nuisance, and I shall not write any more until I get some from you. The appointments for Non-Commissioned officers were read at Dress Parade last night and mine was among them for 1st Sergeant, and tomorrow I suppose I shall receive the warrant. I hear they are to send another Regiment from Western Mass if they do I wish I could get a chance in it better than what I have now. There are a great many Lieuts in this Regiment a great deal bigger fools than I be, however I suppose the curse of ill luck will forever hang to me. I get a great many compliments for prompt attention to my duties, but so I always did in other business but it never amounts to anything and compliments don't pay.[8] There goes the Tattoo, so I must bid you good night. give my love to all the family and respects to everybody. tell them I should like a letter from some of them before I come home. I suppose you did not get my letter in regard to my Spy Glass, as you did not send it. Give my love to Aunt Lu, tell her to write. Mat asked in her letter if she could get to Richmond I don't think she could at least not at present but we are going to open that road in the course of a week or two, and if she wants to go there she had better wait, till we clear the rebels out as they have a great fancy for insulting ladies and stealing their clothes +c +c. I will leave this open until morning, as perhaps I shall have something to add.
Friday morning

We find ourselves all safe and sound this morning again and the night has passed without alarm. I am better this morning but the doctor thinks I had not better drill nor go to the fortifications today. Cal K is also on the sick list but he is up and round the camp same as I am can't Mary knit me a worsted cap like those

skating caps she used to knit I want it to sleep in. please ask Bill Kingsley if he will answer if I write him a letter. I'm not going to write any more to people that don't answer. Ask Tom why he don't answer my letter. tell him that if he will come to Washington again about these days he will have a chance to see a battle. The sun shines again this morning it is 6 oclock and I have just got up two hours later than common. you need not send me New York papers as we get them here in fact all our war news comes from them love to all again very affectionately your son

Charlie

6

Head Quarters 10th Regt MV
Camp near Brightwood
September 3rd 1861

Dear Aunt Lu,

I received your kind letter in due season and was very glad to get it. I intended to answer it before but we have been very busy for a few days. last Thursday our Co had to go on Piquet, and Friday we worked on a new Battery and Saturday we were on Police Guard, and Sunday we had to work on the Battery, the first time we've had to work since Sunday. this Battery is larger than the first one and has two or three pivot Guns. Monday we changed our tents on to higher ground, and yesterday we were reviewed in Brigade by Gen McClellan. the whole Brigade were marched up to our encampment as we have the largest and best ground. there were nearly 4,000 men, so you see I have not had much time. I have also received a letter from Mat and one from Mr. Boland. it is a difficult matter to write a letter for there is no news and nothing to write about every day is just like the day before and it racks ones brains to find material for a letter. I cannot gain any information in regard to any way to get past our lines and into the rebels, but I really wish you could get home and make Mr Campbell over into a Union man for this rebellion is going to be squelched and I am afraid he will lose all he has left after it is over. how can he be so blind to everything as to take sides with the rebels. you have heard of the glorious victory in No Carolina.[9] Mr Jeff will have other things to attend to besides sacking N York and Philadelphia this fall and winter. how I wish he had his halter about his neck but he will get it, sooner or later Our camp is said to be the handsomest round Washington I wish you could see it. they are talking of having some Photographs taken of it and if they do I will send you one. I wrote a few days ago about our

sleeping on our arms one night. it is rumored since that we were to have made an advance that night but *Blow*regard[10] heard of it somehow and retreated six miles the government seems to have started in earnest now and is clearing out the traitor spies both male and female and the rebels will not probably know of all the Federal plans before they do themselves, hereafter. I secured a loaf of cake and some cookies from Cousin Lucy when George's box came also my spy glass. I have received the papers you sent also, and I believe I wrote Mother that she need not send any more New York papers. I would like all the Republicans if you take it now and the Northampton papers. The NY papers are sold here every morning. I sent you a Washington paper a few days ago also one to Mr Boland the weather is hot as fury today almost as hot as it was when we came we have been having very cool weather and a great deal of rain. my face bothers me most to death I had to get up at 12 o'clock last night and go up to the doctors I wanted to try the experiment of having two or three pulled but the doctor would not do it in the night but gave me some pills and some Chloroform to put in my teeth. it does not trouble me at all in the day time but the minute I lay down it commences and I have to get up and travel around. I am going to have one tooth pulled to day anyhow. I think Abner has perhaps made a wise decision in regard to going to war, but then there are things to be said on both sides. I had written so far when Doctor Chamberlin[11] came along and I went with him and had one of grinders pulled out, so I think I shall get some sleep tonight. there is a big battle going on somewhere today probably at Balls cross roads as Mortars were sent there from Washington yesterday, but I wish you could hear the firing once in about two or three minutes comes the roar of the cannon heavy and loud as thunder and then volleys of musketry and the popping of the muskets as they fire by file, that is two men (front and rear rank) at a time, we have heard it more or less all day, but now about 6 $^1/_2$ o'clock it is very loud and rapid, roar after roar comes rolling over the hills. it makes ones blood quicken to hear it but it awakens no sensation of fear yet although for ought we know we may be counted in before morning. I am the sole occupant of the two officers tents, as the Co has not got in from the Batteries yet but I think I can hear thier drums now so they will soon be here and then comes tea, and next roll call, and then to bed, to get up and go it all over again tomorrow. I really wish you could come to Washington. I should so like to see you and I wish I could get some information but it is impossible at present, but aint you afraid they will mob you when you get home I should think you would be for they are such barbarians. I like your letters because they are longer than the others tell them to write everything whether it appears of any consequence or not to them. it is to me the Piquet has arrived and I must close Give my love to all Mother the girls and all the neighbors Lieut Remmington of the Greenfield Co and a Sergeant of the Springfield and a Corporal of the Shelburne Falls Company have gone home to recruit 511 men for the regiment. I

don't know but I might have got a chance if I had known of it sooner. we have not been paid off yet, all owing to laziness at Head Quarters I suppose though I don't know anything about it but we are fast learning to live without money. one man of the Westfield Co died at the City Hospital and was buried day before yesterday. Cal Kingsley has been pretty sick but is getting well now. Lewis Day is sick as is also Lathrop Smith of our Co it has got so dark I cannot see so good night ever your affectionate nephew

Charlie.

7

Head Quarters 10th Regt Mass Vol
Camp near Brightwood DC September 11th 1861

Dear Mary

    I wish you could imagine the situation I am in just now. it is about 11 oclock at night and I went to bed at 9 but my jaw ache came on and I have rolled and grunted until I could stand it no longer and finally have got up and am seated here writing to you. you may wonder how I can write under these circumstances but it does not trouble me nearly as bad when I am up and hardly at all in the day time. it is a terribly stormy night the rain comes down in torrents, and beats upon the roof of the tent, and the wind blows furiously, but this would be a pleasant music to me if I could only lay still, and be lulled to sleep by it I received your last letter to day and was very glad to get it. I also received one from Dwight Palmers wife, a first rate one, reading just as she talks, and telling all about the family +c it was very kind of her, she tells me Dwight has been very sick, and has not been to the store for two or three weeks. To day has been a very exciting day. we have heard tremendous cannonading all the afternoon, and this evening, it is reported that Munsons hill is taken, and that our troops are in pursuit of the rebels. Major Marsh brought the news from the city and says it was all excitement down there and that the city fairly shook with the cannonading as I should think it might by what we heard here. it is also said that the troops have gone from Kalorama, where we first encamped. still this may be all rumor, and tomorrows paper may contradict the whole of it, but it does seem as if there must be some truth in it this time. we expected to have been paid off to day but have not and I don't know as we are any nearer to it than we were two months ago, though our Regiment of our Brigade has been paid to day or at least it is rumored so. Fred Clark has just come in from the boys tent and says they are all drowned out up there. they are situated on the hill about 100 paces from the officers tents. I am sorry for them,

and it is hard for the poor fellows out on Guard tonight. Fred has camped down with us and I wish there was room for all of them but that is impossible. I am glad our boys are not on guard to night, but they have been out nights nearly as bad though I think this is about the worst we have had. I should have liked to have been there to Mothers picked up dinner but the veal I think is not so good as we had for dinner. viz Fried pork + Eggs and boiled Potatoes bread and coffee. I am sorry Mother has sent the old Bed Quilt as we have been restricted to ten wagons, and when we move shall have to leave much stuff that we have now, and undoubtedly Mats trunk will have to share the same fate. I have written to Luke twice about getting me a chance in the new Regt but, I guess there are more officers than men, though I think he might get me a chance and perhaps he will. a corporal in the city guard has had the offer of a Lieutenantcy in that Regiment and a private here has been offered the orderlies berth in a company in it. Another corporal in the same company has been appointed a Lieut in a Maine Regt and is only waiting to be paid off before taking it. it is over the river beyond Alexandria I don't see why anyone should dislike Col Lee. I liked him the best of any Col we ever had he was Col when I joined the Military I don't know as I wrote that we have had a visit from Porter Nutting and W A Hawley. the latter looks as natural as life. they stayed one night in the camp, and yesterday we had a visit from Mr Briggs the one that married Ann or Carolyn Clapp I don't know which, he also staid over night. Tell Mother that I am much obliged for the piece of flannel as twill come handy for cleaning my gun but as to mending my pants with it, I have a better way for they are plenty large enough to be drawn in to any amount and I have made them pretty much all over once, and as to the flag of truce we don't hang them out at all, no flags of that color, I don't know of anything I should rather find in the trunk when it comes than you and Mat. you sympathize a great deal with a young man that was sentenced to be shot, more perhaps than you would, if you had to sleep in camp and lie down at night, and sleep depending upon the vigilance of the Sentry's for your life and perhaps for the lives of the whole camp however I am glad he has been pardoned, as I had no doubt he would be, but the next one will not get off so easy there is to much depending on sentinels, to have them get into the habit of sleeping on their posts, and they have to keep awake only 8 out of 24 hours, and then very seldom oftener than once a week. his mother if he had one as you say would undoubtedly feel very much worse than if he had fell in battle.[12] (Mine would I know) but that is his fault, not the fault of the laws. Give my love to Nellie Parsons and tell her I should like to have a letter from her. Tell Aunt Lu I believe she owes me a letter, and she must not put it off for anything else, if it is true that our boys have commenced in advance, we shall soon have the way open for her to get home, and if she will wait til we do I will try to get leave of absence, and go with her. would'nt that be a funny way for me to make her a visit, after all that has been

said about my going there. I'm afraid they would not like to see me now. tell her
to send them any message from me she likes, if it would do. it is so provoking to
have them take up on the other side but then they will see things in a different
light one of these day's I think I get all your letters, I guess I have got the one you
call your long one, but I don't think any of them are very long compared to mine.
I am very happy to hear of Mrs Daisy's recovery, and think there is a prospect of
her dying by the hand of the "Soger boy" when he gets home. I hope you would
ask Mother to send me a receipt [recipes] for making Indian Pudding, Johnnie
Cake Griddle Cakes Pancakes +c anything that we can boil or fry. these are the
only methods of cooking we employ now, but we may perhaps have facilities for
baking sometimes, if we should stay long in one place, and it looks to me as
though we had a fair prospect of spending the winter here now, even if we go out
to fight I think we shall not break camp this is all uncertainty though,—I sent a
letter to Mother this morning and thought I should not get ideas enough for
another letter for a week, so you may thank my neuralgia for the length of this
one and also for its coming so soon. Give my love to all. tell Julia Clark I think
she should write first. give my respects to all Mr Clark's family also Mr Kingsley's Mrs Cook's and all the neighbors,—it still continues to pour in torrents, so
good night yours with all kinds of love

Charlie

8

Camp Brightwood DC
Sept 16th 1861

Dear Mother
    I meant yesterday to have written you a long letter, but it was the busiest day
we have had for a long time first in the morning we had company inspection, and
then got ready for Regimental inspection by Major Gen Buel at 11 o'clock and he
did not come until nearly 2 o'clock. after that we had to fall in for the funeral of
Lathrop Smith who died yesterday at about 12 o'clock. his body is being
embalmed and is to be sent home tomorrow he died of Typhoid Fever. his
brother got here the night before. the co have to pay the expenses, which are
some fifty dollars this is the fifth that has died of that fever within two weeks. I
should hate to be considered unfeeling but it is establishing a precedent that we
shall not be able to follow in going to this expense to get his body home, for we
cannot have but very few such instances, before it will take all of the pay of a
private to meet the bills this of course you will say nothing about as I shall pay my
proportion as cheerfully and as willingly as any man.[13]

Capt Joe arrived Saturday night to gether with Ike and Brewer Musgrave. they have been here ever since and are going home to day.

it is early morning and I am writing out doors, and have not time to write more this morning but will try to write a longer one to day or tomorrow. the goodies came to hand all right. the cap is just a fit, and the pies taste first rate. the bread had got mouldy. the watch was all right but I dropped it the first morning and it stopped it has not done any business since. I shall try to go to the city to day and get it fixed. I received Aunt Lu's letter, and shall answer it next. I have not time to write more this morning. love to all

Very affectionately yours
Charlie

9

Camp Brightwood DC.
September 22nd 1861

Dear Mother,

I have been intending to write you all day but have not got to it until now, about 7 oclock in the evening and it is awful hard to write now as the Capt has got the tent full and they are walking round the floor and shaking it, and talking a half dozen at a time so that I cannot hear myself think. I don't have half as easy time to write as I did have. Oh dear now the Capt has gone to reading Psalms, and I cannot do anything at all. I have almost forgotten the contents of your last letter so you must not be surprised if this does not seem to be much of an answer, or if it is a short letter. I noticed your remark about Gen McClellan but I presume his Sunday order is all for effect, at any rate we do not experience much of the rest spoken of on the Sabbath now a days for instance last Sunday we were reviewed by Major Gen Buel.[14] he ordered it at 11 oclock in the fore noon and did not come until 4 or 5 oclock in the afternoon, leaving us in a state of suspense all day not knowing when we should be called out, and consequently we had no rest at all as the review occupied all the rest of the day, with the inspection, and if the powers that be had any of this great respect for the Sabbath they would not have ordered the inspection on Sunday, for they might just as well have had it any other day, so you see that like all other great pretentions to religion, it is done for effect on the country at large, and as for all the stories of McClellans going to be prayed for in Cincinati and in all that sort of stuff I don't believe it any more than I should any other Newspaper lie.[15]—you are mistaken about our being excited here there is the greatest absence of excitement of any place I was ever in in fact,

there is none at all and if we have got to stay here three years we shall all die of euni [ennui] and it looks very much as if we were to stay here all winter at least for they have commenced to build a chapel to hold services in on the Sabbath, and I hear that all the Wagons are to be drawing boards this week to make barracks of still some things look as if we were going to fight, as for instance our ambulances have all been sent off but one still I suppose we might be ordered out of camp to fight and afterwards return to the same place to camp. it don't seem as if all these troops could stay here always and not have a battle. McClellan has issued an order to all the troops on Picket not to fire on the enemys Picket unless first fired on by them, so you see in addition to all the rest our poor fellows are to wait and be shot before they shoot anybody, as for any effect that will have on the rebels I think it is all bosh for the savages have no honor nor any sense of humanity, or any morals for such an order to have any effect what ever, we might as well make it a war of extermination on both sides and then there will be some survivors north after the other side is rooted out. they have no respects for the laws of nations, or any other laws human or devine, nor for their own word or solemn oath.[16] tell Sarah that I have given her message to Juba,[17] and he sends his respects. our house has quite an interest in the war now has it not all the dwellers there in have a relation in the Army yourselves May Phil and Sarah, quite a list to be sure. Capt Joe has not been very smart since he came, but I think is improving you speak of the responsibility of my position, but I should rather have one of less responsibility and more pay. there is a mighty difference between my pay and that of the next rank (2nd Lieut) $20 and $105.50 per month. I had a letter from Luke Lyman offering me the same position in the new co that I have in this but says he could not get me a commission as those have to go to the men that raised the company. I wonder if that is the case how they came to offer a lieutenancy to Hen Dwight, and give the captaincy to a boy from Amherst. it don't look very clear to me, but I suppose it is my usual good luck and another case of *professed* friendship, but I do not think I shall be at the expense of coming north to take the same position in another green company and go through the mill again for anybody elses benefit. there is no possible chance of promotion here and I think that if "patient waiters are no losers" neither are they any gainers, and as to the danger if I get into another Regt, I expect the danger and I can't see why I should not better myself, if I could because it might be more dangerous I had a letter from a friend of mine from Haydenville he is a member of the band in the 7th Maine Vol and is stationed in Baltimore. I had another from John D Isbell who is Quarter Master Sergeant in the 18th Mass Vol it does seem as if the men who knew the least about the military got the best chances. I presume it is a judgement on me for joining the military when you did not want I should. I don't see why you'd need have any certificate of my being here as it is paid by someone in Northampton and they know what I am serving in this Regt,

however I will get one if that is all that is wanted to get it, but probably the only reason is so we shall have another example of our good fortune. the cap sent by Mary is first rate just the thing and so is the night cap, it has been awful cold here to day and very uncomfortable without an overcoat. am much obliged for the recepts [recipes] and shall get Juba to try them. you did not send any for griddle cakes. tell Aunt Lu I have not forgotten her I think I should have written this to her, but I commenced before I thought, as I believe I owe her two, but tell her not to stop writing on that account, by any means. don't show this to anyone out of the family as everything I write gets back here whether it is printed or not.[18] we received no bundles of Gazzettes this week though I got one from you. it is time to put out the lights so good night, give my love to all, from ever your affectionate son

Charlie.

10

Camp Brightwood September 25th /61
Head Quarters 10th Regt MV

Dear Mary
  I have just received yours and Mothers letters and thought I would answer immediately although there is not much to write about. we have had another funeral this afternoon of a member of the band named Chase. this makes the sixth I believe, one of whom is buried here under a tree in full view of the camp, and speaking of this makes me think you have written to me several times about Fred Wrights being sick, and I have written you as aften that he is not sick. he has been no more sick than merely ailing for a day or two, and is apparently as tough and hardy as any man we have. Cal Kingsley has been sick for a couple of weeks or so, perhaps threatened with fever, but has not been in the Hospital nor kept his bed, is all merely excused from duty, and he is now well and has been doing duty for a week. If anybody is dangerously sick I shall let you know but as for paying any attention to such stories if people have any sense they will not.
  Things in camp all point to some movement of importance. what it is I cannot tell, but some new order is promulgated every day and every man is being provided with everything necessary for the field and march. we are ordered to have one suit of clothes, and one change of underclothes and all the most minute details are entered into in everything. all officers and soldiers wives are ordered out of camp before the first of October, and tonight everybody is excited in camp and bets are freely offered that we shall start before morning, but I do not

apprehend that we shall start as soon as that. the adjutant told me to night that he was sure we should go in the course of ten days, but he always has some bug bear story when there is any excitement of the kind, but nobody knows anything at all about it, and when the word comes we shall all be taken by surprise. I hope when we do go we shall break camp though I presume we shall not as Henry Wells brother to George Wells in our company belongs to a New York Regt, and they were sent over there and laid out two weeks without any tents, that will be pleasant won't it?

We have something to amuse us now as the Artillery attached to our Brigade comes up to our Parade Ground to drill, and it is great fun for us it is a Battery of 4 pieces six pounders. they are not very well posted up on the manuvers yet but the guns make just as much smoke and noise as though they were, and it is a great Blessing to us as it breaks the monotony of this hum drum life. Our company is out on Picket to day and our quarters are deserted. Captain Joe send his respects to all. he is improving I think, he has been out on horseback pretty much all day and has gone out to call tonight consequently I am monarch of Company Cs Headquarters just now we have received seven new recruits and our company now numbers 101 men. we have but very little sickness just now though our little drummer boy is in the Hospital but is getting along first rate I send you a picture of a group we had taken but tis a miserable picture but is good as can be expected I suppose with the conveniences they have for taking them. it was taken in front of the tent which is my home you will notice it has a double roof which prevents rain from beating through it all The artist took a picture of the Artillery yesterday and when he gets them done I shall try to get one to send home I think by your description the new Company is the off scouring of all humanity.

I'm sorry if Abner has enlisted with such a sett and I'm afraid he will bitterly repent when it is too late to, to think of his having to go into a tent with twenty of such a lot of Podunks devoid of common decency it almost made me cry to think of it. I should have thought he would rather have come on and joined this Company if he must go. I should rather he would have joined the regulars and then his comrades would be obliged to keep clean and decent while in camp or on duty at least. I am so sorry that he will know nothing about choosing his mess [?] but will go just where they put him I'm afraid, without opening his head. the Amherst company by what I hear from there is a better co, as I know many of them and they are nice fellows. still there may be a good proportion of those that are good men as of course I have only heard the names of the scamps, but I suppose it is useless for me to report or moralize about it. nobody could convince a boy that even if he had been through the mill no not an angel from Heaven they have all got to try for themselves I know from experience. I don't know but I judge to harshly of the co, as I said before but I know that there are certainly a

dozen of the company that are the lowest of the low, and to think of Aunt Rachels son as one of them makes me writhe, but enough said on that subject.

Mother speaks about thinking I should have more pride than to join that co as Orderly so I should if I had not thought I could have a better sight in the future but when after Lukes making such plausable excuses to me, and then offering a lieutenantcy to Hen Dwight, I gave up all idea of that, although I don't understand why Hen Dwight should consent to take the S. Major's post and refuse a lieutenantcy as a Sergt Major is only one rank higher than mine, and one dollar a month more pay while a Lieut gets six times as much, and ranks much higher, and is a commissioned officer which the Sergt Major is not. it does not seem as though it could be true, and besides a Sergt Major is not in line of promotion though that does not make much difference in the Volunteer service for if a man don't know anything he is qualified for promotion in that service.

I have been in camp alone all day and meant to have written a dozen letters but this is the only one I have accomplished as I had a lot of stuff to draw from the Quarter Master The Ordnance Officer and the Commiserat to fit out the new recruits and some of the old ones who had lost their clothes in part I never saw or imagined anything so heedless as some of them are just like children and no more capable of taking care of themselves. they would lose or throw away their heads if you did not watch them and then come to the Orderly Sergt for another. tell Sarah she need not worry about Juba he is all right safe and sound. Mother said she was in distress to know about him. I send some message about him every time I write. it seems as if you did not get all my letters I sent two last week one Monday and one Wednesday, you do not speak of having received but one. Juba cooks only for the Officers and myself now. they have taken him away from the company as they refuse to pay him anything after cooking for them two months, and the Lieuts paid him, and then took him to wait on them exclusively. he is safe for I just saw him asleep in his tent right back of ours.

Why did you not send along that note you found I should have liked it very much. I shall send the certificate if the Colonel gets up in time tomorrow morning if not, I will send it in my next. Mother knows what it is. we went into camp at Springfield the 12th of June so Mother can reckon the number of weeks I should think she ought to draw three dollars per week or at least two dollars though I don't know what the law was. the Harpers you sent was a prize indeed for me although I forgot to mention it in my other letters. I have read it through from beginning to end. I wish I could get my library into my knapsack I should send for it. I appreciate the motive in sending the first book but I cannot say I appreciate the books or ever did. oh dear! I'm so sorry for Uncle Edward do give my love to him, and tell him if Ab has not taken the oath to get him home again, and tell John if he wants any information about the Orderlie's business to write what and I will let him know but first of all he wants a copy of the Army

Regulations I have been ever since I started learning it and have not got it learnt yet but he is excused from a great many ardous duties which were put upon me, and will be likely to be on him, if he is not posted. I have not but just found it out myself but he is just from studying and can commit the regulations to heart, while I could learn the main points. I never wrote to Luke that I would accept anything less than I have got now but I wrote I should rather serve in the same capacity under him which I then thought I should, but after what has been done by his influence in that Company I would cut my hand off first, and then I would not. we shall have a reckoning some day if we both live through this war and meet again there is no one discontented only in so far as they should like to better themselves if they could, which I do not think is discontentment there is no one in this Regt that would exchange for the same in that, so that settles that matter and I would say good night as Capt has got back, and it is past time for lights to be out, and I will finish in the morning.

Thursday morning.

I have just been up to the Col's quarters but he has not got up yet and I am afraid I shall not be able to send the certificate but if I do not I will send it in my next we find ourselves all safe and sound this morning as no doubt we shall for a long time to come it is a beautiful morning and the companies are all out for morning drill and take them and the white tents on the hill with all the green woods for the background and the bright sun shining over all, it makes about as fine a sight as ever one could wish to see, and you can hardly realize that it is any part of war, but I must close with love to all and lots of it. I have written this letter partly to you and partly to Mother and I do not suppose it makes much difference who it is directed to as it is for all of you so good bye and let us hope that it will be less than three years before we meet again. yours with all love

Charlie

PS of course you will not read or show this letter to anyone

II

October 3rd 1861 Camp Brightwood DC

Dear Mother

I sent one letter to Aunt Lu this morning but as I am on the sick list and being better today I thought I would write you a few lines and send tomorrow. I do not get but two letters a week now from all sources but I presume it is because I write

less than I did but it is impossible to make letters out of what material we have now. We had a visit last week from a friend of our Company we made in Springfield. I don't know as you ever heard of him his name is Samuel K Lee he was in the next store but one from Rockwoods in Springfield when I was there and a great friend of J D Isbell. You may have heard me speak of him, at any rate he took the greatest fancy to our Company while on H Park,[19] and made us presents there, and used to come up and spend almost every evening with us, afterwards he sent us a box to Medford with presents of every kind in it. There is a candlestick now on this table that he sent us there after that he came down himself and staid till we sailed with us, and has kept up a correspondence with us, all along, and as I said before, he has been on and staid four or five days with us. he is the best fellow you ever saw, and a perfect gentleman. he made me a present of a splendid prayer book on here [?] with his name on it, and Capt Joe and myself have private services out of it. I don't know but I have written you that John Isbell is Quartermaster Sergt in the 18th Mass Regt. they are stationed over the river.

I have had pictures given me to day so I thought I would send them home for you to keep in case I should ever come home one is a picture of the Battery Artillery attached to this Brigade and takes in two or three lines of Companies tents in the background, but Co C is not among them, but they are all just alike for that matter it was taken the first day they came up here to drill and just as they were getting ready to load, the tents hardly show at all against the sky for a background.

I wrote to Aunt Lu in a hurry last night and I was sick tired and sleepy so I suppose it will not be a very interesting letter. she wrote that she was intending to start for home very soon and was coming here. I should be so glad to see her but I do not want to have her start for home yet, as it will be so difficult to get there and we shall certainly make it easier travelling in Virginia before a great many days, than it is now, and I do not know of any possible way for her to get into Va from here, in fact I know there is none, and when we make a start (we means McClellan) we shant come back until the job is finished. at any rate that is my humble opinion, for the alarm I wrote you about in my last proves it, for no sooner do the rebels make any suspicious movement than immediately the whole vast Union force is under arms in less time than it takes to tell of it, and ready to march at a moments notice in any direction and if they come on before McClellan is ready to advance, their cake is dough, and when he gets ready, the order will be forward till the thing is settled.

The Comfortable is very comfortable, in fact to much so, for when we march we shall have to leave everything of the kind and sleep on the ground with one blanket. I cannot then have even my shawl and I'm afraid the change will be to great, now I sleep as cosy as I ever did at home. I received some last weeks papers

to day I suppose they have been delayed as we have received our bundle of this weeks Gazzettes all right. I shall write to Mr. Boland tonight or tomorrow I sent him a paper this morning. I said to Aunt Lu that her letter was written on the Prests fast[20] but I see by the date since that twas not, but I suppose its just as well, I never look at the dates of letters, so I when she wrote about attending church I jumped at that conclusion without thinking. it is now evening in the camp is at rest again and everything is quiet and peaceful as you could wish, how soon to be broken by the din of battle one alone only knows. Another Regt passed here on its way north to day. it was said to be a Philadelphia Regt and going to Coleville some twelve miles north of here. there must be a great many troops on the road to H Ferry now. I have got to the end of my paper and will close. remember this makes the third letter this week. give my love to all reserving the lions share for yourself, from your aff son

Charlie.

I forgot to state that Capt Enos Parsons and Porter Nutting arrived here during dress parade tonight on the everlasting Post Office business I suppose I can't see why they cannot let it alone fooling away thier time and money over it.

12

Camp Brightwood DC October 9th 1861

Dear Mother

I received a good long letter from you to day, with a short one from Aunt Lu, for which I am as glad as you can think. I sent Mattie one yesterday morning with a account of Henry Parsons death.[21] his father arrived here to day but I did not see him as myself and Alvin Rust got permission to go out shooting, and had taken our target and gone when he came. he staid but a very few moments and was gone when we came back. Henry died very suddenly indeed, as no one considered him dangerous until noon of the day he died, at least no one in the Company. there appeared to be a difference of opinion between the Doctors. Doctor Holbrook said the day before he died that it was a bad case of Typhoid but Dr. C thought differently, as I told Mattie in my last I was in the Hospital Sunday PM and sat with him quite a while and he appeared to me quite smart and nothing seemed farther off to me than his death, but there seems to be something that our Doctors don't get hold of. the city guards had a man die in the city Hospital at about the same time, and one died at the same place from the Shelburne Falls Co, and to day Howard one of our men, has died at Columbia

Hospital. you remember I wrote of his being sick in my last Sergeant Bishop is said to be getting better. we received a message from S B Curtis, about him yesterday and I walked a mile and a half up to Brigade Head Quarters with the answers. I learned from your letter that Mr Curtis boards at our house you can tell him that D C says Bishop is better and he can see no reason why he won't get along.

It is considered certain that there will be at least three more deaths in this Regt within twenty four hours one from each Company B D + K are lying at the point of death now the two former at the City and the other here. in regard to my own health I am well and hearty again and you would have thought to have seen me trudging off to day with a great big target on one Shoulder and a musket on the other, which I carried a mile, and part of the way up a hill steeper than anything I know of in Northampton. A Rust was with me as I said before and we made some splendid shots at three hundred yards I hit the circle of less than the size of a mans head, which is doing first rate with a common musket, as they are not remarkable for accuracy we are going to try it at eight hundred yards tomorrow. I have not had an attack of Neuralgia for a week, and for two days I have felt first rate, not withstanding we have had a sudden change in the weather and it has been so cold to day that I have worn my overcoat all day.

I cannot get over Henry Parsons death. it came so sudden and he was a particular friend of mine, and he and myself had, many a confidential talk together and always worked together from the first, and he was in my squad until I came to tent where I am now, so that it takes hold of me more than the death of almost any other man in the Co unless it is Cal or John Cook. I cannot make the death of this last man nor of the first seem half as bad to me though I suppose it is just as bad for thier friends. it is half past eight and I have had to stop writing to go up and call the roll. Tattoo is at 8 and ¹/₂ o'clock now. I came very near having a chance to come home with Henrys body, if Erastus Harris had not been coming and his father had not come on I had the promise of going with it, but it was my usual luck, nothing ever happens right for me. I should so like to come home and stay a few days, but probably shall not until the war is over as McClellan won't grant a furlough to save a mans life. it has been tried in Lewis Day's case who is no more fit to be here than you are. I believe he is going to apply for a discharge which he can probably get. Aunt Lu writes that she is going to start for home, which in my humble opinion is just about as foolish a thing as she can do for the Lord only knows how she is to get there, and they will probably hang her the first thing when she does get there. Give my best love to her and tell her not to start.

There is a rumor in camp tonight of the capture of New Orleans but nobody places any faith in it. we have also a rumor of a fight in Banks department which lacks confirmation. Cal Kingsley is tough and hearty now. he and myself and

Johnnie Cook are going to have our pictures taken together when the man comes round again. give my best respects to Mrs K + Mr K also to Mrs Cook and all thier family John I believe has not seen a sick day since we have been in service. give my respects to Mr Clarks family also and all the neighbors. An attendant from the Hospital just stuck his head into this tent and says Howard is not dead after all, but is raving crazy so I presume he will die before morning. they made some mistake at the Hospital in the city and it is someone else that is dead, but I don't think there can be much hope for him as almost all of them are taken crazy before they die, but Henry Parsons was not and I suppose did not think he was going to die ten minutes before he did. I must close for tonight and if I think of anything else I will write in the morning so good night.

Thursday morning

    I am twenty eight years old to day. I don't think I should have [thought] of it if you had not reminded me of it in your letter. In regard to my being in any of those pictures, it is not so. it was probably Lieut Shurtleff who you saw in the tent, so you need not dispute any man about that. I should suppose that the town might pay that sum without so much fuss as they make about [it] but I do hope and pray that some of those old skinflints will have to be drafted and then see how they will like it. I guess [?] come to bring them down to 6 hours drill a day they would be willing to shell out to get away from it news has come this morning of another victory at Hatteras Inlet. We shall probably hear of more victories before long. Capt Joe is out in front of the tent drilling some new recruits and the rest of the Company have gone out Target Shooting you would think if you could hear the noise here just now that there was a fearful Battle going on, but they are only learning to send the ball strait to the mark to be ready when the time comes. It [is] cloudy and cold this morning and looks as if it was going to rain. I must close now as I have my morning report to make out Give my love to all and write often to

Your aff son
Charlie.

13

Camp Brightwood DC Oct 15th 1861

Dear Pary

    As to morrow is my day for sending a letter, I thought I would write you although I have nothing to write about. we are still in the same camp though we have expected almost hourly to march, and the Col told us at Dress Parade last

night that he had no doubt that we should go over into Virginia within three days. he made us a long speech and said that after our first review Gen Mc-Clellan said this was a Brigade he could depend on, and said we have the name of being one of the best Brigades in the service, and says he we know we are the best Regiment in the Brigade. Major Marsh says that Gen Buel who is in command of this division is a very ambitious man, and knows he has good troops under him and he keeps urging the matter to have us called into the service, that he may get the credit of what we may do if we should do ourselves honor as I suppose he thinks we shall. if we go over there we shall have a hard time enough of it. we have had orders to night to put all tools of the Regiment in perfect order Shovels Pickaxes Axes + Hatchets so you see they are laying out plenty of work for us. if we don't have any fighting, they say that the troops over there have to work like everything making roads building earthworks, and cutting wood. We had a rumor last night that from 30,000 to 50,000 men have landed at the mouth of Occoquan River, if that is so we are probably to have busy times very soon, and what a battle it will be when they come together there must be over 200,000 men on our side and probably not much less on the other, and it will be hot work when the tug comes but we are going to have the victory unless by some special dispensation in the rebels behalf. we have heard nothing to day of the aforesaid troops and it may be true that it may and it may be not, though it is no sign that it is not, because the papers don't mention it for if it is of any importance to keep it secret they would not be allowed to publish it. The supposition is that when we move forward Gen Banks will move also and also the troops that are said to have landed below, and all three are very large armies indeed But after all nothing is known and nothing certain will be known until it is done, and if Gen McClellan comes up to the scratch and does what is expected of him he is thereafter the man of the age.

But to return to ourselves and Company C. Sergeant Bishop has been discharged from the Hospital and is considered well but has not got strong enough to do any work yet. Howard, who was reported dead once is getting better Sergeant Day has applied for a discharge from the service, and will probably get it he tried to get a furlough of three weeks but could not, and he never can get well here. I will tell you what the doctors say though you must not tell of it on any account at home. he has got the consumption they say and one lung is gone. be sure and not speak of it at home for I don't know as he knows it himself—my health is first rate and I can sit down any time and eat a horse. I am hungry all the time and eat more than I ever did before in my life. you must be sure and let me know if you receive the picture of the camp I sent Monday and I believe you have not said anything about the pictures I sent last. oh yes! Mother did in her last Cal Kingsley and John Cook[22] are both well and have both had a letter stating that Aunt Lu was going to start last Monday if so she should have

been here before this, but I cannot believe that she will, but if she is coming I hope she will come before we move over the river, as she cannot get over there to see me and it is doubtful that I can come over to see her, as the orders are very strict now and no relations of soldiers are allowed to go over to see thier friends, on the other side, which I consider a gratuitus cruelty, but our so called superiors don't consider that common soldiers have any of the feelings of humanity I suppose. I don't know as I aught to say that either as spies are so plenty and the authorities cannot spend time to examine into every individual case, but if Aunt Lu should come after we have gone over, she must let me know by mail and I shall make a strenuous effort to get a pass to come over and see her.

when you write me let me know all about the new Regiment if there is one, and whether the 27th Regt has gone yet or not. we heard they were to start Monday and afterwards they were to start Wednesday. I suppose they are to go to camp on Long Island it is said that the troops that landed on Occoquan were one of the expeditions that was supposed to be going south. Charlie Wells is still getting better and I presume he will get well though when I asked the Dr about him this morning he had not seen him I gave Mothers message to Mrs Minch and she sends her love I suppose though I don't know whether she said to or not

Give my love to Aunt Lu if she has not gone and tell her I do not want to see her bad enough to have her start for home yet, though I would not fail to see her if possible if she does come I know she must feel dreadfully about the last battle but let us hope her family were none of them in it. Mrs Minch experienced a great deal of sympathy for her. give my best love to Mother, and this letter is as much to her as anyone and so are all the letters I write home so you need not any of you put on airs when my letters are addressed to you. we have a deaf and dumb tailor in camp and he has drawn a splendid picture of our camp, and is going to have it lithographed, and when it is done I shall get a copy for home.[23] it is the most comical sight to see him round among the boys talking by signs. he also carrys a slate so when he cannot communicate by signs he writes. he is everybodys friend and everybody is his. he is a sort of Regimental pet, we are having most beautiful moonlight nights, so bright that I can see to call the roll at Tattoo (8 ½ oclock PM) by the light of the moon.—we are drilling almost entirely in four ranks which looks a little ominous as I suppose that fighting is pretty much all done in that way. we are to drill in skirmishing tomorrow morning with blank cartridges which we have not done before. I have written this letter with a tent full all the time and could hardly hear myself think, so you must excuse all mistakes as I have not time to read it over Give my love to all as usual reserving a large share for yourself from Your Aff brother

Charlie.

14

Camp Brightwood DC Oct 23rd 1861

Dear Mattie,

I received your long and welcome letter, and was more than glad. it was just such a letter as I like to get only I like them longer, if anything I have been alone in the tent all day to day, as Company C is on grand guard or Picket as it is popularly known and they are all gone but me and three or four men up in the quarters. we are living on in the old style with nothing for excitement. we had intended to change the location of the tents to day towards yesterday morning there came up a tremendous rain storm and lasted until this morning. we move the tents once in a while for sanitary considerations as it is considered unhealthy to keep them in one place a great while at a time. It is now 5 oclock PM and the wind is blowing a perfect hurricane and it is so cold that my fingers are actually stiff. the boys will have a tough time tonight lying out by the roadside. Erastus Harris got back last Saturday he brought a number of trunks for the boys and they got the goodies out and shared them round and then we gave three rousing cheers for old Northampton which roused the camp.

by the way Henry Parsons gave me his pistol, but as it was locked up in his carpet bag and the key lost it was carried back to Nhampton and his father gave it to A J Harris to bring back. he says he left it at his (Harris's) fathers house. I wish you would go and see if he did and get it as I am very suspicious that he has sold it, especially as Capt Parsons gave him $10 to pay expenses connected with carrying those corpses home and when Henry's father came on he told Harris he might give it to his (the Captain's) wife but Harris spent it and Capt is minus, and I am afraid he has sold or pawned the pistol. at any rate I wish some of you would see about it. Major Marsh has been trying to get a furlough to go home but has not succeeded and I think it is doubtful whether he will as they are very stingy with thier furloughs

We have had intelligence of the battle of Leesburgh but can hardly make out which side got the victory. we had another time of expectation night before last and yesterday night before last the cooks were all night cooking three days rations and we have the customary orders to be ready +c +c but I suppose it was on account of that Battle. The Tammany Regt which was engaged in it was the one we camped side of at Kalorama and that gave us tea the night we lay on the ground the Fifteenth Mass Regiment which was also engaged went by here but a few weeks ago and Col Raymond Lee made a call at our Colonels, and staid quite a little while. The regt rested in the road in front of our camp. Col Lee is among the missing. he was a gray headed man and his whiskers were white as snow.

I have just got through my tea and feel pretty well but it is so cold my toes

ache. although I have just got a pair of new boots with soles one inch thick the government shoes are miserable things and cannot be made to last the month and all that merchants will allow in exchange for them is 75 cents though the government price is $2.10 each Soldier is allowed four pairs a year. I drew two pairs so it brought my boots down to $3.50 in money, as this price was $5.00 they charge outrageously for everything in Washington I had to give sixty two cents for a hairbrush no better than I have sold hundreds of for a quarter or less I cannot tell how much obliged I am to Tom for the interest he takes in my welfare and I do so hope he will succeed. if he wants any recommendations from Capt or the Colonel he can have them Capt says he will recommend me for anything military or for *anything* else, and I have not the slightest doubt that the Col would also. I hope Mr Hayden will take an interest in the matter as that makes all the difference in the world. I am glad John has got so good a chance. there is a great difference between a second lieutenantcy and the Orderlies, one is all work and no pay and the other is all pay and no work

Fred Wright is anxiously waiting for his transfer and is aching to be on his way home. Cal Kingsley has been to the city to day. I don't know as I wrote you anything about my visit to the city I went all over the Capitol and saw the pictures Mary tells so much about, but I should like to stay there and look at them a month. you can tell Mary that all the floor under the one where the pictures are is one vast Bakery, with thousands of Barrels of Flour packed up in it, and teams constantly arriving and carry off loads and loads of Bread. this Regiment has a thousand loaves or more every day and other Regiments the same so you can judge what an amount of business they do there we have a Butcher established at Brigade Head Quarters and kill our own beef. Capt is going to get a stove for our tent. the ladies have one in theirs and so does the Colonel. Bishop has got pretty well and has gone to duty again. Charlie Wells has been out once we have had no new cases of sickness in our Company very lately and I hope we shall not have. I am going to stop now and play a few games of Euchre and will finish afterwards. It is now 9 oclock and I have just come from playing Euchre with Fred Wright and he has been talking about going home, which makes me feel a little homesick. So Aunt Lu is really going to start or rather has started to day I am afraid I shall not see her but I hope I shall. I don't see what she wants to stop in Philadelphia for. I'm afraid I shall be ordered off before she comes the officers have been making bets that we shall be ordered off within a week I sent Tom two papers to day I have sent him some before I wonder if he received them. I received the papers you sent. You have no idea how cold it is tonight. it is a real November night I have been copying Orders and finishing the pay rolls to day and my hand is so cramped that I can hardly write at all

I am glad you are so rejoiced about the liquor question, but it is no great thing,

as I have no particular desire for it, but every other man in the Company but Lt W and myself drink daily if they can get it. I should have excepted Lt Shurtleff though as he very seldom drinks, but some of the men do get so confounded drunk and raise pluto that I was determined that they should not have the fact that I drink too, to throw in my face, if they had to be put in the Guard House, and I might have to do it. you mentioned what the ladies are doing I am glad to hear that they are knitting socks, as those are the most acceptable things they can send for the Government Article is worse and are poor things enough and stockings of real knit stamp will be hailed with delight, if you have a chance I wish you would send me a couple of dozen of boxes Olmstead Leather Preservative and I will send you the money when we get paid off. it is the best thing to put on Boots and Shoes that there is made and will prevent them cracking out. I succeeded in buying a box of one of the men to day although he did not want to sell it. Give my respects to Bill Kingsley and tell him to come down and spend Thanksgiving. I expect we shall all be mighty homesick on that day I almost hope they won't appoint one.

I would send up recommendations if I knew what kind of ones to send, or how to write one but I do not. I wish it had been possible to have got a commission in the same Regt with Fred Wright but it makes but little difference when if I could only get one, I wish the Governor could know the whole story. how I was cheated out of the Lieutenancy in this Company, but I don't know as it would do any good. Capt Parsons had the most beautiful letter from Henry Parsons father to day and the [most] patriotic I ever saw it would ring tears out of stone. he says "I am sorry I have but one to give my country" it was a magnificent letter and I wish it could be published he prays for blessings on us and it seems as if with such fervid patriotism as his to buck us as if we must prevail. Poor Henry. I miss him very much as he used often to come and sit with me when I was in the tent alone as his duties and mine often kept each of us from going out with the Company, but we cannot call him back, and he and his family have given more than any of the rest of us may be called to, for our common country and thier glory is greater in the same. I am grieved for his sisters for I have sisters of my own and I know what thier feelings would be under the same circumstances. how little we thought as we sat on the steps of his fathers house one day but a short time before we left what would happen in a few months We were up on the plain to drill and during a rest we went over there and got a luncheon if we had been told that one of us would be taken in a few short months I think we should neither of us thought that he would be that one but so it is.[24]

I cannot imagine why the people of Northampton allowed the traitors Lathrop to go from them for of thier treason I have no doubt. I should think somebody would make it thier business to follow them and see by what means they can get home for if there is a way for them there is a way for other traitors

and it should be looked to. are they afraid of them on account of their wealth and standing or what is the matter. it is my opinion that somebody has neglected thier duty in that matter

Johnnie Cook has got possession of a young Oppossum somehow and it is a comical looking thing, half Woodchuck and half Coon I should say shouldn't you know he would have it if anybody, but I believe it has been doomed by the boys in his [tent] as not being an agreeable mess mate I saw a boy of another compány have one to day and I rather think it is the same one. you can tell Miss Miranda Cook that I saw Cal rolled up in the blanket she sent him, and he looked as if he would have a very comfortable night he and another have been to the city to day consequently they are not out with the rest of the Company to day. I wish you could see with what eagerness we watch for the mails and what a blessing it is to get letters. I think if you could, you would write every day it is the chiefest of our pleasures.

I wish also that you could see our camp by moonlight. I have written often about it but I cannot describe. I never tire of looking at it and it has the addition tonight of a large fire before the Guard Tents, which are usually shaded by the woods, but the fire lights up the whole front and adds a great deal of beauty to the scene. it seems strange to see anything so beautiful and peaceful connected with "grim visaged war"

Tell May Phil I am very much obliged for the papers she sent. they were a great treat. I must close now give my love to all and my respects to all the neighbors especially to Mrs Clarks family Mrs Kingsleys and Mrs Cooks and Miss Miranda also Mrs Strong with lots of love your aff brother

Charlie.

15

Camp Brightwood DC Nov 10th 1861

Dear Mary

I received a letter from Mother and yourself yesterday also one to day which was written October 24th It is the missing letter of week before last. just came to hand I can't think where it has been all the time as it was directed plain enough but I am sure I wish it had come when it ought to for I was disapointed enough at not getting it. Last Friday we had a grand Review at the grounds near Columbia College where we hold our Brigade and Division drills. it was a grand affair. there were in all about 10,000 men and the President + Gen McClellan were there. I did not see the President to know him. we started at half past eight in the

morning and got back about six oclock at night. it is four or five miles from here, and we were with knapsacks on about 10 hours, with hardly any rest at all, yet we have got so used to it that we were not very much fatigued. Not much like the old Military when we used to stop and rest every quarter of a mile. I have sent a paper that contained a notice of it. we have a little news of the fleet this morning and it is supposed that they have succeeded very well we are anxiously awaiting further intelligence from them. I suppose you have received my letter containing my recommendations and you will observe they are pretty strong, but I think there is no possible doubt that I shall get a 2nd Lieutenantcy in this regiment as there will be 4 vacancies very soon one in Company I one in Company D one in Company A and which one the other comes in I do not know as yet, but the Adjutant is very sick and to day the Doctors report that he cannot live. to day consequently they will have to promote a 1st Lieutenant to his place, so I am quite certain that I shall have a chance. the 1st Lieut of Company A has got the delirium tremens, which kills him for remaining any longer in this Regiment. he has already been cashiered, before he got sensible of his condition. I presume my Lieutenantcy will be in that Co which is the worst Company in the Regiment, but I suppose it don't make much difference so long as I am a Lieut. though I wish it was in this Company. I hope to know something about it this week, but this Red Tape business takes a long time. Mother hopes that I can get an appointment in Fort Warren, but that would be impossible and besides I don't want to be up there loafing around. I don't call that going to war. I should think that Frank Conkey would feel cheap enough to Volunteer for any such safe service as that. I think it is worse than not Volunteering at all. but I don't want any such service as that its to much like Home Guards, and I don't think I'm adapted for a Home Guard. Conkey will get well laughed at I have no doubt.

I had a nice long visit from Aunt Lu last Thursday, in this way we were all ordered down to Columbia College in the afternoon. we were to fall in at one oclock. we were all at dinner when up drove a carriage with nigger driver attached, and there sat her ladyship as large as life she sat down and took dinner with me and I got excused from the drill, so we had a visit all alone all the afternoon except a little while that she was gone to see Mrs. Merrick. she sewed some Orderlies stripes on my blouse, and we had a first rate time generally, and wished many times that you were all here. she returned to the city at 4 oclock. she said that she should be at the review on Saturday, but I did not see her.

it is Sunday evening and the Camp is in the wildest excitement. Cheers upon Cheers rend the air and everybody is shaking hands and slaping each other upon the back and Cheers come floating through the air from the Camps of the 36th NY and 7th Mass for a report has come that the American Flag floats over the Court House in Charleston SC, or Beaufort, or some other place down there the news is almost too good to believe, but the fleet has made a strike somewhere,

and you will probably know all the circumstances before this gets to you. But to return to Aunt Lu, she seems to be in good spirits as one could expect, and is in very pleasant circumstances, and the folks where she is stopping are most kind to her. Cal K and John Cook and all are well and growing fat. Major Marsh starts for home tomorrow. The news has settled down to the fact that our troops have silenced 3 Batteries and landed, and the Stars + Stripes float over the Court House at Beaufort,[25] and they are marching inland. I would not wonder if we were sent down there, as it is known that troops are sent off somewhere pretty soon after they have had a grand review But there is too much excitement in Camp to write any more tonight if I can get time in the morning I will add some more or will write another tomorrow I hope the good news of tonight will be the same in morning. so good night Your affn Brother

Charlie

16

Camp Brightwood DC November 17th 1861

Dear Mother

It is Sunday morning and our Sunday duties to the Government are over until Dress Parade at 4:30 PM so I have taken my pen in hand to write to you, though my fingers are so stiff and cold that I cannot make them go very well. it is a regular blustering windy November day and although the sun shines as brightly as in July still there is no warmth in it and the wind cuts right through a fellow

Friday night our company was detailed to garrison Fort Mass during the night (they send one company in there every night) and as Lieut W was unwell, and Lieut S was on Court Martial and Capt Parsons Officer of the day, I was sent in command of the company so you see if I don't get the pay of a Lieut, I can do the duties. there are no tents or Barracks in the Fort, and nothing to sleep on, but the bare earth, consequently we did not sleep at all, and had to keep running round to keep warm at all, as no fire nor light is allowed, and although there is a large church right in the center of it it is kept locked and no one allowed to enter it. it is a perfect humbug sending anyone there, as one man is just as good as 500 for no enemy can get within 25 miles of it in force, still we have to go through the ceremony. I slept a large part of yesterday. Col Lyman paid us a visit yesterday. he looked quite natural. he says Abby is getting well. he was going to see Aunt Lu when he went back. he did not stay but a short time, he says they expect to go with the next force to reenforce Gen Sherman. I have heard nothing more about our going, and do not know as there is any foundation for the rumor, that we

were. We have not been paid off yet and I don't know when we shall be I don't see any more prospect of our being than there has been for two weeks past. we all supposed we were going to be yesterday, but we were not and that's the most we know about it. we have been promised a new uniform for two months but it has not arrived yet and I don't know as it will. our old one is getting quite ragged, and if it was not for the Jackets we wore from Northampton, we should suffer from the cold, but one wears them under our blouses and are quite comfortable. we are all very anxious to go south and I should not wonder if we got a chance. they are having Oranges and sweet Potatoes and all sorts of good things down there.

There were 9 contrabands arrived in camp last night.[26] they ran away from some place twenty miles above here in Maryland. I don't know whether anyone will come after them or not, but if there does not nobody in the Regt will make it thier business to send them back. Col Briggs did not come out here to hunt niggers, and can't see that it is any part of his duty to send them back so if they do not come after them they will stand a good chance of getting free, and so they will if there does, as the men will afford them every facility for getting away, and you may rest assured that they won't be fired upon if they run by the guard. this war is playing the Dickens with slavery and if it lasts much longer will clear our Countrys name of the vile stain and enable us to live in peace hereafter. the effect at Port Royal of our landing there shows how much all the talk about niggers fighting for thier masters amounts to, and I should not wonder if our large arrival was one of the immediate effects of the talk about that affair.[27]

Geo Bigelow is under arrest by the General *and all for nothing,* he was on Grand Guard, what we used to call Picket, and since the cold weather came on, they issued a foolish order that they shall not have any fire. George was out Thursday night and stood it as long as he could without a fire then built one. a Rhode Island Captain was Field Officer and he reported him to General and the Gen had him arrested. George relieved a Co of the R I Regt on the same duty, and found three fires that they had. I think it is about the meanest thing that ever happened but Rhode Island will have to toe the mark and not miss one iota of her duty in this Regt and let us catch her at it. if they do they will get snapped up short. George says he never will draw his sword in this Regiment again, and I don't blame him as there is nothing in the Articles of War or Regulations against having a fire on Grand Guard, unless in close proximity to the enemy, but old Buel must promulgate an order, that they should not. he considered it his duty to make soldiers just as miserable as he could but thank the Lord they have started him off into Kentucky and we shall have no more of him

I wish you would write all about what hope there is of my getting a commission up there as I do not think there is any hope here. there has been two Orderlies promoted here within a few days which makes three in all, so you see all the talk about my being the best, where considered the best is a humbug, and I

don't want to hear any more of that stuff. I have endeavored to do my whole duty and if I have failed it is not my fault and certainly I have had no reprimands, nor any fault found with me. I do wish I could get home to Matties wedding, but it will be impossible. Majors and Col's and big officers that are supposed to be of some use here, can get furloughs, but privates that would not be missed among the thousands of them cannot, but thats Bible doctrine that they that have shall be added on to and they that have not shall be taken away from, even that which they have.[28]

I have just written a letter to Aunt Lu. I am going to try to go and see her when we get paid off. she carried off Capts Picture, of his wife and children, when she was here and has not returned it yet. how like her that was now she wants me to pay the postage on a lot of slips of [mail?] which she wants to get of Mrs Wendell and send to Mary and I suppose I shall do it, if she ever gets to it, but at the same time I think it is a humbug. since I commenced writing a rumor has come to me twice that I had gotten an appointment as 2nd Lieut in Co A, but I don't think it is so. Don't build any hopes on it I must close now as Capt wants the table love to all write long letters to Your aff son

Charlie

17

Camp Brightwood DC November 21st 1861

Dear Mary

I received your welcome letter yesterday or rather last evening and should have answered it so as to send this morning, but we had just got back from Brigade Drill and were very tired so I went to bed instead. well it is Thanksgiving and I have thought of home many many times to day although it has been quite like Thanksgiving at home. we had a roast Turkey and Oysters, Cranbery Sauce Sweet Potatoes, +c +c, and had Mrs. Capt Joe to dine with us so we had all that anyone has even to the Company. the boys all had roast Turkey, and we have had no drill, and have passed the day very agreably indeed. Cal Kingsley had a big Turkey sent him from home and his mess got up a great dinner day before Thanksgiving and had Mrs. Col Briggs, Major Marsh + wife and Capt Joe + wife and had a grand good time generally. Company I from Holyoke + W Springfield had an enormous quantity of things sent them. they had 80 chickens 20 Turkies with Mince Pies, plus Cakes plus Cheese. it made a pile about as big as a tent. it was all cooked, so they rigged up a long table on thier Co Parade, and all ate dinner together, so you see we have made out quite a Thanksgiving, but

there was not one but what thought of home, and I could often notice a moistening of the eye as home and friends were mentioned.

I wrote an answer to Aunt Laura's last letter but have received no reply. I should have written to her to come out to dinner to day but we were so busy I did not think of it. Mrs. Parsons is going in to W to see her and Lieut W and myself expect to go to Annapolis and shall go to see her on the way. we have got permission from the Col + Capt and if we can get the Generals we shall be all right We hear nothing more about our going to South Carolina, but I suppose we shall not even if we are to go until day before we start. we get no news of any importance. I cannot think what Mr. Seward[29] meant in his conversation with Mr. Wendell at any rate his prophecy did not prove true, and I suppose he knows about as little of the war movements as anyone else—

The weather here is just about the same as it is at the N in November, warm + cold windy and stormy, as November always is We were paid off yesterday and I enclose $15 Mother made a suggestion in a letter some time ago. you can tell her to carry it into effect when you get this. I should send more but I cannot tell what may turn up and I may need it before another pay day. you must be sure and acknowledge the receipt of it as I should be afraid it was lost if you did not and I wish you would write longer letters and I should like them oftener. I have had no answer to my letter to Abby. I suppose he has not got well enough to write yet, but I suppose I shall see him this week or next. The Camp is quite lively with ladies just now. besides the three mentioned there is Capt Ives wife and the Adjutants, or rather the acting Adjutants wife, and Lieut Shurtleffs wife and some others are coming. If I had a wife I should request her to stay at home for I don't think the camp is any place for a woman, but still they will be tagging around after the men you know, and you can't make any guard keep the ladies off. I verily believe if all the "secesh" women in the south could walk right into any camp without any challenge at all.[30]

Lieut Col Decker has been placed in command of the 7th Mass Vols and will probably make Col of it. In that case Maj Marsh will probably be promoted and I should not wonder if Capt Parsons was made Major. in that case I should certainly get a Commission in our own Company, but you must not say anything about this as it is Castles in the air, and may not happen at all. the Belchertown part of our Company have had a box of things from home as big as a common [?] it contained comfortables and Blankets for all the Soldiers from that town in this Regiment. it seems as if every town took care of its own Company but NHampton and they take care of the Hospital when there are not a dozen sick ones in all. the quartermaster has got enough of such things to fill our Parlour that have been sent to the Hospital, and when there is a Company out on Grand Guard on a cold night Col Briggs sends out the Comfortables + Blankets to them, and that is all the real benefit derived from them.

Captains wife thinks we are a great deal more comfortable than she expected and I am glad she came for she will not feel half as bad when she gets home

I wonder if this war will last three years and if I shall see home before the end of that time, or if I ever shall again. if things don't go on much more rapid than they have yet, it will take much more than three years to end the war. it is said the President is going to call for 200,000 more men in that case Mass will have to furnish half as many more than she has, and where is she going to find them. they will have to go to drafting them certain. I suppose you have heard of the great Review of troops over the river yesterday 70,000 men it took from 11 oclock AM to 4:30 PM for the line to pass in review.

I cannot think of anything more to write tonight so I will close, hoping to hear from home soon and often. Please find out if it will help matters for me to get a recommendation from Col Briggs, and let me know if it will. Give my love to all at home and all enquiring friends, and write soon to Your aff Brother

Charlie

18

Camp Brightwood DC November 24th 1861

Dear Mother

I received a letter from you and Mary last night and was glad to get it as usual. We have just got through with Thanksgiving week and have made as much of it as possible under the circumstances but it did not seem much like Thanksgiving. It is Sunday night and snowing like fun it is the first snow we have had but the weather is much warmer than some we have had. I suppose it will not last much longer than our first snows at home. I do not know where the reports came from of my being appointed a Lieut. there has been a great deal of such talk here but I have not got one yet though everybody says I shall I don't know whether I shall or not. Col Briggs is so slow that I don't know what to think it is "hope deferred that maketh the heart sick"

So Mattie is really going to be married and I cannot be there. how I wish I could but it is no use wishing or hoping for anything. you know when you get up just what you have got to do during the day, and that night you know you have to get up and go through it all over again tomorrow. we have our daily duties varied about twice a week by a Brigade or division drill at Columbia College. We have got a new General and like him very much. he appears to have great consideration for the men. We had one of the drills last Friday and almost the first order he gave was "Colonels will be very careful to improve every moment of oppor-

tunity to rest the men" consequently, after every maneuver, we ordered arms and waited for the next which was a great relief, and every little while he would order "prepare to rest" when we stacked arms, and sat down or moved round, all of which makes the tedius hours of drill pass off very quickly and the men learn more and do better, than when they are kept at it hour after hour as we were under Gen Buel, ten hours upon the stretch, and with knapsacks on at that, and then Gen Keyes[31] orders the drills in the morning and gets through by three oclock, but when Buel was here, we had two or three hours drill in the forenoon and then started for the other drill about 1 oclock, and staid until about 5 oclock and got completely dragged out by the time we got home. The prospect now is that we shall winter here. the Col has given permission to the men to put stoves in thier tents which he refused before, and I guess we are not likely to move from here. if we should stay here and I could afford it I should try to get a furlough this winter but it would use up two or three months of my present pay. I expect to go to Ananapolis on Tuesday to see Ab. if I can get a pass, which I guess I can as Sergeant Braman has been, or rather is gone there now. his pass ran out to day but he has not returned yet.

George Bigelow has been released and had his sword returned to him without a trial as it appears that he was partly justified in building a fire. he will probably soon be first Lieut as Lieut Keith will probably be Adjutant in O Edwards place, as Edwards has got an appointment on Gen Buels staff it is said, whether it is true or not I do not know.

Col Lee of the 27th Regiment has been here to day. he thinks they will go south very soon. we are all quite sure that we should go with them at one time but begin to doubt it now, as I said before you mentioned that Aunt Lu was afraid that we had gone over the river, as she did not hear from me. I answered her last letter, but as I had lost the number of Mr Wendells house, I directed it to his care and it is possible that she did not get it at any rate I have not heard from her since and don't know what has become of her. she sent Capt Joes Picture back but wrote not a word to me. Capts wife spends most of the day in camp. she is boarding at a Mr Reynolds about a mile from Camp with Majors wife. The Col + wife occupy the tent erected for Mrs Merrick. Everybodys wife is coming that can afford to have her come. I went out about a half mile this PM to a house where we have got acquainted and made a call with PW Kingsley. we sat quite a little while by an old fashioned fireplace had some apples and some mince pie, the people keep a small country store, and I bought a new cord for my tent, and he bought some butter and eggs, and we came back to quarters. they are very pleasant people, but not "right smart".

There has been a nigger, a slave of one of the families here round with a paper to raise 800 dollars to buy himself. we all told him he was a fool not to take "leg bail" and save his money. I guess his master sees that there is not much help for

slavery and want to get his money for him before there is no more slavery. I am a poor judge of the value of such property but I should suppose to look at him that $800 was a small price for him, for he was a *right smart* nigger to look at.[32]

Company A that you ask about is the Great Barrington Company. It has got the meanest Captain of any Company in the Regiment but I don't care, for that as if any fellow could get in there and bring the Co up to the standard of Co C. it would be a great credit to him, and I don't see why the men are not so good a set of men as any other, only thier Captain don't know anything. I don't esteem the victory you are pleased to call it, anything to brag of, there is a great difference in that matter between the camp and the town. I presume if I had a hundred meddling friends round here to urge me not to drink and watch to count the number of times I did do so and then go and get up a parcel of lies about me to hide thier own faults I should never have left off, but here nobody cared and nobody asked me to leave off so I left off. and the less congratulations I have on the subject the better I like it. it is one thing to govern yourself, and know it and another to have others think they are governing you, but I don't know as you can appreciate the difference and with regard to the good influence you attribute to Capt Joe I can only say that he keeps his black bottle and resorts to it frequently, and if he had any influence at all it would be the other way so I hope I shall hear no more of good influences and all that sort of humbug. I don't believe in influences anyway. if influences amounted to anything I should suppose the example of two Lieuts and his Orderly ought to prevent him from drinking which they failed to do, he puts it on the plea of medicine which is all a humbug, as I know a man is better out here without it and the Doctors say so too. Still the Doctors drink![33]

Please write me all about friend Lee and how you liked him. he is a splendid fellow, and I know you will like him. I am sorry I did not have the chicken pie that would have been thanksgiving indeed, but then we had enough to eat. Mary wanted this letter directed to her, but I wrote one and sent it to her last Friday morning so it is your turn. I suppose Mat would not have time to read it if it had been to her. Give my best love and heartiest wishes for her future happiness and the dear girl deserves it, if any ever does. how glad I shall be to see her. tell her to make short calls in Philadelphia. Give my respects to Bob K tell him he had better take Washington on his route home the cake was very good indeed Lieuts S + W and myself demolished it at one sitting. Be sure and inform me if my last letter arrived in safety and let me know if you have sent any papers lately, as I have not received one for three weeks I don't know what is to pay. I have stockings enough, but I should like a doz papers of Mount Eagle Tripoli and that Leather Preservative. it is not Blacking. we have got Blacking enough and I should like if you should send them a few boxes of Mass Matches. the matches they have here are not good for anything.

I am writing in the Lieuts tent where they have a stove and it is warm and cozy as your own dining room. we are going to have one in ours tomorrow. give my love to all and write soon it will probably be longer before you get my next as I shall probably be in Ananapolis when your next comes and shall not be able to answer it quite so soon but you must not wait but write as usual to Your Aff son

Charlie

19

Camp Brightwood DC Dec 4th 1861

Dear Mother

I received your kind letter to night and was very glad you did not fail to write because you did not get one from me although I was afraid I should not receive one, for I thought you might be too busy to write. I suppose Mattie is married and is now Mrs Boland. I have thought of her many, many times to day, and imagined all about it, and while the ceremony was probably going on I was trudging round the plain down at Columbia College at a Brigade Drill. We have to go three times a week now and it is hard work enough I can assure you.

It is now decided that we are to go into winter quarters here and tomorrow the Regt is going to work felling timber for Barracks, and our Co is to take charge of the camp. Each Company is to have two Huts 16 × 24 feet, 48 men in each. it will be awful this winter and I suppose I shall have to go into one of them though I don't know what arrangements are to be made I don't see why we could not remain in tents as they must all have stoves in them and are very comfortable I think much more so than the Barracks will be. We all thought there would be a great battle this week but I don't know. I doubt whether there ever will be a battle at all. It seems as if it would be a great job to keep this large army all winter doing nothing but I don't know but they can do it. Another of our Castles has fallen to the ground. Lt. Col Decker has returned to this Regiment and an army Officer is appointed to Col of the 7th so there will be no promotions on that scene in this Regt Major Marsh will remain *Major* Marsh. Captain thinks I shall get promotion somehow, but I must confess I see no probability of it, though the vacancies still remain unfilled, but Col Briggs is very slow a vacillating I think. Capt Joe and Lt W are on Court Martial and Lt S is in command of the Company, and I act as 1st Lieut at the drills. Capts and Majors wives took dinner and tea with us to day. When Capt came on he brought a boy for servant from Whately, and he has proved the biggest thief you ever saw. he stole $55 from Lieut Shurtleff and a Pistol from each Jas Braman a man in Co I a deaf and dumb man and myself.

Lieut received $25 and Braman his pistol, the rest is a total loss. I forgot though the man in Co I he got his pistol back. The Capt has sent him off to day without searching him any more or anything.

It is after Tattoo and I am writing in the tent with a fire of Green Walnut wood and it is hot as your kitchen or dining room. I don't know but it is too hot to be healthy but it will be cold enough in the morning to make it all up. I thought I should freeze this morning it was so cold everything was froze up, and it was as cold as Greenland, but the weather has moderated to day and tonight it is not near so cold. You say Doct Chamberlin told Mr Hall that the rebels could take W. in his opinion all I have got to say is that Doct Chamberlin is a fool. they can't take W nor get within 10 miles of it, and that he ought to know or any other "numbskull". I have not received any of the papers you speak of sending for more than three weeks, so I think perhaps you had better not send any more. I don't know what the matter is, as the letters come regularly enough and others get papers.

we have got the Presidents message[34] but I don't think it amounts to much he don't talk nigger enough, but its no use mincing the matter. Nigger has got to be talked, and thoroughly talked to and I think niggers will come out of this scrape free. Juba is still here but I don't like to interfere with his affairs about sending money. why don't Sarah write to him herself? I have not had any letter from Aunt Lu since I saw her last Thursday but she has sent me a number of papers. My Watch keeps very good time and is a great benefit to me. I saw Johns letter in the Gazzette. I should like to have Uncle Edward come on here very much. When does John expect to leave Pittsfield? Tell Pary I should have written this letter to her but I did not think of it until I commenced and it don't make any difference. What will you do without Mattie it will seem as though half the house was gone. Do write me all about the wedding +c +c. Cal K is tickled to pieces at the idea of her coming on. I hope to have a Lieuts tent of my own to welcome her to, but I have not got it, and don't suppose I ever shall have. John C + Cal are well Cal is on guard to night, I wish I could come home and see you all but I don't know when I shall. Give my love to all, and write often. Remember me particularly to Mrs Clarks family, and Mrs Kingsleys and Cooks so Good night from your aff son.

Charlie

20

Camp Brightwood DC December 8th 1861

Dear Mary

I received another little note from Mother tonight. Little notes seem to be the order of the day now but I thought as I had not written you for some time I would try and see if I could not get an answer of some length from you. But it is harder than ever to get anything to write about. we are in as much uncertainty as ever as to what we are going to do. we had made up our mind that we were to go to winter quarters here, and they had commenced to build Barracks for us when all at once we were refused lumber to build them of and last Friday we had another Grand Review of the division by Gen McClellan, and now there is a story in the NY Times, that a strong force under Gen Keys is to be sent down on the extreme right flank of the enemy, near Springfield VA. The Paper has a map of the country round there. Then to day there is another story that one of Gen McClellans staff was to be married a week from next Tuesday, and that Gen McC told him if he was going to be married it must be next week as it would be impossible for him to be the week after and so it goes. meantime we stay here at Camp B, and go through the same dull routine of daily duty, and blindly grope for some knowledge of the future. Mrs Parsons is still here but is going home next Tuesday day after tomorrow. Meantime Mrs Shurtleff has arrived, and I pray the Lord we shall be ordered over the river if for nothing but to get rid of the women, for if we don't go pretty soon we shall be over run with them and have more women than men and I don't know but they would follow us even over there, for women will tag after the men you know, wherever they go. We have had one of the warmest and most pleasant days you ever saw, as warm as September. We had Divine service in the open air and it was uncomfortably warm. We hardly know what to make of it. We have had some very cold weather but no snow except a few scattery flakes that hardly staid half an hour, but it has been cold enough to freeze pails of water almost solid in three or four hours. I am anxiously waiting to see Mattie and hope she will be here tomorrow but don't hardly expect her before next day.

Mother did not write much about the wedding and I want you to write me all about it and how you get along without Mattie. I heard from them in NY Joe Hawley has made us a visit and he was at the wedding and passed them in New York. I hope they will not make a long stop in Philadelphia. Joe H has got an appointment under his father of Asst Brig Quarter master at a salary of $75 per month, so his *patriotism leads him to sacrifice himself for his country.* it seems as if everybody got their nests feathered but me, at any rate every body that can't earn thier living any other way. I wish I had not have been so patriotic but had staid where I was well off but I suppose it is necessary for some to make fools of

themselves, and I suppose I am one of the destined ones. We also had a visit from
Mr Crane the Baptist minister he took dinner with us, and said grace before it
the first time we ever had a Camp meal Blest. he is a very nice man. he told me he
sometimes thought he aught to go for a chaplain, and I think he would make a
very popular one for he would take a heart interest in his business, and be the
friend and counsellor that the boys want for I believe that men might be lead into
religion from the camp that could not be reached any where else, but my opinion
in such matters is worth very little. Doct Chamberlin has returned he speaks of
having bowed to you or Mattie in church I could not understand which, he is just
as conceited as ever and knows just as little. We also had a visit from our
represenitive in Congress the Hon Chas Delano, in fact yesterday was a Calendar day in our history, but I would give more to see Mats little finger than all the
rest of Northampton except you and Mother.

All the boys that you know in our Company are well. Cal and John Cook are
tough and hardy, but Cal is getting most to fat to move round much. He is bigger
than Uncle Henry Strong, (by the hi way I wish you would give my respects to
him and his wife) in fact all the boys are growing fat as pigs, and if we stay here all
winter they won't be fit for anything in the spring, but I hardly think we should
stay here. if we go where the NY Times said we shall be right in the face of the
enemy and have enough to do to keep us in fighting order.

I have not heard from Aunt Lu since I wrote last. I hope to see her out here
when Mat comes. I cannot think of anything more to write give my best love to
Mother and my respects to everybody especially Mr Cushing and family so good
night from Your aff brother

Charlie

PS Dear Pary I wish you would see Mrs Ed Daniels and give my respects to her
and find out what her husbands address is and let me know in your next letter. I
received 2 S Republicans to day, the first papers I have got from home in 4 weeks.

Monday morning
I have just got up and called the roll it is a most splendid warm morning do
not need O Coats at all. I hope I shall see Mattie to day write often Yr aff

Charlie

21

Camp Brightwood DC December 14th 1861

Dear Mother

I received your most welcome letter this PM and it was the first real good letter I have had from home for a long time. I sent you or Mary a letter Thursday morning as usual. You cannot imagine how glad I was to see Mattie. it was the next thing to going home. You expressed great fears about our going over the river but I would not get very much alarmed yet as we are now engaged in the operation of building log Houses for the winter and start off into the woods after Co Drill in the morning and spend the day in cutting logs and drawing them into camp. all sorts of Plans were proposed and finally the order was to build them as we please, only each Co as near alike as possible. our Co has got the walls of one up. I have been out in the woods most all day but have not injured myself with work. we are cutting in a larger woodlot it is all yellow Pine, tall and straight and we go in and cut down a tree, cut one or two logs off twenty to feet long and go on to the next one. I am glad that I do not own any woodland in this region, for armies cut and slash, just where it is most convenient, without regard to whom it belongs to, and necessity is law for everything. I have not heard from Aunt Lu since Mattie was here but presume she is well, or I should hear fom her. I shall try to go down in a few days when I shall see her and perhaps she will be out before that.

Well dear Mother I suppose the long desired promotion will take place very soon as the Col has decided to promote Lieut Shurtleff to a 1st Lieutenancy in Co A and I shall take his place in this Co, at any rate the Captain advises me to write for my uniform tonight. Mr Boland said when he was here that he would be responsible for it until I could pay Daniel Kingsly made my uniform that I wore from N Hampton and I want he should make this. I suppose he knows what the regulation uniform is as I believe he made Capt Parsons Tell him I want the pants a *trifle* larger round the waist than the others were, and if he can I wish he would put a welt of light Blue cloth in the seam instead of a cord. I don't know as he can produce the light Blue cloth but I have seen them made so and it is much better than a cord as the cord wears off. I want them made of good stout cloth or Cassimere, and of a good shade of Blue, I don't care to have them very fine, but his own judgment is best and what he selects will suit me. As to the Coat also he must use his own judgement, only to be sure and make it of a good Blue, and be very particular to have them well and strongly sewed. I want also a single breasted Blue Cloth vest, same as he made for Capt Parsons. I don't know whether he can get the shoulder straps for a 2nd Lieut. without sending to the city if he cannot, he may send it without and I will get them here. I shall want also, a sword, and sword belt, and I shall have to ask someone to get them there

as they can be bought cheaper at the Manufactury in Chicopee, and if you do not think it is asking too much to ask of Mr B. I wish you would ask him to buy me the Regulation sword for a Lieut. (The Manufacturers will know what it is) and ask him to be particular and get one with a scabord without a seam (they will also know what that means.) and I want a good sword belt with a plate that will not tarnish easily. The sash I think I had better get here, in Washington, and when these are sent I want you to put in that Pistol and Cartridges if there were any that H Parsons gave me. I write all this to you because I don't know when Mr B will get home and if he should not until after you get this I wish you to tell Mr Kingsly what I have written, and have the uniform making, and have him get it done as soon as possible.[35]

I don't see any possible doubt as to my getting the commission as the Col has spoken to Lieut S to day, and Lieut has agreed to take it, and I shall certainly get the appointment when he does, probably both recommendations will be made to the Governor at the same time. Corporal Munyan told me some time ago that his brother wrote him that they heard I had got a commission and wanted to know if it was so as they wanted (some of the boys) to present me with a sword + sash, perhaps they would now if they should hear of it but the difficulty in that matter is that I have not quite got it, that is, I have not got the commission in my hands though the Capt says there is no possible doubt about it, nor do I as Col is not a man to commit himself as far as he did with Lieut S to day and then retract. You express fears as to the danger and about Lieuts having to go on guard. they do have to but a fellow can sleep very warm even in the woods with a commission in his pocket.

In regard to the dreadful sufferings of Co C, I had not heard of them though we are very much in need of New Coats which I suppose M Clark is now making. we should have suffered very much if it had not had the Jackets we wore from NHampton, as our blouses are nothing but one thickness of thin flannel, and most worn out at that. The Government cannot get uniforms made fast enough, on the other hand it is true that Co C has had less than any other Co in the Regt with the exception of Bartons Roughs, every other Co has had boxes upon boxes of Comfortables, + Blankets, stockings and mittens +c +c, and the Belchertown part of our Co had a box of such goods as big as our kitchen almost, but Northamptons efforts you know have all been in the Hospital line, which does not benefit us at all. The Hospital is stocked with Comfortables Blankets Pillows and everything in that line and so is the Quartermasters Tent, all sent to the Hospital but they cannot be given out to Companies, you know. I was down to the Hospital tents a few days ago, and they were opening a large box just received and Charlie Wells told me he had so much now that he had no place to put it, and did not know what to do with it. Our Co as a Co has not received a single box of anything. Many of them individuals have got Comfortables though

sent them by their friends. My old Muster Comfortable has worn out and given up. It was literally worn out in the service but if I get a commission I can carry 80 pounds of Baggage and shall get me some more Blankets. that will make another want, namely a trunk which I shall have to get, but I don't know as I shall be able to until the payday after the next.

as to our camp being a lonely place, I had not thought of that but now it is spoken of I guess it is rather a lonely place but I think as there is a thousand of us here we shall be able to make a line [?] of it, and it is considered the most beautiful place in thier diggings, though it is rather bleak now the leaves are gone. the weather is beautiful, and I can hardly realize that it is winter it freezes some nights but it is very comfortable in the day time without an Overcoat, but we have had 2 or 3 days of very cold weather and expect to have more but when I cannot inform you. Please give Respects to the de Brewer girls and Jennie Clapp when you see them. In regard to any important movement about here I am sick of hearing anything about it. the indications so much talked of still continue, but the indications have been that something important was about to take place for six months past and we don't put any trust in indications any more and have voted indications a humbug

Don't you think your opinion of Gen McClellans being a second Washington is a little influenced by his not ordering the Couch Brigade over the river, just a little you know. I don't think myself that he comes up to Washington just yet. he just set the example of returning fugitive slaves to thier masters, you know.[36] Captains wife went to see Aunt Lu the day that Aunt Lu came out with Mattie, and whether they met after that or not I do not know. I don't think Dodi [?] Shepards sayings worth minding and probably the reason why he won't pay his Northern creditors is because he has not got anything to pay with. he'll sing a different tune before many days.

You wrote me a good long letter and I think I have returned it with interest. I am in the tent alone. it is Sat night and Capt Joe is out with some other Captains and the Band seranading Col Frank P Blair, who is at his Fathers house, about half or quarter of a mile above our camp. The things I wrote for will have to be sent by Express unless I should get the appointment before Corporal Brown comes back, and I will write again before they are sent and also to Mr Boland. it is quarter past ten oclock so with love to Mary + all the rest I will bid you good night Affectionately your son

Charlie

Sunday morning
    The Capt arrived home last night and says perhaps I had better not send for a uniform until he has seen the Col once more you need not do anything about it

until I write again but you can keep this letter so you can tell Mr. K what I want. News has come this morning of the Conflagration of Charlestown and a big battle of Western VA it says we killed 200 of the enemy, and but 30 on our side, but still our forces retired in good order as usual yrs +c

Charlie

22

Camp Brightwood DC December 29th 1861

Dear Mother

I take my pen in hand to write you once more, though it has got to be a most hopeless task. it is now nearly two weeks since I have heard a word from home. I wrote a long letter home telling you of my promotion and telling all about my uniform but I do not know whether you ever received it or not and I have written twice since, but cannot get any answer I have waited and longed + looked for the mail and when it came have been disappointed every day since a week ago last Wednesday. and what is to pay I cannot think, and whether you are dead or alive I do not know. you cannot imagine how heartsick and homesick it makes me to be disappointed so every day. It seems as if you could not have written for I got a letter from Daniel Kingsley to day, saying that my Uniform was done I got the pants by Brown and Hubbard has arrived, but left his trunk at the Depot in the city and the rest of my uniform was in it.

I should not have written until I heard from you but we have got a small pox panic and I knew you would hear of it and think I had got it perhaps we are in close confinement. they have got a story that we have got the small pox, though why I'm sure I do not know for there is not a case of it in the Regt and there has not been that I know of, but we have all been vaccinated and, are not allowed to go outside of the lines nor is any one allowed to come inside. we have a double guard and are cut off from all the world, but you need not be afraid for I have no more idea that there is any small pox in the Regiment any more than there is in your house A man in Co K died last night and was sent home to day. he died of Fever. I went down to the city Christmas morning and staid all day and all night with Aunt Lu. Geo B went with me. we had a fine time, and just in time for next day the General informed us that we had the small pox and must have no communication with anybody outside of the lines

My commission has not arrived yet, and I don't know when it will. Col Briggs tells Col Decker to make the change when he went home but he has refused to do it, and some of the Officers of the Regt have got up a petition to the Gov to

have promotions made according to the roster, but you don't know what that means, but it is nothing about me, only in relation to Lieut Shurtleffs case. I don't know that the whole thing will fall through, but Capt says it will not and I guess when Col Briggs returns and finds out what they have been doing interfering with his business, he will make Rome howl. Aunt Lu feels dreadfully she has tried again to get a pass and could not succeed. I had a letter from her last night. she says she has not heard from you for a long time and feels bad about that to, and says she thinks it cruel that you do not write I think it must be that the fault is in the mail, for I cannot believe that you would fail to write for so long a time. I shall certainly give up if I don't get a letter this week. I wish you could have seen them being vaccinated to day. we were all marched down to the Hospital, and the roll was called and as fast as a mans name was called, he stepped in and bared his arm Dr. Holbrook seized his arm, and cut it in all directions with a lancet, and Dr. Chamberlin and C Wells daubed it over with a brush and he was finished. it was a laughable sight, although the funeral was going on at the same time, not half a doz paces off.[37]

Cal Kingsley is well. He gets letters regularly, and his last one stated that you were all well. John Cook is also well. We have got our Barracks almost done. we have made ours ourselves even to the shingles all the others bought boards to cover thiers, but went into the woods and split and shared the shingles and have got the building most covered with them.

I cannot write any more for I have no letter to answer and cannot think of anything more to write. there are no indications of our ever having to fight, and no indications of a fight anyway and I don't know as there ever will be any. do please write often, and direct them very plain and as usual, so good night frm aff your son

Charlie.

23

Camp Brightwood DC Jany 2nd 1862

Dear Mother

This PM I was rejoiced at receiving two letters from you and although they were somewhat old they were most welcome, for I had begun to despair of ever hearing from you direct again. It was two weeks yesterday since I had heard a word from you. one of the letters was dated Dec 21st and the other 26th and I cannot but think there must be another one on the way, as not withstanding I received nothing, I continue to write once a week, and there has been time since

your last for you to have written again. My commission has not come yet, and I don't know when it will. the Col has not returned from Massachusetts but is expected this week, and when he comes I think he will put us in our destined places without much delay. he ordered Col Decker to do it but he has not, and I rather think there will be some music when he gets back.

I have no news to write. I wrote you about my going down to spend Christmas with Aunt Lu we had a very nice time but although Aunt Lu was cheerful I do not think she enjoyed Christmas much. she feels so bad, and it is impossible to think of anything to comfort her, for her case hardly admits of comfort. The last news from Western Va completely upset her, and I don't wonder, though how it was possible for a man of intelligence as we supposed Mr. Campbell to be, to get mixed up with the rebels to the extent of fighting for them is more than I can account for, and I'm afraid it will go hard with him when we have whipped the rebels. It seems we must humble ourselves before England and give up Mason + Slidell, and all for nothing too, for she is bound to have a fuss with us and we may as well make up our minds to it first as last, and she will not be long in finding some other pretext for a quarrel. I only wish she would wait until we get through with the south and then we would give her such a thrashing as she needs and as we compel her to mind her own business in the future.[38]

In relation to our present war, things seem to move as slow as ever, and we seem to get no near to the end, and it seems to be a war for the preservation of slavery more than anything else. McClellan is said to be sick abed, or I conclude he is as the Chaplain prayed for him as such tonight. We have got our Barracks nearly completed, and our camp looks like quite a village as it is. You mentioned the cold weather, and think we must be suffering from the same cause but I rather think you would have changed your mind if you had been here yesterday. it was warm enough to go round in shirt sleeves and be hot at that. to day it is colder but still not very uncomfortable out of doors, the weather is very change-able however, but we have had not much severe cold weather and no snow whether we are to have any winter or not is more than I can tell, it seems as if it was about time if we are.

I had a letter from Matt this week. she seems to be enjoying herself very well. I should like to call on her in her new home. how strange it seems to write of it. I cannot realize that our Mattie has gone out of our house forever. We have been mustered for Pay this week and shall probably get our pay next week. I want to send you some but I shall have so many little things to buy that I don't know whether I can or not but I shall be able to next pay day if you can get along until then, the 1st of March.

Tell Mr Boland that if he has not done anything about my sword he need not as I suspect the boys are going to give me one, as one of the Sergeants called me one side the other day and asked me if I had spoke for one, and told me I need

not if I had not. You ask if I shall remain on Capt Joe's tent when I get my commission. I shall not. when I get that I move into the Lieuts tent and have a right to half of it. it is only next door though and we all eat together. I thank you just as much as though you had sent me a Christmas present, so you need not worry about that. I must draw to a close as it is after 9 oclock. the Capt lays here abed and asleep and we have to start to a Brigade Drill to morrow morning at half past eight. we have been relieved from them this week, so far, on account of a small pox panic, but the small pox case proved to be eresyphylas and our embargo is taken off and the panic has ceased.

Cal K and J Cook are well though John has cut his knee slightly and does not drill just now but he is sound and not laid up in it. Give my respects to Mary Phil and all inquiring friends, with much love to Mary and Mattie, I remain Very aff your son

Charlie

PS Don't fail to write on the accustomed days.

Friday Morning

it is about half past six I have just been up and called the roll. it quite cold this morning. The Capt getting up my Lieutenant very soon in about two hours we start for the Brigade Drill. the place is about 5 miles from here and we shall get back about 1 oclock. I did not go to the last one as I had the pay rolls to make out.

I dread the drill to day but we have got to take it, it is nothing but drill, drill, all the time and all for nothing too. it seems for there is no possible sign of a battle ever taking place in this vacinity. I forgot to wish you a Happy New Year last night, but do so now so good morning Yours +c

Charlie

24

Camp Brightwood DC January 9th 1862

Dear Mother Dear Mary

I have been anxiously expecting a letter from you, both yesterday and to day, but am again doomed to disappointment, and I presume that I shall be for two weeks to come. it does seem to bad that I cannot have my letters as other people do but it seems I cannot and as I have no doubt that you have written me and that I should have received it before this. I have seated myself to write to you. I received two letters from you as I wrote Mother in my last and was glad to get

Second Lt. Charles Harvey Brewster, soon after he received his commission in December 1861. Reflecting the local bonds of Civil War units, soldiers in Brewster's company donated fifty dollars toward the purchase of his uniform, including his sword and sash. *Courtesy of Jonathan Allured*

them at last though they were very old when they came. All doubt is over about my commission as it is on the way, probably keeping company with my letters from home. I saw it in the list of Commissions issued in the Boston Journal, and Col Briggs has got home and brought a copy of the petition. he found it in the State House at Boston when he was home and sat down and made a copy of it and made it all right with the Governor, and the Commissions were immediately issued. the Col is very much offended and two or three of the Officers who signed it have been to him and apologized, but he expresses a good deal of contempt for them, but its all settled as far as I am concerned and I shall probably take my post tomorrow.

And dear Pary, my heart is full to overflowing tonight as I will proceed to tell you.[39] I have just had a peek at some presents that are to be given to me tomorrow. You must know that as soon as the boys heard that it was all settled and that I was to be thier Lieut, they immediately started a subscription to procure me a sword +c and as the result sent P W Kingsly (Captain K's brother) to the city and he has just returned with a sword costing $20, a sash costing $20 a belt costing $7 and a cap costing $4.25 a better set of equipments then there is in the Regiment, and tomorrow they are to be presented to me and the only drawback to my perfect happiness is that I shall have to make a speech which I dread most fearfully. Several of the boys have seen them and have said that they only regret that I did not wear them from Northampton when we started, but its something to have earned them you know. I had no idea that there was such a good feeling for me, as in the six or nearly 7 months we have been in the service, I have had many a fuss with most all of them, and punished some of them, but it is a remarkable fact that those are the ones who have insisted upon giving the most for the purpose, every man in the company put his name down, and I am very glad that it is so for there will now never be cause to refer back and say I showed partiality on account of anything that happened at this time I know you will all rejoice with me at the stroke of good fortune as well as evidence of my standing in the affections of the men, who although there may be some enemies among the subscribers, there would not be such a spontaneous outbreak if the feeling were not general. all the Sergeants have been congratulating me and it seemed as though it was wicked for me to feel so glad at such an amount of good fortune and they not to have any. I could hardly say a word and what I am to do tomorrow for a speech I cannot think. I imagine it will be short and sweet don't you?

Sergeant Bishop takes my place as Orderly which is a great offence to Sergt Braman who stands next to me on the roll, and expected to have it, but there is no difference in the rank of Sergeants other than the first or Orderly Sergt and any one of the four has just as much right to it as the other. it is for the Capt to decide which is the best man for the place and I think he has decided wisely.

Corporal Munyan is promoted to be a Sergeant, which I am very glad. in fact I urged upon the Captain about as persistently as he urged my promotion upon Col Briggs, though urge is not the proper word to use in regard to his efforts with the Col, and the topic between them was Lieut S and not me, but the captains object was to make a place for me. Markus T Moody is promoted to Corporal, Sergt Braman was so mad that he brought his sword down to the Captain and said he would not be Sergt any more, which was very foolish, as he will find to his great sorrow as soon as he gets over his mad fit, which I presume he has by this time as he is now holding a confidential conversation with the Capt in his tent, and I presume the upshot of it will be that he will get his sword back and conclude to remain a sergeant if he don't show a proper spirit tonight there will be another sergt appointed tomorrow and he will bitterly repent at his liesure.

I am writing in *my* tent. I have not slept in it yet but am going to tonight. Lieut Weatherill and myself have been arranging things all day We have made new bunks and I have left the Capt and taken up my residence in my future home, where I shall be happy to see you at any time and will entertain you and your friends to the best of my ability. Tattoo is beating so I must draw to a close. Give my love to Mother and Mat and respects to all the family. tell Mat not to forget that she owes me a letter, and don't fail to write on the regular days, as I shall probably get them sometime.

Remember me to Mrs Clark Mrs Clarks folks Mrs Kingsley and Mrs Cooks John Cook + Cal are well, Cal is helping to build a bridge across a creek, to draw wood over. I am entitled to 2 ¹/₂ cords of good hard wood per month and I wish I could share it with Mother—But I must bid you good night, write often to Your aff brother

Charlie.

TWO

My Contraband

January–March 1862

Brewster spent the first of his three winters at war in Camp Brightwood, on the edge of Washington, D.C., coping with boredom and sickness and determined to protect fugitive slaves from their former masters. This extraordinary experience exposed both his racial prejudices and his antislavery sentiments. Before Brewster ever encountered battle, in his own way, he understood that he was fighting a war to free slaves.

25

Camp Brightwood January 15th 1862

Dear Mother

It is Wednesday night and in the past times when mails came regularly I use to be made glad on this night by a letter from home, but have received none to day, nor have I since I wrote you last, and don't know as I ever shall again but I thought I should write you a few lines tonight as I know you have written to me and will be disappointed if you do not hear from me.

I have appeared in my new uniform today for the first time, as the long expected Commission came last night. We have had no drill to day however, as it has rained most all day, in fact it rains or snows pretty much all the time now and we do not do much now but sit indoors and pass time away as best we can. Capt Parsons has been in the city and returned this PM he went to meet Dwight Kellogg but he did not come—

he went to see Aunt Lu and she is in distress to have me come down and show myself, so I am going to apply for a pass tomorrow and if I get one am going to see her. I intend to buy a trunk if I can get one to suit me. My commission dates back to Dec 5th and they say I can draw pay on it from that time. if so it will be quite a sum in my pocket, some $85, which is quite an item in addition to my next two months pay. they all say there is no doubt about it and I presume there is

77

not. I feel quite like a free man once more, now that I am a commissioned Officer. it is wonderful what a difference two little straps on the shoulders make, but you must experience it in order to realize it. I cannot tell you what it is but this much that before I had lots of work and very little pay and now I have very little work and lots of pay. I am to be "Officer of the Guard" day after tomorrow so you see I am to get a taste of the unpleasant part of my duty immediately, but it only comes about once in two weeks, so I reckon I can stand it very well.

It is raining quite hard and comes pattering down on the roof of the tent, but I have a warm fire of Hickory wood and it is comfortable as in your own dining room. Lieut Weatherill lay snoozing in his bunk just back of me. we have rigged up bunks like the berths of a steamboat one over the other. shelves as Matt called them once. the first time she slept on a Steamboat, and we slept very comfortable. I have got two more heavy woolen blankets from the Quartermaster and have plenty of bedding.

I have got a "Contraband" he came from Montgomery[1] 13 miles north of here. his master whipped him in the morning for something or other and he took leg bail in the evening and landed here night before last. he is a bright looking mulatto, 17 years old and says his master paid $400 for him six years ago. he was the only slave his master had and his master never will have him again if I can help it. I was on the lookout for a servant as I am allowed $13 dollars extra for subsistance and $250 [2.50?] for clothing per month if I have a servant, and it does not cost half that to keep him. I wish I could get some of my old clothes to put on him, especially my old overcoat. I do not suppose you will have any chance to send them, but if you should I wish you would, he is very near my size, but I don't know if it would pay to make a bundle of coat Pants O Coat and vest, of mine and send them along, and then I could rig him up so his master would hardly know him. But I am sleepy and it is hard work writing, when I have no letter to answer so I will bid you good night, with love to Mary and Mattie and respects to all the family, and to all the neighbors from Your loving son

Charlie

26

Camp Brightwood DC January 23rd 1861 [1862]

Dear Mary

I received your welcome letter written on Monday the next day which was a very quick trip. I intended to answer it last night but just as we got through Dress Parade Captain had a letter from Dwight Kellogg that he should be in Washington that evening and as the Sutler was going right down and coming back this

Officer of the 22nd New York State Militia and his servant, a Virginia freedman. Despite policies mandating the return of escaped slaves to their owners, the use of "contrabands" as personal attendants became common among Union officers in 1861–62.
Brady Collection, National Archives

morning I got a pass and went down to meet him. Capt could not go as he was "Officer of the Day" to day. I found him at the National Hotel where we staid last night, and came up to day. we called upon Aunt Lu this morning she has had a letter from Mattie Campbell and is very much rejoyced thereat, although it tells her that many of her friends are dead among whom are Jessie Gilmer and Mary Flemmings husband. Aunt Lu was going to have one more interview with Seward and if she did not get a passport this morning was going back with Dwight Kellogg when he returns, so I think you may expect to see her before long as I have no idea that she will get a pass if she had come on here a rabid secessionist and had been arrested and put in prison for a few days she could probably taken the oath of allegience and got a passport, but being a good and

loyal woman it is of course impossible. it seems to me that our whole set of
Officials are a set of incapables, at any rate, to obtain any favor it is only necessary
to be secesh or an Englishman. they don't dare to refuse Lord Lyons anything
and if he says such a person must have a passport south of course they must, and
Seward bows and gives it.[2]

The weather here still continues rainy and cloudy and we have forgotten how
the sunshine looks it did try to shine once to day but did not succeed and tonight
it is as cloudy as ever. I went to the Opera last evening. it was very fine and this
morning I saw the mother of the "Prima Donna" Mrs Hinckley at Mr Wendells
I don't suppose it will be possible for me to get a furlough as there has a new
order come out that the Government needs every man in the field at this time,
and no more furloughs will be granted unless for very urgent reasons indeed. it
seems very funny to hear of its being so cold up north and of so much snow for
we have had hardly enough to cover the ground. I think you must have had a fine
time at the sleigh ride, and I wish I could have been there to dip into those
walnuts. I have had two half bushels from the city but they are all gone now. I
enjoy cracking them these long evenings very much.

I saw Will Hawley down to the city to day. he enquired after you and he
wanted to know if Stone had taken the whole Colton family in charge, pretty
good was it not. I am very much rejoiced to hear that Mrs Douglass is dead. Now
you need not to be shocked at that, but I think she aught to have died long ago.

They are beginning to revive the stories about our moving and going somewhere else but I do not think there is anything in them and I don't believe we
shall move from here, at all. I long to hear from Burnside and what he is doing
for I expect great things from him. it seems he has gone to North Carolina, and I
would not wonder if he got behind the rebels at Manassas and we shall have
them between two fires and can whip them more at leisure, but I don't know as
we shall and our General Buel is pushing matters in Kentucky, so things do move
after all, if it is but slowly.[3] it seems as if we must have some hand in the drama
before the last scene, but I don't know as we shall but I shall have the satisfaction
of knowing we did all that we were ordered to at any rate, and more than that we
could not do. I think we should be able to recruit a good number to render a good
account of ourselves in a fight but if they don't want us to, we must even do
without one.

Cal Kingsley and John Cook are quite well and flourishing Cal continues to
grow fat. he is a perfect giant and if the war should last three years I cannot
imagine how large he would be. to day they discharged the last man from the
Hospital and the whole regiment has not a man in the camp Hospital now. I
believe there is one or two in the Hospital in the city and that is all, which we
consider a mighty good thing and I don't believe any other Regiment in the
Army can say it. I am glad you have written to Will Robinson. I wish I could go

over and see him, but I suppose I cannot. I've had several friends from over there to see me but it is more difficult to get from here over there. I wish you could open my door and walk in and see me this evening I am all alone in my tent and fire burns cheerfully, and I hear the hum of conversation in other tents around me. it certainly is as comfortable as anyone could expect, if one only had something to do I have got a contraband though I believe I wrote you that before. he is quite smart for a nigger though he is quite slow but he is willing and I think has improved a good deal since I got him. I have not heard anything of his master, and if I do I shan't give him up without a struggle.

I must close now as it almost time to attend roll call and after that I am sleepy enough to go to bed. My best love to Mother and Mat. I wrote Mattie day before yesterday. my respects to all the family, and to all the neighbors and so good night from Your aff brother

Charlie.

27

Camp Brightwood DC Sunday PM February 9th 1861 [1862]

Dear Mother

I received your most welcome letter, the first one by mail for three weeks yesterday PM and was very glad indeed to hear from you once more though I am sorry to hear that your + Mary's health are so poor. I am glad you liked the pictures but you do not say whether they look natural or not. I have ordered some more and I will send one to Dwights wife next time I write. I think you must have enjoyed Matties visit very much indeed and I think it is a great pity that I could not be there too I cannot imagine why any letters would not come directed to me, but such seems to be the fact. the next one you send under cover to Capt P. you had better have the inside Envelope a little smaller than the outside. We had come in from Dress Parade and gone into my tent where we take our meals and eaten our supper when we adjourned to the Capts tent to take a smoke, and found the letter directed to him. I said I'll bet that letter is for me. he says I guess not. he took it up and opened it by tearing off the end when he drew out a letter wrapped in a piece of newspaper I said I still believe it is for me but I should think Envelopes were scarce. Captain opened it and read Dear Charlie and then handed it to me. The inside envelope fitted so tight that he had torn off the end of both and I did not discover it until sometime after I had read the letter. I think that a emetic must have done the Desk the world of good.

We did not think Dwight staid very long, and he did not go down to the city

but twice while here. we kept him as long as we could, and he seemed to enjoy himself very much. I wish Uncle Edward would come down and make us a visit he can come from New York to Baltimore and return on one of the Perhams Excursion Tickets now for 8.00 and the fare from Baltimore to W is 1.50 each way I think he would enjoy it very much tell him he can have my bunk, and stay just as long as he likes if it is until the 4th of July. if we don't have to move before then and I don't think we shall I had a letter from Aunt Lu last week she was visiting at a Mrs. McCauley (or some such name) and was intending to start for Mass the forepart of this week she has had two letters from Mr Campbell since I heard from her last. I still have my contraband and he gets along first rate. I reckon he never imagined such an easy life as he has now. he has only to keep wood cut for one fire and brush my Clothes + Boots and keep my sword bright, and he appears to be perfectly honest, and I *reckon* he is a *right smart nigger*. I do not have the Neuralgia much not enough to speak of, and am quite well in all other respects.

That piece in the papers about the City Guards Officers is all humbug. it was put in by some of the men who cut up a shine and got put in the Guard House for it, as they deserved. the fact of the matter is as Geo Bigelow said one day that every man in that Co thought he ought to have been a Brig Genl, and that he had done the country a great favor in coming at all, and therefore aught to be allowed to do pretty much as he pleased. And you know nothing is easier than to write complaints and get up a row at home among the friends of the soldiers there.

I don't believe there is so lenient and easy a man in Camp as Capt Lombard and I presume thats just whats the matter. he has probably endulged them so much that they think he must. I know those poor fellows must have had a terrible time with the Burnside Expedition I should rather fight my way back than to go by water in the way that we came, and our trip must have been a pleasure excursion compared to thiers.

We received the news from Tennessee yesterday and everybody is jubilant thereat and prophecies a speedy termination to the war, but my humble opinion is there has got to be many such and many greater victories before the end.[4] You wish I was safe at home again but I do not see how I could well be in a safer place than this. we have settled down in to the opinion that we are not for use, but for ornament and that we shall be mustered out of service on this very ground.

I received your letter by C Wells and have written once or twice since. We also have had several days of sunshine but no relief from mud. to day is a beautiful day, but rather cool but much like a March day. I have not seen any Geranium leaf and could not make out whether you sent it in the last letter or one before. I did not see how dirty this paper was until I got the letter half written I should think it had been used for a door mat by the looks of it but I cannot write it over

for it is most time for Dress Parade and I suppose it does not make any great difference how the paper looks, as it is the writing you are after.

We had new blue frock coats and light blue overcoats given out yesterday, and are to have new pants tomorrow. the pants we are very much in need of as the last we had were good for nothing at all and have been condemmed.

Cal + John C are well as are all the rest of the Company and most all the Regiment, only three in Hospital and we have been quite a while without anybody in Hospital. Dr Holbrook our former Asst Surgeon has been appointed Surgeon for the 18th Mass Regt, and we have got a new one whose name is Geo Jewett, I don't know where he comes from.

You did not say whether Julia Clark had received my letter or not. Give my respects to all the neighbors love to Mattie and Mary + Mr Boland and Uncle Ed don't forget to tell Uncle Edward to come to W. We have got new and more strict orders, so I don't suppose I shall see Aunt Lu again before she goes back. we are cooped up tighter than ever. I cannot think of anything more to write. With much love from Your aff son

Charlie

PS 10 oclock PM The stories about our going to Kentucky are rife again to night, whether there is any foundation for them or not I do not know, but everybody is wide awake again and the expectation that something is going to happen. Buel I understand is to have 30,000 troops from somewhere, so Good night with love

Charlie

28

Camp Brightwood DC February 15th 1862

Dear Mother

I received your welcome letter of the 13th this PM and was glad to find that I could receive letters directed in my own name again. I wrote to Mary and mailed it Thursday or rather I sent it by Captain Parsons who I suppose has arrived in Northampton before this. I have not much more to write about as it was only day before yesterday and nothing of any importance has happened since. we had a little excitement this morning though immediately after Guard Mounting the Guard was dismissed and the Regiment called into line and we thought orders had certainly come, for us to go somewhere or do something, but it was only to read an order calling for volunteer sailors for the Western Gunboat Flotilla.

Immediately over 200 volunteered but as they could take only about 18 many had to be disapointed, but 2 are going from our Company. Viz Corporal Brown and a private named Frank Bois I believe the men would volunteer to go to the "old scratch" himself if they could only have a change. they are so sick of this kind of life, and I don't blame them much. You say you hope the 10th Regt will not have to go to Kentucky, but I cannot say I agree with you for it is awful to stay here in this old pasture and hear of the glorious deeds that are being done elsewhere and to think that we have no part in them. I cannot imagine any possible use we are to the cause, in any way shape or manner and we are just as safe as we could possibly be in Mass. I have to go on GG with the Company tomorrow. it has snowed all day to day and will rain tomorrow I presume, and we have to go out and sleep in the woods and in Fort Slocum, and all for no possible purpose only to make ourselves just as miserable as can be for 24 hours, and then come back to camp again. It is a perfect humbug. We could endure it cheerfully if it was for any good purpose but it is not and that makes it ten times worse. We should be glad to do it if there was the least danger connected with it just enough to make it interesting.[5]

Lieut Weatherill is quite sick tonight but the Doctor has been up and does no[t] consider him dangerously so. Charlie Wells is again very sick he was taken yesterday and we were quite frightened about him this morning but I believe he is better tonight. You must not say anything about these cases as it would only alarm thier friends for nothing and the Dr does not consider Lieuts sickness anything more than a severe cold

We are all rejoicing over the glorious news from Burnside and from Tennessee + Missouri, and we think things indicate a speedy termination of the war, which I hope will happen. Our Regiment have been furnished with new O Coats + Frock Coats and present quite a fresh appearance. I had got so far in my letter when the Tattoo beat and I had to go up and attend to Roll Call, and have just got back. it is now half past nine o'clock and the camp is as still as an empty church. I shall have to go to bed soon as I must to be up early in the morning for inspection and then depart not to return until Monday morning.

I have a sense of how anxious everyone must have been up there when the news of the Battle at Roanoke came for we were quite excited here and when we heard that our Mass Regt was cut up, we were afraid it might be the 27th, but have since learned that it was the 25th and the 10th Connecticut which suffered most but the later accounts do not make it half as bad as the first did. Albert Kingsley wrote to Cal about his fathers sickness and Cal feels very badly about it but he hopes that Al exagerated it a little. he + John Cook are quite well. I think there can be no doubt but that Gen Stone is a great traitor and I do not think they can be too soon about hanging him and all the rest of his stamp. I see the Burnside prisoners are to go to New York I wonder what they will do with them.

The Report has just come that Fort Donelson[6] is taken but whether it is true or not I cannot say I hope it is.

I presume you have seen Capt Joe before this and have given him all the messages you told me. The Geranium leaf came safely to hand and was very fragrant and suggestive of home.

I think the idea of those Havelocks is first rate and hope they will be sent. I wish we had them to wear tomorrow on Grand Guard there is every prospect of a rain for our benefit and they would be very comfortable.

Please Give my respects to all the neighbors Mrs Kingsleys family and Mrs Clarks, Cooks, Strongs + all also to Mr Cushing plus family. I should like to be there to Mrs Clarks silver wedding very much. I am glad the pictures pleased you so much. I am much fleshier than I used to be and I am enjoying good health in every respect.

My love to Mary + Mattie tell the latter she owes me a letter I got some papers from her to day. I wish you would send me the Gazzette plus Republicans as I hardly ever see one now.

But I must bid you good night. with much love Your aff son

Charlie

29

Camp Brightwood DC February 19th 1862

Dear Mother

I received your welcome letter this evening and as usual was most glad to get it. I also received one from Cousin Jane. I have answered hers and have got quite sleepy but will endeavor to make out something for you though I can hardly think of anything to write. The all absorbing topic of course is the late news from Tennessee, which we received with all the exaggerations, attendant upon first reports, night before last, yesterday morning the line was formed immediately after Reveille and we formed square when the Col read us the news, and we gave nine such cheers as Yankee lungs only are capable of while the guns of Fort Massachusetts belched forth a salute of 34 guns, and we gave ourselves up to general rejoicing.[7] meanwhile it continues to rain and the mud continues to reign, in this part of the country, and I should not wonder if the war in other parts was finished, while the Army of the Potomac continues stuck in the mud. as I sit here in my tent writing the rain patters down in torrents on the roof and it looks out of doors as if it had set in for a long spell of weather. I took the Company out to drill this morning, but we have not been out since. and the [word] tonight is that we shall not drill any tomorrow.

It is quite nice being in command of the Company as I do not have to go on any Guard but Grand Guard and that comes only once in twenty days. I was out Sunday and Sunday night and shall not have to go on any Guard again until Capt comes back.

What do you think of the glorious news that is coming every day now. it begins to look as though this terrible war will be finished up in a short time now and we should return to our homes and then what are we all going to do. I wish I could get an appointment in the regular army but I don't suppose that is possible. There is nothing new in camp and we see no signs of being called into active service though we may take part in the advance of the Army of the Potomac, if that ever takes place, if it does not then we shall have saved our bacon, and nobody can doubt our courage, for if there was ever a party spoiling for a fight it is the 10th Regiment Mass Volunteers.

I am sorry to hear that Mr Kingsley is so low, and I am sorry for Cal I did not tell him what you wrote but he knows how his father is for Al wrote him, and Charles Rogers wife wrote him and he told Cal, and I don't know but it is just as well that he should know it for if he should die it would be a terrible shock to him if he knew nothing about it. Cal is fat and hearty as ever and is just about as much of a pet with the boys as he was at home. They call him the infant. John Cook is well, is doing duty as cook, and just as careless as ever.

I see by your letter that Mattie is possessed with the insane idea that I owe her a letter. you tell her it is not so, but exactly the reverse. And she had better send me a letter directly or I shall put her in the Guard House. This a military order and must be obeyed.

Jane writes that she has got a young lady for me pretty and good, so if you should see any young ladies after me, you can tell them I am spoke for.

We have discharged one man to day on account of Physical disability. he has run down to a shadow within a month, and no one knows what ails him. his name is Levi Elmer, and he was one of the recruits that Lieut Remington got. he is from Ashfield. he cried like a good fellow when he came to go away.[8]

I suppose Capt is enjoying himself greatly. I don't know how he got his furlough but he seems to get anything he asks for. I don't suppose I could get one if you were all dying.

I have not heard from Aunt Lu since I wrote you last. I suppose she had got home before this but I believe she was intending to stop at Thomas Russells on her way. You know Gen Lander has been driving Rebels out of Winchester but I don't know whether that is any where on her way home or not but I presume the time will not be long now before the whole state of Virginia or at least the western half will be cleared of Rebels. I guess the Rebels have made up thier minds by this time that man to man is about as many as they want to contend with, and that 5 of us to one of them is about 5 too many You must write all about Ab if he writes home about the battle.

It seems so funny to hear what you say about the snow for we have hardly been able to realize that it was winter at all.

One of our boys has got the mumps. have I had them I have if I recollect right.

Please write often, your letters seem to come all right now, though how long it will last it is impossible to say Give my love to Mat and Mary and tell them both to write There are three letters here for Capt Joe. you can ask him if I shall send them to him though I suppose it is no use, as they are all from Northampton.

Give my respects to all the family and all the neighbors. I should like to have been at the silver wedding. Give my respects to Mr + Mrs Clarke and tell them I hope they will live to have a Golden one. But I must bid you good night as it is after "Taps", and the end of the paper. So I will close, with much love Your aff son

Charlie

30

Camp Brightwood DC February 22nd 1862

Dear Mother

I received your letter of the 20th this PM and was glad to find you were so particular to write to me. I wrote a long letter last night sent it this morning. in it I told her pretty much all the news, to day has been a general holiday. we have had no duties to perform, except this morning we formed a square and the Col read Washington's Farewell Address, and the rest of the day has been spent in Target shooting. It is now eight o'clock and most everybody has gone to bed but as I have two more letters to write tomorrow I thought I would write to you to night. It has just commenced to rain and the mud which is now quite deep will be deeper tomorrow. it has been almost dried up several times but there comes a cold spell and the ground freezes a little and we have a little snow, and then more mud, and I don't see as there is any prospect of its ever being any better.

My Contrabands master came after him to day, but we got wind of it and I sent him over into the woods, and his master hunted all round, and finally came and knocked at my door. We were playing Euchre and I sang out come in. he opened the door and asked if Lieut Brewster was in. I said that's my name, and asked him to come in. he rather thought he wouldn't so I went out and went back of the tent with him, and he asked me if I had a boy named David. I said yes but I did not know where he was. he said he was with you this evening wasn't he. I said no I have not seen him this evening it was about 4 o'clock rather early in the evening and I had not seen him for two hours. I guess he considered it a tough case for he said well that's all and I turned on my heel and left them standing

there, there were two of them, they went off and David has reappeared but his name won't be David any longer. I am going to rechristen him immediately his name is going to be Harry Hastings, hereafter, and then I shall not have anybodys boy David.[9] I think that the two Nigger hunters would have got such a pounding as would have lasted them one while if they had staid in camp. the boys wanted to give it to him this PM, and they wanted to take David up into the Quarters, and said they would warn me his master would not get him, but I thought it was better not to have any fuss as long as I could get along without just as well. the boys have got 3 or 4 contrabands up in the Quarters, and the man that takes them away will have a good time I do assure you. Col Briggs never gives them up if a master finds his negro in camp the Col tells him if he wants to go with his master he may if not he need not, and you can judge what the answer is.

I should like very much to be at home when Capt is there and the rest of them he must be enjoying himself greatly. Somebody has written that he was at church Sunday last and had on white kids that tickled the boys greatly.

I wrote to Mattie about Mr Wendells being out here and telling me that Aunt Lu had got a passport. I was very much surprised indeed for it was hardly two weeks since she came out to bid me good bye, and was going to start immediately for Mass but Gen Dix was an old schoolfellow of Mr Wendells and when he took the passport business in hand she got one immediately. I have not heard a word from her since she was out here I should think she would write. Mr W says that slavery is done for in the border states. he says that a man eighteen months ago tried to sell him a negro and his wife and child and asked $2,200 for them, he came to him a few days ago and tried to sell them to him for $400.00 and he told him he would not give him $2.50 a piece for them. I think slavery will be abolished in the District of C before this session of Congress is over, and it must soon follow in Delaware and Maryland.

I am very much pained to hear such accounts of Mr Kingsley. I dreamed I saw him last night, and he looked just as poor and thin as I suppose he does in reality. Lieut W + myself had a letter from Captain and are going to answer it tomorrow. I had a letter from Willie Robinson yesterday which I am going to answer tomorrow. he is expecting an appointment as 2nd Lieut every day as his 1st Lieut is gone and his Capt has recommended him. I suppose he is in pretty much such a fit as I was a couple of months ago. Give my love to Mary and tell her she cannot be too quick about writing that long letter you say she is going to. I think those havelocks must be a very good thing indeed. I believe I told you in my last that I had had a letter from Cousin Jane. I meant to try and get a pass to go down and see Aunt Lu to day but the General sent up word that no passes would be granted so it was of no use.

Cal K and John C are well but Cal feels quite bad about his father I did not tell him what you wrote before and I don't know as I shall what you wrote this time. I

don't think this Regiment will ever see any fighting, at least it don't look like it now. the papers this morning said that the Rebels were leaving Manassas, and if they leave then the Union army will soon be in Richmond. Give my respects to all the neighbors and your household love to Mattie + Mary, and don't forget to write often too Your aff son

Charlie.

31

Camp Brightwood DC February 26th 1862

Dear Mary

I received your nice long letter to night and was very glad to find that you were in the land of the living as I had not had a letter from you for a long time.

It is terrible dull here and I have not much material to make a letter of. We have had day before yesterday a terrible wind, which has done a great deal of Damage, it blew over a large Chesnut tree just behind our tent and it fell across the back End of Captains tent and directly across the middle of the next tent to it. Lieut Putnams of Co E. and smashed it all to pieces. the Orderly Sergt was in the tent and got his face very badly scratched. he had a very narrow excape. The wind also blew down a log House in the 36th NY Regiments Camp and killed an Orderly Sergt. it blew down every tent in the 2nd Rhode Islands Camp, and in this camp it blew down the Quartermasters tent and the Officers Eating tent. It was the hardest wind we have had since we have been here and that is saying a great deal for we have some terrible ones.

My Contrabands master has been after him again to night he bribed one of Company F to entice him out of camp but he did not succeed. I have just been up to see Capt Lombard about it, and he says he will fix his hash for him in the morning. his name is Hogan and if ever he comes under my command in any military capacity he had better look sharp and not fail in the smallest thing of his whole duty. if he does he will wish he had never seen a Contraband, for Command Officers have a great deal of Power if they have a mind to use it, and it is absolute, and I should not have the least hesitation in using it to the utmost on any man that would be guilty of aiding any master to reclaim any slave. if Davids master comes here again, I shall tell him to clear out and if he don't go I shall "let loose the dogs of war" We have got some five or six Contrabands in our Company now. the last time I was on Grand Guard John Cook marshalled about six of them and brought out Coffee to us. I thought I should split when he came into Fort Slocum at the head of such a party of Grinning Darkies, of all colors

ages and sizes. it just suited him though! One of them has got feet that are about 24 inches long and they turn out both ways and such a comical looking Nigger you never saw. he washes clothes for the boys and I guess makes quite a good thing of it. One squad have got a boy, the smartest and brightest darky I ever saw, and he makes a great sport for them in singing and dancing. the boys raise pluto with them, and one great sport is to get them butting each other with thier heads. two of them got at it the other day just as the Company were forming, and set them all in roar, of course I had to scold them but I thought I should split myself. they looked so comical, just like sheep butting at each other.[10]

We have got another story in camp that we are going to move but I do not see anything that indicates such a thing but we do not have to guard the forts any more the 59th and 76th New York Regts have been detailed for that service, and as that was the only thing that offered any reasonable supposition of necessity for keeping us here, it looks a little as though we might be on the eve of moving somewhere.

I have at last had a letter from Aunt Lu written just as she was starting for Fortress Munroe. she wanted me to write her there but I do not see her any probability of her getting it if I do. I do not know how she is going to get home but I trust she will get along somehow. Poor Aunt Lu when shall we ever hear from or see her again. I am sure I cannot tell.[11] How funny it seems to think that Abbey Parsons should get into Battle before I did does it not. I should like to write to him but I do not know how to direct, and John too gone to Ship Island where he will see more of the southern country than I probably ever shall it seems almost like a dream. I wonder why John never wrote to me. I am afraid he must have had a harder time than ever Ab did for they must have been out in the terrible gale we have just had. it almost seems as if Providence favored the Rebels, for we have had a terrible gale just after every Expedition has left. I am not able to reconcile it with our ideas of the right side. We cannot believe that Providence can favor the wrong, and yet we cannot believe we are not right in this struggle both sides pray earnestly to the same god for each others destruction, and as far as the elements are concerned he seems to have answered Rebel prayers so far.

We have been at work to day fixing up the camp and putting everything in first rate order which is one thing that makes me think that we shall be ordered away, for we never have taken extra pains and slicked up camp yet, but what we had to move from it right off. it is raining light guns tonight so I guess we shall not go tomorrow.

The Court Martial adjourned yesterday and Lieut W resumed command of the Company to day, but the Col has ordered them to commence again tomorrow so I shall be in command again until Capt Parsons comes.

You need not bother your heads about my going to Mr Blairs, as I have no idea

that they want to see me any more than I want to see them. I am very sorry to hear such bad news for Mr Kingsley and I do not know what to do about telling Cal. he is a little unwell himself today. How I have been favored with good health since I have been in the army hardly anyone has had so little sickness as I it seems strange when such great strong fellows have been sick so much, I am getting to the end of my paper and it is long past bed time Lieut W has been to sleep a long while, so I must draw to a close by the way is it paper rather scarce that you have to cross your writing as you did in your letter. I wish you would take a little more paper and not cross the lines, as you know that bothers me. Give my love to Mother and Mattie and respects to everybody. With lots of love to yourself I remain Your aff brother

Charlie. PS Write again very soon

32

Camp Brightwood DC March 4th 1862

Dear Mother

Capt Parsons has just got back and I have received your most welcome letter together with one from Mattie, and a pair of stockings and last but not least a picture of Mat + Mary which I value above all the rest. You cannot think how glad I was to receive that, but why did they not have you in it somewhere. I wish they had I should have thought they would. I should have written you before but Sunday I was on guard, and yesterday I did not feel like it as I was sleepy, and to day I have had a very bad headache, which still continues and will probably make this letter short.

We have another grand excitement the day after I wrote Mary last. We had about noon positive orders to get ready to march the next morning at 3 o'clock so as to be at the Depot in Washington at 6 o'clock AM. the whole Division was included in the order. Infantry, Cavalry, + Artillery we had a Dress Parade in the afternoon, and formed square, and had prayers and a speech from Col Briggs, telling us that might be our last Dress Parade for a long time and that the next time we formed square, it might be with our faces outwards and with charged bayonets +c +c everyone felt good and noone had the slightest doubt that we were at last to take the field, and have a chance to try our spunk. each man was to carry 4 days rations and 100 rounds of Cartridges but in the evening after the Ammunition was all distributed and, every mans knapsack packed, and everybody waiting anxious and ready, the orders were contermanded. Oh it was discouraging I can tell you. We were to go to the reinforcement of Gen Banks if

he needed us it was the day he crossed the river but the Rebels did not show any fight and consequently we were not needed, and we had to settle down quietly again to our usual avocations. Erastus Slate + Henry Dickenson were here and they were at the Depot to see us off the next morning but we were not there. I must leave this letter for to night for my head aches so I cannot write more.

Thursday Morning.

I feel some better this morning. I had the Doctor last evening and he gave me something which carried off my headache. We had more marching orders yesterday in so far as to be ready to start at any moment, with 2 days rations and 100 rounds of Cartridges, and everybody thinks we shall go in less than a week. I don't know but I shall be discharged, as the whole Regiment is almost in a state of mutiny on the Nigger question. Capt Miller the pro slavery Captain of the Shelburne Falls Co undertook with Major Marsh to back him to drive all the Contraband out of camp. he came to me and I had quite a blow up with him. Major Marsh took the Regiment off the camp to drill yesterday while they were gone Capt Miller searched the camp for niggers, but did not find any, this morning they are all here again. this morning placards were found posted around the camp threatening direful things if they persisted in driving them off, which is a most foolish thing, but the men did not come down here to oppress Niggers and they are not quite brutes yet, as some of thier officers are. I have nothing to do with any of the trouble except that I refuse to order off my own servant, in this I am not alone, as Capt Walkley of the Westfield Co has done the same thing, the Officers are divided into two parties on the question, and most bitter and rancorous feelings have been excited which will never be allayed. I do not know how it will all end but I should not be at all surprised if they made a fuss about it and should prefer charges against me, Capt Parsons, Lieut Weatherill, the Adjutant, Capt Walkley, Capt Lombard, Lieut Shurtleff, + our one or two others hold the same opinion that I do in the matter. I should hate to have to leave now just as the Regiment is going into active service, but I never will be instrumental in returning a slave to his master in any way shape or manner, I'll die first. Major Marsh well knows that the slaves masters are waiting outside of camp ready to snap them up, and it is inhuman to drive them into thier hands, if you could have seen strong men crying like children, at the very thought as I did yesterday you would not blame me for standing out about it nor can one blame the men for showing sympathy for them, for they are from Massachusetts and are entirely unused to such scenes, and cannot recognize this property in human flesh and blood.[12]

You may wonder where the Col is in all this and I do also. we have all offered to give our servants up if he gives the order, but nobody knows that he has given any such order, and he is off camp all the while, attending a Court Martial, and

the whole thing seems to be the doing of Maj Marsh Lieut Col Decker and Capt Miller, the last has been threatening to have the men sent to the Tortugas for mutiny, and perhaps he can do it, but I doubt it. I must close now and send this to the office in order to get it off by this mornings mail. please write again as soon as you get this, as I do not know as we shall be in this camp to receive more than one more letter. Give my love to all. I shall write to Mattie some time to day With much love Your aff son

Charlie.

33

Camp Brightwood DC March 5th 1862

Dear Mattie

I received your most welcome letter accompanying the stockings, and also the pictures for which I cannot find words to express my thanks. I have to look at them fifty times a day. I am in camp alone to day as the Company is out on Grand Guard to day and as I went both of the last two times with them I managed to stay in this time. I have been slightly unwell for two or three days but have got pretty much over it now.

We have had another grand excitement over orders to march which we received last week. They were positive and we were to start at 3 o'clock in the morning but they were countermanded before 8 o'clock the same afternoon, and we are still here, but we are under standing orders to be ready at a moments notice, and to have 100 rounds of ammunition per man, and two days rations cooked all the time, and daily expecting orders to start, every man also is ordered to take an extra pair of shoes in his knapsack so it looks as if we were to have a long pull when we do move. Capt Lombard got a furlough the other day and started for home, and got as far as Washington where he got such information as convinced him that we should march in less than a week and he came back and gave it up. We were intended the other day to reinforce Gen Banks but the Rebels made no resistance to his advance and consequently we were not needed, and when it is proposed to send us next I am sure I cannot imagine.

We have had quite a row about giving up slaves and about the secessionists in this neighborhood and it threatened to be quite a serious affair for a time but things are quieter now. Capt Miller of Shelbourne Falls undertook to put all the Contrabands out of camp and myself and several other officers refused to give up our servants, at his order for we doubted his authority in the matter, as the Col had heretofor given us to understand that he was not opposed to our keeping

them, and had appeared to be quite anti Slavery in his views, but he took the matter in hand and read the order for thier expulsion at the head of the Regt and pretended to consider it a mutiny and altogether got himself into a terrible rage about it, and went over to the pro Slavery side body and soul. so it seems that the prime object of our being in this country is to return niggers to thier masters. I don't think Massachusetts blood was ever quite so riled nor quite so humbled before, but we had to submit. I was mad enough to resign, if I had not thought it would please our slave catching brutes too much. we have a good many of that class among our officers, and I believe Major Marsh would go further to return a fugitive slave than he would to save the Union.[13]

The stockings you sent were first rate. I have not put them on yet, but they look like just the thing I want

Friday Morning

I wrote as far yesterday and the regt was called out to drill and it was so long since I have seen any trainers I thought I would go and see them so I did not get to finishing this letter yesterday. This morning Capt Parsons tent took fire from the Stove Pipe and burnt half up he has not got in from Grand Guard yet, and does not know it. The fire Companies men promptly on the spot but as it was very windy they did not succeed in saving much but the frame.

I suppose Aunt Lu is now in Va but how near home I cannot tell. I had a letter from her from Old Point Comfort. The Contrabands left here night before last have got back. I don't know what will be done with them they say they went as far as the Susquehanna and they would not permit them to pass, and somebody tried to take them. I don't know what will be done with them I am sure. I had a letter from Mary and one from Mrs D W Palmer day before yesterday. Cal K + John Cook are quite well and I believe is everybody else you know. I meant to have got some pictures to send to you this time but did not get to it, but will try to send them next time

Give my love to Mother and Mary, and my respects to everybody. the mail will close very soon and I must send this to the Office. With much love Your aff brother

Charlie.

34

Camp Brightwood DC March 8th 1862

Dear Mother

I received your welcome letter to night and I think you must have received two from me before this time as I have written regularly though one of mine was delayed in consequence of your last (before this) having been sent by Captain and I was on Guard when I got it, and so I could not write in time to send it Monday morning. I expected you would be in a fever when the news from here reached you but we have not gone yet, but we are expecting our orders every day. part of our division has already gone and we shall soon follow. we have had 2 Regiments of Regulars added to our Division, and they are the ones that have marched, but where they have gone to or where we are to go to nobody knows. You must not be alarmed at any reports that come from here as you cannot possibly hear any truth unless you have it from me, and you know we have got to go and take our part in the struggle. that's what we came for and we aught to be thankful that we did not have to meet the enemy while we were raw and undisciplined and not ready for battle. it is said that we are now about as well trained as well as can be for Volunteers and certainly we know everything that is in the book for Infantry tactics. The weather is getting warmer and the ground begins to settle and it seems as if the army must make an advance very soon if it ever does. We are as ready as we ever can be, and perfectly willing, and if God rules shall I truly believe render a good account of ourselves when the time comes. I am more concerned about the reports that will go home when the Army does move, and you cannot have even a shadow of truth to guide you and yet you will believe everything that comes. I could almost wish for your sakes that, all communication of every kind was cut off between here and the north.[14]

We have not been paid off yet, and I don't know as we ever shall be again. The government has no money, and it takes three weeks just to sign enough paper money to pay 4 days expenses, and how they are ever going to catch up at that rate I am sure I do not know.

The Regiment drills every day now with Knapsacks on each containing 1 Shirt 1 pr Drawers 1 pr Stockings, 1 pr Shoes, 60 rounds of Ammunition 1 Blanket 1 Overcoat and whatever else each individual has in mind to put into it, but what I have mentioned he is obliged to carry any way. They trot round the lot here on the Double quick over fences through ditches, up hills and down dale, and when you take into consideration that besides what I enumerated before, each man carries his Cartridge box containing 40 Rounds more of Ammunition strapped on one side and his bayonet scabbard on the other, together with his haversack, containing (on the march) from two to four days provisions, and his Canteen containing 1 quart of water, and to wind up with his musket. you may consider

that the boys are pretty well toughened to it now and in addition to all this the Sergeants wear a long Sword that reaches from the waist almost down to the heels. *Do you wonder that I wanted a commission*

Capt Parsons is houseless and homeless just now, his tent having taken fire day before yesterday morning and was about half consumed before it could be put out, and he has not got another yet.

The Officers are ordered to reduce thier baggage to the smallest possible amount, as each Regiment is allowed only 4 wagons. You can judge something what the difference is when you reflect that we had 25 wagons when we came out, and had them all full how small in time they are ever going to get the baggage down to 4 wagons is more than I can see but it has got to be done and will be somehow I suppose.

I saw in the paper that the Missispipi with the 31st Mass Regt. ran aground and had to be partly unloaded and put into Port Royal to be repaired so John has his share of hardships. it does seem as though everything that went by sea was doomed to some mishap. it is thought that the Captain of this vessel ran aground purposely, and if so how in the name of all thats mysterious can such a man in command of a Government transport. I wonder how he happened to have such a fine passage out. it seems as if this was a peculiarly favored Regt and let us hope that it will continue so until the end. I presume it has more prayers offered for it than any other in the service.

I had a letter from Mary from Hartford and I shall write to her next. I also had one from Mrs Palmer the same day I shall answer that soon. she says that Fisher has been sick a long time and Dwight has had no one to help him. I don't hardly see how he gets along without him, but I suppose trade is not so lively while the war lasts.

I believe I wrote you that I had to give up my Contraband. well he started off with the rest of them the same night, and the next night three of them arrived back. they had been within ten miles of the Pennsylvania line, but a white man stopped them and questioned them so closely that they got scared and turned round and came back. we gave them a good dressing down and scolded them well for thier cowardice, and tonight they are going to start again. I told mine not to be taken alive, and if anybody undertook to kill him if he could, but they are most of them poor cowards, and I don't know but they are just as well off. I don't know as they are many of them capable of taking care of themselves it don't seem possible that men would get so near to freedom and then turn back to, a certain doom as they do.[15]

I have not heard about any 60,000 troops going to Fortress Munroe, and I reckon it is all gammon, but troops are moving all the time throught the city and we are undoubtedly on the eve of great events, and you certainly could not wish us to lay quietly here and take no part in them. they would hoot at us when we came home.

Captains wife writes that everyone out there says that the war will be over by the 1st of July, but its a mighty short time to then, and it will take a long time to settle things after the fighting is over. I heard the Quartermaster say today that we should undoubtedly have our orders tomorrow but I don't suppose he knows anything about it any more than I do.

You see I have not followed your example and written a short letter, which fact you will please bear in mind when you write next. Give my love to Mary and tell her I shall write to her next and I hope we shall have moved and I shall have something to write about. I wrote to Mattie one day this week Give my love to her and tell her not to delay in writing, and you must direct your letters as at present, until you hear from me, as our letters will probably have to still come to Washington after we leave here.

Cal K + J Cook are quite well John is as full of mischief as ever which is putting a cartridge in a fellows pocket and setting it on fire, to day proves. I expect he will get his head knocked off in some of his performances yet. I am sorry that Mr K is no better. I have said nothing to Cal about it.

Give my respects to all and write me a good long letter often. I must go to bed now, so good night, with much love from Your aff son

Charlie.

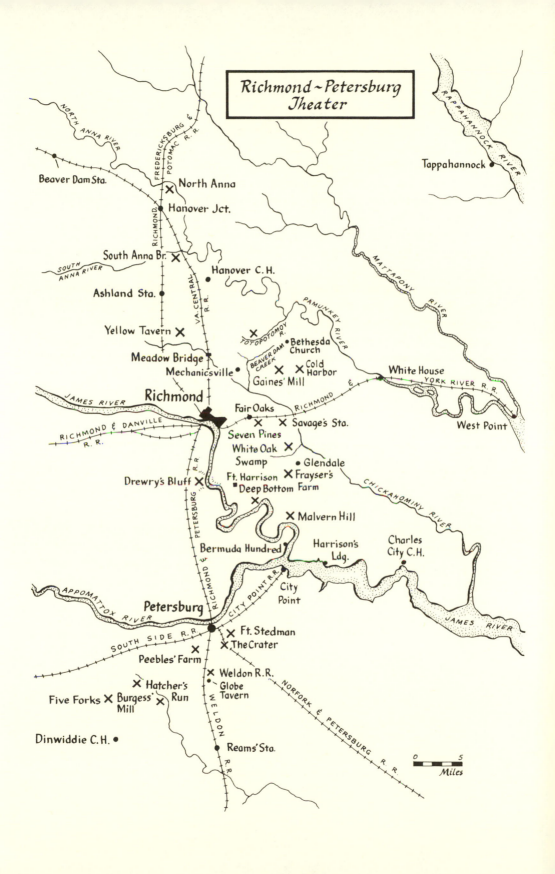

Richmond ~ Petersburg Theater

RAPPAHANNOCK RIVER

Tappahannock

NORTH ANNA RIVER

Beaver Dam Sta.

FREDERICKSBURG & POTOMAC R.R.

✗ North Anna

Hanover Jct.

RICHMOND,

MATTAPONY RIVER

SOUTH ANNA RIVER

South Anna Br. ✗

VA. CENTRAL R.R.

Hanover C. H.

Ashland Sta.

PAMUNKEY RIVER

Yellow Tavern ✗

TOTOPOTOMOY R. ✗

Bethesda Church

BEAVER DAM CREEK

Meadow Bridge ✗

Mechanicsville

✗ ✗ Cold Harbor

Gaines' Mill

White House

JAMES RIVER

RICHMOND &

YORK RIVER R.R.

Richmond

Fair Oaks ✗

RICHMOND & DANVILLE R.R.

✗ Savage's Sta.

West Point

Seven Pines

White Oak Swamp ✗

• Glendale

Drewry's Bluff ✗

PETERSBURG R.R.

Ft. Harrison ✗ Frayser's Farm

Deep Bottom

CHICKAHOMINY RIVER

✗

✗ Malvern Hill

Bermuda Hundred

Harrison's Ldg.

Charles City C.H.

RICHMOND & CITY POINT R.R.

City Point

JAMES RIVER

APPOMATTOX RIVER

Petersburg

SOUTH SIDE R.R.

✗ Ft. Stedman
✗ The Crater

Peebles' Farm ✗

✗ Weldon R.R.
• Globe Tavern

NORFORK & PETERSBURG R.R.

✗ Hatcher's Run

Five Forks ✗ Burgess' Mill ✗

WELDON R.R.

Dinwiddie C.H. •

Reams' Sta.

0   5
Miles

THREE

Oh It Was a Fearful, Fearful Sight

March–July 1862: The Peninsula Campaign

Brewster survived all the battles of Gen. George B. McClellan's Peninsula campaign in the spring and summer of 1862. After the siege of Yorktown, the battles of Williamsburg, Fair Oaks, and the Seven Days, and while stranded at Harrison's Landing on the James River in July, Brewster almost quit the army. His devotion and the necessity of the situation combined to make him stick it out; but war was now something frightfully real.

35

In the woods in VA March 13th 1862

Dear Mary

I believe I promised to write you next some time ago, but I wrote to Mother day before yesterday so I thought I would write to you this morning. I wish you could see me now. I am writing on a piece of secesh trunk, which belonged to the same Jones[1] who has just damaged our Navy so at Fortress Munroe. We are Bivouacked on his place, which was once a beautiful one but is now a barren enough. there is hardly a tree left standing in this region and the old mansion is deserted and the soldiers go all over it and take possession of anything they please. There is a Regt of Lancers encamped in an Orchard, round the house and they are cutting down the apple trees for fuel. I am writing in a house of my own building. it is about 3 feet high and built of pine boughs and turf. it is not so comfortable as many I have seen but it answers very well. I wish you could see the different kinds of huts the men build. some build neat barns [?] almost impervious to water, and others heap together a few boughs and lie down upon them. others take the bare ground. we have had beautiful weather since we have been here though it rained the first night some. I knew nothing about it however until I waked up after it was all over and found my blanket all wet. it has clouded over

now and it looks as if it was going to rain and it is growing colder with an east wind. We are about 1 mile from Lewinsville, and I have been out there this morning and such a deserted looking place you never saw I should think there were a dozen or fifteen houses and all but one deserted. there is a church there and I should think there had been two stores, and a blacksmith shop, but the doors are all gone and the windows are all out, and not a soul to be seen but straggling Soldiers. the whole army of the Potomac is bivouacked out the same as we are, and are all in advance of us, and what to do, they do not seem to know, for the Rebels have left bag and baggage and nobody knows where they have gone to.

there was a council of war held in W yesterday and our Gen Keys has gone to it but what the result is nobody knows Meanwhile we live here in a state of suspense, to which a battle would be the height of felicity. You have no doubt read in the papers about a house which our Pickets used to occupy day times and the Rebel Pickets nights. we are close to it, but it is now nothing but a ruin we have used it pretty much all up for fuel. it was once a nice place with fruit trees round it Peaches Pears and apples, but there is nothing left but the stumps, in fact the whole country presents a horrible picture of civil war the inhabitants of Lewinsville were most all northerners and the houses were nice white ones with green blinds it looks very much like that part of Florence which is up on the plain by Valentines old silk factory, even to a nice brown cottage to correspond with the Littlefields, you can imagine how that would look if the inhabitants were all driven out and the doors and windows all knocked out, and some of the houses stripped to frames. Some of the men of the 2nd RI Regt found an unexploded shell in the woods yesterday, and were playing with it, and one of them dropped a lighted match into it when it exploded blowing one mans head almost off and severely injuring others. the man died in a few hours. I don't know whether I shall get a chance to send this to day or not. Give my love to all. I shall write again when we get to a new place if we ever do the next Division is some nine miles ahead of us. we are all well so far, what we shall be when this rain is over, I don't know My paper is full so I must close with lots of love from Your aff brother

Charlie.

36

Camp Brightwood DC March 16th 1862

Dear Mother

I know you will be surprised to receive another letter from me at this place after the one I wrote you from Chain Bridge yesterday morning, and I did not

expect to be at this place again. we lay there yesterday in the rain until night when orders came that we might come back to these quarters and await further orders if we wished. So we rallied as many of the Regt as we could find and started, they were scattered over the woods for an extent of 3 or 4 miles drenched to the skin, and in a worse plight than you can well imagine, but we finally got most of our Co together and Capt Parsons and myself started with them for Camp Brightwood a distance variously estimated at from six to fourteen miles and in such a rain as you never saw. it seemed as if the windows of heaven were open, and it actually poured down, and the water in some places was knee deep in the road besides fording creeks where it was waist deep. We got the orders about dark and commenced to arrive here about 12 o'clock at night. we found the Officers tents all down and we are quartered in the Barracks with the men. the men have been coming in all day some have just arrived this evening, but we are all feeling finely and have but two made sick in our Company by the tramp. there were a few men in camp and they heard we were coming, and they got up and made hot coffee for us, and Col Briggs had sent to the city and got three bbls of Whiskey which was served out by the Drs advice. I did not try any of it, but I feel as well as any of them to day, and better than most of them, and ready for another pull which we expect tomorrow or next day, but where we are going to or anything else about it I don't know. nor does anybody else. To crown all the rest last night we got lost in Georgetown and went a mile or two out of our way, and had to retrace our steps. I did not stop to rest during the whole march. I suppose we had as hard a time the last week as any part of the army has had during the war and everybody says we endured it nobly.[2]

We started Monday Morning and got back Saturday night having been in the open air during whole of that time sleeping in the rain two nights. it rained almost all night the first night we lay at Chain Bridge. I lay between Capt P and Fred Clark, and pulled up my blanket and went to sleep every once in a while the blanket would get down and the rain would come pattering down on my face, and wake me up, and I would pull it up and go through the whole performance again.

I had on the worsted cap Mary made for me, and I got up in the morning and took it off and wrung about a pint of water out of it. I was terribly sleepy that night for I had been up on Guard the night before, and then started at 7 o'clock in the morning and Marched to Chain Bridge, where we waited all day for orders and when they came they were merely to lie down where we were and wait for further orders.

I wrote you that we were going up the Rappahannock but it is not known where we are going and I find that was merely a report, and without foundation Our two days mail has just come in and brings no letter for me, which of course makes me feel very bad, as if we should move off tomorrow I cannot tell when we shall have another chance to get a letter. I cannot think of anything more to

write. I believe I forgot to tell you that we found the bodies of two dead Rebels in the woods out on Prospect hill. they were much decayed and we did not know where they belonged. the buttons were all cut off thier coats, our boys buried them, how horrible it seems. they were probably wounded in some Picket skirmish and crawled off and died. you must know that we were right on the ground that was debated so long between the Pickets of the two armies.

I wish I could inform you when we are going where we are going to and when but I cannot but I am in good health and spirits, and ready and willing to go anywhere. I cannot discern that I have ever taken cold in this trip, and I would not have lost the experience for anything. it is reported now that we are going to reinforce Burnside, and almost everything else is reported, and nothing is known, so you are as wise as I be in the matter. I suppose you have all sorts of rumors up there but you must not believe any of them as it is impossible to find out anything reliable even here, so you can judge what it must be up there.

Tell Mattie I shall write to her when I get a chance to write two letters at once, but I know how much you will worry, so I have written you or Mary as often as I have had a chance. Cal + John Cook are well and have stood the march first rate, though Cal was a little sick one day. John was perfectly happy, for he could build a fire just where and when he had a mind to. We had a rumor one day that Richmond was in flames and the boys said it was because they heard John Cook had crossed the Potomac.

But I must bid you good night for my eyes utterly refuse to keep open With much love to Matt + Mary and respects to all Your aff son

Charlie

37

Washington DC National Hotel March 26th 1862

Dear Mother

Yesterday morning we started again from Camp Brightwood for the purpose of embarking in this city we marched down to within one mile of here and waited until night and the transports which were expected did not arrive so the whole Brigade went back again. The whole camp was torn to pieces, so I came on down to the city, and slept last night.

It is six and one half o'clock AM and the Brigade is ordered to report here at the foot of sixth st at 7 o'clock I suppose we are going to Fortress Munroe and I don't know when I shall have another opportunity to write but shall do so at the earliest chance I get. I reckon we are going up James River and you will probably hear of us in Richmond before a great while.

I do not know certainly as we are going there but that seems to be the general impression. I have received your letters and Marys you must continue to direct to this city until I can inform you differently.

Tell Mary I received her letter yesterday while we were lying on the ground out on the 7th st round waiting for orders.

I have not time to write more this morning so good bye. I don't know when I shall have a chance to write again or where I can hear from you again, but I hope it will not be a great while.

Cal + J Cook were well and smart last night and we are all in first rate spirits at going. You have no idea what a number of troops have gone, and there are one or two Divisions to follow us, but as I must bid you good bye, with love to all from Your aff son

Charlie.

PS I sent some money to D Kingsley to pay him and told him to pay over the balance to you. I should have sent more but we are going into a strange country and I wanted to have some in my pocket and I have a great many small bills to pay, but it is not a great while before the next pay day when I shall send you some more.

38

Hampton Va. March 29th 1862

Dear Mother

We have just arrived here having left Washington yesterday AM. I came with the last boatload, being on Guard at the time we left. Co C came on another boat and I have not seen them yet. we are right at the ruined village of Hampton which is nothing but a mass of chimneys.[3]

I have but a moment to write as the man is going over to the Fortress, and will take this love to all Aff yours

Charlie

Don't know where we are going but there are thousands upon thousands of soldier here

39

Hampton, Newport News or some other place in Virginia
Sunday Mch 30th 1862

Dear Mother

Again I have a chance to send a letter which I hasten to improve. Our Sutler who came on with us is going back to Washington this PM and I shall send this by him. I have written every day since we left Camp B but one and that was the day we were on the Potomac. We arrived here last night just at dark as usual, and in the midst of a pelting rain, Capt P and myself made ourselves as comfortable as possible with a hut made of Rubber Blankets. it is situated in the midst of a great plain, with mud in any quantity as it was plowed land. We slept very comfortably last night, although it rained torrents all night and continues to rain still. Capt + myself are seated flat on the straw under our blankets, both writing home. Our heads press against the roof of our shelter and about two feet off on either side is a great big mud puddle, just the same as it would be in the middle of the road in front of your house, during a heavy rain. I sent a letter home the day we arrived here, and one to Mary yesterday by Syd Bridgman but I suppose this will arrive before Syd does. We are entirely in the dark as to where we are going or when.

We marched out here yesterday PM, which is about 5 or 6 miles from Hampton and two miles from Newport News. There are soldiers ahead, Soldiers behind and soldiers[4] on each side of and all around us the country is fairly alive with them our troops occupy Gt Bethel there were 15,000 Rebels there but they fled upon the approach of our forces. I suppose Richmond is our ultimate destination but by what route and when we do not know. the men are all in first rate spirits and appear to enjoy themselves first rate, and they do not grumble at all, whereas they were growling all the while when we were in nice comfortable Barracks at Brightwood, but this is something new. We left Lieut W on Guard at the wharf with the baggage. I was on Guard at the wharf when we left Washington, and until 4 o'clock on board the boat. that is from 4 PM Thursday until 4 PM on Friday. there are 2 or three Lieuts in our kind of guard one kind of guard or another all the time, so I suppose our time will come pretty often.

John Cook + Cal K are well and in good spirits so are all the rest we discharged our only sick man when we left Washington. Our Regt occupied three boats coming down and each boat towed one or two Schooners or Barges and all loaded with war material of every kind. Horses, Cannon Ammunition Wagons Pontoons, and Bridge Material and everything you can think of. We saw the Monitor in the Harbor, near Fortress Munroe lying there with steam up ready to start at a moments notice. she does not look as though she could harm a fly, but the little thing is the sole protection of that great Harbor, and the great

Fortress and the hundreds of ships and steamboats lying there, to say nothing of the many seaports outside. thier safety all lies on that little box with a handful of men and two guns wonderful is it not?[5]

I cannot write more as I am all cramped up and both feet are asleep and I have so much to write about that I cannot think of anything. I do not know where to tell you to direct letters but I suppose you must direct them to Washington unless you can write two at a time and direct one to Fortress Munroe and one to Washington.

Give my love to all, with lots for yourself from Your aff son

Charlie

40

Camp W F Smith near Hampton Va Thursday April 3rd 1862

Dear Mother

We are still in the same camp from which I wrote last but are expecting to move very soon. I received a letter from you yesterday written on the 29th of March, also one from D Kingsley acknowledging receipt of money and I suppose he paid over to you what I told him to. I should have sent more but I had so many things to get, to prepare for the field and so many little debts to pay that I could not feel safe in sending any more as I wanted some in my pocket. as you know Officers have to buy thier board as they go along. Our Regiment has not been paid off yet and I got my Voucher discounted at a Bankers. I had to pay $10.00 for it but I could not march without some things, and without money.

Our Regt with the rest of the Brigade started a week ago last Tuesday from Camp Brightwood and marched to within a mile of the city, and waited there all day for the transports, but they did not come up so at night they marched back to Camp B again, but I got permission and put on down to the city and staid over night. I went and called on Mrs Wendell in the morning and found them very well and very glad to see me. The Regt arrived in the city again the next morning and staid there by the wharf all day until about 7 o'clock PM when they commenced to go aboard, and finally got loaded about 10 o'clock PM, on two boats. Co's C G + E on one and the rest on the other they lay by the wharf until morning, when the Sea Shore containing the three Cos above mentioned, steamed off down the river, leaving Lieut C H B behind as officer of the guard, finding the other boat the Ariel too crowded they procured another and put two Companies H + F on that and they steamed off finally, we picked up the last straggler, and shoved off the plank and the Ariel containing the other five

Companies started off down the Potomac. I was about the last man on board. It was a most beautiful day and we enjoyed the sail very much. we kept on our course all that day and night, and arrived at Fortress Munroe the next day about 11 o'clock, and came to Anchor, after dinner, we steamed round to the village of Hampton (that was) but there were so many boats before us that we could not land at night so we slept aboard that night. Companies C G + E had disembarked that PM and slept on the ground. the next morning our part landed and I went in pursuit of Co C. my way led through the town of Hampton which you know was burnt in August last by Col now Gen MacGruder of the Rebel army, and such a picture of war + desolation I never saw nor thought of, and hope I shall not again, but I have written you about it before. I pass through the church yard round the celebrated Hampton Church, the oldest one in use in the United States it is completely destroyed all but the walls and they are useless. The toombs and vaults around were in many instances broken open, and the bones exposed to view. it was horrible. Well we staid around there until afternoon, when we took up our line of march and arrived at this place just at night in a heavy rainstorm as usual and here we have been ever since. it is in a level plain of vast extent. there is but one house to be seen, but of the thousands + thousands of soldiers you can form no possible idea. they have been coming for 10 days before we started, and they have been coming ever since and they are not done coming yet.

Yesterday all day long regt after regt followed one another up the road past us, and where the end of them is I am sure I do not know. We had a visit from Willie Robinson yesterday. I should not have known him. he has just been promoted to 2nd Lieut. he has improved most wonderfully since I saw him he had received a letter from Mary since he came here and I read it. the letters came by way of Washington but in future you may direct letters to Fortress Munroe.

It is supposed i believe that now our first battle will be at Yorktown but nobody knows or cares if they will only send us somewhere but we are awful sick of lying here and holding Company + Battallion drills, as we have to, and the curses of the men at having to drill are both loud and deep. they can bear any amount of hardship and privation if they are marching on but an hours drill kills them off completely and no wonder for they have done nothing else for nine long months and looked forward to the time when they took the field as the time when they would have a change and a relief from drill and now to have all the intervals between marches filled up by drills, is discouraging enough. I have been as great a stickler for drill and disipline as anyone but I know that you cannot learn volunteers any more after they have arrived at a certain proficiency, and the very word drill disgusts me now.

The Rebel gunboats came down and fire shells into the woods where Smiths Division is just ahead of us and some of them have burst within a quarter of a

mile of us. I do not think of anything more to write to day, but as I cannot send this until tomorrow I may think of something else. I have just been detailed for Guard duty to commence at 4 o'clock this PM Since writing the above we had orders for a Review at 2 and one half o'clock We marched out but before it took place the order was countermanded. I went out to the Guard mounting and found that there had been a mistake in the detail and that I was not to go on Guard duty to night. We have got orders to march at 6 o'clock tomorrow morning, and are probable destination is Yorktown.[6] there is said to be a Rebel force of 90,000 men but I can hardly credit it, I reckon we shall have work to do tomorrow or next day, and now dear Mother do not worry yourself, but just consider that my chance is as good as anybodys, and what is to be will be. I had some misgivings about writing you at all until it was over, but I thought I would as I do not know when I can write again. It is fast day in Mass but how different from a Mass fast day it is here amid the sounds of Drums Bugles neighing of horses, braying of mules, and the hum of voices of the innumerable men, under a broiling sun, which makes clothing of any kind a nuisance. I have had my Coat off all day and suffered with heat at that. I have just received a letter from you. I wonder at Lieuts Clark + Spaulding coming home, but you can depend upon it. it is no Recruiting service they have either resigned or been discharged I do not know which I presume it is some trouble between them and Capt Vance.

We had a tremendous Thunder shower last night. I lay dreaming and I thought it was cannon. I thought we were marching towards it, and could see the smoke and I wondered why the balls did not come, finally I woke up and there came a clap precisely like the firing of cannon, and I expected to hear the long roll, but when I heard the rain pattering on the tent I concluded that it was all right, but I must close as I do not think of anything more to write and the next time you hear from us you will probably hear something worth hearing, at least I hope so and I reckon if we beat the Rebels they will not get much rest after it I presume. we have as many as 150,000[7] men here, and cannon in any quantity.

Give my respects to Mr Boland, love to Mattie and Mary, and respects to everyone else, J Cook and Cal are quite well. I can hear Cals voice outside now. We are to take two days rations tomorrow and day after that we expect to dine in Yorktown Don't fail to write often and direct to Lieut to CHB 10th Mass Vols, Keyes Corps Fortress Munroe Va. And so good bye with lots of love from Your aff son

Charlie

41

In the woods near Warwick Court House Virginia Sunday PM April 6th 1862

Dear Mother

I wrote you last Wednesday telling you of our intended march the next morning. well we marched as ordered at about 7 o'clock AM, on a most beautiful morning. The sun shone as bright as a morning in June at the north, and the peach trees were in blossom in every direction. We marched on, ever and anon hoping, as the road became clogged by the thousands of soldiers who were ahead of us, passed Newport News at about 10 o'clock, and turning to the right, took up our line of march up the James River, and continued along a road that runs parallel to it, and about 40 rods from the bank. The country is very low and level, but a ridge rises up on the very bank to a heighth of about 15 feet. Here we passed the relics of the bivuoac of the Smiths Division who had started on before us. About 11 o'clock word came back from him (Smith) that he was in sight of one of the enemies batteries, and requesting permission to attack them. Gen Keyes gave the required permission, and he fired one shell, when they left in Double quick time. we sent on two Brigades of our Division to support Gen Smith, and halted on an open plain that had been the Piqcquet[8] lines of the enemy the night before. There was a house, or rather a group of houses, which were deserted, we staid here two or three hours, and I went over to them. They were entirely empty and the wells were filled up, the foundation was most all gone and in an outhouse I found a lot of old letters, but they were all dunning letters and addressed to a man named Marion Colbert. The Woods here were full of Secesh hogs and pigs, which had been let loose and the boys went after them with a rush and soon returned bearing its junks of fresh pork, and building fresh fires, sat down and feasted upon pork steak, broiled upon the end of a stick held over the fire. We went on as far as we could that night and turned into a pine woods after dark and stacked arms, and threw ourselves down on the ground behind the rows of muskets and were soon lost to all sense of our troubles, in sound sleep.

When we started I left all my blankets and everything else. But my Overcoat + Haversack, and as the roads are terrible and we had but two wagons anyway. I found myself without anything to sleep under and it had clouded over and bid fair to rain like guns in half an hour. Lt Weatherill brought his blankets on his back, so I turned in with him. We had just got completely asleep when Capt P came and roused him up and communicated the joyful tidings that he (Lt W) had got to out to go out with him on Picket guard. Of course he had to take his blankets, as Capt did not bring any so I had to be [?] up and seek quarters elsewhere which I did with some of the boys, 5 or 6 of whom were nestled together behind some brush and logs. I woke up in the morning feeling first rate,

as Providence had spared us any rain in the night. We took up our line of march at sunrise and made slow progress, as there were many awful mud holes, and places where the Rebels had cut down trees and felled them across the road and at other places crossing creeks in single file on a log, or a plank thrown across. About 9 o'clock we came up to the Batteries taken by Smiths Division the day before, and thought to ourselves if we had been in them and they outside it would have cost them something to get in.

Before this it had been raining, almost ever since we started and now, it grew dark and thundered and lightened and the rain poured in torrents, but we struggled along through the mud which was of the consistency of thick molasses on a hard floor, and awful slippery. You have no idea of how formidable the works were here. it was a stockaded fort. I hardly know how to describe it. As we came across a long plain we came to a large mill pond on our right, and the road went down in a sort of ravine, and right across from the dam on one side to the bank on the other was a line of logs about 4 inches in diameter and firmly planted in the ground close together, and at about 10 feet hight cut off and sharpened to a point. Where the road went through there was a strong gate, right behind this a high bank, crowned by a fort with embrasures for two guns. There every knoll was crowned by a breastwork for rifle men and stretching away as far as we could see were breastworks with embrasures for cannon, and behind these were the Barracks, enough to contain 4 or 5,000 soldiers. The place is called Shooters Mills, named I suppose, from an old Grist mill which stood in the center. We slipped and slid through this place and our Regt and the 36th NY made a wide sweep to the left, making a straight line through the plowed fields and woods and here we had the toughest time we had seen yet. It appears we had to reach this point at a given time and the sun had now come out, and it was hot as July at home, and the mens cloths and knapsacks were wet and yet we hurried on.

Men fell out completely exhausted and were left on the ground where they fell, and still we pressed on. We would come out on an open field, and make for the wood on the other side, plunge into them and struggle through, those that could not keep up fell to the rear, and the ground became strewed with knapsacks, O Coats, Blankets, Boots + Shoes, Pants, Shirts, + Drawers, and all the articles which go to make up the soldiers outfit. We kept on in this way until we arrived at a piece of woods about noon, and where we halted and took about an hours rest, and the stragglers most of them came in. Then the Bugle sounded again and we fell in and marched through this woods, down a steep bank, across a slab + log bridge over a marsh, in a cove which sets back from the river up the other side and through a small piece of woods, and out upon an open field. As we came out we saw the 2nd Rhode Island Regt just disappearing in some woods on the right with guns upon the right shoulder, and at the Double Quick. Straight out we came and on our left was one of our Batteries with guns unlimbered and

men at thier stations ready to hurl thier iron hail at an instants notice. We took a turn to the left, and the order was given "On Right by file into line" and out of chaos (as it were) came the 10th Mass Vols straight across the field, in line of battle, and after them came the 36th NY, and took up and extended the same line to the left. Word was passed along to look to the condition of the tubes,[9] then came "load at will" and there we stood.

Presently up the straight road (which we had left in the morning) came the 7th Mass Regt and formed in line right behind us about 100 rods before us was a piece of woods, directly before us a road and on each side of this a Va Rail fence. We stood there a while and then half a doz men tore down two lengths of the fence and we doubled on the center, and passed through and formed in line in the next field near the woods, and there we stood, formed as we supposed for our first battle, with steadfast gaze upon the piece of woods in front out of which we expected to see the Rebels come or to hear the roar of musketry every moment. Presently the right and left Companies H + G deployed as skirmishers and went forward to a fence on the edge of the woods, and kneeled down behind it. We waited there I should think two and one half hours, and all this time we could hear the Artillery off on our right as they poured the shell into some place invisible to us *but not a Rebel came near us.* Next day called in the skirmishers and we took up the line of march up the road past Warwick Court House, which is about half as big as our barn and built of brick. As we passed the open door we could see a safe broken open and any quantity of papers strewed about. The village consists of a store, Tavern, Ct House, Jail and one or two houses. Down a little hill and through a creek up to our knees, and then over a half mile of road in mud up to our ankles, into a piece of woods we went. The cannon sounded nearer and nearer, and we expected at any moment to arrive in sight of the fort, which we understood they were shelling, but the order came "Right about" march, and in an instant we were marching directly back. Wc "filed right" into an open field and here was one of our Batteries stationed again, and we formed in Battle array, stacked arms and threw ourselves down upon the fresh earth and waited for the next order. Here we staid until after Sundown last night, then we took up our line of march back past W Ct House and closed up in column by division in an open common, of hard clay with water standing in puddles all over it. Here we stacked arms and were told to make ourselves as comfortable as possible where we were, as we might be ordered to move in 5 minutes, and might not until morning.

There was an old house in the village, and in the 15 minutes there was not a board left on it, neither roof floor nor anything. One of our boys received enough for himself and the three Officers, and we made a floor and down we laid, and were soon fast asleep. this was about 7 o'clock or half past. The next thing I heard I was being shaken by the man who slept next and shared his blanket with me.

"Lt Lt, the Bugle has sounded" up we got tired and hungry (for all this time since we started I had not had anything but a few crackers and a half a dz cookies which I put in my haversack when we started Thursday morning. Our suttler, on whom we depended, owing to the press of wagons and the worse than awful conditions of the roads, had not been able to come up with us) We strapped on our equipments, the poor men shouldered thier knapsacks and off we started. It was just 9 o'clock PM. We took a bee line for the same woods we had faced when we first formed in the afternoon.

The whole Regt was detailed for Picket guard. Into the woods we went, dark as Pocket, posted little groups of men 4 in a group, 2 or 3 rods apart and extending for 3/4 of a mile. This being done and instructions given them I threw myself down and composed myself to sleep. Pretty soon Capt came along and threw a blanket over me, it was a light thing which he had picked up during the day. At three o'clock this morning I woke up nearly frozen, and went and got permission to build a fire, and with the help of two or three of the boys took down three or four lengths of a rail fence, and soon we had a rousing fire, blazing half way to the top of the trees. The rails in this country are all made of pine and make spendid fires. I was glad to see this mornings sun. About 9 o'clock AM our Company was sent off on a two days duty of some kind I don't know what, and soon after six more Co's were ordered off to build a road somewhere, and the other three have lain here all day, in the warm sun They are Companies C, F, + A (C Northampton, F Springfield, A Gt Barrington) and I assure you we congratulated ourselves on our good fortune.

The inhabitants here have fled leaving everything and the woods are full of cattle, horses, and hogs. Our boys have been bringing in quarters of beef all day long. They build up a fire, hang up the beef on a stake and soon are revelling in roast beef, or beef steaks, or Pork or mutton as the case may be. How different from a quiet New England Sabbath is this Sabbath in the army. As I lay here writing to you on the side of a hard cracker box, I hear the booming of cannon, the bursting of shells, and ever anon the crack of the rifle, or the volley as the case may be, and in future accounts of this battle or skirmish, or whatever they call it we shall be named as participants I suppose, and yet I know almost as little of it as you do in your far off New England home. I know that we have got or rather they in the front have, a number of secesh prisoners, I know there is a Battery there, and it is supposed that we have got the Rebels penned in, and that they may try to retreat this way, and that we are to stop them. It is also said that they are trying to get around our left, and another story has it that they are being reinforced from the other side of the river and are trying to get in our rear and cut us off from Fortress Munroe, but we know nothing certain. I know this however, that our Quartermaster has been informed that he will draw his next supplies from vessels at Yorktown, and we have not got Yorktown yet, and we took but six

days provisions, and could not bring half of them. I presume that the whole thing will be in the newspapers before you get this but you will have the satisfaction of reading a *long* letter written while the battle was going on.[10]

Another report has just come in that the Porters Division has taken 300 Prisoners. I have written this not knowing when I shall have a chance to send it, perhaps from Yorktown, perhaps never, but I know it will be interesting to you if you ever get it, so I write on. Part of our Suttlers wagons arrived this forenoon and our wagons with my Blankets, which will go on my back hereafter. I have a full stomach once more, and again feel first rate, never better. I have been through lots of privations or hardships but on the whole I like it. You will wonder I suppose how I felt when I thought we were going into Battle, but I cannot describe it. it was a queer sort of feeling, but rather pleasant than otherwise, but then the bullets did not come, and we did not see the enemy so I suppose I do not know much about it. I shall close this letter here
[the next line is on the fold and is illegible]
send it back to the Fortress tonight if not I shall probably write more before it goes if there is anything to write. Cal and J Cook are here and tough and hardy.

Give my love to Mattie + Mr B tell her she must look to you for news from me at present I can find time to write home only. Love to Mary and respects to all with much love from Your aff son

Charlie

PS Six o'clock PM One of the Suttlers men is going to the Fortress in the morning and I shall send this We have not got the Battery yet there are said to be 10,000 men in it. Col Decker went within half a mile of it to day and was shot at twice with a shell. One struck within thirty yards of him. 12 regiments are said to be ready to take at a moments notice. a column is moving up York River also.

42

Warwick Court House VA Wednesday April 6th 1862
Camp Winfield Scott
10th Mass Vols, 3rd Brigade
Couch's Division, 4th Corps
Army of the Potomac

Dear Mother
    Above you have our full directions and titles which you perceive makes quite a large stream in the aggregate. Well, I have not much to write. we are lying here

where we were when I wrote you last, and the army is engaged in throwing up Breastworks, and getting heavy seige guns into position. The enemy are very strong in numbers and position and are constantly receiving reinforcements. it is said they have more than 500 Cannon, and I presume they have as it is very near Norfolk where the treacherous commander of the Navy Yard gave up so many in the beginning of the war.[11] I presume it will be some time before the great battle takes place the enemy open upon us occasionally with shot and shell and yesterday they drove in our picket in Smiths Division. they fire upon our Pickets constantly. I went over to a house in Smiths Div yesterday to grind my sword. it is about 2 and ¹/₂ miles from here and is used for an Hospital. I saw a number of men who had been wounded on Picket. Some had lost thier arms and some thier legs +c +c they all agree that lots of the enemys Pickets are negroes.[12] probably the chivalry do not like to expose themselves to such dangerous business The word has come to fall in immediately with arms and equipments. I shall have to stop.

Saturday April 19th

I closed this letter on Wednesday last buckled on my sword and pistol and fell in with the Company it was about 10 o'clock in the forenoon and hot as mid summer at the north we marched on about 3 ¹/₂ miles towards Yorktown and stacked arms in the woods, and waited all day, until about 9 o'clock at night. We had started out without our knapsacks and had no blankets nor any overcoats nothing but our arms. we were expecting a battle about 9 o'clock at night. we marched back to our last camp and packed up our worldly goods strapped them on our backs threw ourselves on the ground about 12 o'clock and slept until 2 o'clock when up again and marched back to where we were the night before. there we made our coffee in little tin cups and made out to eat a couple of hard crackers, and then we fell in and marched about a half mile further, and waited again, finally we took up our line of march again and went on a half mile farther and debunched upon an open plowed field formed line of battle fronting some woods, there were also dense woods on the right and left, then came the order "Capt Parsons + Capt Day (Greenfield) deploy skirmishers". out went Companies G + C, loaded and deployed and into the woods in front we went about 150 yards. we had orders not to go any further then we were told to keep a sharp look out ahead, and wait for further orders. we threw off our knapsacks. (Officers and all have to wear them now) and threw ourselves on the ground there was no shade and the sun beat down until it seemed as if the scorching rays of heat would burn through us we got no further orders until night and the enemy did not appear. at dark we moved forward further into the woods, gathered in parties of four, with orders for two of each party to keep awake all the time, and to allow no one to pass us either way, and if anyone came from towards the enemy to

challenge them, and if not answered properly, and immediately to shoot them and in addition to this we had the assurance that in all human probability we should be attacked before morning.

well part of us threw ourselves down and covered up with our blankets and part kept watch. I was with the 3rd group from the right, and had Sergt Munyan with me on the right of our Company was Company G and on the right of them were the Pickets of the 7th Maine Regt. we were about half a mile from the enemy's entrenchments and the line of the 7th Maine Pickets run by the entrenchments of the enemy at about 800 yards distance. I threw myself down on my blanket and covered myself with my overcoat and went to sleep. about 12 o'clock I woke up, and got up and visited two or three posts of the Guard, came back, and laid down again. I had got most asleep when I heard off to the right of us the firing of guns. Pop - Pop- Pop Pop Pop- and running into a regular roar of musketry. we sprang up and strapped on our knapsacks in quick time and the boys seized thier muskets with a firmer grasp and we were ready for them, but much to our regret they did not come. the firing was by Berdans Sharpshooters[13] and the 7th Maine. our troops are engaged every night in throwing up earthworks in front of the enemys, and after the Maine row that night, the Rebels brought out a Brass field piece in front of thier works with the intention of shelling our men but the sharpshooters were ready for them and before they fire it they had picked off the gunners and the rest of them ran inside and left the gun and they have not been able to get it since These sharpshooters are the greatest terror to the enemy and well they may be for no sooner does one of them the Rebels show himself then plunk goes a bullet into his body, and he is done from secession for this world.

This part of thier works is on the bank of a creek and before them is an open field and our men have thrown up earthworks nearer and nearer every night until they have got within 400 yards of the enemys works and behind them are posted Berdans sharpshooters, and they can hit the size of a man's head or hand at this distance every time and they have killed quantities of them so that they have not fired a big gun at our side for two days, for the moment a gunner shows himself to load a piece that minute dies. there was one big nigger the day before yesterday got up on a parapet to swab out a gun crack went a rifle, and he fell outside of thier works and there he lay all day long and they dared not come out to pick him up and they could not for it would have been certain death if they had. I went up there twice yesterday, and there was not a living thing to be seen about the rebel works they dare not show so much as a coat tail.

I suppose when all things are ready we shall have to make a grand charge over them and take those batteries. I wish some of the grumblers at the north that are in such a hurry to have a fight could come down here and try it on. I am willing to exchange my share of this life with them, without any compensation to boot.

we get to sleep at night jump up three or four times in the night and form line of battle, find it a false alarm and lie down again, get up in the morning and strip off our clothes and go to digging Wood Ticks out of our flesh, then wash all over, and as likely as not have to perform the same operation again before noon. we are all covered with little sores caused by these wretches and there is no help for it. they are as thick as leaves, and thicker for every leaf is occupied by half a dozen of them. they are hard shiny backed fellows and it takes a hammer and chisel to kill one of them.

The Rebels have a line of Fortification from river to river lined with sharp-shooters and bristling with cannon and I think if some of the grumblers who are spoiling for a fight and crying why don't you advance, were here they would be glad to turn tail and go home, and let the military leaders do the business in thier own way. In addition to this there is from James River a sort of deep ravine runs across the peninsular almost to York River and the rebel works are all on the bank of this ravine. they have dug a canal for York River, which is higher than the James and have dammed it up and at any moment they can let the water in and flood this ravine to the depth of six and eight feet and through this ravine we have got to go to storm thier works and yet these fools at the north who have staid at home and not risked a hair of the head of thier precious carcasses, would have us rush ahead regardless of everything else as long as they are safe in thier homes if they are so anxious for loss of life why don't they come down and loose thier valuable ones in a useless assault upon these entrenchments.[14] there never was a better opportunity to show thier valor and to sacrifice thier lives to thier countrys cause, when all things are ready we shall move upon these works and there is hardly a doubt that we shall take them, and we are not afraid to go to day if so ordered, but as long as we have competent leaders who have made it a lifes study how to do these things, I think the cowards who have staid at home had better cease thier senseless noise and let them have thier own way. I have not had any letters from home this week. I don't know why. please write often if you do not hear from me, as I write every opportunity. I must close this immediately as the mail is going all well, love to all Your +c

Charlie (over)

I was too late so this will have to wait until the next chance which will not be for two or three days perhaps I am sorry but could not help it. I send you enclosed a secesh postage stamp which was found on a letter in a deserted house on our march hither. I forgot to tell Mary to send that cap to Fortress Munroe and to make it smaller than the other a little. It is going to rain and I must stop to make some preparation for it about my shanty. I did not have any last night nor night before nor night before that. I may think of something more to write before I can send this.

Tuesday April 22nd

I have had no chance to finish this letter since I stopped last Saturday. that evening the rebels made an attack on our Pickets and we were called into line we stood in line of Battle until about 2 o'clock Saturday night, and then broke ranks and crawled into our huts with our equipments on. we had hardly got into them before Pop Pop went the guns again and we had to turn out again and stand out in line the rest of the night. it rained like fun all night long and the next morning presented the sorriest lot of fellows you ever saw. it was Sunday morning, and we threw ourselves down all soaked as we were, with equipments on, and during the day we had to fall in and get ready to receive the rebels twice.

at night we moved our camp farther into the woods towards the rebels, and took turns acting as a reserve for the picket. Company C went on at 1 o'clock AM night before last and staid until morning a terrible cold North East wind blew and we had a tough time yesterday I was sick and laid in my bunk all day. it cleared off in the night and is very pleasant this morning it has rained almost incessantly since Saturday evening and we have been up in it $^2/_3$ of the time. our lines are not over half a mile from the rebels anywhere and just to the right of us they are only 350 yards. we have three batteries of Parrott guns there behind some earthworks which our troops have thrown up nights. I saw Willie Robinson last Sat. he was in the fight the other day when the 3rd 4th + 6th Vt Regts tried to take one of the rebel batteries and one man killed in his company. they are right close under the rebels nose, and our brigade is detached from our division to support them. I went down within 400 yards of the rebel works where I could see them as plain as you can see the railroad from our house but they could not fire at us for one sharpshooter kept such a lookout that they cannot even show thier heads without getting a bullet in it. they showed a flag of truce while I was there and just as soon as our side acknowledged it you should have seen the heads pop up over thier breastworks. they looked just like the bees when they swarm on the outside of a hive. they wanted permission to bury thier dead, which was granted and our side went forward and got our dead and wounded who had lain there between the two sides since Thursday when the fight place. our sharpshooters had shot lots of them since then and there they had to let them lie, until they smelt very badly as to go after the bodies would be certain death. I don't know when this is all to end. we have just received reinforcements of 10,000 men from McDowells department[15] and it seems as if we might whip them out pretty soon. there comes the order to form the line of battle again so I will stop here Give my love to all and do write I have not heard a word from you since week before last Yours with much love

Charlie

43

Camp Winfield Scott
Warwick Ct House, Va Wednesday Apr 23rd 1862

Dear Mother

I have just been made glad by the receipt of a letter from you and thought I would commence an answer to day even if I did not finish it. I closed the letter yesterday by telling you of the order to form line of battle again. well we slung our knapsacks this time, and we were encamped on the edge of the woods about a mile and a half from the enemy the order came, "by the left of Company to the front" and forward we went straight through the woods towards the enemy. we knew not what it was for nor how far we were going, and whether there was to be a general engagement and we were going into position or what was going on. we went on about a mile, and halted and lay down. the skirmishers went on until they could see the enemy's works, and then we marched back. it was only a reconnaisance, and for no particular purpose that we could discern. we came back to camp and threw down our knapsacks, and very soon the order came again to fall in which we did and marched back some 4 miles to this place where I commenced writing my last letter which as you know I finished up then. it seems we have been detached from our division for a week we were sent up there to support the Vermont Regiments on Thursday last when they had thier skirmish with the rebels. we have now got back where we can have a little more quiet, and not be roused up every night to stand in the rain and wait for rebels who never come. The 7th Maine whose pickets joined us on the right had a skirmish with the rebels the same forenoon that we made the reconnaisance.

The picket line is formed by groups of three men about 100 yards apart, or nearer when occasion requires, and both armies place a line of these out towards the enemy. they are to inform the main body of any movement of the enemy and to hold them in check as long as they can when they retreat and rally on the main force, if the enemy follows up in force it brings on an engagement but they often come out and draw in the pickets some distance but do not follow unless it is a general advance. this is called a reconnaisance. We yesterday forenoon [saw] two regiments of Niggers came out from the rebels and drove the Pickets of the seventh Maine Regt. they succeeded in surrounding one of the 7th, and notwithstanding he gave up his musket, they shot him through the head and bayoneted him half a dozen times. a small squad of the 7th seeing this determined to avenge his death and they sallied out upon this party right in the face of the enemy and securing one of them a big nigger they chopped him all to pieces. the 7th had two killed and two wounded I saw one of the wounded brought in on a stretcher. it is a notorious fact that the rebels have any quantity of niggers in their service. our pickets have seen them and have shot them. they not only have them to work on

Fortifications but they are organized into Regts and are armed and do the most dangerous part of thier fighting but Oh! won't they catch it when we get at them they are rousing a spirit of revenge in our boys that will show them no mercy when thier times comes.[16]

Our men are just mounting heavy guns upon our right, and we expect any day to hear the booming of them but they have not opened yet. We are getting impatient but must content ourselves to wait until everything is ready for there must be no failure here. You wonder where Aunt Lu is I presume if her husband has done as the secessionists in this part of the country have, she will be dragged off further into secessia and her home will be deserted as the houses in this country are, and very likely will eventually be torn down to furnish shelter for Union troops but if he is wise enough to stay in his house he will probably come out all right You do not suppose it is possible that he is Union at heart do you and that he was obliged to write those letters but I suppose it cannot be, or his sons would not be in the rebel army.

I don't know how long we shall stay here but I wish this war was over with I know that much and how it is that we can stand such hardship and not make us all sick is more than I know. I never took into my calculations of war this being without tents and without anything to eat but we have enought to eat now such as it is and get fresh beef occasionally. the suttlers are reaping a great Harvest such as have been lucky enough to get thier goods landed. they asked twenty cents a pound for cheese fifty + seventy five for butter one dollar for Tobacco and everything else in proportion. I should like when the war is over to hang all the suttlers gathered together and let the soldiers surround them and give them a few volleys of minnie bullets. there are some good ones among them though such as the suttler of the 4th Vermont that we came across in the woods. I wrote you about it. he did not charge any more than a fair price for anything and appeared like a human being and not like a vulture.

I was mighty glad to hear that Mattie had sent me some Maple Sugar. I read in the papers about New Maple Sugar two or three weeks ago, and I have had a terrible hankering after some ever since. I don't know what made me but I have thought of it almost every day since and wished I could get some. Sergt Nims has not arrived yet, and I don't know what has become of him and I should be disappointed enough if I do not get him when he comes he has been long enough on the way to come here forty times I believe I wrote you that I would send you a secesh Postage Stamp in my last but I forgot it but will endeavor to send it in this. it was taken off a letter in a deserted house in this vicinity. our Pickets yesterday captured an Orderly Sergt of a Georgia Regiment, and it is also stated that a Major of one of the rebels Regiments had deserted and ridden into our lines and stated that there were two or three Irish Regiments among the rebels who swear that they will never fire upon the US Flag.

I went over this forenoon to see one of Prof Lowe's Balloons, which is stationed about half a mile from here. they made two ascensions last Saturday, and were intending to make another to day but the wind is to strong. Genl Porter got carried away in one of them a few days ago but managed to get safely back.[17]

You asked me if I have ever seen Genl McC. The day we were on Picket up in the woods pretty soon after we came here we had just got our men stationed when he and his staff and Body Guard came along the road we turned out the guard and presented arms and he sent back a Major of his staff to inquire what regt we were his Head Quarters are about 4 miles from us now but they are only a very short distance when we were up to the right.

Our boys do not like it at all that they are sent back here but I suppose they are just as near the enemy here as we were up there but we are not quite as active on this flank as the right has to be forced first but we are within a mile or so now and can go out and take a look at them at any time now. This is the greatest country for reptiles and creeping things of all kinds that ever was heard of. I got up this morning and went out and went to a rotten pine log to get some of the knots to make a fire of. I took hold of the end of it and pulled it to pieces it was very rotten and nothing but the heart and the knots held it together as I raised it up there lay one of these Black snakes with a ring round his neck. You better believe I jumped. a few mornings ago the patients in the Hospital found one of them between them as they lay on thier blankets on the ground. he had crawled in to warm himself I expect we shall be overrun with them when the ground gets warmed into thier holes. then we have the wood ticks, and scorpians and the Mosquitoes and the Mosquitoes begin to sing, and what next I am sure I do not know.

I do wish it was possible for me to get a furlough and come home. I looked at Mat + Marys pictures a long time this morning and wished I could see them but wishing does no good.

I have just been up to the Suttlers cart and made my dinner of ham and bread with a cup of coffee to wash it down how I do hate and *loathe* ham + Salt beef. but I have to eat it or starve. the ham is sliced up in a pan placed on the head of a barrel. I walk up to a pile of tin plates secure one and a knife and fork a tin cup and spoon then go to one of the cooks and he puts a piece of ham on the plate. I then get a pc of bread which feels as if it had been cut six weeks and dried in the sun. then I go to the fire and get a cup of coffee then return a few rods to pine log, straddle it and cram it down, hungry as a bear, and yet it seems as if I could not eat a mouthful of it I munch away a while on it and just get enough to take care of the craving and chuck the rest into the bushes, drink the coffee and back as hungry as I went. I would give a five dollar bill to get into your Pantry this minute.

I miss the papers about as much as anything though we get them about every

other day but the days drag heavily when we have nothing to do and a paper would help them along very much.

This country is a constant wonder to all Yankees. to think that we are in the oldest settled part of the United States and yet the country is almost all forest, and the houses are miles apart, and here at Warwick Court House, which contains records as far back as 1640 and I don't know but farther, and yet the whole town or rather village consists of a store a tavern, jail and Court House, and when I write Court House, don't picture to yourself anything so imposing as one of our district school houses but an edifice of brick about the size of Mr Lewis Strongs office, situated in a noble grove of oaks, that look as if they were a hundred years old and I suppose they are and more, and this is the county seat. there is no reason why this should not be as thickly settled and thriving as any county on the face of the globe. the soil is good the climate too, and everything grows here that we could wish, and it would be a magnificent region, but for the curse of slavery which has blighted it.[18]

Capt Joe sits here reading his Psalams. he sends his respects to you and all. I must stop now and perhaps before I have a chance to send this I should think of something more to write. We are now going to pull down our habitation and build it over. give my love to all and be sure to write *very* often, to Your aff son

Charlie.

PS Thursday 5 o'clock AM
I am detailed for Fatigue duty and am off soon where I don't know when nobody in the company up but me. have no time to write more, so good morning yours +c

Charlie

44

Camp Winfield Scott
Warwick Court House Va Sunday May 4th 62

Dear Mother
It is Sunday afternoon and our camp is about half broken up and half not. Our enemies evacuated Yorktown last night, and most of the Grand Army is following them up. we had an order to march at 1 o'clock to day but about fifteen minutes before the time came it was countermanded and we were ordered to cook 3 days rations and be ready to march at a moments notice.

We heard last night or rather commencing yesterday afternoon, a very heavy

cannonading, which was going on lively when I went to sleep about half past 10 o'clock. this morning appearances indicated that the enemy had vamoosed and our forces went over, and found it was true.[19] our forces are now in Yorktown, and how much further than that I do not know. they will probably retire some distance and throw up another sandbank and we shall have to go to work and build more corduroy roads, and move the heavy guns into position again, and then away they go again and so they will worry us out. the firing last night was terrific, and although it was some 7 or 8 miles off, we could distinctly see the flash of the guns, and then in 28 seconds would come the sound of the report, followed in 4 or 5 seconds by the report of the bursting shells. What they were firing at, and whether they had any battle or not, I do not know. All the cavalry and light Artillery in our division has gone to the front. I presume we shall stay where we are until tomorrow and then I presume we shall go on especially as it looks very much like rain, and we always have to march in the rain.

It is sometime since I have written home because I get no letters from home. I have not had one since Mary wrote about the flood I wrote to Mary and Mattie a few days ago, on the same day. Cal Kingsley has had a letter informing him of the death of his father. he feels very bad indeed, and I am so sorry for him but it is a case that admits of no consolation. I think it too bad that he could not have a furlough. P W Kingsley also in our Company has seen the death of his father in a newspaper and one of the boys had a letter telling of it, but he has not heard a word from home himself but his mother wrote to the Col asking for a furlough for him, but he could not grant it. his case is rather harder than Cals for he did not even know that his father was sick and I suppose he was not, but he died in a fit. I rather guess it must have been Cals mother though that wrote to the Col for Capt Kingsley died very suddenly and this letter speaks of the father being very low. he has probably got the confounded.

What glorious news we have from New Orleans and Fort Macon.[20] We also have a rumor in camp that the rebels have evacuated Norfolk but I presume it is not true. it seems as if the rebels would have to give up pretty soon, but I don't know but they will hang on and fight to the last. if they do we shall have to stay our three years out, but I reckon they will make up thier minds to abandon Virginia pretty soon for if they do not they will get most awfully cut up.

An Orderly has just rode up the Cols tent and I should not wonder if he had brought marching orders. I guess not though for I do not see any stir made. you would be surprised to see how quiet the camp is to day. The order has come we are going to——Mills and I must close. give my love to all my next will be dated from some other place probably. so good bye from Your aff son, in haste

Charlie.

45

Williamsburg Va Wednesday May 7th 1862

Dear Mother

I wrote you last Sunday and was broken off very abruptly by the order to fall in. We had previously had an order to cook three days rations, and had just put them over the fire, when the order came to take all the rations we could scrape together and march immediately. it was then past the middle of the afternoon. we started accordingly and took up our line of march and just before dark we arrived at the rebel entrenchments and it is the greatest wonder in the world that they ever left them. I shall not attempt to give you any idea of the strength of them for I cannot but they were situated on the bank of a deep ravine which of itself was almost perpendicular, and I should think it was 50 feet high and the entrenchments were 10 or 12 feet high, on top of that, the ravine was full of timber fallen in every direction and I don't believe we could have taken them without the loss of 5,000 lives, and perhaps 10,000 and we saw but a small part of thier works, as we passed a long distance to the left of Yorktown. But the rebs were gone neck and heels and we pressed on our roads that were cut up into ruts by the Wagons and Artillery, and through new roads cut in the woods. it was cloudy and very dark and as we stumbled along, many a soldier measured his length on the road, as the stumps were left standing. we pressed on until about 10 o'clock, when we reached a place called Lebanon, or Eden. some say one and some the other, *but I don't believe it could have been Eden.* it consisted of a church one house, and a Distillery. here we filed off into an orchard and threw ourselves down on the ground (which it seemed to me was particularly hard in this place) to get what rest we could. we had but just got down when it commenced to rain, and it rained all night. in the morning we got up, and packed our knapsacks and after a bit of hard bread, and making a cup of coffee we slung our knapsacks and started on, my blankets were both wet, and it seemed to be they weighed a thousand pounds.

The roads, and the fields by this time were worked up into mud, knee deep and it would start my long boots partly off, at every step, the roads were crowded with Artillery and wagons, and we made slow progress, but we kept on, now dodging between wagons, and under horses noses and then turning out into the woods, and sometimes by a shorter cut across lots we made what speed we could. we had heard the sound of Artillery all day growing nearer and nearer as we advanced, and about 5 o'clock we arrived at a large open field. This field which is now historical and famous, presented a beautiful appearance as we came out of the woods. it being covered with growing wheat, which had got up to the heighth of the knees, in the center stood a large two story house painted white, with a red brick chimney outside at each end, and the field was covered by lines

of cavalry and infantry drawn up in battle array, and dotted here and there with Artillery Caissons and thier horses, all standing there silent and firm. The field was surrounded with woods, and a ravine just in the woods on one side, and from this came the incessant roar of artillery and bursting shells, and cracking of musketry, with sounds exactly like popping corn only louder. we immediately formed in lines of battle, and Col Briggs rode along the line saying "Boys the only rest I can give you is to tell you that you are needed tonight." as soon as we had formed Gen Keyes rode along the line and said "Well you have arrived at last, and I am glad to see you"

we were immediately ordered forward and advanced in line of battle to support Hookers Brigade, who were engaged on our right. we had just gotten into the edge of the woods, when we were ordered back and sent off at the best speed we could make to the extreme right, to the support of Hancocks Brigade who were then hotly engaged and it was supposed that we were needed there most. it was four or five miles, and through such horrible mud, that you cannot by any possible means get any idea of it. on our way we passed three rebel forts, that had been taken during the day, and arrived at our destination just at dark, but the battle was over and the victory won, but a more completely exhausted lot of men than we were were never seen. it had rained incessantly all day long and every man was soaked through, but down we lay upon the battlefield in mud up to our ankles and slept soundly until about 4 o'clock or earlier in the morning, when we stood to arms until daylight, which revealed such sights as I hope never to see again. the ground was strew with dead men in every direction we lay close to one of the rebel forts, and about a quarter of a mile off to the right was another, and a little to the left another, and between the two but further off still another that stretched away the right and left until hid by the other two. between us and the nearest ones was a line of pickets (these forts had not been taken the day before) and at sunrise Co C and three companies from other regts were ordered out to relieve these pickets as we marched out through the growing wheat at every few steps we had to step over the body of a dead rebel, as they lay in all different attitudes, taken in thier last agonies. Oh it was a fearful, fearful sight, and ever and anon the fatigue parties passed us having wounded men who had not been found the night before, and had lain through that fearful night, in the rain and cold, alone with thier agony. the rebel dead in this part of the field outnumbered ours ten to one but there are parts of the field where the proportion is the other way. our troops here destroyed and captured 2 or 3 regiments of rebels, but language fails me, and I cannot attempt to describe the scene. if I ever come home I can perhaps tell you but I cannot write it.[21]

We (Co C) arrived at the line of Pickets and relieved them, and now all eyes were directed at the rebel works in front, were they still there or had they gone, we could see no signs of life about them. we were ordered not to advance any

farther than this line. we sent back for permission to go on and see if they had gone but it was refused, pretty soon out from the woods on our left came a line of skirmishers and we saw them creeping towards the fort pretty soon they gathered together and then they made a rush and mounted the parapets, and then up went the stars and stripes.

They were all deserted. The Pickets were called in and we took up our line of march and proceeded about a mile to this place where we rested last night and probably shall tonight as it is almost night now. It is the second day after the battle and most night and the dead are not nearly all buried yet, though they are as busy as they can be all the time. Sixty thousands troops have gone on but when we shall I do not know, I do not know what our loss is, but of the 1st NY Regt the Quartermaster told me this morning that of 908 men who went into the battle only 140 came out whole. we are bivouacked about 1 mile from Wmsburgh. it is a town about the size of EHampton, most of the inhabitants have deserted it. You will learn more about the battle than I can tell you from the papers before you get this. I send you some secesh money which I got from some prisoners taken in the battle. you will please share it with the girls. the poor prisoners many of them have faith in it yet and refuse to part with it for less than the full amount but of course it is worth nothing except for curiosity. this I send is especially valuable as I got it on the battlefield from the prisoners themselves. Mary wanted some relic from Yorktown but I have not seen Yorktown and probably never shall. part of the battle yesterday was fought in old Revolutionary rifle pits, and in some parts of it the dead lie in ranks. I must close now as I am writing lying flat on my stomach in the hot sun. Give my love to all and write soon.

It is now 8 and ½ o'clock in the evening. I have been up to the city or town of Wmsburgh since I wrote the forepart of this, it is a very old looking town, I find that there are a good many of the inhabitants still there. there is a guard stationed in every house I received your nice long letter after we had fallen in to march Sunday PM also the papers, and the cap from Mary tell her I carried it in my hand four miles without opening it, and finally opened it sitting on a rail fence, before the first line of rebel forts, and near where the men were killed by the percussion shells buried by the rebels. I think it is a beauty, and am ever so much obliged. The rebels buried those shells all along the road and men were stationed to tell us where they were I think we aught to kill every prisoner for they bayoneted our wounded, and beat thier brains out after they were wounded and helpless, and they raised a flag of truce and when our men stopped firing and came up to them they fired on them and killed lots of them in that way, and they raised the stars and stripes and did everything else that no nation but savages would do[22] but I must close, I will just say that we have got a rumor that Macgruder has surrounded Smith has surrendered with 15,000 men but I am afraid it is not true. I am glad to hear from Aunt Lu, but I do not blame our

soldiers for taking the poultry or anything else they wanted. I should do it myself if I was as hungry as I am now. we have had hardly anything to eat since Sunday noon, nothing at all but hard crackers and not a quarter enough of them. our supplies have just begun to arrive tonight but I must bid you good night with love to all, I don't know where I shall be next time I write. NB This letter is not to be published under any circumstances for I do not wish to be laughed at here as "our own correspondent" My respects to all the neighbors and so good night With much love Yr aff son

Charlie.

46

In the woods 5 miles from West Point
Sunday May 10th [11]62

Dear Mother

It is Sunday PM and just a week since we started from Warwick Court House and it has been by far the most memorable week of my life as well as the hardest. We staid at the place below Williamsburg where I wrote you last Friday until morning and going round the town to the left, commenced to march to Richmond, and of all the hard marches that we have had the one of that day beat the whole. we halted considerably in the forenoon as we had to pick out the way as our Brigade was ahead on this road, but about noon got back on to the main road and our miseries commenced. it was burning hot and dusty and they drove us along without halt or rest, until almost sundown. men fell out by the way by the hundreds and when we arrived at our Campground we had not two hundred men in our regt. some companies had but 4 men and the rest came straggling along through the night. We had just dropped down on the ground when an order came for Company C to go on Picket. that was "the unkindest cut of all". but there is no if nor ands in military and the poor tired fellows had to sling thier knapsacks again and go off for about a mile into the woods for a night of watching, without even the hope of seeing an enemy for there was 60,000 or more troops ahead of us but we have to go through all these ceremonies whether there is any enemy round or not. I was completely exhausted and the skin was worn off my ankles clear to the bone and Capt said I need not go and so I with one man in camp to take care of me were left in camp in the morning at 7 o'clock we took up our line of march again, and our company was the rear guard. we marched on until about 1 o'clock yesterday when we stopped in this place and have been here ever since. I don't know where we are any more than we are near

Soldiers of the Sixth Vermont Volunteers rest after burying troops killed during the early days of the Peninsula Campaign, spring 1862. *Courtesy of Vermont Historical Society*

West Point which is 35 miles from Richmond. when we shall leave here I cannot tell. we have any quantity of astounding rumors but do not know what to place any faith in. It is said that the rebs will make thier next stand in a place called mud Bottom 15 miles from Richmond, but I guess by next Saturday night we shall be in Richmond whether they make a stand there or not. As soon as we got here yesterday I was detailed for "Officer of the Guard" and had to go accordingly in the night I was taken sick with a very bad diarorhea and it has weakened me so that I can hardly stand up and if they should march from here today I am afraid I should have to remain behind.

This is a beautiful country we are marching through and we passed lots of pleasant residences, some of which are deserted but most of them have a flag of truce hung out and are occupied by women but the men are all off in the rebel army. still we have to pay the highest prices for anything we can get of them, but the men cannot be entirely restrained from helping themselves I do not blame them for I think it is a most absurd idea that we must protect these rascals property that are fighting against us. we seeking thier lives and they ours, and yet

we must go starving through thier country and not touch a thing it is ridiculous Corpl Brown who is Gen Devens orderly has just come and says Norfolk is taken and the Merrimac run ashore and blown up[23] the work goes bravely and it cannot be very long before we shall have cleared Virginia of rebels I think it likely that we shall have a bloody battle before Richmond however and I dread it for I have seen all I want to of battles and blood. I shall never forget the sights that the battlefield of the 5th of May presented and though I am not afraid still I wish it could be settled with as few such scenes as possible in one place there is one hundred and eighty graves of Union Soldiers in one row and the rebels loss is much larger than ours. I meant to have written a longer letter but am too weak. I have not had a word from you since last Sunday a week ago. I wrote you last Wednesday and enclosed some secesh money. let me know if you got it. Give my love to all and write often to Your aff son

Charlie.

47

On the road to Richmond, one mile beyond New Kent Court House VA
Wednesday May 14th 1862

Dear Mother

I wrote you last Saturday [Sunday] from our last Camp Ground where we staid until yesterday morning I was sick and on my back from the time I wrote until we started myself and Bishop, and I took more medicine in that time than I have taken before for three years. it took all my strength away, and my flesh too, but I am coming out all right I guess. We started from that camp yesterday morning at 7 o'clock, and were on the road until 12 and ¹/₂ o'clock last night, though we did not march but a very short distance as the road was blocked by a long Pontoon train, which we are taking along with us. I marched until about 12 o'clock yesterday, without knapsack or haversack, and then Dr Chamberlains man (Newton Taylor) let me have his horse and I rode until 10 o'clock last night, when I got off and marched until we arrived here about half past 12 last night. I expected to be down again to day, but I woke up about half past four this morning, and found myself feeling very well. I got up and made a cup of coffee, and ate three hard crackers, and felt so comfortable that I thought I should commence a letter to you. it is now about 7 o'clock AM we have got within 22 miles of Richmond and our course is still onward and this letter may be mailed there, as I do not know when I shall get a chance to send it.

we are expecting a battle to day, as it was reported last night that the rebels were posted in a swamp ahead of us 20,000 strong. we have not so many as that

here but shall have before noon twice that number, but it won't make any difference what our force is, as if they do not "skeedaddle" we shall attack them if they are two to one of us, and they will have to move on. I have seen a Springfield Republican of last Saturday. it speaks of the 2nd RI and the 7th Mass Regts being in the battle of the 5th inst. they were not in it any more than we were but just the same. they did not fire a shot nor did we, but we were all in the battle.[24]

New Kent C H which we came through in the night is like all the Virginia towns and consists of some half a dozen houses, and hotel. I did not see the Court House to recognize it, but I suppose it is there. there is a Rail Road here somewhere, though we did not see it but I heard a whistle this morning and it did not sound more than a quarter of a mile off. it sounded quite natural. I wish some of the grumblers that staid at home could be here and share some of our pleasures in these days. You cannot realize half what we have to go through and I cannot tell it. We have been through about every hardship known to man. I would have given 50.00 to walk into your front door last night. Added to all the rest we left our baggage at Warwick and it has not arrived yet and we are here without a change of clothing, a clothes brush or anything else. We have received three mails this week but not a letter nor anything else for me, though most all the rest had something I am afraid you do not write only when you get one from me, whereas you aught to write every day whether you get one or not so that I should get something every day. Tell Mat she aught to write more. She has nothing else to do. Tell her I am much obliged for those papers she sent. How is Tom I have not heard anything from him lately. Give my respects to him, and tell him if he wants to enjoy life to enlist, and join the Grand Army of the Potomac. Tell Uncle Edward that this is the greatest farming soil he ever saw, if the Government confiscates I think I shall try to get one. I have got to the bottom of this page and as this is all the paper I have got here and begged at that I will stop writing for this time. if I should have to send this without writing any more you must consider the rest said.

48

Thursday May 15th 1862

After finishing the other sheet yesterday morning I went down to a small brook and washed myself all over and when I came back I found the whole regt had been ordered out on Picket. I was not strong enough to carry a knapsack so I staid in with Bishop and Corpl Prentiss. In the course of the day the rest of the Brigade was ordered forward and so we have been alone here during the night. I feel very much better to day and I hope to regain my strength so I can keep along with the regt this is the first time I have ever staid behind when the regt moved

the regt is on the advance now and they move forward only 20 feet in five minutes, so you see they are very cautious. Our army captured 400 of the enemies cavalry yesterday.

I have been down to Cumberland Landing on the Pamunkey River, about 1 mile from here this morning. I should think that between here and there were as much as 300 pieces of Artillery I never saw such a sight in my life. I shall close this letter now seal it up and wait for a chance to send it I don't know when it will be as everything is uncertain nowadays. Give my love to all, and respects to all the neighbors with much love from your aff son

Charlie

Friday morning.

I have received a letter from you and Mary last night so I have opened this to let you know it you cannot think how glad I was to get it, for it was more than two weeks since I had heard from home. I am very much surprised that Kingsley should say that I told him I should go home if I was he. I merely told him that I presume that there would be nothing done about it if he did and I don't think there will but I did not advise him anything about it. he ran away and will have to suffer the consequences if there is any. we (that is Bishop and myself) have moved on to the regt about two miles from where we were yesterday, but there is nothing but the right wing here. the left is all on Picket and has been since day before yesterday. it has rained like guns ever since then, and I have not seen Co C since then the Col said that they were coming in this morning but it is 10 o'clock and they have not arrived yet. if they do not come in I shall try to find them today and resume regular duty, and I do hope I shall not be sick again while this war lasts. We have not seen a paper since the 8th inst and know nothing about the battle in Western Virginia, and we did not know that we had been mentioned in the papers. though we knew we aught to be if the 7th and the 2nd RI were for we were in the battle as much as they. I wish you would not borrow any trouble about my not getting your letters, but write the same as usual or oftener and I shall get them sometimes and you must direct them to Fortress Munroe until I tell you otherwise I should have got the last one sooner if you had directed it there. I suppose we are now about 18 miles from Richmond and they are filling the woods full of men to day and advancing slowly I don't know why they do not go on faster but I suppose it is all right.

I expected to be in Richmond before this but I don't know now when we shall be. the roads are in a terrible state again on account of the rain and why the men do not all die is more than I can understand but I think the Lord must be on our side, for although there are a great many sick there are not half as many as I should suppose there would be under the circumstances for they have every thing to go through and one would think that the life we lead would kill wild

beasts. I notice what you say in regard to living with Mat, but it does not seem to me best at present, for if I live through this war I hope we can make some better arrangement, at any rate do not decide until we see whether the war is going to last always or not. if it should last a year longer I can save enough out of my pay to go a long ways towards paying off the Mortgage, and then if I can get a situation we may do pretty well.

I do wish that we could see a paper we have had them regular all along until we made the last advance and we are hoping to get some to day John Cook has not been sick to my knowledge, and he is out with the Co and doing duty regularly Cal is well, and tough and hardy, he felt very badly indeed about his fathers death and I was very sorry for him. tell Mary that she aught to thank her stars that she cannot see any more of the soldiers than she does. the soldiering that we are doing now is a very different thing from the home soldiering, and if she should see how rusty, black and grimy we are she would not think much of the glory. and then if that did not sicken her, it would only need the sight of one battlefield to put on the finishing touch. I wrote you about that after the last battle, but I did not tell you I believe of the experiences of that night we arrived close by one of thier forts, just after dark it was when Gen Hancock repulsed the enemy, with the bayonet. They picked up all the wounded they could that night and brought them into the fort, and there they lay all night lying in the mud, with no covering, and rainy and bitter cold it was horrible to hear thier groans they fairly made night hideous and if we had not been completely exhausted, we could not have slept at all. Many of them died during the night.[25]

We have passed any quantity of Wagons that they left in the road, many of them stuck in mud clear up to the bottoms of them and of dead mules and horses there is no end, and the stench is horrible. I have just heard that our company is not coming in so I am going to try and find them they supported a battery of Artillery last night, and are directly before the enemy, and I cannot stay here and know it, so I will close again If I do not get a chance to send this before long it will get to be a pretty long letter so love to all again from your aff son

Charlie

49

20 miles from Richmond
Sunday May 18th 1862

Dear Mary
As the last letter I received was from you and Mother both I suppose I must direct this one to you. I wish you [could] see me to day where I lay here in the woods. I have just completed my habitation and I will describe to you the process

as I have a splendid house, and all built with my own hands with the aid of a stout Bowie knife, which I am possessed of. the first thing is to select a suitable building lot which is all important, and the only thing to look for is a knoll which is a little higher than the ground around. I found it in this case at the foot of a tall pine tree. It is necessary to get high ground because in case of a shower or rain if I were in a little hollow, I should soon find myself in a soak I next procured six crotched sticks, about the size of a Broom handle, two of which must be longer than the other four, as the ridge pole is to rest upon them. after crowding them into the ground, I procured 3 poles about six feet long and laid them across, in the crotches and the frame of my house is complete. then I commence on the floor for which I procure a lot of young cedars and trim off the small boughs, until I consider it of sufficient depth, for floor and bed also. then I take my two Rubber Blankets and pin them together, and stretch them over the poles fastening the edges by little sticks driven into the ground. then I stick up a few cedar boughs at one end and my house is done, and a very comfortable one it is, not very magnificent nor very lofty, it is good house for countries when they have earthquakes. I have to get down on my hands and knees to get into it and then my back is apt to hit the roof.

I am writing in what you would consider a very uncomfortable position, lying flat on my side, with my Woolen Blankets folded up for a table to write on. this comprises my furniture. My pantry is an enamelled cloth bag, or rather a double bag, and its contents just now are two pounds of sugar, one half pound of Coffee, one tablespoon full of salt and half a dozen hard Crackers, 3 papers of Tobacco half Dozen Envelopes, 1 Doz Sheets of paper one Ink stand one pen + holder, two Woolen Night caps (*made by my sister Mary*) one Rubber O Coat, 1 Opera or field Glass (to spy out Rebels when on Picket) and one pair Cork soles. this pantry is provided with a strap which goes over my shoulder and suspends the whole institution at my right side, when on the march the military name for this concern is Haversack and it has caused my poor shoulder many an ache, and will cause it many more. this comprises my whole outfit of housekeeping except, a tin cup of one quart capacity, which I buckle on to Haversack when on the march. And thus I have lived and a hundred thousand others for the past two months, except that often when we arrive at a camping place at night and are to start in the morning we dispense with the house altogether.

It is most 4 o'clock, and I shall get my supper pretty soon. Do you want to know how I shall do it. Well, this is the way. I have considered the matter like any careful housewife, and have concluded to have some rice. so I must go about half a mile to Brigade Commissarys, write him an order for half a pound of rice, stating that it is for my own use, when he will sell it to me, then I come back and go to the spring half a mile the other way and get some water. then I shall build a little fire of twigs, put a little rice is the aforesaid cup and sit down on the ground and stir it until it is boiled, then I shall put sugar in it and eat it, then clean the

cup and make a cup of coffee and drink it and then I shall be ready to go to bed, and then if the Rebs don't attack us, or we are not ordered forward I shall sleep until morning when I shall probably make my breakfast of hard cracker and coffee. When I am in camp, we often have fried ham and sometimes fresh beef, and Juba cooks it but I am on detached service. last night after I had got into a comfortable doze the Sergt Major came round and says Lieut Brewster, you are detailed for one week for Guard duty at the General of the Corps. (Keyes) to report at 7 and $\frac{1}{2}$ o'clock tomorrow morning. so this morning I came over here. I have 15 men one Sergeant and one Corporal from our Regt, and the same from the 36th NY Regt making 30 privates 2 Sergeants and two Corporals, and have got to stay here one week commencing to day. it is a very light duty, as we have only to post a guard of three men round the Generals quarters, and when he moves on we have to guard his Baggage train which consists of 5 Wagons.

My principal duty is to lie on my back or otherwise, but I do not like it and it will be a mighty long week for me. if I only had something to read, I should stand it better, but I have nothing and can get nothing. I have not seen a paper later than the 8 inst. We arrived in this place yesterday afternoon (the Regt is about half a mile from here) it is about 5 miles from where I wrote my last letter. the rebels were here about 20,000 strong last Thursday but they have run as usual. They crossed the Chickahominy and burnt a bridge about two miles from here. we are now engaged building another which will take about two days they say and then I suppose we shall be after them again. Many of the houses on our route are deserted and many are not. there are some of the most beautiful places I ever saw but the houses are generally mean looking concerns. There is one very large and handsome one close by here however it stands in the middle of a very large wheat field a long ways from the road, the field is nearly I think quite a half mile across and last Thursday the Rebs were drawn up in six lines of battle stretching clear across this field. we can see where they stood and tread down the wheat. they were going to give us battle here, but finally took the more prudent course and *"skeedaddled"*. we should have had a severe fight if they should have wanted for there is only one division here which consists of Peck Graham + Devens Brigades and several Batteries of Artillery.

Our Regt is Bivouacked in a camp just left by the Rebels we found some pieces of a Richmond Dispatch giving an account of the Battle of Williams-burgh, and as usual claiming a great victory for thier side, and that they took 900 prisoners, and 11 pieces of Artillery. I reckon a few more such Victories will finish them up. There are Guerrilla bands on our rear, and they have shot two Wagoners off thier Wagons. it is said that 9 of them have been taken. if so I think they aught to give them a short shrift, and a stout cord, but I presume they will be more careful not to harm them than they are our own men, and they will be allowed to take the oath of allegince, and be let loose to murder more of our men. All the families that remain hang out a white rag or flag of truce as it is called

which ensures them protection, and we are not allowed to take anything from them even if we were to starve, and yet in nine cases out of ten, the men of the families are all in the secesh army. I think it will take ten years of Sundays to restore the Union by any such kind of war as this. the whole aim seems to be to hurt as few of our enemies and as little as possible. I go for driving every mothers son and daughter of them out of the country and settling it with Yankees. they are always going to hate us, and we them and they will take up arms again, at the first opportunity.[26]

I suppose you may be somewhat anxious about my health but I think it is fully restored, and we have got up where there are more hills and less swamps so I think there is not much danger of fever. The country here is much like New England, but is destitute of the ranges of mountains which you always see in the distance there. How I should like to see her dear old hills and mountains again. you never can see anything in the distance here. you come out of the woods into an open field, and all you can see is straight across it into another woods and you plunge into that and come out again to go over the same thing again, and again, occasionally varied by the sight of a farm house or a Negro hut full of grinning darkies. I wish you could see the darkies. they range themselves along side of the road as we go along and then they stand and bow, hat in hand, and they keep thier heads abobbing until all have passed. One old darkie woman gave vent to her feelings as we went by in this wise. "O Lord! I did not know dere was so many peoples I nebber seed haf so many" And I have no doubt it did look like a great many people for there had been a constant stream of soldiers by there for two days and there were thousands behind us.[27]

I sent another specimen of secesh money and motto which was probably cut off some Rebel Envelope or little paper. it is just as it was found in the rebels where we are now. it is a picture of a rebel flag, and the motto you will see is very appropriate, under the present circumstances for they are on the run all the time.

The country here is putting forth all its beauty. the trees in full leaf and the woods and fields full of flowers. I have seen any quantity of Honeysuckles but never anything but the pink ones just such as we have at the north. they are most gone now though I have not seen anything growing in the way of crops, but wheat, except one field of corn that we crossed night before last. it was up about three inches I suppose it is not half planted at home, but these fields of wheat where the army has crossed will not be worth much, as a troop of cavalry horses make quick work of it.

It does seem as though I might get a letter from home oftener as we get a mail almost every other day. I don't believe you write as often as you used to you are afraid I shall not get them but you must write if I don't. I shall get some of them and probably all. I would give a dollar to see a late paper. we heard that Buell had been killed and Halleck defeated with a loss of ten thousand men.

I do wish this war was over. I do not like this perpetual "pick nick", and I have

lived a savage life long enough. the boys are all pretty well. John Cook and Cal never better. I have written you a good long letter so you will please take notice of it and act accordingly Give my love to Mattie and Mother My Respects to Tom, and all enquiring friends, and the neighbors.

I will now go about the aforesaid supper so good night, with much Your aff brother

Charlie.

PS We hope to get to Richmond this week but I dare not predict anything.

50

In a clover field, 12 to 14 miles from Richmond
Wednesday May 21st 1862

Dear Mother

It is just sunset of a most beautiful day, though it has been dreadful hot. I was relieved this morning from my Guard duty at Gen Keyes Hd Quarters, and joined the regt and immediately took up my line of march with them. we came on about two miles or perhaps not quite as far as that, and bivouacked in this field which is the best place we have had since we left Warwick. our small Brigade is in the advance and we have to go out on Picket frequently. Rebel prisoners are taken every day and as I lay here, I hear every few moments the boom of cannon and bursting of shells, and another battery has just gone by on its way to the front. we may be called upon to support it tonight, probably not though. Since I commenced this and while I write this line, two squads of Rebel prisoners have been brought in and are now going by. We do not know anything of what is going on in the world outside of our own camp, how I wish I could see a late paper. We have got a rumor that there has been a battle at Corinth and that Beauregard and 23,000 men are prisoners but I presume that there is no truth in it. Our Artillery had a skirmish last night in the swamp in front, and silenced one of the enemys Batteries.

We are expecting a great battle here but I reckon that little Mac will make his dispositions for it, and the chivalry will take a distant view of his preparations and then "skeedaddle" as usual, if they don't they will get a terrible licking though it is reported that they are concentrating everything there and have got 140,000 troops there. A contraband that came in yesterday says that they are talking terribly fierce about burning Richmond and fighting over the ashes, but thats all bosh.

I must stop now as we are detailed for Picket and have got to start immediately 4 Companies under Maj Marsh so good night. will finish when I get time. thank the Lord it is a pleasant night and we shall not need any shelter, but it is hard to have to break up and go just as we have got all ready for the night.

On Picket, Bottom's Bridge Thursday morning May 22nd

Dear Mother

I bid you good morning seated on an oak log, just on the edge of the water in the Chickahominy about two rods from Bottom's Bridge which the Rebs burnt and our men are now engaged in rebuilding. the Rebel Pickets were here yesterday morning and are now about two miles from here. Our Brigade is the first to cross and Col Russell of the 7th was the first man. there is one Regt ahead of us on Picket, and Co C + Co A were ordered out here last night with orders that if the Rebels drove the Pickets in not to let them get to the Bridge anyhow. We had to cross the stream one at a time on a log or rather the trunk of a tree which was felled across. it is about 50 feet wide and 5 to 6 feet deep. the Bridge will be done about noon today and then our Division will cross. They are very anxious to get some Artillery across as we have none on this side. A Cavalry squadron is just crossing and they look funny enough holding up thier feet and the horses swimming. this is one of the places where the Rebs were going to make a desparate stand but concluded as usual that the discretion was the better part of valor. It was dark last night when we came across and some of the boys fell in and got a ducking. We hated to come out last night, but everything turns out for the best. if we had not we should have to be making corduroy roads in the hot sun to day, instead of lying in the shade.

Capt and myself slept under the same blanket last night on the ground in front of the muskets, and it was harder than Pharaoh's heart, but it promotes early rising for it is now only 7 o'clock AM and I have been up over three hours. We have to sleep with Arms and equipments all on when on Picket and it is not the most comfortable thing in the world. Our boys have had lots of fun the last 3 or 4 days. they got a Gazzette that had that Shaw boys letter in it bemoaning his fate in having to eat bread and molasses, and telling that he would not eat salt ham at any rate, and telling also how brave he was. I wish you could hear the boys remarks. You know how much I love salt ham when at home or any other salt meat, well it is the greatest luxury I have now, and it makes me disgusted to hear that fellow growling because he cannot have anything better than bread and molasses when so many of the soldiers in this Army have often times been without anything, for instance the 7th Regt Mass Vols came out here Sunday night without knapsacks or Haversacks and stayed here until last night lying out without anything to shelter them in the rain and nothing to eat but a few Hard

Crackers sent out to them, and having to exercise sleepless vigilence for the wary foe was but a few rods ahead of them, watching any opportunity to pick them off. they had three wounded and one taken prisoner within three rods of where I sit the prisoner was taken. The Regt I spoke of is now going back and crossing the log one at a time. it takes a long time to get over in that way. I wish you could see what a splendid morning this is. the trees are in full foliage and the Birds are singing in the trees and the water ripples and sparkles at my feet with the sun shining gloriously over all, and if it were not for the Regt I see before me each with his deadly Enfield rifle on his shoulder I could hardly imagine that there was war in the land.[28]

It was 11 months yesterday that we took the oath to remain in the Army of the United States and how few expected that the war would last until this time, but it has and I don't know but it will last as much longer. I wish we could hear something that is going on in the rest of the world. Capt and I made our frugal breakfast this morning of some cold ham which was fried last night and a couple of Hard Crackers a piece. I made the coffee in our drinking cups which answers all the purposes of your store furniture. I don't know as you will be able to read this as I have written it on my knee. I could not find a piece of board to write on. I do not think of anything more to write. Gen Keyes and staff have just appeared on the other side of the creek. Give my love to Mat + Mary, respects to all the neighbors, and tell all who have friends in Co C that they are well. With much love Your aff son

Charlie

51

In an Oatfield, nobody knows how far from Richmond
Saturday May 24th 1862

Dear Mother
The mail has just arrived and as usual brings nothing for me and in my wrath I vowed I would not write again until I got one from home, and as usual I have taken pencil in hand to drop you a few lines. the trouble is that you do not write any oftener (if as often) than you did when the mail came regular whereas you aught to write twice as often so that when the mail does succeed in reaching as it would be sure to bring me something.

I wrote you last from Bottom's Bridge. we staid there until yesterday and at 4 o'clock PM and then the Regts began to cross. we had completed the corduroy bridge and the Topographical Engineers has brought along a trussle Bridge and

thrown it across and then the whole of the two divisions (Couch's + Casey's) crossed. First came the Artillery and then the infantry it was said to be 11 miles from there to Richmond and we marched from 4 o'clock to six at a very rapid rate with hardly a halt for a moment, and it is said we are 12 miles from Richmond but I do not think it can be much more than 9 or 10 at the most. I had the best view of the army in motion there that I ever had as they came down a long slope of low hills to the creek and then up on the other side and as we arrived at the top of the latter slope I turned and took a look back and could see the long line, looking like an enormous snake winding back for two or three miles and bristling with Bayonets, and at short distances the Stars + Stripes, and the flags of the different states and the Guidons +c presenting a scene that occurs but once in a great while. it is raining like great guns, and the order has come to pack up and move on. I hoped and we all thought that we were to stay here over Sunday but on we go, so I must stop

Sunday May 25th 5.30 PM

Dear Mother

We packed up yesterday and in the midst of a pouring rain and in mud of the usual depth and tenacity we marched out on the Richmond Road about 3 miles.[29] as we marched along we heard the booming of cannon and bursting of shells growing nearer + nearer, and finally we stopped in an open field where they were coming back the wounded and, close before us was our Batteries roaring + crashing away, and occasionally a shot or shell would go whizzing over our heads from the enemy. I tell you they make a fellow begin to calculate what his chances are of getting out. They made a noise much like Bill Clapps Foundry when they are blowing off, or like a circular saw buzzing through a log and when they burst they tear up the turf I assure you. I saw where one had cut off two young oaks that grew close together and they were about 5 inches in diameter and another place where one went right through a larger tree. But soon after we got there they stopped firing. our Batteries banged away six or eight times more, and then limbered up and on we went.

The skirmish was commenced by some of Casey's Div but his troops are almost all new ones, and they could not get some of them up to the scratch. it is said they refused to go into the woods towards the Rebels so they sent for 2 reliable regts from Couchs Division and the 10th Mass + 36 NY were selected. We went on behind the Batteries until we got to this place and formed in line of Battle and another Regt and the 8th PA Cavalry scoured the country for some distance but the enemy had taken themselves safe off so some other Regts were ordered up to take our place and back we had to toil to our old encampment through the rain and mud, and it was a ploughed field we had left, which was all

mud now and we were wet to the skin, and the boughs were all wet too, but we had to stand it and after frying some ham and making some coffee, which was accomplished by Juba, and then a ration of whiskey and quinine was served out, and we turned in and I for one slept soundly all night. I woke up once and found my feet in thin stockings stuck out of the end of the tent in the mud and I was quite cold, but I was too tired to be kept awake by any small miseries and drew in my feet and went to sleep again. this morning we expected to have a rest all day but were disappointed as we took up our line of march at 10 o'clock and marched up here where we were yesterday and here we found thousands of soldiers, and lots of cannons and here we all are on a large open field with a fine farm house, and negro huts in the center, and we are all in line of Battle, and the wagons are all ordered to the rear, as the enemy are enforce about two miles from us, and tomorrow I suppose we shall have a battle, and we expect to give them a dressing, but we may not have any. Oh dear a large mail has come in and everybody has got something but me. I cannot write any more under such circumstances, so good bye give my love to all, and if you can any of you spare time please to write me a letter with much love Your aff son

Charlie.

Tuesday May 27th

I had no chance to send this as all correspondence has stopped press and all so I thought I would finish out the sheet. I had but just stopped writing Sunday night when there came an order, "Co C for Picket" most of the co had got laid down for the night, but we had to get up and pack knapsacks and start off with one Company from each the 36th NY 7th Mass, + 23rd Pennsylvania. we got out where they were to post us and found 4 companies already there they were ordered to go 500 yards further to the front, and we took thier place. the Aid de Camp went back and we had just arranged again for the night when he came galloping out again and ordered us all into camp again so we packed up again and went back. we expected to fight next day, but were disappointed though once during the day we packed up everything and got ready to march and then we stacked arms and made our shelter again, just after we went to bed last night it commenced raining and before morning it perfectly soaked us out. I had the doctor to see me just at night and he said I must take a powder of quinine + morphine, and a hot whiskey sling and I did so and about 3 o'clock this morning I woke up and the water was leaking through our Rubber Blankets, and had also soaked through the Rubber Blankets under us, and through our O Coat besides. I had a touch of chills and it was very beneficial to be soaked with water in that style.

We are only 7 and $\frac{1}{2}$ miles from Richmond, and are daily expecting a battle,

when next we march it is ordered without knapsacks and with 20 extra rounds of cartridges in the mens pockets, and we are also enjoined to depend greatly upon the *bayonet*[30] it is said that we have formed a junction with McDowell but I don't know whether it is true or not, but I do hope they will fight soon for we cannot lose so many in battles as we shall by this terrible exposure. all the wagons have been sent to the rear and all the sick and feeble, but men are constantly taken down sick, and if we do not fight pretty soon they will have to send a lot more to the rear. It is trying hard to clear off to day but I do not know whether it will make out or not. It is said that in Caseys Division out of 13,000 men that landed, there are now but 7,000 fit for duty and they have not been in a battle yet either. they have been cut down by sickness and who can wonder at it, with the terrible exposure we have all been subjected to. Co C is all going out digging rifle pits this afternoon, and forces are engaged cutting down the woods all round here so it looks as if we were to hold this position, and not advance any further but I do not know anything about it perhaps before I send this, the battle will have been fought.

Wednesday May 28th

No mail is allowed to go yet. Yesterday Porter + Franklins Divisions had a battle on the right they fought from 1 to 6 o'clock PM with heavy loss on both sides and ended in a drawn battle, neither side gaining any advantage. they have sent down for all the Ambulances belonging to this Division. we are engaged night and day digging rifle pits and throwing up earthworks, all of which is very discouraging. it does not look to me as though we should get Richmond for a long time to come yet. my diarrhea still hangs on and I am without any strength at all, if I don't get better soon, I shall resign and go home Any one that is sick here gets no care at all, and if they cannot not go on they are left to live or die just as it happens.

To day the suns shines brightly and it is brazen hot, but at half past two this co has got to go out, and dig in the trenches for two hours. one thing is very certain if they do not take Richmond soon, they will kill the whole army by this ceaseless exposure + toil.

I wonder how the 27th Regt gets furloughs all the time. they hoot at a man that speaks of a furlough in this army, and we hear all the time of somebody who is home on a furlough from the regts in No Carolina.

We thought Sunday when we made the last advance that certainly we should have a battle this week and either get Richmond or get licked but it does not look now as though we are any nearer than we were two months ago. You may think it strange that men should long for a battle but so it is every one thinks that thier chance to live would be better in a hard battle than they are to lie round in swamps in this way. Time passes here without incident of any kind and there is

nothing to write about. so I will close for the time and if anything happens during the day I will write it though when I can send this nobody knows.

Thursday May 29

To day is calendar day in our record, for to day we received letters from home and NY Papers of the 27th inst by the newsman. NY Heralds sell from 15 cts (when plenty) to $1.50 a piece when scarce. I received your letter of the 22nd and a few moments after your note by P W Kingsley I was overjoyed as you may well believe as I had not heard from home for a long, long time. the salve arrived, to late as my ankles have got well and become calloused they have brought me many a mile since I wrote you that they were so sore, but I have a Boil on my leg, which has taken thier place and fully makes up for the deficiency. We have advanced about a mile again to day, and are getting quite close to the Rebel stronghold, but I shall have either a victory or defeat to chronicle before I can send this. We are joined with McDowell and have possession of the Richmond and Fredericksburg Rail Road. Major told me this morning that our forces took 1300 prisoners, when they got possession of the Rail Road. Our regt went out on an armed reconnaisance yesterday. they went in sight of the Rebels and they threw shells at Company C which was ordered in advance, for skirmishers. they threw five, and they all burst within ten rods of them. I was not there as I was just getting over another attack of the diarrhea and had no idea that there was to be any such work. they did not return the fire, as they merely went out to cover the operations of a Topographical Engineer who made a sketch of the Rebels position. This morning the Major of the 98 NY was killed at the same place by a shell from the same guns.

We have heard of Banks defeat, and of the 2nd great uprising of the north.[31] Does Northampton send any volunteers this time? I was very glad to get Aunt Lus letters she does not say anything about me. I would write to her if I thought she would like to have me, and if I live to get to Richmond I think I shall anyway. I can't tell anything about whether the fight will take place this week, but I rather think they will wait until Monday morning to avoid the Sabbath as the fight may last a week if the Rebs show much pluck. I think this must be a perfect paradise for roses and berries in thier season for there are perfect thickets of bushes here. the roses are budded and the berries half grown, but we never get any, for there will always be a man watching for every berry to get ripe. there is a house surrounded by cherry trees near here. the cherries are half grown and beginning to turn red but the men have stripped the trees and I presume dysentery will follow, but they would eat them if they knew it would. The nice and clean appearance of this paper is accounted for by the fact that I carry it in my pocket and it is 4 or five days since I commenced it. I cannot think of anything more to write tonight so I will wait another opportunity.

Saturday, May 31st.
5 and one half o'clock AM

I have just heard that the mail is going this morning so I hasten to finish this nothing of any interest has transpired since day before yesterday but there was skirmishing pretty much all day about half a mile from here. We had a tremendous thunder shower commencing about 4 and $^1/_2$ o'clock yesterday and lasting until I went to sleep last night. I never heard nor saw such Thunder + Lightening in my life and the rain poured in perfect torrents. Co C was out making Corduroy when it clouded up. together with a detachment from two other regts and Gen Devens sent out for us to come in and leave all the tools where they were. we were mighty glad of that, for we all expected a perfect drenching. I do not know what was accomplished by skirmish yesterday. it commenced by the Rebels driving in our Pickets and then our troops were ordered out and drove the Rebels back again, and reestablished the Picket line. I hear that our side lost 7 men. We see little squads of soldiers sent by most every day. I begin to think that we shall not have a battle here unless the Rebels come out and attack us, at any rate we shall not until little Mac gets fully ready, and has made success as sure as human means can make it. He has also provided against any rout if we are obliged to fall back, by repairing the roads and fortifying every advantageous position about $^3/_4$ of a mile back of here. we have a line of rifle pits and earthworks, nearly two miles long. we never expect to have to use them but, they can never drive us back of them. I reckon that MacClellan will finally worry them and scare them so that they will conclude the better way is to leave. Whatever is thought elsewhere of Mac, he is the idol of this army, and so is Keyes of this corps.[32]

It is cloudy this morning but I hope it is not going to rain all day, and I do not think it will. I wish you could have seen me last night but you can imagine yourself sleeping in a swamp under two umbrellas and in a harder storm than you ever saw. thats the nearest to it of anything I can illustrate our condition. many of the boys were completely drowned out, who had built thier shanties on low ground but I managed to keep dry. I should not think Capt would have written home any such story as Mary say's he did. it is true I am very much reduced hardly anything but skin and bones but I have no idea of being left behind, for if I had fully made up my mind that I could not keep along I should find some way to get home. I should give up and try to get a furlough but you know the brave ones that staid at home would call me coward and all that so I must stay here until after the fight at any rate. My diarrhea does not trouble me as much as it did I have taken to eating strawberry leaves and I think they have done me good.[33]

And now in relation to the coming battle if anything should happen and I should get killed, you will be entitled to my pay, there is three months due me now but if I should not get paid off before anything should happen my pay will

be in two places that is from the March there will be fifty dollars per month in the state treasury of Mass. which I have allotted there subject to my own order. the rest of my pay is drawn from the U S pay master the same as usual.[34] in addition you will be entitled to a pention [pension] of $15 per month as long as you live, so you see you will not be left unprovided for. I write this that in case anything should happen you will know what to do or to have done, but let us hope it will not be necessary. Don't fail to write very often and give my love to Matt + Mary. Respects to Uncle Ed, Mr. Boland and all friends. I must close now as I have not been to breakfast. With much love Your aff son

52

6 miles from Richmond Va
Monday June 2nd 1862

Dear Mother

I presume this letter will find you most anxiously expecting a letter from me. I am sitting in the hot sun and can write you but a few lines.

Last Saturday afternoon as we were lying quietly in camp the guns began to crack just in front. the fire grew hotter + hotter and in just a few moments the order came for us to fall in which we did and immediately moved forward in line of battle. we were in this direction for about 50 yards and then moved to the left, and took position in some rifle pits, immediately behind Gen Casey's Divisions camp, and Oh Mother, I cannot begin to give you any idea of the terrific storm of bullets, shot + shell, that poured over us as we lay behind those pits. we could not get into them for they were full to brim of water, but we lay right behind them in the mud. after half an hour of this, the firing ceased and we were ordered forward behind some fallen woods, which had been cut down, and had just got our line formed, when in the woods at our left, and rear appeared the Rebels. Co G was the left Co and Co C came next and I never shall forget the moment when I turned and saw them through a small opening hardly three rods from me, taking aim at us almost directly behind our backs. it was but an instant and there was a roar, and a perfect rain of bullets came pouring into us. I felt the wind of them on my face and men fell dead + wounded on every side. the line was hardly formed and of course it was immediately broken.[35]

I tried my best to make a face to the rear toward them, and to add to the general confusion it was a matter of great doubt whether they were rebels, or our own men, and we restrained half our fire in that account. the order was immediately given to fall back and form some more fallen brush just behind us, but it was impossible, everything was in confusion and we could not see 3 rods from us

in any direction so the order was given to rally on the camp, which we did. Capt Parsons was wounded at the first volley, though I did not know it at the time nor until we formed in front of the camp again, which we did as quick as possible, though with greatly diminished numbers, and were immediately ordered to the left again into the rifle pits where we were before, and here we crossed the field again in a perfect torrent of shot + shell and every other missile of destruction. we lay here for some time again and here we had two or three more wounded.

Pretty soon the firing broke out very hot on the right and we were ordered across the field again to the right. across we went and formed behind a low ridge and faced them, and fought our best, but they turned us again on our right and left, where we had no support. we fell back over another ridge, right in our camp and here we faced them again but twas a hopeless task "a forlorn hope" then Col Briggs fell and was taken up and carried to rear entreating and commanding his bearers to stop, and put him down. he would not leave the field, but they kept on. what few there were of us rallied round the colors and retreated through a strip of woods in which was our camp, but we could not stop to take anything with us as the foe were right on our heels and pouring in a perfect storm of bullets. as we came out in an open field in the rear of this woods we found the remnant of a regiment, the 93rd NY or Pa, I do not know which, NY I think, though they hailed us to form on thier left and go in with them and make one more effort. Capt Miller of Co H (Shelbourne Falls) was in command of the shattered wreck of the once glorious 10th, and there was one other Capt, Smart of N Adams. We hesitated a moment for we knew it was useless, but Massachusetts men were not to have it said that they refused when anybody else made a stand, so we went in again.

Forming lines, back we went, urged on by Gen Heinztleman, Keyes, + Devens,[36] the latter on foot with a shattered leg. I had of Co Cs being in command 3 Sergts, Bishop, Nims, + Munyan 2 Corporals Loomis + Moody, and 4 or 5 privates which was all the company I had, but they were true grit and knew not fear, and this little remnent of two Regts went in to those woods again, and met the host of the enemy, and held them at bay for a short time. it was the hottest fire I was in during the day. Co H suffered terribly here, losing thier 2nd Lieut Leland and four sergts. they were on the left of the line and in the road that went through the woods, consequently the most exposed. the rest of us being partly protected by the woods. Cousin George was in command of Co F also in this last tug and had about the same number that I did. His Capt would not go in the last time. *I guess that George and I have kept the old Brewster blood in good repute,* at any rate we did not shirk from duty, until Gen Devens himself told us to fall back behind the other line of rifle pits. I have written you about them I put a letter of twenty pages which I have been writing from day to day while the departure of the mail was prohibited, but I expect it is in the hands of the Rebels

as I cannot learn certainly but the general impression seems to be that the mail was not sent that day before the battle, if so I hope it will put thier eyes out when they read it. I have lost everything that I had in camp, except what I had on my back namely my clothes and my sword and pistol, and so have all the Co. My Haversack, Field Glass, Knapsack, Blankets, Rubber O Coat, and the pretty cap Mary sent me last, are all gone to the benefit of the occursed Rebels. What I lost there cost me over thirty dollars, fortunately my valise containing my sash, clothes and pictures of Matt and Mary +c was back with the team behind the Chickahominy.

We had but 7 Companies in the fight the other 3 were on Picket. our loss in the regiment is 27 killed, 84 wounded and 14 missing, total 125, or one out of four of the strength engaged. in Co C, we have lost in killed, wounded and missing, 21. Capt Parsons will be home before this reaches you. I did not see him from the time we went into the battle when he was wounded until just as the cars having him on board left yesterday I sent word by him to make it his first duty to tell you that I was safe. Lieut Wetherill is in Hospital sick, and although I aught to be, I cannot leave the co, as I have to make requisitions for a complete fitout for the co and everything else in my hands. Sergt Braman was killed by a Cannon shot or shell when we fell back the second time. He had been wounded in the leg, but was able to go until the shell or shot took his shoulder and arm completely off. he was brought to the rear and lived until about 8 o'clock that evening. He did his duty and died a hero. He was sensible to the last. he is buried in a garden close by here and in the best order that could possibly be done under the circumstances. I did not see him after that fight and did not know of his death until morning. Private Putnam, another of our dead, is another hero. he died while being brought out on a stretcher. his last words were, "Tell Capt Parsons I died a soldier". he was the man I have written you about once or twice as sharing his blanket with me +c +c. a generous open hearted, whole souled soldier of the Union, besides him and Sergt Braman, it is almost positively known that Francis W. White and Perry N. Coleman are dead, but there is a bare possibility that they are wounded and prisoners.

Yesterday Sunday, they had another and it is said a harder fight on our right, and tis said they piled up the Rebels like cord wood I suppose we have the Rebels cornered between Richmond and the Chickahominy and that these battles are thier last desparate struggles. We are now lying behind a long line of rifle pits with an open field of 50 acres or more in front, and all the Rebels in Dixie cannot drive us from here. I have slept under a Rubber Blanket two nights by favor of the boys, and am liable to sleep without anything for some nights to come. I don't know whether Capt W is going to get well enough to take command or not but I hope he will for if there was any other officer here with our co I should go somewhere. I have been sick for three weeks and yesterday when I went into the

fight it seemed as though I should not be able to stand a half an hour but I went through hard labor enough to kill a man if it were not for the excitement, but still now that it is over it seems as if I could not keep around. I was down at the hospital and saw Lieut Wetherill yesterday afternoon, and he said he should be up this morning but it is noon and he has not appeared I cannot succeed in giving you any idea of the battle, but I know this much that I had no possible hope of coming out alive, and I thought it all over how terribly you would feel and all that, but I came out without a scratch. I look back upon it and I cannot think how it can be. it does not seem as though any man that had been there could come out unhurt.

Capt Smart of Co B (No Adams) is killed. he was killed in the last struggle last night. Capt Day of Co G (Greenfield) is killed. He was killed in the second stand we made. I presume this must seem like a very confused account but I cannot make it plainer until I can tell you by word of mouth about it. There are so many incidents crowding my head, that I cannot write clearly at all and even when I sleep, the minute I get into a doze I hear the whistling of the shells and the shouts and groans, and to sum it up in two words it is *horrible*.

Cal K was sick and did not go into the fight though the fight came to him. he and Johnnie Cook are all safe and sound. Wm Mather was shot through both legs. Wm M Kingsley (Geo Kingsley's son) was shot through both legs and a number of others whom you would not know were very severely wounded and we have a dozen men that were hit but not hurt who were not included in the list of the casualties. You must tell Cals folks and Johnnies all about them or show them this letter and don't fail to write me often and let us hope this horrible work will be over soon. We are under marching orders, that is to be ready at a moments notice all the time and may have to go at any time. There is fighting all around us today as it sounds like it, for we hear cannon in every direction. We had two alarms and stood to arms in the night last night, and 3 o'clock PM is the latest we sleep mornings now. I wish the scoundrels would once show themselves on this open field. we would give them all they ask for and more too in the way of reception. the great trouble is they have got us in this miserable country, half swamp and they know every inch, and we know nothing about it. however if the right wing gets behind them we shall have them, dead or alive. we have taken lots of prisoners. they are coming in constantly. in the fight on the right yesterday, they took 350 including a Brigadere Gen, several Cols and several Lieut Cols. it is so hot I cannot write any more. Give my love all and pray for the end of this war, with much love Your aff son

Charlie.

53

In the mud near Richmond Thursday, June 5th 1862

Dear Mother

We are still here behind the rifle pits from where I wrote you last which was Monday I think. I do not know whether you have got it or not as we have no means of sending the mail so I gave it to a sutlers man he says he sent it and I hope he did.

We are in about as pitiable a plight as you can imagine, with no blankets or shelter, except a few blankets we picked up on the battlefield, which the Rebels did not carry off, and we are lying in the mud and it rains incessantly and not such rains as you have in the north, but torrents, such as you never saw. The Chickahominy has risen and overflowed its banks so that teams cannot cross at all and the Rail Road is washed away, though it was expected to be repaired yesterday.

The farmers in Northampton would call it cruelty to animals to keep thier hogs in as bad a place as we have to live and sleep in I am daub with mud from head to foot. my clothes are wet and have been for 3 days and nights, and from appearances they will be for some time to come I have not got a change of clothing and do not know when I shall have.

We have heard nothing from the Rebels since the battle and we have not got to Richmond and I think it is doubtful if we ever do. You can never realize the severity of the battle and I hope it may never be my lot to go into another one. Four times that day I stood in the thickest of the fight when bullets rained like hail stones and the last time the most desparate of all. I had but nine men all told. I have been praised a great deal and I think my conduct on the occasion was satisfactory. Gen Devens was very badly wounded in the leg and his horse was killed under him still he kept with us until another horse was procured for him. As we came down that night I stopped, with the two or three of my Company who were with me and asked him if there were any instructions for an officer who did not know as he had any Company left. He put his hand on my shoulder and said, "Nothing Lieut but get together what you can and report them ready for fight in the morning" said he "I went into a fight once with a regt 680 strong, and the next morning I reported 310 ready for fight again" and he says the 10th is as good a regt as the 15th. He was Col of the 15th Mass you know, that fought at Balls Bluff. He is a splendid man and brave as a lion.[37]

How any of us ever escaped that day is the greatest wonder, for it does not seem possible that a man could have been there and be alive now. We have now relapsed into the same state of uncertainty, anxiety and suspense that we were in before the battle. The ground we lost on Saturday was regained on Sunday but nothing more.

It is estimated that we were attacked by 50,000 to 70,000 men and we held this enormous force in check, until night, not more than 2,000 of us. The latter part of the time I do not know what is to become of us and added to all the rest, my diarrhea has come on again and takes my strength all away. I do wish it was possible for me to get leave of absence for a couple of weeks, and come home and recruit up a little but I don't think it is possible.

[erased section]

Lieut W came back Tuesday night, and took command of the Company. He is half dead with the Rheumatism. Requisition was made for Blankets, Knapsacks +c but it will be at least two weeks before we can get them.

[9 ½ lines erased here]

We have to get up every morning at three o'clock and stand at arms for an hour or two. This morning we were all wet and half frozen, and then when the sun does shine it absolutely melts everything.

Part of Hookers Division went by here to the front last night just at sundown they were the 1st + 11th Mass the 2nd NH and the 26th Pa. They are the ones that fought so hard at Williamsburgh and have been lying in the rear since I saw Seth Clark and had a talk with him as they halted some ten minutes close by here. He is quite well, and looks tough.

I received a letter and a lot of Papers from home Tuesday, for which I am very much obliged indeed. Cal Kingsley did not go into the battle Saturday, but the battle came to him. he was sick and left in camp but he did excellent service in picking up and carrying off the wounded he and Johnnie Cook are both well as they can be under the circumstances We see by the papers that Banks is regaining the ground he lost and I do hope something will be done before long. Oh if we could only fight these Rebels once, where we could have a sight of them, we would avenge the dead of Saturday but I don't know but we have got to always fight them in woods and swamps.

The stench that arises from the battlefield is horrid. they gathered the horses together and piled wood on them and burnt them.

Please let me hear from you as soon as possible. I do not think of anything more to write. Give my love to all, and respects to all the neighbors and friends. With much love Your aff son

Charlie

54

Camp before Richmond Sunday June 15th 1862

Dear Mother

As Major Marsh's resignation has been accepted and he is going home to day,[38] I improved the opportunity to send home my Overcoat, my sash and a secesh epaulette, which belonged to a major in the secesh army.

My Overcoat is much soiled as it has been knocked around from pillar to post ever since we went to prospect hill on the 10th of March. I wish you would have it well aired and cleaned. you had better give it to someone who makes a business of such things and I will pay you for it. Mails arrive here regularly every day but I do not get a letter once a week, and I am at a great loss to account for it or for the fact that you did not get my letter after the battle. this is the fifth I have written since that memorable day. it is the bitterest of all my privations not to get letters from home. if I can have them occasionally I can bear the rest but to be deprived of them is the crowning misery. how little our friends at home when they are wishing they could do something for the soldiers think that almost the greatest thing they could possibly do is to write to them often. You all seem to think that because you have no great events to write about, or stirring incidents that you have nothing. Whereas, it is the little common place incidents of everyday life at home which we like to read. It is nothing to the inhabitants of Northampton that the beans are up in the old garden at home, or that Mary has moved her Verbena bed into the garden, but to me, way off here in the swamps, and woods, frying in the sun, or soaking in the rain, it is a very important thing indeed. you do not realize how everything that savors of home, relishes with us.

We are still lying in the rifle pits. We have received D'aubry tents, woolen Blankets +c and are once more as comfortable as could be expected under the circumstances. Everything here is almost as quiet as Sunday as in N Hampton to day with the exception of the occasional boom of a Rebel gun, and whistling of one of thier pleasant messengers to remind us that they are still at home. Day before yesterday they poured shot and shell into the Brigades on our right, all the forenoon, but although our side had from two to three hundred pieces there they did not reply at all, but when they do get ready to open, I think they will find what they were trying to by the firing the other day, mainly the position of our Artillery.

We have a great many sick at this time and no wonder for if a man was exposed one day at home to what our boys have to endure continually, it would be considered almost a miracle if he was not sick. I often smile as I think of how careful we always were at home to change our clothes if we happened to get wet, and our stockings even if we got our feet wet and here we get soaked through +

through and lie down and sleep in them, and are obliged to, and yet we live through it all.

We have received a Free Press, which gives a report of the battle of Fair Oaks perporting to be from Capt Parsons. I don't know how he can give a report of a battle he did not see, for he was wounded at the first fire, which we received and was not in the fight after that.

George Wells also who he reports as fighting like a tiger all day, ran off to the rear and got by the Provost guard by limping and pretending to be lame, and good honest John Warner, is very much surprised to think that he had such a desparate fight with three Rebels as he has not hardly had a gun in his hand since we went into the camp at Brightwood 10 months ago. he has been hospital nurse ever since and was at the hospital in the rear during the battle or assisting in camp off the wounded, and did not even pretend to fight and could not if he would as his duties were of an other kind. the whole piece is nothing but a creation of the brain.

I see the Capt praises the sergts for thier bravery but has not a word for his Lieuts. well who cares. the men of the Company have more faith in the Lieuts than they have in the Captains, so that makes it all square. I have the satisfaction of knowing that I tried to do my duty, and have the credit of doing it in quarters where it is worth more than any censor or praise than all the Captains Parsons in the army can give. the whole Company are justly indignant at such misrepresentation of facts. Capt Miller of Shel Falls will be promoted to Major in Marsh's place, which leaves Company H without any Officers, thier 1st Lieut having resigned, and thier 2nd Lieut B F Leland was killed. Captain Smart + Day were killed which makes room for five promotions in the Regiment. I hope I shall get one of them, but I do not know. Sergt Bishop I think will be promoted and I do hope he will. it is aggrevating in the extreme to see such men as he filling a 1st Sergts berth and then to see the style of men that go to make up the commissioned Officers. There are some Captains in this Regiment that are not fit for Corporals.

I was yesterday on a Board of Survey to report upon 5,000 pounds of damaged Pilot Bread and some damaged Beef in the hands of the Brigade Commissary of Subsistance. they had fed us on it until we could stand it no longer and the Board of Survey was appointed. we condemmed it all and it was thrown away.

There has been a gorilla attack[39] on the cars in our rear. they were fired upon about 5 ½ o'clock night before last, and about twenty men killed. where they came from, and where they have gone to is a mystery, as they disappeared as suddenly as they came, but they were probably men who have claimed our protection as we came up the peninsular, by raising white flags, of course they received it, and of course they seek every opportunity to injure us when they can do it unknown. I do not believe that there are twenty Union men south of Mason

+ Dixons line hardly. I would no more take the word of a white man a native of Virginia than I would of the greatest lier I ever knew, if he claimed to be in favor of the Union. they cannot carry on war as a system, but they will murder an unarmed man in cold blood whenever an opportunity occurs.

Juba has gone home and I sent by him, a Missipi Bowie Knife to Tom please let me know if it comes safely to hand. I want to send some money but do not hardly like to trust it in this letter. I wish you would ask Daniel Kingsley to let me know the amount of my note as I have forgotten it. I dread to keep my money in my pocket in case of another fight, and I must have considerable about me, for it is the only friend a man has in this country, and I do not know when the next pay day will be, if I did I could tell just how much to send home. I think about the whole though you need not say anything to him and in a few days I will send to him as before, and have him pay a small bill I owe Geo Wells + Son, and then I will tell him how much to give you, and if it does not leave enough for him why he will wait for the balance until next pay day. I have written twice how my pay is disposed of, and what steps you must take in case I get killed but you have not said anything about it so I do not know as you ever got either of them so I will try once more. To begin with $50.00 per month of my pay I have allotted, and it goes to the Treasurer of the state of Mass, subject to my order. it commenced the first of March, and on the first of July it will amount to $200.00 in case of my death. that would go to my heirs, the balance of my pay is paid regularly to me, when the regiment is paid off. that you would have to get of the United States. so you see that if anything should happen the state of Mass will have of my money $50 per month since the first of March last, and the United States will owe me from the time last pay period. Then you will be entitled to a pension of $15 per month, as long as you live, as dependant upon me for support. I thought it well enough to write this though I hope I shall not get killed and there will be no occasion for you to take any steps in the matter, but it is very uncertain how long a man will live in this business.

I can not think of any thing more of interest to write to day. Cal + J Cook are quite well. Give my respects to thier families and to all the neighbors with love to Mat + Mary reserving a large share for yourself from

Your aff son

Charlie.

55

Camp near Seven Pines Saturday June 21 1862

Dear Mary

I believe it is your turn to receive a letter from me, so I have seated myself to try and write one though it has become almost as hard a task as it was at Brightwood to find material for a letter. We are lying in Rifle Pits where we have been ever since the Monday after the battle and where to all appearances we shall stay until our three years are up. Everything is as quiet here as it is in Northampton with the exception of the bursting of a Rebel shell once in a while which nobody pays any attention to. they waste about 50 or 60 per day in our camps or rather over thier heads, but seldom get any reply from us. I see nothing that indicates the speedy fall of Richmond on the contrary for anything I can see it is likely to stand a year. It is just one year ago to day that we were sworn into the United States Service, and things look now as though we should have to stay a great while longer, than they did then. I had no idea a year ago that we should be in the service a year, but now I cannot see the war ended in two years. The whole army is engaged in building Forts even way back here 8 or 9 miles from Richmond we are building them, and have to go out 2 hours per day to work on them. it is killing on the men weakened by diarrhea and other sickness to have to go out and pick and shovel 2 hours in the broiling sun. the place where we work is about 100 rods from here, and I have just got strength enough to walk there with the Company and sit down and broil for two hours and then come back again. I presume this army has built entrenchments enough to reach around the United States if they were in one line.

I received a letter from Mother last night. I had vowed that I would not write again until I got one and I should not if it had been six months. I know you do not write as often as you aught to, for if you did I should get letters oftener. I got a letter from Thomas + Mattie, and have answered it, but this is the sixth or seventh letter I have written home and in answer I have had but two and it is 21 days since the battle. I think it is too bad when letters are the only thing that makes existence tolerable in this God forsaken country.

I have however one amusement, which is entirely new to me, which is, what do you think? nothing more nor less than catching frogs. there is a big frog pond down by the Rail Road close by camp and I go down there with Corporal Coburn, an old Mexican soldier and catch frogs, and then we bring the legs up and Bill Allen cooks them and I can assure you I never ate anything so nice in my life. they are as much better than trout as trout is better than salt pork, so if when you get up mornings you can want to imagine where I am you can just think of me as catching frogs in the swamps of Old Virginny. I don't know as you can either for come to think of it you do not get up until after I get back from frog

catching. We have to get up every morning at 3 o'clock and stand at arms an hour, in order to be ready to repel any attack which the Rebs might see fit to make at that early hour, a thing that they could not possibly do, for before they could get to us they would have to break through the whole force of our lines in front, if they got through them, there would be no use of our making any resistance here, for we are in the rear of the whole. We have a report though that we are to go to the front to relieve Hookers Division. I don't know whether it is true or not, but anything is preferable to building forts. I don't believe Mac-Clellan can take Richmond or rather I don't believe he thinks he can.[40] This grand army we have bragged so much about, never made an attack on the enemy yet, he has always attacked us and surprised us, and generally worsted us in the first place, and nothing but the clear grit has saved us either here or Williamsburgh.

Several of the Officers have resigned and I have a great mind to do the same for it does not seem as if I could live from one days end to the other. Mattie wrote she almost wished I had hurt my little finger so I could have come home but I would almost be willing to lose a leg if I could come home, and when I think of it I am almost disposed to grumble because I was not wounded the other day. I am sure I had as good a chance to be as any one in the army.[41]

There has been a great guerrilla raid in our rear and it is said that every citizen between here and Fortress Munroe has been arrested by our troops. I hope it is true and I hope also they hang every one of them without judge or jury. I have no faith in the Unionism of any man in this state. they will be Union and take the oath to save thier property and the moment the army gets by they will fall upon the stragglers and murder them in cold blood, and seek every opportunity to afford the enemy any information they can gain about the movements of our army, and yet every effort must be made to protect and conciliate these fiends in human shape, and thus this kid glove war is carried on. I am sick of the whole business, if I was commander I would not leave a white man in the country behind me. they are a set of foul treacherous murdering villains, and deserve no mercy whatever.[42]

We have had two letters from Capt Joe, and tell Lieut W he must answer them but I don't know when he will get to it he is not much better than I am and neither one has energy enough left to write a letter.

If all you people that are so engaged sending things to the hospital would sit down and write letters to the soldiers it would do them a great deal more good. they never get anything that is sent to the hospital, and they turn up thier noses greatly when they hear of anything sent to the hospital, but they are very thankful for the shirts that you have sent to the Co. but have no idea whether we shall ever get them or not, in fact consider it doubtful, as government monopolizes everything in the transportation line, but I don't know but they will come.

The Officers have got Wall tents once more and it really seems a little like living again though we have got nothing to put in them in the way of furniture, but then we can get head and feet both in when it rains which is something you cannot do with the little shelter tents.

I have got to the end of my paper and to the end of my ideas so I will close, give my love to Mother and Mattie. Respects to all my friends and all the neighbors. With much love Your aff brother

Charlie.

I sent home my Overcoat and my sash by Major Marsh, and a letter. I don't know when it will get there as I hear he is going to stop in Fair Haven Connecticut. Please let me know when you get it. I also sent by Juba when he went about the time Taylor did a Bowie Knife to Tom. As you did not say anything about it I conclude he must have lost it or sold it. I was afraid it would never get there if I sent by him. Cal + J Cook are well.

56

Camp near Seven Pines Tuesday June 24th 1862

Dear Mary

Your last welcome letter reached me way out in the woods, about 2 miles from here, on the edge of the great White Oak Swamp, where our Co and Co H went on Picket yesterday morning at 8 o'clock and returned this morning.

I could not help wishing you could see me where I was when I got it, lying on my back under two or 3 pine boards, sweating like a Major, and trying to read the NY Tribune, and keep the flies, Mosquito's + other bugs incident to this delightful region, off me. at the same time, John Cook went into camp and got the mail, but I would not allow myself to expect anything consequently I was very happily disappointed.

I did not get much sleep last night as there were but two officers out with the Picket. Lieut W being sick, Lieut Bennett had the first watch last night from 7 to 9 o'clock, mine was from 9 to 11. Sergt Nims from 11-1, and another sergt from 1 to 3 when we all get up. Well from 7 to 9 the Pickets on the right took it into thier heads that they would have a little scrimmage so that kept me awake during that watch, and then I sat down in the dark, and thought of home, and wondered if I should ever see it again, and thought of you all sleeping quietly in your beds and then contrasted it with myself and the thousands of soldiers scattered round in those woods keeping vigilant watch over Uncle Sams farm, peering into the

darkness, crunching down, looking this way and that starting at every falling twig or rustling in the woods, of the wild rabbitt or the crawling lizard, and occasionally as I sat there in the dark, and terrible stillness then would come a-cracking which sounded at first like a volley of musketry, but ends in crack of a falling tree as it comes thundering to the ground, then would break in the barking of some house dog way off across the swamp, then the occasional crack of a rifle off in the night, as some Picket thought he saw some lurking foe. Then would come over the Black + stagnant swamp the sound of Rebel drums, and the rumble and whistle of distant cars, and then I would wonder and surmise are they leaving Richmond? or are more coming in? or what is going on?

thus my watch passes away, and I crawl under the board and draw my blanket over me, and lay my head on my Haversack containing hard crackers, the corners stick up and it is a long time before I can adjust my head so as to lie easy finally I glide off into dreamland to be awakened by a blinding flash, and a crash as though the foundations of the earth were crumbling away. I jump up and knocked my head on the boards overhead, and then comes the rain, in sheets, the trees bow before the blast, and sway and crack, the blinding flashes of lightening, followed by tremendous peals of thunder and by pitchy darkness that you can almost feel, and the rain comes driving in at the sides the front, and pouring through the roof, until we are drenched, but we draw our blankets over our heads and draw up our feet until we are almost doubled up, and lie still, for we must grin and bear it, but what a contrast to an hour ago. then silence, broken occasionally by "the voices of the night" it was almost oppressive, and now, it seems as if all the demons of earth, air, fire and water were let loose and where before all was so still, you can hardly make yourself heard by yelling at the top of your voice to the man who lodges on the next board.

thus passes with an occasional repetition of the shower on a smaller scale two hours more of the weary night, and I have just got into a doze again and the sentinal comes with "three o'clock Lieut" so up we must all get, and stand at arms until daylight, for perhaps, with all our vigilance and watchfulness, the wiley foe has come through some secret passage in the swamp and may be all around us now, waiting only for daylight to attack, and kill or capture us, and we must be ready to make as desparate fight as we may, to warn our friends in the distant camp, that they may be prepared to drive him back, and just as we get the line formed, it really seems as if we are going to have something to do for we hear rapid firing just to the right of us, and each soldier grasps his musket with a firmer hold, and peers into the woods and bushes, in anxious expectancy but all is quite again, and it is now broad daylight so we "stacck arms" and go to making coffee in our little cups and munching hard crackers or "reducing squares" as the boys call it.[43]

Thus the experience of one 24 hours Picket duty. Don't you think pleasant?

and have I not made a long story of it? Yet I did not tell of the pleasant neighbors in the way of snakes, Toads, Lizards, flies mosquitos +c +c who consider these swamps thier lawful domain, and that they have a lawful right to pray upon anyone who enters them.

I have seen a Free Press to day with the mean attack upon Major N. why could they not let bad enough alone? and that story about breaking his sword, and cutting his buttons off +c +c is without a shadow of truth.

And why must people get up such a lie about poor Colemans body. have they no mercy at all for his sorrowing friends that they must add this to all the rest. It is a black lie the whole of it part of the men who buried him, helped take him up, and can take their oath of its identity. I would like mightly well to shoot anyone engaged in propagating such a lie.

You do not say anything about the big Bowie Knife I sent to Tom so I conclude Juba must have lost it, as I was afraid he would. there was a letter sent with it too. tell Tom to find out if he has got home and ask him about it.

I suppose Major has not got there either with my overcoat and sash + letter.

Adjutant Keith in my opinion was a ten times worse coward than Major at any rate,[44] he was not to be found any where, where there was fighting going on after the first struggle, and he certainly was to be found way to the rear. I believe he gets off on the plea that he was ordered there by Major but I have seen plenty of men who say they saw him way to the rear, farther than Major went and before he got there. there were no officers of Co F in the last fight but Cousin George and I heard (and so did all who were there) him urge Capt Miller not [to] go in again, and tell him twas nothing but murder to try to make another stand, but we did try, and got an especial commendation for it, and not only that but we stopped the Rebels for that night and next morning they were driven back.

It does not seem as though the great battle could be postponed many days for we are drawing nearer and nearer. our whole front was advanced 300 yards this morning. I heard last night about sundown about a dozen very heavy guns in the direction of James River. we are ordered to keep three days rations, cooked constantly on hand and are expecting every day to march. We were all ordered to be ready at an instants notice this morning, and had equipments all on and ready to start but did not. Some think they are evacuating but I guess not since Sat night until last night everything has been as quiet as Lonetown, not a gun was to be heard night or day. We have just had another *t-r-e-m-e-n-d-o-u-s* Thunder shower, and since that stopped we hear cannon occasionally at the front it seems to be a favorite time to have fights during a thunder storm.

I do not get much better of my diarrhea, though I am not quite as thin as I was owing to rest and having somewhat better rations. Bill Allen cooks griddle cakes for my breakfast + supper, and they are first rate, only not quite as light as you make them at home.

I have now had five descriptions of Sergt Bramans funeral besides hearing all the boys read theirs so I guess you need not write or send any more of those. Why don't Matt write again, and why don't you all write oftener. I see there is an order for all sick and wounded officers to report at Ananapolis immediately is Capt Jo going. If I was at home wounded I would resign before I would go there and lie in Hospital, even if I was able to travel, I should think Fred Hillman that went home with Capt had better make tracks back again before he is taken for a deserter. the boys who remain here grumble at him a great deal for shirking his duty so, and he is nothing more nor less than a deserter while he stays there. Cal K + John Cook are both quite well and hardy. Cal is as fat as ever and appears to stand the rackett as well as the best.

It is quarter past seven and I have just lit my candle. there is considerable firing going on at the front. I hope we shall not have to fight to night, but the very atmosphere is crowded with battle nowadays and it may break out at any moment. our army draws closer + closer upon them every day, and they must fight or run very soon.

The woods here are a perfect forest of Whistleberry Bushes loaded down with green fruit. we pick and stew them as you do green Currents at home, and I think they are better if anything than the currents. the open lots are also full of Blackberry bushes and they are getting quite large, but I do not think we shall be here when they get ripe. I never imagined such quantities of them as there is here.

It is almost 4th of July again. what is N Hampton going to do. is she going to celebrate. I guess not though for I believe it is not quite 10 years since she celebrated it last time, is it? I forgot to tell you that I had quite a narrow esccape while on Picket yesterday. our Pickets join on to those of Kerneys Div and as I was going round by a road to visit some of our posts, I passed near the line of thier Reserve, and one of the sentinals levelled his gun at me, and would have fired but his officer stopped him. I did not know it at the time or I should have been tempted to shoot him for being such a fool as not to know that an enemy could not come from the direction I did, at any rate I would have given him and his officer such a blowing up as would make him wish he had shot me. I passed on all unconscious and did not know of it until afternoon. One of our Pickets was in to Head Quarters and told me.

Cousin George is unwell and off duty. I don't think Dr Chamberlain knows beans. here I have had the diarrhea for two months, and every time I go to him he gives me an opium pill which stops it for a few hours and gives me a headache instead, and thats all the good it does. I think he is a great humbug.

I see by the papers that Col Briggs has been nominated for a Brigadere General I don't see what they want any more Brigaderes for. they have got more than they know what to with now, but I think he deserves it well. Lieut Col

Decker is very slim. His rheumatism troubles him a great deal, and I am afraid that if Col B is confirmed they will send some Boston Monkey to command this Regt if they do you will see me making tracks for home. Gov Andrews sent one to command the 7th Regt after Couch was promoted, and he was drunk all the time, was dismissed from the service, went down to Washington, and drank himself to death. they have got an army officer, Col Russell, who was a Capt in the Regular Army they like him very much. he is the roughest looking man you ever saw. he has got a great scar across his face, and dresses in such style you would think he was a teamster, but he is a nice man very particular in matters of disipline, and very cool and brave. he is not afraid of man nor devil.

Well I think I have made out quite a long letter, and shall expect as long a one in return, *immediately* and also an answer to the one I wrote you a few days ago, and tell Matt, that there will be a quarrel in the family if she don't answer my last "right strait off" I agree with you the Mr Caleb is not much like Bill Clapp. he is just as much of a gentleman as Bill is hog. Give my love to mother and Mattie, and my respects to all the family and neighbors.

By the way I forgot to say I have seen two more of my letters in the papers. if I see any more in them, I shall stop writing altogether. I had not seen it until all the boys were laughing at them and calling me Our own Correspondent. I am in earnes, and won't have them published, so look out now if you want to get letters from me then keep them out of the Papers.

It is about time to retire to my couch of Oak leaves so I must bid you good night, with lots of love I remain Your affectionate brother

Charlie.

57

Camp near Seven Pines Thursday June 26th 1862

Dear Mother

Your interesting letter came to hand about noon to day and I am glad that you are beginning to wake up in some measure to a realizing sense of what is required of you in the way of lengthy letters and I think if you keep on you will get so as to write letters of some length after a while.

Well I have been in another battle, or rather skirimish and am happy to say am safely out of it. I have spent the hardest and most trying 24 hours that I ever spent in my life. Yesterday morning about 9 o'clock the Regt was ordered to rig up and be ready to march at a moments notice there have been brisk rattling of Infantry firing all the morning and it grew hotter + hotter and it was imme-

diately in front of us apparently on the same ground as the last battle at about
half past 9 or 10 we were ordered to fall in, and shortly after took up our line of
march towards the scene of conflict followed by the 2nd RI the 36th NY and the
7th Mass. we marched to Seven Pines and closed en masse by Regiments and
stacked arms and seated ourselves on the ground and waited further orders. we
sat there and listened to a terribly heavy firing of musketry and looked at the
dead and wounded being brought back, and the dead being buried. but a few
hours ago they went out full of life, and now we see them brought back on the
shoulders of 4 or 5 men carrying the pick and shovel. they deposit thier burden
on the ground, and dig a grave or rather a hole, put the body into it cover it up,
and the soldier rests among the thousands of his friends + foes who fell in the 1st
battle of Seven Pines or Fairoaks and whose graves are almost as thick over this
plain and in the woods and swamps, as they are in the burying ground at
Northampton. In addition to this we were right in front of a house which was
used as a Hospital, and to quiet our nerves I suppose they would occasionally
send out an arm, or a leg from the windows.[45]

Well we waited there until about 2 o'clock I should think, and then we took up
our line of march past Caseys old camp, and passed the crowning battlements of
the forts which had been thrown up on that now historical ground, past the long
lines of rifle pits that connect them, on to the woods ahead. as we past out from
the line of defences, a battery of Griffin Guns sent howling and screeching shells
over our heads, diagonally across the line of march and into the woods a mile
ahead. we kept on until we reached the woods, and a short distance into them,
and then deployed and went forward in line of battle. I have called them woods
but they were nothing but underbrush and scrub oaks, intersperced with tall
pines, so thick in some places that we could hardly get through, but we pushed
on to about 10 or 12 yards of an open field beyond halted dressed the line and lay
down. the second RI followed us in the same order and took thier position some
15 yards behind us. we were on the right of the Wmsburgh turnpike, and the 7th
Mass + the 36th NY deployed in the same manner on the left of the turnpike.
they then brought up the road a section of a Battery of U S Artillery, and we all
moved forward to the very edge of the woods, and now we were on the very line
of Caseys Pickets on the morning of the Battle of Fairoaks.

the guns immediately commenced plying the woods on the opposite side of
the field with shell and grape + cannister. the field I should think was about 400
yards wide at this point, they banged away for a long time and got no reply, and
sent back and got more ammunition, when finally we heard the bang of thier
cannon and a shell came whizzing close over our heads, and struck RI Regt,
killing one man and taking off the leg of another. our Battery limbered up and
went to the rear double quick but the Rebels did not cease thier favors, and kept
on with shot shell and Cannister they would howl and screech just over our

heads, and cut off the tops of bushes, and almost all struck in the ranks of the Rhode Island Regiment. they had 5 or 6 killed and many wounded and with the most horrible wounds one round shot took off both legs of two men at once. another man had both legs and both arms shot off, and a shot in the side thrown in, and yet he lived a little while. we had one man only slightly wounded in the back. he belonged to the Greenfield Co. and I think his name was Stubbs. he was not hurt much only bruised and lamed a little. Both of Gen Palmers aids were wounded one a Col of Cavalry, one a volunteer aid lost two fingers, and the other a Lieut lost an arm, and one of his Orderlies was also wounded.

But thier fire gradually slackened and finally stopped about sundown. We were ordered to spend the night there, and hold the ground if we could, and throw up rifle pits and shovels were sent up to us for that purpose. we had retired about 15 yards from the edge of the woods, so we laid down to spend the weary night under the very nose of the enemy in great force and the other troops all but our Brigade went back into the fortification. it was as dark as the thick woods as you can well imagine and an awful place to dig, the water was almost even with the surface of the ground, and full of roots and logs, tangled and twisted and tied up in every shape and manner, but the men toiled on up to thier knees in mud and water. 10 from Each Co working a half hour, while thier comrades lay with musket in hand to drive off the enemy or hold him at bay.

well about 11 o'clock the Rebel Pickets approached and our Pickets commenced firing on them, or at any rate our Pickets commenced firing whether they saw anything or not, and some of our Pickets came running in over us as we lay on the ground I was right behind the centre of my Company and Lieut W was superintending the rifle pit. I cautioned the men to be cool and not to fire until the Rebels got right into them, and had got them all right closed up together and ready to receive the enemy when somebody on the right called out fall back. it was not Col Decker for he was behind at the rifle pit and Major Miller was ahead, as he was field officer and had charge of the Pickets. I think it was Keith, but cannot swear to it, but whoever it was he deserves to be shot without any ceremony, for it caught like lightning among the men and they jumped up and over my head they went, quicker than thought. Oh if ever I was mad twas then, I called them fools and cowards and everything else but up I got and after them fortunately the rifle pits had got so they made quite a show and were not any more than 25 feet back of where we lay, and we stopped them there and formed a line as well as we could, and laid down again down behind them and set them to work again.

they worked away for some time and the Pickets had kept tolerably quiet, only an occasional shot being fired. But all at once they broke out into a terrific volley again, and the Rhode Island Regt commenced to fire and they were almost in the rear of us though they had moved a little to the left, but they must have killed

and wounded a great many of us if they had not fired very wild. Col Decker had left the field, hardly able to move with the Rheumatism, and unfortunately Capt Barten was left in Command all the senior Captains being on Picket and Barten is nothing but a boy anyway. I believe he is not 21 yet, we were lying behind the embankment and in a first rate position to hold the Rebels in check, when he like a fool gave the order to fall back again, I did not know he was in command and I tried to prevent Co C from pulling back, but they jumped up and they fell back with a vengeance, back into a swamp where the mud and water was up to the waist. I yelled and ordered, implored and entreated them stop but could not arrest them, neither could Lieut W, until they had fallen back about 10 rods, when we got ahead of them and managed to stop about 20 of them, and got them back to the rifle pits again, again set them to digging. one of our men Co C E T Mally of Shel Falls had his finger shattered here and it had to be amputated, there are some 4 or 5 slightly wounded in the regiment.

I'm afraid that this last nights work will get unfavorably reported in the papers, yet we held the rifle pit until we were ordered out of them at half past three this morning. it will be too bad if our reputation which went up like a rocket should come down like the stick. But noone can blame them for we had no officers, and no orders to stay there if we could not hold the ground.

all night long as we lay there we could hear the Rebels bringing in regt after regt and could hear thier orders, and the rattle of thier Artillery as they brought it up, we expected that every foot of the woods where we were would be raked by thier artillery this morning. When we came away this morning we were marched down into the fortifications, which we reached about 4 o'clock and I threw myself down on a pile of brush wood and went to sleep and did not wake up until 7 o'clock. When the sun became so hot it burned my face and I woke up, we had to wait here until 11 o'clock AM when tired and hungry + sleepy we took up our line of march back to our camp, glad was I to get under the sheltering roof of my tent again.[46]

to add to our comforts, there were lots of dead Rebels scattered round in the woods yet unburied and the stench was intolerable as we marched by an open space to day I took the idea into my head to count the graves. it was just back of Caseys old camp. the space is no bigger than our garden + yard and I counted 51 graves, many of them I presume contained from 6 to 10 Rebels. the graves were not generally dug more than a foot or two deep and then the earth piled over them. sometimes no hole at all was dug but the earth just thrown over them, and anybody can get thier full of horrors by going over that battlefield.

it has been very quiet to day until about two or three hours ago. they commenced firing heavy guns on the right and it still at half past seven PM going on it is the heaviest and most horrific cannonading I have heard since I have been in the army. it is thought to be Porter trying to cross the Chickahominy, other

reports say he crossed yesterday while we were calling the enemys attention this way. I do not know which is the correct report. Our loss in killed and wounded yesterday is reckoned at 300 though I suppose it is not known yet.

I have just counted and thier heavy guns are firing at the rate of 24 a minute, and whenever those big shells are falling at that rate, it is a very hot place to be in. Cal K was with us yesterday, and is as cool as a cucumber. John Cook was not with us as he is slightly unwell.

I shall send in a few days to you a lot of pictures of Camp Brightwood which have just been sent on. we subscribed for them several months ago. they are for the friends of different members of Co C, and will be called for as the boys are going to write to thier friends where they are. it will make you some trouble but we cannot do anything with them here, and there does not seem to be any other way to send them, two of them and I think you may give Madame Boland one of them, there is one for Mrs P W Kingsley which Matt is to take out and leave at Capt Kingsleys until it can be sent up to her. they are all marked on the back. there are three from Dr Chamberlain and all to go to Mr A J Lincoln the directions are on the back for what is to be done with them, one is for himself. Elbridge can take them up to him. it is a very good picture indeed and Matt can point out to you where your "shon" spent the last summer and winter. it is the fifth from the left of the Officers tent, the same artist has drawn a picture of the winter quarters at the same place which will be out in about three weeks.

The story about all those terrible things that were done to Major is all Bosh. there was nothing of the kind done. And I never heard of Capt Millers holding a revolver to Keiths head but he did give him a mighty blowing up on the battlefield and Keith I suppose did hide behind a tree.

Hurrah! Hurrah! I guess the grand day has about arrived for an order has just come to have every man serve with 60 rounds of ammunition to night, and three days rations, and this together with heavy firing on the right, looks as if things were coming to a crisis. well let us hope for the best. we are on the eve of stirring events, and no one knows what the result will be but I hope the vile city will be in our hands before Saturday night.

I can imagine how Miss Pary flew round when she saw the O coat + sash, and I wish I had been in the Bed room to be found. Oh dear I am so excited I cannot write I hear the cheers, thousands upon thousands of men they rend the very ear and there must be some good news, and it must be something concerning the firing that has been going on which has been growing more distant and now is very far off. I guess Porter is going into Richmond to night. Oh how thankful I shall be if our weary labors are to be rewarded with victory. I cannot write I must go out and see what I can see. Bonfires are springing up all through the woods. The news has been carried to every regt but this but I cannot find out what it is. Some say Jackson and his whole command are taken and some say Fort Sumpter

is taken, and some say Porter has driven all the Rebels on the right into Richmond, and some say Richmond is evacuated. why we do not get the news officially is more than I can tell, so I will drop the subject.

The Cape to my O coat was left at Brightwood in my trunk Capt Joe wrote he is going to send for his, and I wrote him to send for mine and Lieut W.

Give my love to Uncle Ed and tell him I wish him much joy. I had forgotten to say anything about it before, it was because I had so much else to think of. I would have given a hundred dols to have had him in command of this regt last night because he would have been so cool. I think now that it is a pity he did not go into the military, because he would have made a splendid Col. I don't pity John much for being in command of his company and I don't believe he does for I know a 2nd Luff likes to have command once in a while and he gets $10 per month more when he is in command, and being on guard in camp or Barracks isn't very hard for the Officer of the Guard. But I don't see how they can get furloughs, an Officer in this Army cannot if he is ever so sick.

What has become of Johnnie Wilson? you wrote that Uncle Ed keeps no man or boy. Is Capt Joe going to Ananapolis? I am afraid the Bowie Knife is gone for good. I expect that Juba went to Brightwood and married a Darkey girl there. If I ever go there I will choke him for I was almost afraid to send by him and I told him he would get drunk and lose it. Tell Mat I don't owe her any letters for I wrote her a long one after the one I got from her and Tom.

I think it will be safe to set down anything Bill Clapp says about the army as a lie. he aught to be suppressed as a nuisance, and when I get home I will tell him so, if I ever have a chance.

I have written two long letters to Mary this week, tell her I shall expect her to "govern herself accordingly".

I have finally got the good news which is that Stonewall Jackson came down our right flank at Mechanicsville[47] and has been badly beaten so now we can have MacDowell and his forces to help us I suppose.

I don't see how the Rebs are going to get out of Richmond now, but I guess we shall have a severe fight,[48] but you will know all about this good news before this letter gets to you while I shall have to wait until Sunday when tomorrow's NY papers will come and I shall know all about it.

Give my respects to Mrs Kingsley and to Bill tell Bill I heard to day that he is going to enlist this fall but I hope there will be no more soldiers wanted by that time, not even me. Give my respects to all the neighbors and all the family. It is quarter past 10 o'clock and the Bands are playing at all the Generals Hd Qrs so I conclude the late victory must have been a very important one it certainly is if it has disposed of Old Stonewall, and if our Gun boats will only get up James River it would trouble Mr Beauregard to get into Richmond with his reinforcements. I think more wonderful things will happen this week, but the Rebs have not left

here yet for I hear a popping of muskets up where we were last night. We shall have to go up there again Saturday night and I suppose though I understand that Couchs Division have got to do the Picket on that part of the line the while now, as Hooker has done it ever since the Battle of Fairoaks.

The 1st Mass Regt was in the Battle yesterday and lost a great many men, but I think Seth Clark is all safe as Capt Newell went to thier camp to day and he say's somebody there enquired after me. I have not seen Willie Robinson since we left Wmsburgh he is up on the right somewhere.

But I must go to bed or rather to *ground.* Give my love to Mary Mattie + c, with a large share for yourself I remain Your affectionate son

Charlie

PS Don't you forget that you will get no more letters from me if you publish any more of mine. I think I have made out a lengthy one this time.

58

Camp near Harrisons Landing VA July 9th 1862

Dear Mary

I wrote a letter to Mattie this AM, and an Official letter to Washington, then went out for two hours fatigue duty in the hot sun, perhaps you don't know what "fatigue duty" is well its all kinds of labor done by soldiers except thier regular duties, such as chopping, digging, intrenchments +c.

Our business this AM was clearing away the brush + trees from before a redoubt which we have been building, and the hot sun beating upon my head has given me such a headache that I can hardly sit up, but although I get no letters from home I thought I must write to you or there would be a row in the family. I have received a letter from you dated June 26th, and I received one from Mattie dated June 30th two day's before I received yours, which is the last intelligence I had from home. it is hard not to hear from home oftener, with all the rest we have to endure but I suppose I must bear it as long as I stay here. how long that will be. If present influences are to rule this Regiment I don't know. We have the Lieut Col Viele[49] of the 2nd RI Regt placed in command of our Regt and a man whom the whole Regiment cordially hate.

I have been in command of the Company since the Battle of July 1st[50] as Lieut W has been sick. he has resigned and if his resignation is accepted I don't know but I shall follow suit. I am sick tired and disgusted and how I ever got through the retreat is more than I can account for, in addition to all our other troubles,

the last day of the rout we had a drenching rain which made the roads knee deep with tenacious mud, and it was as much as I could do to pull one foot out after the other. We thought we were to get some rest when we got here but were set immediately to work chopping and digging intrenchments which work goes on night and day, and yet I would bet $100.00 dollars that there never will be a gun fired over them at an enemy, if we fight them we shall have to go out miles in front of them and fight them hand to hand. it is reported that Burnside is coming up the river today but we have heard so much about Burnside that we do not believe there is any such man in the world.

President Lincoln arrived here yesterday. he rode round the front of the lines, some 40 rods from where our Regt lays but I did not go to see him as I suppose that he was showing himself he would ride round in front of our Brigade but he did not, so we did not see him, small loss though.[51]

I don't know whether he has gone back or not. Has Cal K arrived home, or have you seen his arrival anywhere in any of the cities he came over to the landing and must have got aboard one of the boats. I saw a Dr Seymour one of the Volunteer Doctors he is from Enfield, and stationed on board the Vanderbuilt. he says there was a Kingsley on board that ship when she carried the first load from this landing. We have had a letter from one of our Companies who was wounded in the same battle and went on the Vanderbuilt, and arrived at Washington. I want you to tell Johnnie Cooks folks that he is sick. he has an intermittent fever the doctor calls it. I believe the Dr does not consider him dangerously sick, but Johnnie wanted I should see the Dr and find out just how he was and write to you to tell his folks. he is better today than he was yesterday. I succeeded in buying a bottle of jelly down to the Landing the other day of a sutler, and I gave him some and he relished it. Oh dear it is a tough place to be sick here, no comforts and no nothing, and they will not allow any sick to be sent away now. I think it is outrageous. if a man gets his little finger wounded in battle he can go home however strong and well he may otherwise be, but a sick man be he ever so sick he cannot go anywhere away from the Regt. I cannot imagine why it is so but so it is. You must tell them not to be afraid, as the doctor says there is no danger. Oh dear I must lie down a little while, my head aches so I cannot write but will try finish bye and bye.

6 o'clock PM   My head is not much better and I can write but few words more. We were mustered for Payment this PM and it was a mournful sight to see old Company C that used to turn out a front of 45 files now turn out with a front of 10 files or twenty men rank + files + 5 sergts and 1 Officer. it almost made the boys cry to see it and they are all reduced to shadows and look as though they were on thier last legs. They have a dreamy, listless look as though they were without hope.

You do not approve of my signing Major Marsh's letter, but I thought it was a

little thing to do and he promised on his word of honor to make no use of it until he had confirmed with the officers of the Regt again and had heard from them, and the next we heard from he had it in the Gazzette. It does not seem to do him much good. I see by Col Briggs letter that he speaks of the middle of the afternoon as being much the most severe part of the battle. he is very much mistaken for he did not see the severest part of that battle nor did Capt P nor a great many other Officers. it was the last stand made by the 10th or part of it, and part of another Regt, and just at sundown that was when Co H suffered so severely and a part of the battle that Col Briggs knows nothing about.

I did not speak of the Hospital Garments at all I meant the little goodies which have been sent from time to time which I have no doubt go to fill the mouths of Hospital nurses, and stewards a great portion of them, but I don't want you to say anything about this, and have no doubt that they do somebody a great deal of good, but when I see poor fellows like Johnnie Cook lying on the ground and dozens of others, and see sick men hardly able to walk at all and would not be if at home, struggling wearily through the mud as I saw them during that fearful march, and see them stop in the mud to gather strength sinking deeper and deeper into it, and then think of the work you do that goes to some sanitary commission and, your own sons and brothers can get no good from it, it seems not exactly right but I see no help for it. we cannot get them here and we aught to be thankful that they do somebodys sons and brothers good.

We have received none of the things you have sent since the Battle of Fairoaks, nor do I know that we ever shall. I don't know why for Adams Express boat runs regularly but it sometimes seems as though this Regt was accursed in every respect this and the 36th NY have been in all the battles and have been cut off, while the 7th + 2nd RI have escaped almost everything they laid all day during the last battle in a perfectly safe position seperate from the rest of the Brigade. I don't know whether there is any management about it or not but it looks like it. I am much obliged for the description of Mattie's house. You no need to have sent Sarah away on account of wages as I could pay her easy enough as for my sending a decent contraband I don't know how I could send one but there is a boat load of them down to the landing, and a funny sight they are indeed. Some of them look very neat but they would have to have wages, as well as anybody else, for they are free now, and my experience of contrabands is that they are the laziest worse good for nothing, of all Gods created creatures that boy I had at Camp Bright-wood could not turn round once a week, he was slower than any snail.

Tell Mrs Clark I am just as much obliged to her as though I got the jelly. it was very kind of her to send it, and I thank her ever so much and still hope it will come.

I don't blame Cousin Edmund for not liking Keith I think he is a coward and a hog. I saw him the other day while we lay under the Artillery fire in the ravine I

wrote you about we were perfectly safe but he got off 50 yards to the rear and sat down behind the biggest tree he could find, the whole Regt was laughing at him and he mysteriously disappeared before the fight was over, and he has been sick ever since, but he looks as tough and hardy as an ox. it is getting dark and I must close. Give my love to Mother Mattie and Thomas, and respects to all the friends and neighbors Very aff your brother

Charlie.

59

Camp near Harrisons Landing
July 12 1862

Dear Mother

I received your little note of the 8th inst and although letters to me are like "Angels visits few and far between" I thought having plenty of time just now that I would write you this PM. I am afraid that you take it for granted after every battle that I am killed and so do not write whereas you aught to write still longer letters and if I am really killed why there can be no harm because somebody will get them and send them back.[52] We are resting just now, waiting for Richmond to fall I suppose the most perfect quiet prevails, and with the exception of an occasional Bang from the Gun boats off on the River and the familiar sight of arms, Uniforms and munitions, we should hardly realize that we were engaged in a bloody war. The Rebels have left us in perfect quiet since the first morning after we reached the river, and now we have so entrenched ourselves that the Rebels in the south could not make us budge an inch. the Army is in camp in one continuous line for I don't know how many miles and in front is a line of breastworks of large logs with earth thrown up on the outside.

that mark represents them and the crooks in it are strong forts with very heavy embankments and over these embankments appear the mouths of long and large guns, from 30 pounders to 80's and great gaping mouthed Howitzers the straight lines represent breastworks that connect them and over these look the smaller fry in the way of Parrotts, Griffins and Napoleons, and in the case Mr Reb pay's us a visit in addition to these will glisten the barrels and bayonets of the deadly Enfield, Springfield Austrian Belgian, and Saxon Rifle with a stout hearted soldier behind it, for they are there but a few paces behind the breastwork ready

to spring at a moments notice, soldiers from every state now, side by side the soldier from Maine New H. Vermont Mass. RI. + Conn. stands the stalwart warrier from Ill. Ind. Ohio, Iowa Mish. + Wisconsin and intersperced with all the men of NY Penn + New Jersey. There they stand elbow to elbow there they lie side by side at night, desiring nothing so much as that Mr. Secesh would pay us just one visit, just make his boasted attempt to drive us from his sacred mud and dust. Oh don't we wish he would just try it on, but no when we fight him again, we must go after him he knows better than to attempt it here.

Meanwhile we lie here and rest and recoup, and gather strength for the next attempt, and little Mac has been through the lines and says "we give them one more turn boys, and that will be the end of it". I wonder if it will though it will be the end of it, for many of us, no doubt of that, and so we wait and wonder, and go up to the breastworks and peer off over the fields and into the deep shades of the woods, and wonder what next? and when? Ah well it will come sooner or later, soon enough for some. I see it all the march in the noontide sun, the watchful anxious vigils of the nights, the hunger, the thirst, then the crack of one musket, two! quicker! faster! the war the smoke, the whistling bullet, the screeching shell, the shouts and cheers and then the silence, and the survivors gather together and relate the wonderous tales, the narrow escapes, with a pitying word and lowering voice, for the missing companion, then the shovel and spade, and hasty burial and the survivors move on.[53]

It has all to be gone through with again. Three long months, Thousands upon Thousands of lives Millions of Treasure gone, lost and to what end. As far, yes farther from Richmond than at the beginning.

Somebody most certainly has blundered, but nobody is to blame. Why in Thunder don't they go to drafting? Where are all the brave ones who were "coming after us, when they were actually needed"? there were thousands of them when we came away. why don't they come on? Don't they think they are needed yet? I can tell them that if this is not the time they never will see it, but enough of this they cannot be expected to come. it is not half so pleasant to be out here in the woods and swamps as tis to stay at home so I don't wonder at them much only there were so many coming "when they were *really needed*" that I almost wonder that the fifteen thousand from Mass are not on the way already. perhaps they have not heard that they are needed.

Well we have finally heard from Cal as I suppose you have before. he is in Washington in the General Hospital Judiciary Square. he writes in pretty good spirits, but says he would rather be here than there. I think it mean enough outrageous, that they don't let such cases go to thier own houses. I would not like to say it before the men, but under the same circumstances I should be strongly tempted to start for home, leave or no leave, noble Cal how I wish I could shake his hand. It was good for the eyes, of an *"East Ender"* of the old race, to look at

him in the battle the other day, so cool, so brave, and so intent upon the business in hand. he was just what I knew Bill would be, and as I watched that day I thought of Bill a hundred times. Poor Johnnie Cook was not in this fight, but he kept the reputation of the old neighborhood good in the others we have been in and his trials were worse than ours sick and weak riding in a wagon, that would kill a well man to ride in. (I always prefer to walk rather than to ride in one of them) He has been sent to the Hospital and at the Landing to day where he will be more comfortable, and where I have no doubt he will be sent north, and once in the land of civilization he will get all right again, but I don't think Johnnie is strong enough for a soldier. I have this morning made out papers for his discharge and hope to get them through. Poor fellow, I asked him if he wanted his discharge, but he would not say yes. To much pluck left for that, but I could see the longing look and I thought it best, and we shall try hard to get them through and shall punch the Dr up all I can. All I could get Johnnie to say when I asked him if he wanted it was "you know how I have been this spring" brave fellow he would not ask for it himself. I am proud of the old neighborhood it has furnished no cowards for this army unless its me. I can answer for myself, but no others that I can swear to.

I can tell a different story of some Northampton boy's. Fred Clark for instance has been lining some for a month trying to get a discharge and playing sick, but he is all together to healthy to lie still long enough to make any kind of a show of sickness in fact there is not a tougher healthier man in the Army of the Potomac and now I see he ranks as wounded in the late battle he was not wounded in the battle one of our wounded wanted to speak to him as he lay behind the company the next thing he was gone. he did not wait to see the end of the battle. he was seen the next day all right and the next thing he sent word that he was accidentally wounded in the hand by a revolver. nobody doubts that he shot himself. I don't want you to say anything about this for I do not want it to come from me, but he is small loss he was a trembling little coward anyway.[54]

My health is much better than it was and I hope it will continue so. If I could only have a furlough for two or three weeks I think I could come back with a good heart for the work. Ask Tom if he can get me a Captains Commission with Authority to raise a Company for one of the new Regiments. I wish he could for then I could visit you at least.

I hope what you hear about Burnside + Pope is true, but we are so situated in a dense woods that we know nothing of what is going on out of the woods world behind us. I did hear that Burnside had landed on the other side of the river and I saw in the NY Papers that he was on his way here but I place no kind of confidence in anything which I do not see myself. if one Millionth part of the stories I have heard in the past three months had been true We should now have killed and captured every "Secesh" and the war would be over. The shirts have

not got along yet but I hear there is much stuff for this regt and the EX Boat at the landing just arrived but will not be unloaded until Monday. I hope it is there, but have got so used to disappointment that I hardly expect it is.

I should think Col B + Capt P had better come back if they can kite all over the country at the rate they are doing. I am glad to hear that Mark Moody is getting well he is one of the best fellows in the world I am afraid he will not come back to Co C though. has he lost one or two fingers on his hand.

Perhaps it is to your prayers that I owe my safety at this moment, for certainly I've been where death was thick and close around me. I should like to write to Uncle Henry but I have written so many letters and never had any answer I do not know whether he ever got them or not and shall never write any more to him until I get one from him, you may give my love to him when you write and tell him so, besides I don't know his direction and if people want letters, they must write letters. its hard keeping up a correspondence all on one side, and if he cared much to hear from me he would write to me. What has become of poor Aunt Lu. I wish she had not gone home. Give my love to Uncle Ed and tell him I wish him great happiness. Give my love to Nell If I am going to stay in this Army and it is going to last always I shall have to have a new Uniform. the one I have is about played out. it is covered with dirt and pitch and faded into light green. Remember this is the third long letter since the battle, and I have not had but one from you since so look out give my love to Mat Mary + Thomas Respects to all the neighbors, especially Mrs. Clark Cooks + Kingsleys.

And don't take it for granted that I am dead and stop writing until you know the facts. With love I remain Your aff son

Charlie.

60

Camp near Harrisons Landing VA Sunday July 13th 1862

Dear Pary

You are a jewel. I have just received your splendid letter of the 9th inst and if you knew how much good it has done me you would write me every day. It has made me feel so well that although I sent a long letter to Mother yesterday I have immediately seated myself to commence a letter to you it is now about 8 o'clock in the morning, and comparatively cool and comfortable for this country. I have been up since 4 o'clock this morning and I often get up long before most of the Company and always as soon as any. in the morning and evening are the only parts of the day a fellow can move about unless he is obliged to. The orders

prohibiting music are suspended now and we have regular bugle calls there is not a drum left in the Regt and our Bands are played out and are going to be discharged but we have a few Buglers left and have Reville + Tattoo and the hours regular once more and it seems as though we were are a Regiment once more, and then there are Bands all round us and a little music sounds cheering enough after the months of silence, the whispered fall in! fall in! and not a pleasant sound to cheer us in the least. But now we have the Bands playing, the stirring notes of fife and drum and the clear and resounding note of the Bugle in all directions. it would set you crazy to lie here in my little shelter tent at night and hear the Tattoo as it breaks out on the still night air now close at hand, then the next Regt growing fainter and fainter like an Echo as it is taken up by one Regt after another in the distance and again breaking out in some Regt quite near and going through it all again as the time varies in different encampments. As I sit here writing, while all the noisy, and confusing sounds of the week day are hushed for singular as it may appear the same hush comes over the Army each day that there is in the far off towns to the north on Sabboth morning, that is when the sacreligious foe are not near to break the quiet with thier yells, and the cracking musket and roar of Artillery with them there is no respect for the day. In fact they generally make more noise on that day than any other, but as I commenced to say as I sit here writing a Band in some Regt not far off is discoursing the sweetest music, sounding like the opening services in the churches in far off New England, and this is the day that went unmolested, the soldier sits and dreams of the loved ones at home, the whole day is given up to rest and quiet and all unnecessary work is prohibited. I don't know why it is I see none of the sanctimoniousness of much of the religion at home and the men are all of them or most all of them irreligious and many of them of the roughest cast of sinners, or would be called so at home. Yet all are quiet and decorous on this day. I suppose it is the force of old associations and habits of New Englanders, be they Saints or sinners.[55]

We have an inspection at 9 o'clock this morning, and that lines up all duties ordered for the day After that I am going down to the Provost Marshalls Office to set him to looking after P W Kingsley who "skedaddled" from the Co while on the march the day before the battle of July 1st and has not been seen since, the miserable coward. if we have another battle and I get him started for it he won't run from it alive. I can tell him that if he is afraid to face the enemy and take his chances for life and death, I'll make it a certain thing for him if he undertakes to run away. Oh how I loathe these cowards and there are some in all Regts. Every member of the Co curses him and I am afraid he has defrauded the Co of much money in the position he held while at Brightwood perhaps that is what makes him try so hard to get away. he ran from the battle of Fairoaks and was gone a week or more, and he ran from the night skirimish June 25th and in short I

believe he is a despicable coward in every way but enough of him, it is not a pleasant subject for he and I have been good friends and I am indebted to him for many comforts I should not have had, but I'll put him through for all that. I think you spread on the soft soap rather thick I am glad if my reputation is good at home but I am no more deserving than thousands of others you know, who did as well, and thousands who did much better. therefore I think you are desposed to magnify my merits. I endeavored to do my duty to the best of my ability, and though it is pleasant to be thought well of at home, still I am afraid you think I have done a great deal more wonderful things than I really have.[56]

As we are resting now of course there is nothing to do but make stories. We have a rumor this morning that the gun boats went up the river with a flag of truce yesterday, and that there is to be no more fighting for 30 day's but I guess that is all moonshine, and I reckon there is plenty of fighting in less than 30 days too. I have had an inspection since writing so far and have been out to Gen Couch's Hd Qrs and sent a note to the Provost Marshall to hunt up Mr Kingsley and send him to me under guard and if he is round in this vicinity he will be brought to time very soon.

You ask about Johnnie Cook but I have already (yesterday) written all about him, and so you will know before this gets to you he is now at the Hospital at Harrisons Landing and I presume will soon go north on some of the steamers. I also wrote that I have got his discharge papers started and I hope to get them through. you must do as you think best about telling his mother about this. it might awaken hopes that make the disappointments more bitter if the papers should not go through, but I have strong hopes that they will and so has the Dr. if the boys could only be sent home when they are taken sick it would be the means of saving lots of them. give my respects to his folks and tell them the Dr does not consider him dangerously sick and he is now in a comfortable Hospital on the river bank.

I am surprised that Cal should not accept his furlough to go home. I think I should go if I could not stay but one day. it does seem to me that it is about time for some of those fellows who were wounded at Fairoaks to be coming back but I suppose they want to stay just as long as they can and I suppose they can see no reason why they should not stay as long as the Capt does and I suppose there ain't any. I should have been very glad to have got a slight wound, and gone home and staid 2 or 3 months but I am afraid that is wicked, but I do so want to go home and see you all that it seems as if I could not stay here.

I heard that the 27th + 21st Mass Regiments were at the Landing last night, but do not know whether it is true or not it would not be strange if they were, for all reinforcements are sent to the front and I think they aught to be for we have had our share of the fighting and Burnsides men will see such fighting as they did not see in No Carolina. I'll warned you but still the Rebels back was pretty

well broken in the several Battles while we were retreating, or to speak more
politely while we were changing front to the rear.[57]

if you read in the NY Papers the Rebel accounts of the different Battles you
will see that the Battle of Malvern Hills July 18th was the only one where they
acknowledge a defeat or a repulse. they would not call it defeat if we had slain
every soldier in thier Army. this Battle was the one that we were in it was called
at first the Battle of Turkey Bend. you will notice that they claim all the others as
victories, and claim to have driven all before them until then. Confound them
they found when they met Couchs Division that they got hold of a kind that did
not know how to run. I guess that the No Carolina fellows must begin to dread
our Brigade by this time, though we happened to meet them at Fairoaks, and we
took 80 names of the muster roll of that squad of No Carolina Cavalry that met
us and after we crossed White Oak Swamp and again we met No Carolinians at
Malvern Hills and destroyed 3 or 4 Regt of them some of the prisoners taken
then wanted to know what kind Ammunition Couchs Div used they said we
made no wounds but shot to kill I have a very realizing idea how the Minies must
have sung even among them while under our fire. I suppose Mr Trumbull thinks
he is very cunning with the last two letters he published I had just as soon he
would publish my name as to publish them that way. it is not the people at home
I care about it the letters coming back here and being laughed at by the men in
the Army, for let me tell you no two men see a battle alike and my impressions
are not the impressions of anyone else, you know and then I always mix up a
great many things in my letters that I don't want anyone else to see, that you
know.[58] Capt Parsons cannot be any more indignant than are some of the
Officers of the Regt at the proceedings and making promotion. they were many
of them outrageous, but the men have been assigned thier positions although
thier commissions have not come. I consider many of them very unjust indeed,
but Lieut Storer of Gen Devens staff, and since acting on Gen Palmers, took
Bishops name to Boston and I have no doubt he will get taken care of.

I have got the pictures all in my tent ready to do up and send when the orders
came to pack up that day over at the rifle pits. they were all paid for but I had to
give them back to the Artist and he put them all in the box again, and put them
on the wagons, fell in and marched with us that night, got strayed away from the
Regt was picked up by the Provost and was forced to go in with a NY Regt and
fight, got his finger shot off and where he is now nobody knows. I saw by a
Springfield Republican that the deaf and dumb Artist had been in Springfield
selling his pictures of Camp Brightwood. that is another view he got up
subscriptions in the Regiment and we paid him for his when we subscribed and
those we have never seen. I think it would have been as well if he had supplied us
who had already paid him first. But I don't know as we shall ever get them.

George Bigelow has been quite sick and I believe was not in the battle the
other day. he is getting better now and has been promoted. I believe 1st Lieut in

Co H. He says he has had a letter from Aunt Dorinda and she has sent him a box with a couple of pair of stockings in it for me. they will be quite acceptable as I have got reduced to the government article, which are not just much as I like by the way while I think of it I wish you would get me two good heavy collared woolen Undershirts and two pr Drawers to match and send them on by somebody that is coming also tell Capt that it would be a good thing if he could bring on a half ream of fine emory paper. the guns are in bad condition and we cannot get anything to scour them with. I agree with you that I wish Bill Clapp and the others you speak of could be drafted especially old Bill, and I wish you could get no substitute.

I think Johnnie Cook is much to blame for not writing home and I have scolded him about it always when you have written anything about it, but he has not been able write for the last three or four weeks. that is he has had no time nor place nor anything else until we got over here and then he was too sick but he asked me to and I did write to Mother and told her to tell Mrs Cook.

Please give my respects to Mrs Bailey when she comes in.

I am ever so much obliged to you for your first rate letter, and hope you will continue in well doing, for letters are our only comfort. we get the NY Papers every day, but I wish you could send me all the Springfield Republicans every day for that always has something interesting and I want to hear all about how the enlisting goes on. Have you heard anything from Amherst lately. I have not had a letter from there for a long time.

I believe not since Clara sent me Birdie + Frankies picture. Your and Matt's picture is a great comfort to me and I often sit by the half hour and look at it. I wish I had Mother's too. It is now about supper time but I do not feel very hungry, as we had fresh beef today and I ate a pile of Beef steak + potatoes that would astonish you. Sickness is quite prevalent in the Army and doctor told me this morning that he is afraid of yellow fever. I think that would cap the climax if we should get that among us.

I heard at Couchs Hd Qrs today that our Pickets advanced a mile and a half yesterday. that don't look much like no fighting for thirty day's.

To all the neighbors Especially the Clarks Cooks + Kingsleys tell Mrs Clark I guess I shall get some of the current wine tomorrow, at least I think it is at the landing. The stuff is to be unloaded for this regt tomorrow, and brought up.

Give my best love to Mother, + Mat + Thomas and regards to all the family Aren't the sweet Apples most big enough to bake and can't you send me a bowl of baked apples + milk. I have not seen any milk for 4 months except such as the sutlers sometimes bring condensed milk in cans.

But I must stop now and I think you cannot complain of a short letter this time so good bye and do write often to Your aff brother

Charlie.

61

Camp near Harrisons Landing VA July 22nd 1862

Dear Mother

I suppose you will be expecting a letter from me although I have not had one from home since last Wednesday and have written 2 or 3 since I received any. it is very singular that my letters do not come from home. I got one from South Hadley yesterday, from one of our wounded men, written last Saturday and if you have written I cannot conceive why I should not get them. We received yesterday the long expected box from Northampton and could the genereous donors have seen the joyous faces of the boys as the contents were distributed I think they would have been well paid. it was just what we wanted and needed and those nice shirts give the Company a so much neater appearance for you must know that the government furnishes only white flannel shirts. that is called white by courtesy but they are not white, and no power on earth can make them white. they always look dirty whatever amount of cleaning they may have undergone and then the towels handkerchiefs combs brushes paper pens and Envelopes were just exactly things needed for they were just what the boys lost at Fairoaks, and just what the government does not furnish, and the sutlers prices for such things is just about thier weight in gold. I have seen hundreds of common cotton handkerchiefs such as I have sold lots of them at six for 25 cts. sold here for 25 cts. each and this is a moderate price compared to some things. Mrs Clarkes currant wine came to hand last night, and myself and Lieut Buddingly drank it to our health, it was right good. the jelly had almost all leaked away. the cookies were very good. there was a box for Johnnie Cook and you may tell Mrs Cook but I took the liberty to open it, and confiscated the cookies, and gave the towels and hdkfs to the boys as I presume she would wish me to as Johnnie is no doubt at home by this time. There were two letters in it for Johnnie and one that came by mail which I enclose you will please give them to him. There were also two bundles for Cal Kingsley which I have got in my valise for him.

I yesterday sent in my resignation but I am afraid it will not be accepted. I do this because I am sick and tired, and cannot get a furlough. Lieut W has as good as succeeded in getting a furlough of 30 days. Capt and Lieut Buddingly and myself have each been in the service thirteen months yesterday at this time. Capt has been at home more than half. Lieut W has had one furlough before and I have not had any at all, and although Lieut W is no doubt quite unwell still I don't believe he needs rest any more than I do. Captain on all accounts is as well able as anybody needs be to come back and take command of the Company. Whereas it is all left to me without corresponding rank or emoluments, I am not going to stand it any longer if I can get out of it, and I shall try hard even if I have

to take a dishonorable discharge. they cannot dishonor me from my own knowledge of having done my duty and I have been in every fight and trial, and hardship of the regt and should have had credit for it if it had not been for the little mean jealousies of the men in authority.

thank the lord we have got rid of one nuisance Lieut Col Decker has got his discharge. he was the ruling spirit in making the nominations for promotion after the battle of Fairoaks, a battle that he had hardly any part or lot in. Major Miller had some hand in it and I cannot see why he should omit all mention of Co C for he told Lieut W whom you remember was not in the fight and Major (then Capt) Miller was in command that I did nobly, nobly and expressed himself in terms of the high admiration of the conduct of Co C and especially Sergt Bishop, and yet he sits down with Decker and writes the report of the Battle with the Col Briggs, and omits all mention of Co C. perhaps it was in revenge for the dressing down I gave him on Camp Brightwood in relation to the slavery question. he and Decker and Marsh always bore me a grudge for my plain talk on that occasion. The one horse Captains that are left here are terribly afraid that Capt Parsons will come back Major of the Regt I do wish he would he is much better fitted for it than any other man in the regt and has much better military knowledge than the whole of them put together, and thats why they are so jealous of him, and of Co C for there are no officers that ever spent the tenth part of the time studying tactics than we did, and in all disputes we always got the best of them, and so you see little petty jealousies run all through our army of brave defenders of the Union and I suppose that I have my share.[59] its too bad but I don't see how it can all be helped. George Bigelow I suppose got a furlough yesterday or will get one to day. I think he needs it worse if possible than any other man in the regiment for he is quite sick.

Dr Chamberlin has also got a furlough he is a man that was very conscientious about giving to officers who applied to him certificates of illness, in which to ground an application for furloughs and discharges but when he happens to be the Officer who wants a furlough its an entirely different thing. he told us that we must not give up but hang together, and do everything for the good of the regt and yet at a time when if there is any officer needed more than another it is those of the medical department, he gets a furlough and goes off himself in face of his good advise to the rest of us. Gen Palmer has a furlough of 22 days Col Wheaton 2nd RI has a furlough for the frivalous purpose of going to see his wife at Fortress Munroe. but when you get down to 2nd Lieuts Oh they are officers of too much importance to be spared a moment. Oh well. there is the same amount of humbug in war as everything else. I wish they would order us to fix bayonets and march us out of these entrenchments set us on the road to Richmond and tell us to go it, and not stop until we had it.

Well this won't be a very pleasant letter to read, and it is not a very pleasant

letter to write, but I can't help it. I am disgusted with every thing and everybody, can't have anything like anybody else not even my druthers. Give my love to Mary, Mat and Tom. Respects to everybody else, and thank Mrs Clarke a hundred times for the wine, and do write often to Your aff son

Charlie

PS I find this makes so large a letter that I shall have to leave a part of Johnnies until next time.

62

Camp near Harrisons Landing VA Sunday July 27th 1862

Dear Mother,

It is Sunday and yeilding to the force of habit I sit me down to write to you or at least to commence a letter even if I do not finish to day. It rained all night last night and the morning is clear comparatively cold and comfortable, the usual quiet of the Sabboth prevails and for the first time since we left Camp Brightwood, I have to day attended religious services. I have to record with grief the death of one of our bravest soldiers. His name was Edward H. Stanley, and he died in the camp Hospital this morning at 2 o'clock. he had been sick of Typhoid Fever about a week and heretofore was one of our healthiest men, that such seems to be always the case if one of the strong healthy ones is taken sick, he goes by rapid strides to his grave. he has a father and I don't know but a mother, and a wife and certain one child which was born since we came out whom he has never seen, whether he has more or not I do not know. I went over to the 2nd Rhode Island Regt to get the Chaplain, and got there just as thier services commenced, so I sat down and waited until they were finished.[60] I did not know before that there was services on the Sabboth anywhere in the Brigade. It seemed quite like old times and I could not help thinking of you all at home as sitting in the church, and it brought home so forcibly to mind that it seemed as if I must take a short cut cross lots for home immediately I have been quite sick for a few days with dyspepsia. the Dr says and I guess it was for I never felt so mean and miserable and homesick and disgusted with everything and everybody in my life, but I feel much better to day, but I suppose that now I have had it once it will stick to me and I shall continue to have it. I have heard nothing yet from my resignation and don't know as I shall but they are obliged to take some notice of it, they say that no resignations are accepted but those of worthless Officers, so I live in hope that I shall get mine accepted. I did not get any letters from you this

morning and was consequently disappointed but I live in hopes I shall get some tomorrow morning. You must not stop writing because I have resigned because it may not take effect within 30 days if at all, but you are very apt to jump at conclusions, for instance if there is a battle you take it for granted that I am killed and stop writing and I suppose when you hear that I have resigned, you will again stop writing.[61] I meant to have cautioned you when I wrote but did not think of it.

I suppose I shall have to write to Stanleys parents it is a painful task and I hardly know how to do it. how it will grieve them and what consolation can I offer. thank the lord I can tell them he was brave. he was one of my eight at Fairoaks and a braver man we did not have. we have one or two more that are following in his footsteps I am afraid and we can do nothing but stand by and see them die. I hounded the Dr until he got mad to send this man and one other home, and yet I don't know as it was best for we had one man die in New York he got a furlough, but could not go any further. I see by the paper that Nims has got home but I do not see that John Cook has. John Cook started first, where can he be, I thought I saw his arrival in NY in the Tribune, but I saw the same list in the Herald and it did not state thier arrival anywhere but that they were taken from Harrisons Landing at such a date. I am quite sure the Tribune said that they had arrived at NY but when I noticed the difference, I could not find the Tribune. I see Nims did not state the fact that he was discharged but the paper states that he comes to recoup his health but he was regularly discharged on account of having the Consumption and I suppose he concealed the fact hoping to get a Commission, but according to the terms of his discharge he cannot reenlist.

We hear a variety of stories about the new Co from Northampton. some say Spaulding is to be Capt and some say Bill Pratt and some say Edward Bridgman the last is much the fittest man for the place in my opinion, but I suppose you will not agree with me, but he has more military in his little finger than the rest have in both thier bodies put together. I don't know how you explain the hardship as it is rather hard on men past middle age Bill K I suppose cannot enlist at least I should not think he could. Give my respects to him and tell him next to home I would give most to see him.

All is quiet in this part of the Army and looks no more like anything being done than it did 10 years ago. We hear of the Brilliant doings over in Popes Army[62] and then compare them with our doings and although everybody praises us for good fighters yet we can point to no results, in fact to the question what have you done? we must answer nothing and yet we have fought more desparately, lost more men, and endured more hardships than any other army under the sun, and all for nothing. we hear of no advance and there is no prospect of an advance. the winter will soon be upon us and then the mud will again render an advance impossible we shall have a repetition of last years experiences only worse

for here we shall have no shelter, and no comforts whatever. meantime while the north are deciding whether they will volunteer or be drafted the Rebels will force thier whole population into the service, and very likely take Washington. then what movement of brilliant strategy we shall see I am sure I cannot tell. It amuses me or rather disgusts me to read the NY Herald, lauding up McClellan to the sky for his brilliant genious in fortifying and engineering skill, and yet it comes down like a Thunderbolt in Fridays paper, on Gen Sherman because he landed at Port Royal and immediately commenced throwing up Earthworks and fortifying instead of immediately taking Savannah + Charlestown, but its easy accounting for the milk in that Cocoanut. Gen Sherman is a Free Soil, Gen Mac C is not that makes all the difference in the world. It is a wonder to me that there is not spunkiness in all the North to squelch the diabolical establishment as that NY Herald. I should like to assault it once I would show them a specimen of Brilliant Strategy, and not of the McClellan order either.[63]

Half past 2 o'clock PM

We have just buried poor Stanley and that is the last we can do for him poor fellow. it is the saddest thing in the service this burying comrads who die of disease in the Hospital. on the battlefield is different then everybody is engaged in the same business, and it does not seem so bad. The RI Chaplain preached an excellent sermon from Luke 12.37–40 and spoke very earnestly of what we all could but take note of. This mans passing through all the dangers of the march and the battle with us, and then when we got into the quiet healthful peaceful camp where he seemed so safe, he was taken down by disease and died. it is a very effective sermon to say the least. Stanley was married just before he enlisted, which was very foolish in him. I heard him saying just before he went to the Hospital that "he wanted to get a furlough to go home and see that boy of his" poor fellow he never saw him nor ever will in this world. well he is gone and no one knows whose turn it is next.[64]

I am anxious to hear from Johnnie Cook Don't fail to write as soon as he arrives. I do hope he has got home safe. we keep hearing that Capt Parsons is coming and the rest of our men at home but nary one makes his appearance. I don't know what to make of it. the Gazzette says that Capt P will start for his Regt next Thursday, if he did and came along I know of no reason why he should not be here now. other letters say that Syd Williams had started out he has not arrived. we have reason to think that Cal is on his way back as there has a letter come for him from Washington and it looks on the outside as though it is one I wrote him. it would be funny if he should get back before the men who were wounded at Fairoaks, and aught to shame them but I don't know as it would. I don't suppose anything would shame them as long as they have the Captains Example to follow. I have just heard that our Regiment is to go out to support

the Picket to night I wonder whats up. I have heard of nothing of that kind before. Perhaps they are going to make an advance but as I have not reported for duty to day I don't think I shall now go as it might set me back again. Lieut Weatherill expects to get his furlough for 30 days, this week. Oh dear I wish I could get one or my discharge or something it seems as though everyone can get away but me, and I do want to go home so much.

In looking over my Valise I found there two Photographs to save them as they are pretty much worn out now. I thought I would send them home before they are entirely gone. We are expecting the Paymaster every day when I shall send home some money if I can find any way to send it, but the Express Company will take no packages from here and how I shall manage to send it I do not know. I am going to try and make Captain try for a furlough for me when he gets back if he ever does, but still I don't suppose he can do it, but he knows Gen Devens and if he cannot get a furlough perhaps he can get me a discharge, if my Resignation is not already accepted. I see Bill Clapps stupid advertisement in the Gazzette I should like to see him out here I should like to be his commander a little while I would put him through one course of Sprouts I warrent you. I'd make him step round worse than ever he did in that old Foundry.

I cannot think of anything more to write to day so I think I will not write any more until tomorrow, and perhaps I shall get some letters in the morning. I wonder how it would seem to you at home to write a letter as long as this to me.

Monday morning.

The mail this morning brought me no letters as it should if you had written Wednesday. But last night Cal got back and we were glad enough to see him and he was glad enough to get back. I never have seen a person so glad as he seemed to be to get back. I guess that Hospital treatment in Washington was about one degree removed from the infernal regions, and no more. But Cal got his pay while there and consequently he used to doge out and get his meals at a Restaurant, and he is as fat as I ever saw him in my life and looks as tough and hardy and fresh looking. he is a perfect contrast to the rest of us, and so he is the first of our wounded to return. it ought to shame those cowards up at N Hampton who are well enough to come and have been for a month. some of them were not half as seriously wounded as Cal. We were all glad enough to see him the grand handshaking all round the Doctors in the Hospital at W did not want him to come yet but he would not stay there, and I do not blame him all they had to eat was bread and water and little soup or hot water for a change as Cal calls it and all the while a Mr Kellogg from Michigan was there every day begging the Dr's to let him take Cal home to his house pledging himself to take every care of him, but no he must be kept in that miserable furnace of Hospital without a particle of shade anywhere near it, nor anything else to rest the eye

upon. I should like to be a member of Congress a little while, I would make one rumpus I know.

I hope in the course of time to get an answer to this. I send but one picture, as I gave Cal the other. Give my love to Mat + Tom + Mary and my respects to all the neighbors. Please write me how they get along enlisting up there, and whether they will get a Company or not. I can think of nothing more to write, so with much love I remain Your aff son

Charlie.

FOUR

I Don't Know
Where It Is All to End

September 1862–March 1863

Brewster spent most of August 1862 on a desperately needed furlough back in Massachusetts, where he temporarily became a recruiter. He remained on recruiting duty during the Antietam campaign of September, rejoining his regiment as they pursued Robert E. Lee's army in Virginia that autumn. He suffered terribly from chronic diarrhea, was disabled by it during the battle of Fredericksburg in December, fell into a temporary despair, and endured another winter at the front, this time near Falmouth, Virginia. Brewster's physical condition and morale mirrored that of the Union cause during the winter of 1862–63.

63

Camp Day, No Cambridge Monday September 1st 1862

Dear Mother

I am still here in this dismal camp, still hard at work, and still so feeble that it does not seem possible to keep round. I did not write yesterday because we had a great rush of citizens and great excitement all day. in fact there was one continual row all day long. about 500 recruits were sent off on Saturday PM, but the 9th Irish Regt recruits who were drawn out in line to go with the rest refused to budge an inch until they were paid thier $13 advance pay they had received all thier bounties and everything else but this and would have got this only there had not been time to arrange the payroll and the men are wanted at the scene of war, Irish like they refused to go until the last mill was paid, so they were marched back to quarters. I could not but contrast it with the conduct of the Yankee recruits who went off without not only the $13, advance pay, but without the $25 advance bounty, immediately on reaching thier Barracks these wild

Irishmen commenced fighting on thier own hook and have kept it up with more or less intensity ever since.[1] Saturday afternoon, in the first row, they called on the 10th Recruits to help quell the riot and my little squad of 5 who have all the serviceable muskets in the field were called upon to load with ball, but it was finally quelled by arresting 4 or 5 ring leaders and confining them in the black hole, but they commenced another in the same evening but I happened to be in the Barracks at the time and nipped it in the bud. they are in the same building with the 10th Regt Recruits. yesterday afternoon another row broke out among some citizens and soldiers, and we had to shut up 2 or 3 of both, and so it goes day and night. we shall send off a lot more to day, and hope to get the camp a little cleared before long.

George Squiers went off with the 27th party Saturday.

All the recruits are mighty anxious to get off and grumbling because they can't. I often think how mighty anxious they will be to get home again, and how glad they would be before long to return to Camp Cameron, and rest contented, and then to see great men whining round to get a furlough because they have not seen thier wives for 2 or 3 weeks.

There are any amount of affecting scenes here (so called) I call them ridiculous, and every recriut that has got a *lovy*er or sister or any other female friend has got to the last guard in the gate to do thier kissing and hugging and that blocks up the way, and fifty times a day I have to shorten these farewells but the Irishwomen make the most fuss bawling and yelling, +c.

But I must close now and go and see what is going on at the gate. Give my love to Mary + Mattie + Tom respects to all friends, and write soon to

Your Aff son

Charlie.

64

Camp Day No Cambridge Friday Sept 19th 1862

Dear Mother,

I received your note this PM and was mighty glad to get it for I did not know but you were all dead, for if I am not good about writing home you are certainly no better about writing to me.

I have hardly anything to write about as this is the dullest of all mortal places and it is enough to kill a man to stay here at all. The number of recruits now here is but 116 though there are many that have been sent here and have skeedadled as there is no adequate force or means to keep them here, and consequently they

Charles Brewster (*far right*) and fellow soldiers of the Tenth Massachusetts writing letters in camp (date unknown). *Courtesy of Jonathan Allured*

have run off. I don't know who can be blamed for it for certainly, if a man wants to run away there is nothing to stop him. I have nothing about my going away as I have no more idea when I shall go than when I came on. there are a lot of recruits (all we have here) going Monday and I may be ordered on with them, as far as New York, perhaps farther. I don't know but if they send me to NY I shall run away and join my regt. I am mighty sick of this service and had rather go into 40 battles than stay here I live in hopes though that I may get out of this hole and go somewhere and establish a Recruiting Office. I don't know what the poor 10th is to do for men. Barten does nothing in Springfield he has not sent but 10 or 12 men since he established his Office there, and I hear he is not in his office at all. it is too bad and now the draft is postponed to the 1st of October, and they may

postpone it until the day of judgement they cannot get enough men to fill the old regt for the cowards dare not Volunteer for them. if they pay ever so big bounties and I don't believe the war will be ended in five years if they do not adopt the Rebel policy of filling up the old regts.

What a paragraph of lies that was you sent me from the Gazzette. there has not been more than 45 Recruits sent to the 10th and I have not enlisted a man in Boston or anywhere else. I am so situated that I cannot enlist anybody, as I am detailed for duty here and cannot get away from here and there is nobody here to enlist for all that come here are enlisted already. I don't know what is to be done I am sure but it is just my impression that the good people of Mass will find one of these fine mornings an order to commence drafting for the old regts. there seems to be an impression that the old regts are nearly full but such is not the case at all, and when they take in consideration the fact that Mass has 32 regts in the field before the last call with 300,000 and that there are nearly all of them reduced one half, you can judge how many men are required to fill them up. I do wish the Gov would go ahead and draft and not be so confoundedly afraid of it.[2] I believe he is a fool.

Sergt Bliss is here and quite well. I am put on "Officer of the Day" about every other day. I went out on Boston Neck to try and find Mr. Clarks house but could not. I went to the end of the route and then inquired of every store in that vicinity and looked in all the Directories but could not find any Geo Clark Piano Maker and as there are 25 or 50 Geo Clarkes in Boston I was obliged to come back without finding the place. If you will write me full directions where he lives, and I can get them I will try to find the place. I was sorry for I wanted to see them.

I see the news begins to grow less favorable to our side in the late battles, at first they were going to "bag the whole Rebel Army", now they are "driven back into VA" which is not the place to bag them by a long shot, and tomorrow I presume we shall hear that the Rebs have bagged McClellan and all his Army, or perhaps not until Monday.[3]

I do not think of anything more of interest to write in fact there is nothing of interest here. I am sorry I did not see Bishop has he gone back to the Regt please write and let me know if you can find time and if you write Mrs. Clarks address you must do it immediately for I do not know when I shall go. If I get any notice ahead of my being ordered off I shall go and see Col Eustis's wife and offer to take on anything she has to send which will be a good introduction to the new Col, but I am afraid I shall not have more than a half hours notice. I did not have three minutes notice when I was sent to NY and I went without an O Coat and it was cold on the boat and rained like great guns in NY and I caught cold, which set a great decayed wisdom tooth to aching. I bore it until last Sunday night, when I went into Boston to a Dentist. he did not want to touch it in the night

but I urged him until he consented to try although it was the very last tooth on my under jaw so he put on his forceps and gave one pinch and shattered it all to pieces. he then took a machine that looks like one of the hooks like they use in moving boxes and bales. He hitched that and gave two or three twists until I thought he would pull all of the bones out of my body and then informed me that I should have to wait until morning so he put some chloroform in it and I departed. next morning I went in and he managed after lifting me out of my chair two or three times to get it out. he said I bore it well and so I suppose I did. I did not grunt nor groan but I stuck my fingernails into the arms of the chair, but I guess you will think this is a long story about a tooth.

Give my love to all, and when you lecture me about not writing just reflect if you have done any better by me and so good night from your aff son

Charlie.

65

[Envelope says "Western Hotel 9 Cortlandt St NY D D Winchester"]
New York Oct 4th 1862

Dear Mother,

I presume you are wondering what has become of me and why I have not written which I will proceed to tell you in as few words as possible. One week ago last Tuesday I was told that I was to proceed to NY that afternoon with a squad of recruits. after I had started from Camp Day, I received an order from Col Day to conduct each squad to its regt and then report myself to my regt. I had not even time to pack my valise. I came into NY and left some of them for Newbern plus New Orleans and proceeded to Baltimore with the rest. the Quartermaster there told me it was no use to go to Washington as Frederick was nearest to the Army and I must go there. I told them that I knew that some of the recruits belonged to regts that were stationed near Washington, but he said I did not and that all I had to do was to obey orders. so he packed me off to Frederick, Md. from there I had to go on foot 23 miles to Sharpsburgh, and was told that McClellan's Hd Quarters were one half mile beyond. but when I go there I found that Mac had moved 3 miles towards Harpers Ferry. but I found Gen Porters Hd Quarters there and distributed what recruits I had for his corps, but he could not tell me anything about any Mass regts other than those belonging to him, so I marched the rest over to Mac's Hd Quarters also found Burnside and distributed what recruits I had for his corps and next morning I went to McClellans Hd Quarters where I found out that my own regt was in Franklins Corps, and on the extreme right, six miles beyond Sharpsburgh, so I had to take

the recuits I had for the 10th and march back to Bakersville six miles beyond Sharpsburgh and there found that they were still 3 miles off.

I finally found them and staid there that night, and next morning started for the party I had left at Atietam Creek. when I got there I started them for Harpers Ferry 9 miles distant where we arrived about sundown. I took the recruits for Sumners Corps over the river to Bolivar Heights and distributed them to thier different regts and after a very pleasant interview with Gen Sumner, I recrossed the river and having still 28 men left belonging to Heintzle-mans Corps I made a moonlight march of one mile to Sandy Hook where we bivouaced for the night and next day at about half past three took a Freight Car for Washington we were 24 hours going there Meeting 6 or 7 regts on the way, who were going to the front. Some of them were 9 month regts. we arrived in Washington about three o'clock where I proceeded over to Alexandria with what recruits I had for Heintzleman's Corps, and returned to Washington where I went to Gen Wadsworths office and represented how I had been sent off, and they gave me transportation back to Boston.[4] I tried here in NY to go by way of Springfield but could not, and am obliged to go by way of Fall River to Boston, where I shall pack up and after a flying visit to North Hampton shall return to the regt I have been on the trot ever since I started and until now have not had time to write a word. With much love to all I am your aff son

Charlie

66

Camp near Berlin Maryland Saturday Nov 1st 1862

Dear Mother,

This is the first opportunity I have had since I left New York to write, consequently I improve it. I arrived safely in Hagerstown Wednesday night and found our wagons there after provisions I got my baggage on board thier train and intended to ride out to camp with them but I missed them. the wagoners said that the regt was at Williamsport Md so next morning I hired a team and started for that place. on arriving there I found a Lieut of our regt who informed me that the regt had gone back to the old camp where they were when I was here before. The Brigade had been on an expedition up to Hancock but had not been across the river at all. that night orders came to have everything packed up and loaded by 3 o'clock the next morning, which was done and at 5 o'clock we marched we bivouaced yesterday PM about 4 o'clock near Rohersville and this morning at 3 o'clock they had us up again and on the march at 5. we got to this

place which is on the Potomac about 8 miles below Harpers Ferry. Most of the Army has gone over into VA either here or at Harpers Ferry I expect we shall follow on tomorrow. We can hear artillery in the distance across the river. There is a pontoon bridge at this point and although we have come some ways below it, I presume we shall cross tomorrow. we are about 400 yards from the bank on a side hill and the Rail Road Canal and Highway are between us and it.

Marching comes pretty hard to me, after so long a rest. my feet are both blistered on the bottom but I guess they will toughen in a few day's I find the regt in a terrible state without clothes, blankets or shoes and more dirty and ragged set you cannot well conceive of. many of them have to be excused from marching in the ranks because they are barefoot, and hardly any of them have a decent pair. here multi pants are all to pieces ditto thier coats and caps, they look like a crowd of beggars in addition to this, they have not been paid off for 4 months and rations are poor and scarce. I don't know what I shall do myself for I have but little money and I don't know as we shall get any more. if you ever saw a discouraged regt it is this, and about the only expression I have heard is "If I could only get home the Union might go to H-ll". No courage, no ambition, and no hope. I almost wish I had not come back, and the crowning misery is this. every man is covered with bugs, and if it were not so sad it would be a comical sight indeed to see when the regt halts for the night, every man is off with his clothes and commence what they call "skirmishing" which is nothing more nor less than hunting for these disgusting animals and it is not for any want of cleanliness in the men but when a man has but one suit of clothing and has worn that night and day for two months, the animals will take possession of him.

The arrested Officers[5] 11 in number have all been tried but one, but the results cannot be announced until all are tried, the trial has to be postponed when the Brigade is marching. it may be some time before they get thier sentence, meantime they have to follow in the rear, without arms and without command. The regt has never been broken up and put into the 15th nor was the possibility of any such thing ever heard of here. The only conversation here is of the probable duration of the war and the constant prayer is for deliverance from the Army. poor fellows, I pity them, but they lose no chance of blowing the new recruits and regts who have had bounties. I had no idea there was so much feeling about it. Everyone wants to know what the people at the North say, and if they think the war is ever going to end. My letters home will have to be scarce unless you can send me some postage stamps I have but one, and I don't think there is a dozen in the regt, and no money to get any with, either among men or Officers. The men appeared very glad to see me and I guess they were. Capt Weatherill got here a few days before I did.

Cal K is enjoying first rate health and sends his respects. remember me to his folks and all the neighbors. the boys are generally in first rate health and if

decently and sufficiently clothed and fed would be in good spirits. 5 of Co C have volunteered for the regular Army and I reckon about 100 in the regt. The old tent is not home any more, but I must close and see if I can get anything to eat. Give my love to Mary + Mat, + lots for yourself

Your aff son
Charlie

PS There is a rumor of a great battle yesterday but I guess without much foundation.

67

Camp near Uniontown VA Wednesday Nov 5th, 1862

Dear Mother,

I wrote you last Saturday from Berlin Md in which camp we lay until the following Monday we had orders to march at 9 o'clock AM but did not get started until about 12. we crossed the river and marched about 10 miles over the "sacred soil" and bivouaced that night in the woods near no place, next morning at 6 and ¹/₂ o'clock we started again and marched to this place, a distance of about 15 miles. there was a fight here on Sunday and the Rebels were driven to, or through Ashby Gap about 5 miles from here. I believe our side killed about 15 of them and wounded a proportionate number.

Our Corps I believe is in reserve. there are thousands ahead of us, but we may get into a fight at any time. I saw Capt Wright Banks (Mr. J. Banks son) this morning over to the Camp of the 37th Regt he had just been to McClellans Head Quarters where Gen Williams told him that if we did not have a general battle within two days we should have to go back. we are out here without any communication with our rear but wagons and it is impossible to furnish us with supplies and there is nothing in the country. We have two days rations issued this morning, of wormy bread and stinking pork, and although the men were all out of rations they threw it all away. What is to become of us I do not know though I suppose we shall get through with it somehow as we always have but I wish our dear friends at the North who have forced McClellan to move had to share our comforts with us. our wagons have not come up with us yet and I have been two nights without my valise and blankets but Sergt Whitney has shared his with me. I have got such a cold that I cannot speak loud nor taste, smell nor hear anything. We have had a full supply of blankets and a partial supply of clothing but many of the men are without shoes and clothing yet.

I reckon that the US is about played out, as they cannot feed clothe or pay us, but it makes no difference if everyone that remains at home can get a political office. This regt I think would fight more desparately than ever if they got a chance, but if we should have to retreat, lots of them would be taken prisoners rather than stay here any longer. I hear nothing but curses both loud and deep even from some of the best men, men whom I left at Harrisons Landing full of faith and hope. I don't know where it is all to end but it is plain enough what our lot is to be viz. to march starve and fight.[6] I have in my portemonaie an old continental dollar bill and a United States Dollar Greenback at the present day and I wonder how long before they are of equal value. Well I suppose this grumbling will do no good. It is like tooth pulling and we must grin and bear it.

I wish Mary would go up to the Gazzette Office and ask Mr Trumbull if he won't direct the Papers he sends to our Company to Capt Weatherill or me, as they are directed to Capt Parsons and they take them at Head Quarters and we don't get them and I suppose he intends them for this Company. Does Curtis know where the Bishop is he thought when I came away that he was with the regt but he is not. I like Col Eustis very much and the Major too as a man, but if he has to lead us into Battle God help us he cannot now even give the simplest order right. it is too bad and such an outrage on a good regt aught to cost Gov Andrew his place. I meant to have written a longer letter but I have nothing to write about. My back aches sitting on the ground. Give my love to Mary Matt + Thomas. Tell Mrs. K Cal is first rate only he wishes he could get hold of one of her mince pies so do I. We expected to march on this morning but have got no order yet and it is nearly 11 o'clock. Please write me often and tell me all the news.

Yours with much love,
Charlie

68

Camp near Stafford House VA Tuesday Nov 25th 1862

Dear Mother,

I have taken my pen in hand to write you again as I suppose you have written to me although I get no letters. I have received only one from home since I came out. We have been in camp here one week to day and have received two mails in that time but all I got out of them was the package of Springfield Republicans which you sent with the letter I got. We are encamped at a crossroads in sight of nothing but soldiers, wagon trains, woods, and hills, and are patiently waiting

the next move. the Engineers are busy repairing a railroad somewhere and I conclude it is nearly done as this morning we hear the whistle of the Engine and rattle of the cars, though we have not seen any railroad yet. We have been expecting to hear the sound of Sumners Cannon at Fredericksburgh yesterday and to day but it has not greeted our ears yet. what part we are to play in the coming struggle has not transpired yet but I have no doubt it will be a permanent one as they are not apt to slight this Brigade or Division when there is any fighting to be done but we all wish they would move in as we are likely to freeze to death if they do not get us a long ways further South before long. The nights are so cold that most everybody has to get up and stand by the fire half the time to thaw out and then lie down and take another nap. I have got such a cold that I can hardly hear, see, taste, or smell anything. We are kept on "mighty short" rations, which makes us feel the cold worse, and we have no money to buy anything with of the sutlers, so we have eked out a miserable existance on Pork and hard bread. it is reported that Gen Devens has written to the Paymaster to come and pay us off as he needs money himself and his Officers and men are suffering for it, and thier families also. Our Regiment went out on Picket Saturday and came in Sunday. I do not see why we do not get our mails oftener (some folks do) the Philadelphia papers the same day they are published.

This is the most barren and desolate country we have ever been in. there is nothing left, and we have to look to Uncle Sam for everything, and all our cry is more, more.

The weather is very cold and to day it looks like a snow storm. we have had a week of almost constant rain, and the water flooded the flat where the men were encamped and they had to move in the rain and cold in addition to all thier other miseries. how I wish some of the stay at homes could enjoy one winter campaign with us I fancy we should hear less of "onward to Richmond". Our tent is pitched on a side hill and we have dug into it for a fireplace, we gather round it and shiver the time away and try to imagine it is an old fashioned fireplace at home, but the smoke and ashes in our eyes and the cold wind at our backs very quickly dispells the illusion.

I don't know what "Old Burnside" intends to do but I wish he would start about something, or let us build Barracks, or send us something good to eat, or make some change either for the better, or worse, which latter it probably will be when he makes any change. I see by the papers that Geo Bliss has got a Captaincy and I am mighty glad of it for he deserves it, and he has not only got that but he has got rid of 13 months service for when that Regiment is mustered out we shall still have about that time to serve. Hurrah! there goes the Cannon heavy and rapid in the direction of Fredericksburgh I hope old Sumner is demolishing the Sesesh den, but then even as I write it has stopped.

Last night as we sat chatting around our fire we were startled by the stunning

report of a Cannon close by. everyone jumped to thier feet, and we heard no more and it turned out that the men of our Battery had made a raid on a Sutlers cart, that got stuck in the mud near here and among the rest had got a lot of whiskey and got pretty drunk, and took it into thier heads to have an evening gun, so they put in two blanks into one gun and let if off, and it more than woke the echoes in this valley, probably they are doing penance for it this morning.

I have written a letter for the Gazzette which goes with this so you can read it when it is published if you want to.

So the 52nd is off at last and going with Banks. how I wish I were going with him too, if we could only get into a country once which had not been raked and scraped forty times before I should be so glad. Did they make out to a point a Quartermaster before they went. I see Decker got the Adjutantcy. "What a fall was there my countrymen" you know the Adjutant ranks as a 1st Lieut I should think Major Marsh might get a 1st Sergt worth in some of those Regiments. Col Parsons furlough is out. Has he started yet. I wrote to him to bring us an axe if he could but I do not know as he as he was there when the letter got there.

I have been reading some accounts of the climate and productions of Florida and I don't know but I shall go and settle there when the war is over. Do you and Mary want to go with me. that is supposing I am left to go when the war is over. Well I cannot think of anything more to write. Give my love to Mary, Mat + Thomas Uncle Edward + Nell, my respects to everybody else and please write often to

Your aff son
Charlie PS Tell Matt I shall write to her next, though I am almost out of paper and envelopes.

69

Camp near Stafford Court House VA Monday December 1st 1862

Dear Mary,

I received your welcome letter of November 23rd to day and was indeed glad to get it for it is so seldom that they come now that they are great prizes when they do. this is only the third letter from home since I joined the regt and I have written almost every week twice. we get a mail once in three days which is an abominable shame as boats come down from Washington every day, but all letters have to go to Burnsides Headquarters which is 12 miles from here and it takes one day to go and one to come. We are in Gen Newtons Division, Franklins Corps, Left Grand Division of the Army we have lost our favorite

General Couch,[7] and very sorry are we, but glad he has a wider field and full scope for his abilities which I consider second to none in the Army.

We had a dismal Thanksgiving enough and I am glad enough it is over. the boys were mighty blue I can tell you, and I was homesick as a dog. We had for dinner a hash, so called, made of Hard Crackers and the remains of our beef steak breakfast, chopped up with an axe and as we choked it down could not help but think of our accustomed dinners at home, and the comparison, as you may suppose was anything but favorable, and we all hoped that if we spend another Thanksgiving on earth it may not be in the Army. A Mr Birnie from Springfield arrived night before Thanksgiving and brought lots of goodies for the Springfield + West Springfield Companies and two or three little packages for Company C, and some things for distribution to the most needy which amounted to 3 pr Stockings, 3 pr Mittens and 1 pr Woolen Wristlets for Each Company. I took mine to my Co and they began to crowd round sticking up thier bare toes and saying "Lieut I haint got any stockings" and again "I have not had any for three months" +c +c and there were so many needy ones I had to have a lottery and let them draw for them. it was tough not to have enough for all but to day we have got a full supply of clothing of all kinds and our Regt is once more clothed + shod which is blessing indeed for to see men round barefoot when water freezes solid in the day time is an agravating sight indeed.

I am in command of Company E sometimes called Bartens Roughs. the Lieut (Putnam) who was in command was placed in arrest for refusing to obey orders. he was a most inefficient Officer anyway and I reckon will have to budge. The Officers under arrest have not got thier sentence yet, but if they are discharged there will be some chances for promotion in this Regt and I hope if I live to be a Captain before a thousand years. I hear by the other Officers that the Col considers me a very efficient Officer, and I know that he chose me to command this Company in preference to Officer who outranks me. So it looks well anyhow. the Company was a rather disorderly one and the Col said to me "Lieut I want *you* to take the Company and bring it up" I see great efforts are making in the Newspapers to plaster up Ex Col Decker and I saw an extract from the Boston Transcript which details his gallant deeds in taking command of the Regiment at Fair Oaks, and on the 7 days retreat, which is all a lie from beginning to end for he left the field before Col Briggs was wounded and was seen no more that day, and on the 7 days retreat he was not seen anywhere except in the rear with the Baggage, neither was he in the Battle of Malvern Hill else how could Major Miller be in command of the Regiment all that time, and the very fact that he tried to be Q M shows that he wanted a berth out of danger. I have no more opinion of him than I have of Major M. I see also by the papers that "the flower of Hampshire + Franklin has now gone in the 52nd, and our hearts have gone out as they never went before +c +c" all of which may be true, but one thing is certain that Springfield did not have to have a Provost Guard to

protect citizens and property when the 10th was encamped there, which goes to show that, some of the flowers came with us enough to leaven the whole lump.

I notice what you say in relation to the situation of governess and I am afraid you will not be able to endure and as long as my life is spared and I remain in the service I will make the wages up to you to stay at home and take care of Mother. I don't like to have her left at home alone, and I hope this accursed war will be over sometime.

We are lying here where I have written the last two letters. Came here two weeks ago tomorrow, and for all I can see are likely to remain here. though it is said that the troops above Stafford Court House have all gone somewhere, but it seems to be the general impression that we are not to cross directly at Fredericksburgh, and I reckon that things will turn up differently from what some folks expect but I know nothing outside of the 10th Mass Vols. I expect to send some money in this letter. we were paid off yesterday and a joyful day it was for us. I am glad if you like your quote though I am afraid it is not good enough. I expected it would be more. I shall send at least $20.00 and I want to send more but the Lord only knows when we shall be paid off again and I do not want to be out of money again before payday. I want you should pay Stoddard and Lincoln $5.00 for a blanket I got of them just before I came away. I suppose the government is about played out and it may be a matter of doubt whether we ever get any more pay or not. If I should not send it in this I shall send it soon in some other way but if you should want money before another payday you must let me know and I will provide it for you.

We are tolerably well situated here only we can get nothing to eat but fresh beef, Pork and Hard Bread which is tough and we get sick of it when we can have no change. It is almost 9 o'clock PM and I must close for my writing desk (a cracker box) is on Capt Weatherell's bed (the ground) and he wants to go to bed, but I am Officer of the Day to day and I tell him he cannot go to bed until I give him permission. I wish somebody would smash Hen Dwights mug for him. I would like to have him in some of the fights we have been in. he would find it a different business Guarding Rail Roads and raising hens + chickens in No Carolina. he talks about fighting. they have not been in anything more than what we should call a skirmish and never mention it, but I must bid you good night. I am very sorry to hear you have been so sick. you must be very careful of yourself, and now do please write oftener to

Your aff brother
Charlie

PS I have concluded to send $40.00 and if you can spare it besides paying S & S and for your cloak I would like to have you pay D Kingsley $10.00 and ask him to send me the amount of the balance of my account.

70

Camp Misery Sunday December 7th 1862

Dear Mother,

I wrote last to Mary enclosing $40.00 and sent it to Washington to go by Express. I received your letter enclosing the Sesesh on our march to this place. we left our camp near Stafford Ct House last Thursday morning The Wagon trains went ahead and kept continually getting stuck in the mud and hindered us so that we did not make more than 5 miles in all day when we bivouaced on the bare ground. it was colder than Greenland the next morning we started before daylight and pretty soon it began to storm a mixture of rain and snow which wet and chilled us to the very marrow of our bones. we marched in through the mud until about noon when we went into camp in a splendid wood of oak and where there was plenty of water. we had just got the tents up and the fires going when the orders came to pack up. I was suffering terribly from headache and pain in the bowels and I thought I should give up but we packed up and loaded the wet tents onto the mens backs and on we started and I do not think there is a soldier in this Division but would have willing given this glorious Union Stars and Stripes and all for one hour at home, and such swearing I never heard. the men cursed the government, the president, the commander of the Army and the Army itself, the North + the South and everything else. well we marched on about a mile further into this woods which is wholly of pine and no good water to be had and next to impossible to build a fire. meantime it rained and snowed harder and harder, and I grew sicker + sicker. I finally managed to get a blaze of twigs and small dry limbs and down I lay on the soaking ground and it seemed as if I did not care what became of me. Our tent was on the wagon that had not come up and night was coming on but the Company cooks took Capt W and myself in and made us as comfortable as possible. Capt was troubled all night with terrible cramps in his limbs but I passed through more comfortably than I expected but got up in the morning with terrible griping pains in my bowels and my cap was frozen stiff and my boots also, the edge of the blankets where they lay close to the tents were frozen stiff as a board. the ground was covered to the depth of 2 inches with snow. I went to the hospital and got something to relieve the pain in my bowels and came back and nearly fainted away twice. In the afternoon the Dr came round to see me and gave me a prescription and after a while I felt some better. our baggage came during the night and we got our tent up. I passed a very comfortable night last night but got up this morning with the same horrible pains in my bowels but they passed off after a while but I am still very weak, and feel miserable enough.

I am sitting before a miserable smokey green pine fire, and shivering all over and trying to write I am sure I do not know what is to become of us this winter for we have not had anything as bad as it will be bye and bye and we have got to

endure this three or four months longer. the roads are awful and our wagons which went back to our old camp for the rations left there. a distance of only 11 miles have been gone. 30 hours and there are no signs of thier coming back and on our way here we passed lots of mud holes filled with dead mules and horses and barrels of pork and beef and still the North crys onward to Richmond and no winter Quarters. My God! I wish they could be out here and experience one day of our misery. McClellan was right and I believe that this campaign will prove it, and will be only second in horrors to Napoleons Russian Campaign for human flesh and blood cannot endure it. Water in a tin cup beside me freezes almost solid in a few moments, and the piercing wind penetrates to the very marrow, and we have no warmth creating food nothing but miserable hard crackers that a man must gnaw upon all the while to keep from starving and take it all together the prospect is black enough I can assure you. But I suppose we shall live through it somehow, at least I hope so. I do not know where we are now but I know that it is a Godforsaken desert. I suppose not far from the Rappahannock below Fredericksburgh. How we are to make much of a fight I cannot see when we cannot stand but a few moments away from a fire. I see by the papers that the 52nd think they are suffering greatly but the time will come when they look upon thier present trials as luxury.[8]

I am so cold I cannot write more now but I wish you would write oftener I don't think you write very often I received another letter from Matt the same time I received your last for which I am very thankful and shall answer it soon. please tell me all about Marys health when you write I do not think it at all advisable for her to go as governess, in fact she must not. Oh dear how cold it is good night to all and write often to

Your aff son
Charlie.

71

White Oak Church Virginia Wednesday December 10th 1862

Dear Mary,

I received your welcome letter yesterday the one of Dec 4th. I have written one letter since we arrived at this miserable camp to Mother. I have been sick ever since we have been here and have been off duty and under the doctors care although I have been around every day for there is no difference between out of doors and in the house. I don't get any better and if the Regiment marches shall not probably go with them. it was brought on by a hard wet and cold march to this place, with nothing but hard crackers and water to eat and now we have succeeded in getting some potatoes, Mutton Buckwheat Onions and chicken

and Indian Meal and have first rate Johnnie Cake +c. I cannot eat any of them but have to subsist on miserable gruel from the Hospital. this winter campaign is filled with horrors. night before last a man died in our Hospital and day before yesterday a man in the 37th was left behind because he could not keep up as he was sick was brought in murdered and his money taken. the same day a man was killed in the 36th NY by a tree felled upon him, and all the live ones are freezing to death.

Yesterday afternoon we had orders to be ready to march this morning with 20 Extra rounds of ammunition but the order did not come and as it is now past the middle of the afternoon I do not think we shall go to day. this was a dense pine woods when we came here last Friday but it is all burnt up and we have not any wood to burn, and there is no end to our miseries. I have been dosed with Opium Quinine and Morphine + Caster Oil until I have no sense of taste or smell. if the Regiment should march before I get well I am to ride in an ambulance. Lieut Shurtleff has been commissioned a Captain and he has promised to use his influence to get the berth for me but I don't know whether he can or not. I should like it very well, but I don't know much about a horse, but I should like the riding part and I should not have to carry my blankets on my back but it is an office of as much danger and perhaps than any other as far as living is concerned. I should have first rate times if I might eat anything as we have Buckwheat Cakes and baked potatoes, and Johnnie Cake. I wish you could send me a box by Express with some 20 lbs of good butter. I think I can get it now. direct it to Newtons Division, Franklins Corps Washington DC. Please start it along as soon as you get this and let me know by mail when you send it send me the bill and I will send the money on as soon as I get it and I wish you could go to D E Cook and ask him to send me a silver watch by mail, a patent lever or something of that kind worth about $10.00 I want it sure to keep good time and be a good looking watch one that I can sell if I want to, and to send the bill with it and I will send the money for it. I sold the one I had for $15.00 it cost me $3.50. if Tom is in you might ask him to select it. I have not received any letter since I sent the money please write as soon as you get it. I sent it to Washington by our sutler and he has not made his appearance back again since.

It is said that troops have been crossing the river since yesterday, and it is thought that the Rebels have retired farther from the river and entrenched themselves but I do not know anything about the truth of it, we also have a rumor that Gen Peck has taken Petersburgh but we get no papers and consequently do not know what is going on off of this hill. We thought last night that there was surely going to be a battle to day but we hear no sound indicative of any such thing to day. We are four miles from Potomac Creek and vessels come up there with supplies but they are frozen in solid together with a lot of Barges. the snow that fell the day we came here about two inches deep, has not melted a

particle but lays on the ground just as it fell, that is what we used to call pretty cold whether when I was home at the North. We had a recruit from Northampton to day for Company C we could not but laugh at the idea of having one man. he had no tent and we can get none for him. at least not for a month and he is an Irish man while all our boys are Yankees and nobody wanted him to bunk with them. we had rather not have anybody for it don't pay to spend our time drilling one recruit. his name is Dennis Shea. Cal K is well and sends love. Most of the boys are quite well except myself. I don't know whether I shall be able to stand a winter campaign or not. if not I don't know how I shall get away.[9] if I was a Lieut Col I suppose it would be different I think the eyes of the whole Regiment will be ruined this winter with the smoke of the fires. lots of men cannot shut thier eyes for hours after they go to bed they ache so from the effects of the smoke.

Nothing is heard in the case of the Officers under arrest and it begins to look as though there never would be. We should have to move from here by tomorrow at any rate for we shall have no wood at all and without great fires we cannot exist. it is colder than it is at the North very much, and the weather is altogether out of character for the sunny South. I have heard that a letter has been published in the S Republican from Mr Birnie that the 10th is entirely demoralized, which is a diabolical lie. The Regt was never under better discipline in the world but this was probably written under the inspiration of the talk of the Officers under arrest who are most of them from Springfield and vicinity and probably in thier eyes it is demoralized but many of them were the most inefficient Officers we had, and Keith is a sample of a notorious coward and a hog at that, to be sure we have got a Major that don't know putty but every one knows that Capt Lombard showed the white feather at Fair Oaks and was never in any other battle, and Newell went off the field with Col Briggs and was seen no more that day and there were no Captains there at the last rally but Miller + Smart and Smart was killed. Most of the Companies were commanded by 2nd Lieuts.

Col Eustis is a nice man, and understands his business I do not think of anything more to write of interest I suppose if we have a battle within a few days I shall not be there but I suppose I shall be called a coward[10] and never hear the last of it but the doctor says it is no use for me to think of marching with the Regiment if they go soon and in fact I know I could not keep up with them.

Give my love to Mat and Thomas and much to Mother and don't forget to send the things by Express, and you can put in anything else you please. Give my respects to all and write often to

Your aff brother
Charlie.

72

White Oak Church VA Monday Dec 15th 1862

Dear Mary,

I received your welcome letter yesterday informing me of my new dignity of which I do not know what to say and consequently I can say nothing only I hope the new Grandmothers Aunt + Cousins will be able to bear thier new responsibilities with becoming composure. I wrote my last letter from a camp 3 miles from here and the next morning at 5 o'clock our Regiment took up its line of march together with the rest of Franklins Corp I was very sick and feeble with an attack of diarrhea and the night before Dr Chamberlin told me he should get me into an ambulance. the next morning he said there positive orders that no one should go in the Ambulances and I should either have to keep along with the teams or report to the general hospital which was a log house on the road, and he added the comforting assurance that if I went then I should have to sleep out of doors as it was already full. I felt as if I should give up, I did not care what became of me.[11] Well the Regiment moved off and left me sitting there in the dark on my valise, and when the Hospital Wagon started I started with it but as we passed a sutler of my acquaintance he said he should not move for a day or two and I could stay with him so I stopped with him but in a little while he had orders to pack up move on and park his wagon with the rest of the teams, and he carried my bundle of blankets on his team, and so I managed to get to this place where our Division Wagons are, and where the arrested Officers are camped and have been here ever since.

I never felt so mean in my life for the day they left camp our Brigade crossed the River and staid over that night and kept the advance there has been constant cannonading and musketry ever since, and I am lying within the sound of it. I have started twice to go up but as soon as I move the griping pains in my bowels come on again, though I feel pretty well when I keep still. they have been fighting now four days with no particular advantage on our side. the rebels are very strongly entrenched on a range of hills back of Fredericksburgh and our forces are on a large plain before them. they have attempted several times to storm the Rebels Batteries but have been repulsed. our Regt and Brigade led the advance in crossing but have not been actively engaged and up to last night there were only two men wounded in our Regt and one killed in the 37th and two or three wounded in the 2nd RI. it was expected that there would be desparate fighting to day but up to this time about 11 o'clock the firing has not been as heavy as it was either of the last three days. a report has just come in that the Rebels are falling back in the centre rapidly, and we had a report last night that Heintzletman crossed at King Georges Court House some distance down the river with 60,000 men but I do not know whether it is true or not. the Rebels

have got great quantities of Artillery here and we have got great quantities more than they have and I can tell you the sound of guns is terrific. the battlefield is about 5 miles from here and the Officers who are camped here go up every day to look on as they say you can see the whole field from hill this side but I have not been able to get up there it was just my luck to be taken sick just as I had got command of a company. Our side have taken a good many prisoners and we have had a good many killed and wounded but I do not know how many. it bids fare to be the most terrible battle of this or any other war and apparently is not hardly begun yet.[12] it is said that there is hardly a house in Fredericksburgh but what is riddled with shot and shell. Church steeples knocked off and every thing else. our forces shelled it first and when we got possession the Rebels shelled it from thier batteries on the hills beyond. it is reported that Lee says he will either aniahiliate our Army or his own but if Old Burnsides is only equal to the occasion I think it will be his own.

meanwhile I lie here like a skulking coward and hear the din of battle but cannot get there it is too bad. I don't think Dr C knows anything first he dosed me Opium and Quinine until I did not know anything hardly and then he gave me Castor Oil and Turpentine and then Morphine and then some powders of all the drugs in the world combined.[13] I don't know as I shall ever get well, and if I do not pretty soon I shall resign and come home for it is of no use for me to try to stay here and be good for nothing. I had hoped to be able to stick it through and see the end of this confounded war, but this winter campaign is too much for me. I am afraid I have got reduced to one pair of drawers, and I cannot get any here there is only one sutler has got any here and he asks $2.50 a pair for drawers not so good as I bought for 83 cts at home. I wish you would get me two pairs of heavy blue mixed wool drawers size 36 and send them by mail. Get someone to do them up in strong paper and leave the ends open and they will come for newspaper postage. I guess you can get them at Kellogs. I should like to have them ribbed. I don't care what the price is I want you to get the best you can get and I will send on the money for them.

Merritt Clark had some when I was at home that were just the thing and if he has got them now I would like some of that kind his were $2.50 a pair and were worth it. Please don't delay but send them immediately for I cannot change until they come. you did not say anything about the money I sent on so conclude you have not received it please let me know as soon as you do. there is no trouble about sending the drawers by mail as boots and shoes and all sorts of things come by mail they should be well tied up with twine before the paper is put round.

We have not seen anything of Col Parsons yet though it is time for him to be here if he is coming I should think. if he has not started when this gets there you may tell him not to mind the axe as we have got one now and do not need it. Oh dear! How I wish I was at home. I was never been so homesick in my life as I

have been since I have been lying here. I had to come a few rods and then lie down and rest a while then get up and move on a few rods further, and rest again. it was tough I tell you and I thought if I could only get home I would let the Grand Army of the Union and everything else go to the dogs.[14] I don't know but I shall try to get to the front to day but it is doubtful. the musketry have just broken on afresh and is very hot and fierce again. I wish I could write you something definite about it but I cannot. it is said that all the Generals were opposed to crossing the river in the face of such a force in such a strong position but I presume that is not true, but I guess we have got our hands full but it does seem as though with all the men and means we might whip them now if ever. I hope that Gen Banks is coming up the James River to menace Richmond but it seems he has gone further South. I don't see the point of sending him way off to Texas when we can't get Virginia close to our own doors, but I suppose the wiseacres know best. The weather just now is beautiful, warm and bright but it looks and feels like rain to day I hope it won't rain for the roads are in terrible condition now and the rain would make them impassable.

I am afraid the boys are suffering over the river as no wagons have crossed yet though they carry rations to the Bridges and from there they are carried by hand, a pretty slow way to feed such a vast army I should think. in addition to thier other troubles they are allowed no fires and they are lying close to the enemy and the musketry firing breaks out at all hours of the night and must disturb thier rest greatly. I know just how it is for I have been through it all before. we have seen no Papers since the 9th and consequently I presume you know more at the North about the fight than we do here within five miles of it. I sympathize with you deeply in your troubles at housekeeping but I presume the Grandmother has got back now and put things to rights though I suppose much of her time will have to be given to the important arrival at Haydenville. Give my love to the young matron and to my little niece tell her (the mother I mean) that it will be just old enough to play with when its *uncle* returns from the wars if he serves his time out, which will be half out in six days from to day.

The arrested Officers with whom I am encamped are expecting thier discharges every day now. three of them have been notified of thiers already but the papers to enable them to go home have not arrived there are twelve of them Capts Platt (Pittsfield) Pierce (Greenfield) Newell (Holyoke) Traver of (North Adams) 1st Lieuts Remington Putnam + Bennett. 2nd Lieuts Moore Hagar Knox + Crane. Lieut Putnam has not had his trial yet he is the one whose place I was put in and was arrested for disobediance of orders. I suppose I shall get a Captaincy if my health has not failed me and I should prefer it to being Adjt because it is higher rank and more pay. I hear that Col Decker did not go out as Adjt of the 52nd after all. How and why was that did not he think he could have opportunity enough to display his desparate valor, or what was the matter.

Give my love to Mother Matt + Thomas and *the baby*, and write me often and tell me how madam and the child get along. Give my respects to all the neighbors. I shall leave the letter open as I do not know when I can send it and perhaps I may have some good news to write before night.

Very aff your brother,
Charlie.

73

Camp near White Oak Church VA December 23rd 1862

Dear Mother,

I wrote you last while the late terrible battle of Fredericksburgh was going on. I think it was last Thursday, and I should have written before this again but I have been quite busy and I did not get any letters from home either which required a due degree of proper resentment. I joined the Regiment last Friday the day after they recrossed the river, found and congratulated themselves highly about having escaped from a terrible trap and I have no doubt if they had staid there 12 hours longer there would have been very few left to tell the tale of the fate of the Grand Army of the Potomac, and the only reason they escaped was the Rebels waited in hopes they would get more artillery and the wagon trains over in which they were disappointed. The glorious old 10th was the first regt of the left grand Division to cross the river and form in line of battle, and was the last to come back. they covered the retreat, and by both operations they excited the admiration of all the Generals who witnessed it, and gained themselves great credit.

Well the individual who is writing to you is the Adjutant of the 10th Reg Mass Vols.[15] it is not a position of my own seeking, but was conferred upon me without solicitation, the day before Col Parsons arrived so I do not owe it in any way to him or anyone else, but the Col told Col Parsons shortly after he arrived that I was the best Officer in the line which coming from a West Point Officer of 23 years standing and many years of active service in the field, I consider as about the tallest compliment I ever received in my life, especially as it was not told to get to my ears. Our Colonel is a man of the first quality and excited the admiration of the Regt and gained thier entire confidence in the 4 days that they lay under fire before the enemys guns at Fredericksburgh, and as for him he says that "since that experience he has the most implicit confidence in the regt and feels that they will go anywhere he has a mind to lead them". he says that he would not exchange it for any Regiment in the service. But he has been most

outrageously abused by one Birnie who came out here about Thanksgiving, and spent some 15 minutes or half an hour with the Regiment, and some two or three days with the 37th when, and from whose jealousy, he got his head filled with stories about the 10th and thier Col and went home and spread them broadcast and got Judge R A Chapman, J E L King + D L Harris to write letters to the Governor representing him as a most detestable tyrant, and many other things equally outrageous, indeed they hit at the *Lieut Col* and then stated that there is not an Officer in the line whom the men had any choice in electing, or whom they had any confidence in, and went on to state that the Regiment was totally demoralized and praying that some superior power would displace the Col + Lieut Col and appoint someone who would take an interest in the Regiment, and bring it up as it was not fit to go to battle and of no use in its present state. The Governor enclosed copies of the aforesaid letter and sends them to Col Eustis and wants an explanation also to Brigadere Gen Devens requesting a full statement from him in regard to the matter.

meanwhile while these scurlilious letters were on the way here, the Brigade of which the aforesaid demoralized regt comes apart, marched with the rest of the Grand Army to the South upon Fredericksburgh is selected for advance in crossing the river in face of the enemy, and selected to cover the retreat and remain upon the other bank until the whole Army recrossed Pickets Artillery and all, and until the Bridges were all ready to throw off. Then they follow on in perfect order the last to leave, without panic, confusion or fear the Bridges are cast loose. They take them up and the left Grand Division is safe and sound on this side of the River of death as our enemys meant it to be. After all this the gallant regiment goes into camp to find all these diabolical lies awaiting them from home. the Colonel felt terribly about it, but I guess when the reply of the General and Col Eustis replied and the correspondence is published I reckon Mr Birnie will hide his diminished head. I have seen the whole correspondence and Gen Devens praised and sets up this Regiment as they never were praised before.

In regard to myself I am in a quandary. tomorrow I can be recommended for a Captaincy as the list of promotions goes forward tomorrow and the Col tells me he should recommend me above some others whose commissions are older than mine he says to me very impressively, "I want you to consider the matter thoroghly, whether you had not better remain as Adjutant" he says "I will not advise you at all and I shall give you the Captaincy if you want it". but I don't want to consider the matter thoroughly. Well I don't know what to do I am sure if I take the Captaincy it is a higher rank now and a little bigger pay and probably as high as I should get in this war if I live through it. on the other hand rumor says that Col Eustis cannot fail of being a Brig General some day. in that if I should stay here and continue to merit his good opinion I should stand a good chance of being Captain Chief of Staff AAG ADC +c +c in other words a staff

Officer and probably Assistant Adjutant General with the rank and pay of Captain at that. I am sure I do not know what to do, but I rather lean to the Adjutant side of the question. I know the Col wants me to very much so does Col Parsons but I have no horse, and I do not feel as though I could buy one, I am not much of a rider anyway. then you know the old proverb of a bird in the hand +c but then again, I have no guard duty to perform except when the Regt goes in a body on Picket and none of any consequence even then. And I have no drilling to do except when the whole Regt Drills, nor any responsibility of men, clothing equipments +c, then it is pleasant to be at Headquarters so on the whole you need not be surprised if my next informs you that I remained the Adjutant, though I suppose no one at home will believe that I could have been a Captain.

I never saw a man I have more confidence in, or whom I liked better as a superior Officer than Col Eustis,[16] he is a perfect gentleman every inch of him, but he intends to have it understood that he is the *Col* and that is what I like in him. he cannot be wooled nor fooled nor persuaded away from his own opinions and if a man really merits anything he will get it as soon as opportunity offers and if he don't merit he won't get it, and that is the end of it.

Well Col Joe has arrived at last, and oh if you could see the comfort and the satisfaction taken in the good things sent you would feel more than paid and if you could ever see Capt W, myself and Col Joe Sergt Munyan Whitney + Brown seated on the frozen ground round a cracker box, and packing away that chicken pie warmed over it would have done you more good than to have eat it at home. I received your letter of 19th this morning and was mighty glad to get it for seems an age since I have received one. You did not say anything about my letters, in regard to the watch, the butter, or the drawers so I suppose you have not received them, perhaps it would be better to have my gold watch put in order and sent it out the drawers I am terribly in need of and hope you will leave no time in sending them to me by mail as I directed before. I shall write to the young matron at Haydenville before long. I am very happy to hear that they are doing so well, and I should like very much to see the baby, my little neice, but that cannot be a present I suppose. I have got entirely well of my diarrhea and am tough and hardy again, but I suppose it is liable to seize me again at any moment, but I hope not again when there is a battle in prospect, for it lays me open to the imputation of cowardice, which I do not relish at all, although I don't claim to be very brave.

The Officers who were under arrest have been discharged or cashiered all but two of them, one of whose papers have not come and the other has not been tried. I see by Marys letter that you have received the money, but I am afraid you did not have enough to do you much good. you need not have paid D Kingsley if you want the money you could just as well wait until next pay day I am afraid you

will need more before that comes. don't hesitate to write me if you want money and if I have it and if not I will give you a draft on the State House, so you can get anything there and have it charged to me. Mary says you need a dress and if you do I want you to go and get it I reckon my credit is good for either at Kelloggs or S + Lincolns and I want you should have anything you want. It is Wednesday morning and I wish you a Merry Christmas for tomorrow. Bishop is still in Alexandria and anxious to get here. he will probably get further promotion now though he came very near to losing on account of being away although he cannot help himself but the Col says he is going to promote the men who remain with the Regiment and not men who are off. I and Col Parsons made very strong representations and I think he will be 1st Lieut and he would have got a Captaincy if he had only been here for he is the man to suit the Col and in that case his promotion would have been certain. I am terribly sorry that he should be away now we have a Col that can see merit when it exists and will reward it, but the Col is going to apply to Major Gen Burnside to have him ordered back, so I suppose he will be with us before long, now that we are to have a full sett of Officers we shall once more be all right, and the demoralized 10th will yet show that if she is demoralized it would be better for the cause it would be better for the country if she had more of such demoralized regiments.

The Col is one of the best educated men in the United States, and it is worth everything to sit down and hear him talk. it is both amusing and instructive and it is nothing but what he knows, and can give you information on any subject that comes up.

Meantime we are expecting to give these Rebels over the river another turn one of these days, and when the next battle comes off you can look out for a list of killed and wounded that will pull anything heretofore entirely in the shade. I must finish now for it is time for the mail to close give my love to Matt, Thomas plus my neice and to Mary respects to all the neighbors. Cal K is well and more than happy over the contents of the trunk He is now a Corporal I had the pleasure of reading the order for his promotion at dress parade last night.

Thank Mary Fill a hundred times for the walnuts. She knew just what I wanted. I don't know how often this winter I have thought and said I wish I had some walnuts. Major Parker is an old maid in Pantloons, and as big a numbskull on military as ever. But thank the Lord we shall have no more of his attempts to drill now that Col Parsons has got back. Col Parsons rode out to take the Regiment after all had formed the line, and his horse took flight at the colors and threw him off before you could say Jack Robinson.

Now please write me often, and tell Matt and Mary I shall write to them soon. With fingers almost frozen I remain

Your aff son
Charlie.

74

Head Quarters 10th Mass Vols Camp near Falmouth VA Dec 31st 1862

Dear Mary

I received your welcome letter in blue ink from Haydenville and hasten to answer it although I have not much news to write. it is New Years Eve and I wish you all a "Happy New Year" as to myself I am particularly happy tonight, for I have had the pleasure of reading on parade tonight the appointments of Bishop to the Captaincy of Co I Brown to be 1st Lieut of Co K Whitney to be 1st Lieut of Co C and Munyan to be 1st Lieut of Co H and it does me a world of good to have these good and true fellows get thier shoulder straps. they have waited long enough and carried knapsack and gun through thick and thin for a longer time than any of us supposed we would have to stay when we took the oath for 3 years service, but alas the end seems more distant now than it did then.

We are under marching orders as it were and all things point to another crossing of the Rappahanock. we are ordered to be ready at 12 hours notice with 3 days cooked rations and haversacks and 6–8 days light rations and wagons and to keep a 10 days supply of beef cattle on hand. I know that the Engineers have explored a new place for crossing and that Burnside says he will not hold the command of this Army to go into winter quarters. Whether the new place is any more favorable for again crossing I do not know, but it looks to me like a desparate effort, in the dark, to retrieve his fortunes by one who does not know what he is about, and I think the first idea of its feasibility or otherwise that Burnside will get will be when he sees his shattered army drowning in the Rappahanock where triumphantly driving the enemy before them. I don't think he has any definite idea of what he is going to do, but is going to trust his luck and hope for the best, but it is a fearful thing to contemplate a defeat and a rout of this great Army with the river behind them and only the narrow pontoon bridges for escape.[17] it will be the total anihilation of this Army, and the Rebs will not be so sparing of us another time. they will not be disposed to wait for us all to get over, but will let us have it without stint still if the Army does as well as it did the other day that we should force the greybacks out of thier holes, but it will be such a terrible loss of life as has not been seen yet in this war, and I hope that all praying friends in the cause will give thier most earnest prayers that we may not be defeated for that is destruction.

Meantime the weather has set in cold and stormy and may interrupt human calculations, and moreover the Rebels have been flourishing round with one of thier scarecrow raids in our rear, and frightened the timid old granny's in Washington so we may have to dust back to protect that sink of iniquity and the thieves and robbers therein contained, who fatten upon thier countrys woes. I wish Stuart or Stonewall would make a raid in there and carry off some of the political scallawags who are engaged in making a bad matter worse. I have

almost lost all faith in a republican form of government. I who have worked with all my little might to rout a corrupt party in the firm belief that when the republicans got the power they would right these matters and correct existing abuses, and it is only to find that we have routed one set of blood sucking rascals to put into power another set just as bad and 10 times more ravenous, but so it is, honest men won't descend to the little meannesses necessary to get office, and if they won't they cannot get them and so the government falls into the worst hands, but it does not become me a poor first Luff to enter into these matters, for I can do nothing, and I fancy my little sister (although arrived at the great dignity of Aunt) wonders what her brother is bothering her head with all this for, but I can honestly say that I came out to fight for what I believed in, and still believe in, but see no way of accomplishing, but as for voting for anybody in that hope I never shall believe that any man up for office is anything but a scamp, but enough of this.[18]

You must keep your eyes open for a correspondence which will be published probably in the Republican. you know the rumors which have been circulated to our discredit at home and to the disparagement of Col Eustis. well you must know that the matter was brought to the attention of the Gov and he wrote to Gen Devens + Col Eustis both and tonight a very flattering reply has been received with the Governors Autograph, in which he says the correspondence is to be published and if you want to feel still more proud of your brothers Regt you must read that correspondence then write me what you think about it. I have seen the whole of it and it is all true, and it compliments this Regt as I never saw any other complimented and as Generals very seldom do compliment I presume it is published before this and you must be sure and send me the paper when it comes out.

The mail has just come in but brings me no letters from home as usual but it brought me one from Capt Bliss from Ship Island where the 52nd has just arrived. he writes in first rate spirit says "these new recruits think they have a terrible times, but he tells them they do not know what it is to suffer" and no one can tell them better than he, but he said that they are satisfied that they are in the nine months service instead of the three years and I guess they be. the Illinois was the first to arrive, but they did [not] know when he wrote whether destination was Texas or Mobile and were about equally divided in opinion. I was mighty glad to hear from the old fellow and mighty glad that he got so good a place, even at the 11th hour.

My health continues to be first rate and providence permitting it to remain so I shall probably ride a horse into the next battle. I have got a very safe and steady nag the property of Col Parsons a real veteran of the war, she cannot be started out of her propriety by any amount of music, noise of shot + shell or flaunting of colors. she looks upon these things with the indifference of an old soldier.

I was very much shocked to hear of poor Seth Clarks misfortune. he has been badly treated in not getting promotions. I had not heard of it until I got your letter for we got no papers with the list of killed and wounded.

I have not received the watch yet don't know as you have sent it. Willie Robinson (Capt) was here two or three days ago, and told me that Cousin Olive was in S and going to Northampton. Give my love to her if she is there when this arrives. Willie was looking first rate. Cousin George is all right and gets the Captaincy of Co F in the new order of things.

I don't know but I shall be sorry I did not take a Captaincy but I guess not at any rate I am not yet. I enjoyed the letter Mattie sent very much and am anxiously expecting the box.

Another Autographed letter has just arrived from the Governor in which he praises the 10th up to the skies, in fact he spread it on thick but no more than I believe it deserves, for there is no better in the service nor any Regiment that has a better Col. I like him better and better every day but I presume his Officers who have been dismissed and cashiered, will endeavor to defame him when they get home still you may rest assured that the Regiment Officers and men have every confidence in him, but as for myself I think that as an Officer, Soldier or Gentleman this Regiment never saw his equal. Col Briggs could not hold a candle to him, and he has no political interest to serve. Came out for pure patriotism, and left a salary of three thousand dollars a year for less than two thousand, which is proof enough of the fact. his father was a General of fame in the service before him.

You must be careful what you show and what you quote of my letters, as it all comes back to the Regiment. I had a letter shown me the other day wherein it said "Charlie Brewster writes that the soldiers curse the government the Stars + Stripes +C+C" which was all true at the time and probably will be again when we come to some particularly hard service, but these same soldiers will fight like bull dogs when it comes to the scratch, and it is a soldiers privilege to grumble, none grumble worse than the old soldier yet none are relied upon more. but it is not pleasant to have these sayings come back to a fellow when he is in a satisfied mood, as this Regiment is now, in fact I don't think it was ever more pleased and proud of itself than at this moment, and I hope this pride will not meet its fall in the coming battle. I think it is an honest and excusable pride, and not the kind "that goes before a fall".[19]

I have made a long letter out of small material but I hope you will find enough of interest in it to make it readable. We have been mustered for pay to day and I hope it will not be two months before we get our pay this time but I should not wonder if it was for they seem to consider it a small matter whether the soldiers get thier pay promptly or not. if the feeding contractors got thier pay. I wish they would give up a few of these robbers to the tender mercies of the soldiers.

Well it is after Tattoo and mighty cold both for the toes and fingers while you tumble into a warm bed I must roll myself in my blanket and sleep as soundly upon the bosom of Mother Earth, my sleeping arrangements are similar to Camp Brightwood, in one respect as I double (as we call it) with the Lieut Col as I did when he was Captain and I was Orderly of Company C. Poor old Company what with discharges plus promotions, it is dwindling down to a mighty small thing and appears in line with only 11 or 12 files, when we used to bring out from 36 to 40 a year ago, and at the past rate it cannot last a year and a half longer. Well I must bid you good night. give my love and "a Happy New Year" to Mother, Matt Thomas + *Mary Kate,* by the way what a pity my name could not be got in then. My respects to all the neighbors and my friends with lots of love for yourself

Your aff brother
Charlie

PS Remember me kindly to Uncle Edward + Nellie. tell him I do not think I make as good an appearance on a horse as they say he used to. Cal K is well and I hope he gets to be Sergt in the new arrangement of things, but you know I have nothing to do with the arrangement of any of those things in Co C now, but I shall put in a plea for him with Capt W and I think it may have influence. Give my respects to Mrs K + Bill, tell Bill I would like a pitcher of cider if he can spare it, and a couple of Baldwins So once more good night.

Charlie

75

Head Quarters 10th Mass Vols camped near Falmouth and not very near Richmond VA January 10th 1863

Dear Parry,

I received your most welcome letter night before last and was very glad to hear from home once more. It is a terrible cold, stormy, dreary, miserable night such as one makes you all at home huddle round the fire, and bless God that you have a roof over your head, and all the comfort of a home. Our Regiment is out on Picket on the banks of the Rappahanock most of them without shelter, as they did not many of them take thier D'Aubre's and I pity them most heartily. They are under command of Lieut Col Parsons but the Col (Eustis) is on a board of examination and does not go out so he keeps his Adjutant with him, which accounts for the fact that I am in camp under my tent or before the blazing fire in

our fireplace. I never was so satisfied with my decision to remain Adjt as I am tonight. the Regt went out yesterday for a 3 days tour and do not return until Monday AM and it looks now as though the storm would last as long as that though I hope it will not. I went out with them yesterday, and have been out to carry the mail to them to day. they are posted on the very bank of the river in plain sight of the Rebs on the other bank so near that you can almost hear common conversation. I went down to the very edge of the river which is about $^2/_3$ as wide as the Conn at the ferry. I could see them as plain as day, and hear them laugh and talk but I could not quite make out what they said, I did not care to stay very long for although they have agreed not to fire at each other I did not know but some scallawag of a Reb might take it into his head that it would be a good thing to kill an Officer, and so blaze away at me, and as I was not much more than good pistol shot distant I came away when I had seen what there was to see. they are very friendly though and say they wish the privates of the two armies could settle this thing. it would be done up in short time. last night some of our boys went over and exchanged some Coffee for Tobacco, after they returned an Officer of the Rebs visited thier Picket and when he had gone, they told our boys not to come over again as thier Officer had been there and they should have to take them prisoners if they did. that was kind was it not.

There was a Georgia Regt on Picket on thier side yesterday and a Texas Regt to day. It is reported that the Rebs are moving off part of thier troops to day but I do not know whether it is so or not. It looks as though the rainy season had set in and if it has it must put an end to our performances for a while. it rains in perfect torrents.

I must run out to the fire and warm me a little then I will come back and write some more. Our Quartermaster has just returned from the landing at Acquia Creek where he has been for some Express Matter for this Regt but says there is no box for me, so I conclude you have not sent any. You speak very complacently of "while that butter Matt sent lasted" you must know that there are four men in my mess, and anything we have is share and share alike and that butter Matt sent lasted just two days. I sent for the other merely as a matter of economy for we have to pay 60 cts per lb for butter, 30 cts for cheese, 5 cts each for Apples, $2.50 for a bushel for Potatoes, +c+c, and I thought if I had as much as 20 lbs sent it would cost less than to buy it here. You speak of my horse I have not bought one yet though I am thinking of buying Mr Jamiesons (the RI Chaplains) as he is going home. I am using one of Maj Parkers whose name is Tommie and he is a very knowing animal though somewhat lively with his heels. I sent a picture in mine of yesterday. It is mighty pleasant when I want to go anywhere to sing out "saddle my horse" then jump on an gallop off. Wish you could be here to ride with me, and see the sights. I would take you down to the river and give you a look at some live Rebs. there are some Generals wives out here, but I don't think

you would relish sleeping in a tent with Col Parsons and myself, and I cannot have as many tents as a General, though I don't know why I do not need as many. Please send Aunt Lu's letter if you get one. I don't see what she can be doing in Cumberland for that is in Maryland. If you ever neglect to write to me because you have interesting young men or disinteresting young men calling on you I will pull your ears sharply when I get hold of you. I don't by any means acknowledge you get as much on a small sheet as I do on a large. I deny it most emphatically. The flannel Drawers were all right. I found that they could not come for newspaper postage so thats all right too. you can direct to Adjustant if you want to, only remember that the title Adjt comes after the name thus Lieut C H Brewster, Adjt 10th Mass Vols. Capt Ws folks have sent him a big box so I shall get my share of that.

I have sent Merritt Clark the pay for those Drawers and postage. I hope we shall get paid soon as I am getting short again. I do wish they would pay us our money when it is due, and then we could make some calculations for the future but we never know whether it will be two months or six before we are paid.

Give my love to Mother Mat Thomas + Mary Kate, Uncle Edward + Nell My respects to all Cal K is well and sends his regards. Tell Uncle Ed of course I feel big to get on a horse and am getting so I can jump ditches and fences on his back. It is most time for the mail but I dread to have it come for I am afraid I shant get any letters and then I shall go to bed blue. I think that will do as I wrote you a long letter yesterday. Let me know as soon as you get the pictures.

With much love, Your aff brother,
Charlie.

The mail has come and no letter for me Oh dear!

76

Head Quarters 10th Mass Vols Feby 12th 1863

Dear Mary,

I received your welcome letter mailed Feby 8th last night, and was very glad to get it, but very much surprised that you do not get my letters, though I don't know as I ought to be, as the mails are good for nothing anyway. Mother says you have not received but one since I received your box. I think this must be as many as six I have written since Mr Childs was here, and what has become of them I am sure I do not know. it seems as though I wrote almost every day. You speak of my coming home which would be an impossibility unless the government pays us off which I don't know as they ever will do again. we have almost 4 months

due us now and I don't see any signs of any pay. we did think two weeks ago that we were going to be paid but the Paymaster who we supposed was going to pay us did not make his appearance and when there will be another one along no body knows. besides I hardly think it would pay to come home for just 10 days which is the most I could get and it would consume 4 of that going and coming, and cost from 30 to 50 dollars.

Col Eustis, Lieut Col P, Major P and myself dined with Gen Devens last night, or rather at 5 o'clock PM on special invitation. the dinner consisted first course of bean soup, 2nd Roast Turkey, desert custard pie. we had a very pleasant time came home about 8 o'clock last evening. I have enjoyed the high honor of being "Acting Assistant Adjutant General" for this Brigade for one day this week. it did not hurt me much. the Regular AAG was absent on leave. Gen D was commanding the Division, and Col Eustis the Brigade, so he detailed me as AAAG, but that night Col Brown of the 36th returned and being senior Col took command of the Brig, so I returned to the humble station of Adjut of the 10th. My health has not been a bit good for 10 days or a week. I have this horrible diarrhea all the time. I rode up to the Battery on the bluffs opposite Fredericksburgh with Col B this morning, and took a look over into Sesessia saw the Rebs playing ball on an open lot, quite green with grass, but the ride upset me so that I did not go out to Dress Parade to night, if I could get home for 30 days I should like to come.

You want to know what I think of Hooker I don't know much about him we can only wait and see what we shall see. I think when the roads get so that we can move the Army, we shall see fighting enough but with what result noone can tell.

I met Capt Burt of Gen Couchers Staff this morning. he says he goes over frequently with a flag of truce and that I can send a letter if I leave it unsealed, but I don't know as there is any evidence of whether Aunt Lu is within our lines, or the Rebels, and I think it very doubtful whether it would ever get to her or not, so I don't think I shall write but if you want to write I will get him to take it over. if you do, you must be careful what you write. write nothing political or anything that might be construed into information, as the letter will have to be read by the authorities on our side as well as the other. I don't think however that it is of any use, because it seems as if the fact that Aunt Lu was in Maryland, was conclusive evidence that they are within our lines and that being the case it would be of no use to send a letter over. I wrote a tremendous long letter to Mother about a week ago and at the same time sent back Aunt Lu's letters. I don't know as it is of any use to write this letter as I presume you will never get it. it is discouraging with all the rest of our hardships that we cannot have a mail regularly. I presume that Cal K will get a furlough if the others come back. this Regt is allowed 9 enlisted men and 2 line Officers to be gone at the same time but if any of those fail to come back why it takes just so many off and I presume many of them never will come back.

There are two Courts Martial in full blast in this Division trying deserters of which class they have apprehended from 2 to 300 and I sincerely hope they will shoot about one half of them. the bounty men of the new Regiment are much the worse in this respect. if the government had carried out the law and punished desertion by death in the beginning the U S Army would be larger by some 70,000 men to day. our Division has not near as many deserters as the other divisions in this Army. It is almost impossible to get back deserters who get home as the people there befriend them and look upon a man after deserters, as a sort of fugitive slave hunter, and they hide these faulters and resist the Officer +c +c so that it is nearly impossible to get them. I should like to be sent home after deserters and have the people attempt to mob me in the execution of the duty as they have some, and I should like to have a force of a dozen good muskets to back me if I would not give the good people one taste of war, and powder and balls then I am a lier thats all. I should like no better fun than to fire into a mob endeavoring to take a deserter away from me but I suppose it is worth while to pay one and two hundred dollars for men to come out here and then skeedaddle home again. if the people at home would hoot these cowards out of town and not allow them to live at home it would do some good.[20]

I am very sorry to hear that Mother has the Asthma again this winter but such weather as you are having is enough to give any one the Asthma and everything else. We are having just such weather out here one day it rains, the next it snows, the next is cold as Iceland and the next is hot as May, or June, and so we never know what to expect two hours in advance. I hoped to have some money to send home before this but have none now nor any postage stamps that is only two. we could not get the P O Stamps if we had money. I want half a dozen Gents Linen Hdkfs worth about 25 cts a piece but I don't know as you can pay the postage. mine are all worn out. It seems as though the great Banks Expedition bid fare to be a grand fizzle and I suppose if the government could raise 300,000 men they would have to be sent to Oregon or some other place as near outside of the world as they could get. Of course one must not say anything against the government but I guess it is about played out. I see a great deal in the papers about what Gen Hooker is doing +c and I suppose he is but we see nothing of it. but there we are one of the best behaved Divisions and don't require as much attention as some others. Give my love to Mother, Matt + Thomas and respects to all the neighbors. part of our Army is embarking at Acquia Crk and it may be that letters are detained on that account, but theres no need for the Rebs know all about it and thier Pickets frequently call to ours to know when the 9th Corps is going. I am tired and must go to bed, so good night, with much love

Your brother,
Charlie.

77

Head Quarters 10th Mass Vols Feby 21st 1863

Dear Mattie,

I received your very welcome letter last night and although to unwell to get up sat up in bed or rather in ground and read it. I have been down again with my regular complaint, but Dr. Chamberlain got here night before last and he gave me something that has made me feel better for the time being but how long it will last I do not know. I was under Dr Robinsons care for a few days and I guess if I had been obliged to remain under his care, I should not have needed anybodys a great while, but I am afraid as it is that I never shall get over the terrible diarrhea which hangs on to me all the time. I am glad you have got able to go about once more and I have a realizing idea of how you shock the dear grandmothers propriety by proposing to go and look at the dancers.

Dr Chamberlain brought me a letter from Mary and also my sash. The Army is still here stuck fast in the mud and we have no amusement nor excitement, and as if to fill up the measure of our miseries the government has stopped newspapers from coming.[21] I suppose they could not think of any other way to oppress us but to cut off our only comfort that we ever do have except letters from home and I expect they will stop those next. I wish you would send me the NY papers by mail and other papers as newspapers still come by mail, and if you have any novels that you have read I wish you would send them, as we have absolutely nothing to do and now I am sick and have to stay in my tent I almost perish for want of something to read. I don't see why you need to be skeered at staying in your house alone, especially as you have your *daughter* with you I should think she would be enough protection from the fearful perils of Haydenville. I should think now you have got to be the mother of a family you would pluck up more courage and be more like your own mother, who if my recollection serves me right has had very often to go on reconnaisances over the house to drive off thieves and robbers who were coming after her courageous daughter.

I am glad if they have finally started the deserter Kingsley out of Williamsburgh but he never will turn up here, at least I don't think he will. they ought to have arrested him and lodged him in jail and informed the nearest military authorities, Burke too ought to have been back before this, but he has more of an excuse and has at least shown good courage once, which the other one has never done.

I always burn my letters after I have read them so you need not be alarmed about yours. You are really getting to be a giantess, and Thomas will have to have the doors of the house widened I expect and get a four horse team to draw you round. Wonderful! 119 pounds. I think babys eyes must indeed be beautiful if they are "quite like mine". How did you find out that they were going to be

beautiful teeth when they come. You have petitioned for a long letter but evidently did not expect me to follow your example. if you want long letters you should set the example. I should think you followed the scripture maxim in yours that "a short answer turneth away wrath" is not that what it says, but you must know that it don't mean answers to my letters, for they have the contrary effect in that case, so you will please remember that when you write again and govern yourself accordingly.

The Principal excitement now is furloughs and one lot of nine men and two Officers have just gone to take the place of the same number who have just returned. If we ever get paid off and I don't get any better I think I shall apply for a sick leave shall hope to get more than 10 days. I don't think it would pay to come home for just 10 days though I want very much to see my neice, who I expect is altogether the most wonderful specimen of the human race that ever was produced, but don't let Barnum hear of her arrival or he might be after her. seriously though I want to see her ever so much, and I expect that her uncle is as proud of her as any one else. what does Charley Boland say to his new sister. My patriotic younger sister writes to me that she gave P W Kingsley the cold shoulder at the ball, and I am very glad of it but notwithstanding that it did not agree with Mothers views. if I had a brother and he acted as he has done, I'd kick him whenever I met him, and I am very proud of this exhibition of the young Ladies spirit, and I wish there was more of it at the North. it would start some of the skeedaddlers back.

They are suffering terribly with the Typhoid Fever in the 37th. 7 have died in ten days, four of them within 36 hours I don't know but they are all going to die. Lieut Loomis was down here today and said Capt Hayden was quite sick but I don't know as you had better tell his father and mother. that is all he told me except that he was out of his head last night and I am too unwell to go up and see him. I have got a Sergt Major from Haydenville his name is George F. Polly. he is now engaged in making up the bed. he was one of my eight at Fairoaks and is a very nice fellow. Cal Kingsley has got to be a Sergeant which I suppose will please his mamma. Cal is homesick now myself and Munyan have gone from the Company. he wants babying as much as ever, and the Army is a mighty poor place to get it in I can tell you. but you must not breathe a word of this where it will get to his folks but it is too bad that so brave a fellow could not be a little more of a man, and you know that he is not remarkable for soldierly appearance. The drums are rattling off the everlasting tattoo. shant I be glad if I ever get where drums wont sound in my ears all the while.

Don't forget about sending me something to read if you have got anything as I am suffering for something we read over old papers four or five times. Give my love to Thomas and Mother and Mary, my respects to all my friends in Haydenville.

They have built four large ovens to bake soft bread for the Brigade, but it seems as if they never would get to work I suppose they will sometime though.

It is about time for the mail and my tent begins to fill with Officers, who always have to come here about half an hour before and wait for it.

We have rumors that Gen Foster got into a squabble with Gen Hunter down at Charleston and operations are suspended, but I don't know whether it is so or not, but it would be very appropriate. I hope if it is so that they will take both of them and tie millstones round thier necks and cast them into the Atlantic Ocean to stop operations because two pairs of shoulder straps can't agree which is the biggest, but I must go to bed, so good night write often and L-O-N-G letters to

Your aff brother
Charlie.

78

Head Quarters 10th Mass Vols February 23rd 1863

Dear Mary,

I received your welcome letter and the sash by Dr. Chamberlain. We have just had the heaviest snowstorm we have had this winter and the snow lies on the ground a foot deep. I have not got well yet and eat nothing but gruel and medicine though I am some better. I went to George to find out what the medicine was that he says our Doctors have not got the ingredients and cannot put it up but he has sent to Edmund for some I sit up about half the day. my meals are brought from the Hospital Dr C wants me to [go] into the Hospital but I won't have to lie on the same bed with the men who are sick there and they are mighty apt to have bugs on them and I shant go there as long as I can help it. I asked Dr to day if he would give me a certificate of disability but he won't because they have to state that they believe the patient will die if he don't go home he said my case is not serious. I told him I did not know as it was but if I did not get well pretty soon I should go home for good.

I notice what you say about Elbrige. I don't who Col Greenleaf thinks he is, but if a General detailed a clerk from a regiment here and the Col here stopped it he would find himself in hot water directly but I guess there is not much military rule or disipline about those greenhorns down there. I did not like that Col Greenleaf at all when I saw him in Greenfield. Capt Bliss wrote his brother that an advance on Port Hudson was expected daily, and that *Adjutant Decker had got an attack of Rheumatism* I am afraid if there is any fighting his Rheumatism won't allow him to have a hand in it, notwithstanding the white washing they gave him

before he started but he had got a Quartermasters berth as he expected I don't think his Rheumatism would ever have troubled him though Quartermasters are as much exposed to Rheumatism as anyone but not as much exposed to bullets, but his seems to be a peculiar complaint, and exposure to the latter seems to bring on the former in his case.

Nine men and two Officers started off on furloughs last Friday. I think Cal will go in the next lot. he is now a Sergeant.

I entirely approve of your treatment of that mean scamp P W Kingsley and am glad you did not notice him at all. if everyone would that deserters so it would soon send some of the skeedaddlers back though I do not believe he ever will come back he will get into some hospital or other redezvous [rendezvous] for cowards and skulk there, but I am glad they would not let him lie at home. he lied about Bishop for he did not tell him he might go. he told that story at the time, and I proved it a lie at the time and he better not tell Bishop he told him so.

I wish you would send me some reading matter if you have any old novels lying around the house that I have not read or anything else. I am famishing for something to read while lying here all day long with nothing to do.

Dr Chamberlain brought a bundle from Mrs Eustis to her husband and in a pair of stockings which she knit for me just think of that, she wrote to the Col that she was very much pleased with me when I called on her and was glad he had made me his Adjutant.

The NY Times is now allowed to come to the Army but the herald is not, and I am glad of it for it is a treasonable paper anyway and ought to be supressed entirely. You did not say anything about Dr C-s calling on you, although he brought the letter I suppose it was all written when he came.

My horses name is Tommie and I wish you could ride him but I don't think you had better come out for this until we get into some more civilized country where there are more houses, for even if you could get along in a tent with three or four fellows I am afraid those cold feet of yours would suffer more than ever, and besides side saddles are a thing unknown here, and I don't think you would make a good appearance riding a McClellan or Grimsley saddle, for they require one leg each side.

Our Regiment is very healthy but the 37th are dying off at a great rate. 7 have died in 10 days and four of them within 36 hours. all the drs say that Physically it was the poorest Regiment they ever saw these men died of Typhoid Fever. we have none sick in the Hospital but 4 or 5 are there with lameness a sort of scurvy, land scurvy the Drs call it. it comes out in sores all over the body. Fred Hillman of Co C had it and was discharged and so did the former Sergt Major. We shall be mustered for pay in a few days but shall not be paid before the middle of March if we are then.

I should like to have been there to the ball I think it must have been grand

affair but it will probably be a long time before I go to another ball if I ever do. We had a rumor a few days ago that General Briggs was provost martial of Baltimore and was going to have this Regiment there to do Provost Duty but the wish was probably fathered to the thought. that would be too good luck to fall to the lot of the tenth regiment our regiments turn of service will be out in June. the 36th NY they were two years then, and they are happy fellows. I can tell you it is said an effort is to [be] made to induce them to reenlist, but they might as well make an effort to build a ladder to the moon. people don't know what they are talking about when they talk of reenlisting old soldiers. I know plenty of them that would give 10 years of thier life if they knew they had but 15 to live if they could get out of it. people at the north do not realize at all what soldiers life is, but maybe not talk foolishly but let them take a seat and go down into North-amptons meadows and make a habitation of it and see how they would enjoy it. a soldier has more misery in one day than occurs in a lifetime of a civilian ordinarily and thier greatest comforts would be miseries to people at home. I wonder Abner does not get discharged. I should think he could if he was here and sick so much. I should think Luke Lyman could get it for him but I suppose he is too much taken up with the great dignity of Commandant of the Port of Washington. Col Parsons had a letter from him and it was very full of I. Give my respects to Mrs Clarkes family and to Mrs. Kingsleys and all the neighbors please write more than once a week, for I write twice. I had a letter from Matt which I answered day before yesterday. Give my love to Mother, Matt Thomas and Mary Campbell, I think she would know me now if she should see me. Have the Legislature of Mass passed a bill to pay the soldiers yet. Col Parsons is well and thriving I frequently take a breakfast or dinner with him. George Bigelow is well he is getting fat and appears to be quite well now. I am tired and cannot write any more to night, and so good night, with much love

Your aff brother,
Charlie.

79

Head Quarters 10th Regt Mass Vols March 4th 1863

Dear Mother,

   Your welcome letter of Feby 26 came safely to hand and I should have answered it before this but I have not been able to sit up until to day long enough to write an answer, having had another attack of chills and fever accompaniaed or rather followed as usual by diarrhea. it is so easy to say come home for a month

but Oh! how hard it is to get there. 20 days is the most allowed in case, in the opinion of the Regtl Surgeon and the medical Corps director it is the only possible way to save a mans life, and besides that what is a poor soldier to do, who relies upon a bankrupt government for his pay which never comes and he has no money to come with, oh it is very easy to say come home but, to do it is quite a different thing. I suppose I might get a furlough of 10 days just time to go home and come back in but I have serious doubts of the benefits to arise from such a course to my health. Col Joe has no more power to help me get a furlough than you have.[22]

Cal Ks application for a furlough has gone forward to day, and will probably come back approved by tomorrow or day after so you may expect to see him this week or the first part of next. but I must enjoin upon you again not to inform his folks, as I presume you will do the first opportunity as I remember charging you not to once before and you remarked in your last letter that his folks are delighted with his coming home, so I conclude that immediately after reading my letter containing the aforementioned caution you immediately put the letter in your pocket and hurried up there and read every word of it to them as a matter of course as a woman would. Your letter was very short and I shall have to make mine to correspond. The day after I wrote you last the camps between here and Falmouth were all thrown into excitement by the performances of the balloons which had been up most all day and afternoon commenced to come this way and finally got directly over our heads, where it was found to be on a journey, and lots of following it hold a free long brown cords. It came down just beyond our camp, and after a while they raised it up just above the tops of the trees and towed it back again. there is a great deal of ballooning now adays and it looks as if something was going to happen. sometimes two balloons are up at the same time.

Our Rebel friend Stuart untook another cavalry raid the other day and got licked and got back the other side of the river minus 50 men and 2 Officers.

The mud is still unfathomable and it rains almost every other day, which will keep it so until the weather changes it is within 6 days of the time we started for Prospect Hill a year ago but operations cannot commence as early this year as they did last at least not in this region. It seems the Rebels are gobbling up our navy down at Vicksburgh about as fast as we can build it. it seems hardly a week since we had glowing accounts of how the Queen of the West and the Indianola ran the blockade of Pittsburgh and now they are both in the hands of the Rebels.[23] meantime two or three Rebel pirates clear the ocean of our merchant vessels by sending them to the bottom or burning them up and the government goes on building gun boats with Machinery that every scientific man says won't work and it don't. meantime the old Greybeard at the head of the Navy department sets and sleeps, and dreams that we have got a great powerful Navy,

to wake up some fine morning and find that some smart Rebel on a bale of cotton, has captured the whole of it. But I am too tired to write more and must go to bed. By the way I got a bottle of that medicine from Cousin Edmund by an Officer who had just returned from Springfield.

Please give my love to Mary Matt Thomas and the baby, and my respects to all the neighbors. you will think this is a short letter but it is much longer than yours. So good night with much love

Your aff son,
Charlie.

FIVE

We Gained Great Glory but at What a Sacrifice

April–September 1863
Chancellorsville and Gettysburg Campaigns

Brewster spent the summer of 1863 marching and fighting over great distances. His regiment suffered severe losses at the battle of Chancellorsville in May; he learned to face and endure battle, and, for a brief moment, convinced himself that he liked it. The forced march through Maryland to Gettysburg, as well as the aftermath of that decisive battle in Pennsylvania, left many unforgettable impressions. Somehow, the war had taken an important turn, but as a homesick veteran volunteer, Brewster felt disaffected from civilian life and contemptuous of all those who had stayed behind. He had seen the ghastly price of war and now wondered, if he lived, whether a society at peace would ever have a place for him.

80

In line of Battle opposite Fredericksburgh Thursday April 30th 1863

Dear Mother,

You see by the heading of this letter where I am, and probably wonder how I can be writing, but I do not know as I ever shall finish but thought I would at least commence a letter.[1] We had orders last Tuesday night to be ready to move at an early hour the next morning which we were, but it got to be one o'clock and no further orders came, and we concluded that we should not go that day, but at that hour the orders came to form the line at 3 o'clock which we did and picked up our line of march directly towards the river from our camp. the roads and fields swarming with columns of troops moving in the same direction, one of the most glorious sights I ever saw. the day was cloudy and it had rained hard all the morning, and the air was full of a dense mist or fog. we marched about a mile and

a half and bivouacked in the ravines with orders that no fires would be allowed, and to keep away from the brow of the hill, and out of sight of the Rebels. the next morning we started at an early hour and marched out into this place which is in plain sight of the Rebs and the place where we had Picketed all winter. meantime on the right part of our Corps had crossed in Boats (Brooks Division) and surprised the Rebels, drove them from thier rifle pits and laid three bridges. this was at about one o'clock yesterday (Wednesday) morning and our boys were pouring over when we came out onto the plain.

meantime Reynolds (the 1st Corps) met with more resistance on our left about a mile and a half from our Bridges, and the Artillery was firing briskly when we formed our line, but towards 10 o'clock we had the pleasure of seeing the Rebels on the dead run across the plain behind thier rifle pits, and the Engineers laid two bridges across at that point and troops were crossing there all day long. it is in plain sight from our position here, although about a mile and a half distant thus matters rested last night. We have 3 Corps here our own, Reynolds and Sickles, or the 1st 3rd + 6th nobody knows where the other 4 Corps of our army are but last night we heard heavy firing of Artillery on the right apparently very distant. We had a Thunder shower last evening, and it rained all night and is raining hard this morning. this morning orders came at 3 o'clock to be ready to move on in 3/4 of an hour so we got up in the rain and darkness and packed our traps but it is now after eight o'clock and we have not moved from our position yet and as we are waiting round I thought I would write you these few lines. we are expecting an order to go across every moment and the heights beyond the plain look very formidable, but God willing we are bound to have them this time or die in the attempt.

But how I wish you could see this glorious sight the plain is covered and black with men, and the heights back of us are black with men and the plains across the river on our right and left where the wings of the army extend across are black with men. we are in easy shelling distance of the enemy but they have not fired but six shots from thier Artillery since we have been here. I wonder they do not but I cannot believe they are gone but Hooker is putting up some kind of a plane on the right I rather think that our demonstration here is merely a feint but the beauty of the whole thing is that no one knows what is up and if the Greybacks are equally ignorant it is all I ask. they made a desparate resistance to Reynolds men on our left but they had to "skeedadle" and it was a comical sight to see them run across the plain with our shells bursting among them thick and fast but they made quick time, and travelled as though everything depended on thier legs.

I do hope this rain will not interfere with operations again, but there is great danger that it will.

Now for another item which I don't know as I ought to write of which you

must say nothing about until you hear of it some other way. Col Parsons was taken sick with his old complaint two days before I got back and is now very sick indeed. he wanted a green vial night and day. he was sent to Washington yesterday morning. poor fellow I am so sorry for him. he felt terribly and did not want to go but he could not sit up and twas of no use. I suppose people will kill him now sure we are all so sorry for him here but it makes no difference the cowards who have never been to war will show him no mercy I do not know whether there is any chance to send this to day or not but shall try to. Give my love to Mary Matt Thomas and the baby. My respects to Mrs K and family all the neighbors tell Cal that Surgeon Dale has written for his piscription list and it has been sent. with much love and in much haste

Your aff son
Charlie

PS I have written this stretched at full length on the ground with my paper on a knapsack so I don't know as you can read it.

81

Head Quarters 2nd Brig 3rd Division 6th Corps May 6th 1863

Dear Mother,
    I wrote you last from the plains opposite Fredericksburg about a week ago since which we have been through everything that man can endure and live, and have been again doomed to defeat. When I wrote you last we had 3 Corps of the Army with us, but immediately after 2 of them were withdrawn to go and reinforce Hooker way off to the right leaving only our own the 6th Corps with us. last Sat night we crossed the river below F'burg and advanced to what is called the Bowling Green road and after marching all night entered Fredericksburg on the back side about 5 o'clock Sunday morning. I have not time or space to tell you the wild excitement of that beautiful Sabboth morning as we entered the town at double quick amid the bursting of shells and the roar of our own Artillery but in less time than it takes to tell of it we had position, and in course of an hour were ordered to assault the heights behind the town which were the same that the whole Army could not take last Dec. the 10th 2nd RI + 34th NY were detailed as a sort of Furlorn hope and with the right Division marched along the plain before the Batteries of the enemy to draw thier fire and force from the main part of the fortifications. immediately as we started from the lower end of the town many commenced shelling us and I can compare it to

nothing but the throwing of beans or shot by the handful the shells burst and scattered the fragments around us we lost 16 men wounded in that operation meantime part of the rest of our Division charged upon the heights and carried them taking lots of prisoners and 9 pieces of Artillery.

immediately after this was done the Army occupied the heights and took up our line of march on a plank road leading to Chantilly we had got out but 4 miles when we came to another ridge of hills and the enemy were strongly posted upon them we charged upon them repeatedly Brigade after Brigade each in succession was repulsed and the enemy apparently had everything thier own way when our Brigade or rather part of it was ordered forward, Div 10th 2nd RI + 7th Mass. all our troops in front of us were in full retreat and the Rebs following. as soon as our men had passed over us we were up and open fired upon the advancing Rebels. they faultered stopped, and we advanced upon them, and joy of JOYS! they turned and fled to the woods. we advanced to the edge of the woods and they attempted to drive us several times but we held them until darkness came upon the scene and put an end to the strife for that day. we gained great glory but at what a sacrifice 467 men out of our Brigade is the loss and the poor old 10th had 11 killed, 55 wounded plus 12 missing and she now numbers but 268 muskets, and 30 with the Balloon Corps. the 7th Mass lost 179 killed wounded and missing.[2] the 2nd RI 109 ditto, but they are much larger Regts than ours. Col Browne commanding our Brigade was wounded also the AAAG Consequently Col Eustis took command of the Brigade and I took the place of the AAAG, and Aid de Camp. The next day the Rebels were reinforced enough to raise thier force to 40,000 men and just at night they attacked us again and as we had 14,000 men to begin with we had to retreat which we did in good order, crossing the river at Banks Ford. this was made necessary in consequence of Gen Hookers having been repulsed with the rest of the Army the whole 11th Corps which are mostly dutch broke and ran and it is said lost all thier guns to the number of 45. you can judge something of what this Army endured and I tell you that after we got back to Banks Ford 4 men of the 37th and one of the 36th NY dropped down dead of shear exhaustion. Company C has one man killed Constant E Bannerot of Florence, a german and one wounded Josiah Thayer of Belchertown. Capt Shurtleff was wounded again, in the neck, and Lieut Noble from Westfield. It is said the 10th again saved the Army that is this part of it. Excuse this letter for this is all the paper I have and I have got one envelope. shall write more fully as soon as I can get a place. love to all

Charlie.

PS I forgot to tell you Col E got a bullet through his boot and I have the top of my flask knocked off by a fragment of shell of which I am very proud.[3]

82

Hd Qrs 2nd Brigade 3rd Division 6th Corps
Camp near Falmouth VA
May 10th 1863

Dear Mary,

I promised myself to write you a full description of our operations since we left our winter quarters near here one week ago last Tuesday. but as I look back at it now it seems so much like a terrible dream that I cannot realize that one week ago to day, yes at this very hour, I was in one of the toughest fights of my experience. again the old 10th has had satisfaction of turning the tide of battle and driving back the Grey Backs when all seemed lost. again have I experienced the delights of bursting shells case shot and solid shot fired at us by the vindictive foe, again have I listened to the humming of minnie bullets about my ears, and again I have slept upon the battlefield among the dead and listened to the groans and shrieks of the wounded, and yet sitting here the beautiful quiet Sabboth afternoon I cannot realize it at all, but let me see if I can give you an intelligible account.

I wrote you from the Banks of the river on this side about Thursday April 30th well we stayed there and maneuvered in plain sight of the enemy until about dark, when we marched up the river to the pontoon bridges about one mile and bivouacked on the bank and were told to make ourselves comfortable for the night but had not got our saddles off the horses when orders came to fall in and cross the river immediately which we did and formed in a line of battle in the bright moonlight the scene at this point baffles all description.[4] the heights or hills are quite a distance from the river and between is a wide plain or meadow crossed by a sunken road called the Bowling Green road, and as the long dark columns of troops moved off with the moon light flashing from the bright barrels and bayonettes of the guns it was magnificent. we moved on directly across towards the hills and listened with all our ears and watched with straining eyes for the roar and flash of musketry from the frowning hills in front, but it did not come then and we gained the road and turned to the right down a steep muddy hill into a ravine, across a small stream and up the other side. at this moment a staff Officer rode up and said a few words to Col E. and rode off. Col turned to me and [said] "We are going to cut our way through and join Hooker"! then I knew that some of us must sleep our last sleep before night. we kept on over one hill after another until about daylight. we arrived at a hill which we could not see over, in front nor on either side as the road was cut deeply into the hill. here we halted near a house and found it contained a lot of wounded and were told that Col Shaler's Brigade which preceeded us had had a fight here and lost thier Major of 1st Chasseurs of NY. Very soon we made to the side of the

road and two of Batteries 6 guns each passed on to the front and directly we heard dropping shot of musketry from the flankers close to us, and then the roar of Artillery, and then came the word "Forward, double quick" and up the hill we went and lo! we were in the midst of the city of Fredericksburg, round the corner we went up a long street to the Rail Road, turned up the track and into the Depot where we halted in plain sight of the terrible heights rifle pits and fortifications behind the city which the whole of the centre Grand Division could not take last December. this was about 5 o'clock Sunday morning May 3rd amid the roar of Artillery as our Battery poured thier fire at the force on top and rifle pits and stone walls on the side of the roads.

never was a calm waked up so fearfully on a quiet Sabboth morn before. it was but little while before every street was full of blue jackets we staid here until about 9 o'clock Col Eustis having been sent for twice by Gen Newton to see to the planting of some Batteries finally orders came to fall in and we moved up the river to a long street with rifle pits on both sides connecting the houses and every little ways crossing the streets as [we] moved out of the town on the other side onto a long plain the enemy commenced shelling us from the top of the hills and following along the crest of the hills and in the rifle pits keeping even with the head of our column. they had perfect range of us and there was no shelter for us, but the boys never faltered or wavered a particle but marched along as though at a Dress parade or drill amid that shower of Iron and lead the kind of shell they fired were what is called Spherical Case and is a hollow iron ball filled with Musket bullets and when it bursts it throws a perfect shower of fragments of iron and these balls it is just like taking a handful of beans or shot and throwing them all at once only the effect is much more serious if they hit you. we lost one man killed and 16 wounded in about 10 minutes meanwhile as we drew this force down to watch us the troops left in the city formed thier line, and without firing or loading a gun marched up the hill in the face of a galling fire a distance as long as from the end of Gothic Street to the top of round hill. the Rebels poured thier shell and musketry fire into them but stern and silent they marched along men dropping from the ranks but not a lick was spent upon them as the brave fellows advanced. it took "Johnnie Reb" by surprise it was a new feature, but the summit was gained the Rebels fly in all directions the gunners leave thier pieces in our hands some of them with the charge half rammed down and 17 guns, and lots of prisoners fall into our hands. the stars and stripes were planted on the battlements and lusty Yankee cheers rent the air.

I forgot to tell you that when we went up the river on the right our Regt and the 2nd RI were detached from the rest of the Brigade and did not participate in the storming though we lost more men than any other Regt of the Brig except the 7th Mass.

So far all had been glory in victory, very soon after the last exploit we joined

the rest of the Brigade on the heights and after resting a half hour were ordered in again and started on a plank road leading So westerly towards Chancellorsville we marched forward about 3½ miles when a Battery of the Rebs opened upon us from a half mile to the front with solid shot and shell. we were in rear of the column. our column was deployed and skirmishers thrown out and the advance again commenced the enemy were posted on another range of heights called Salem Heights concealed in the woods and as our men advanced they opened a terrific fire of musketry on them that soon became a deafening roar along the whole line. Regiment after regiment formed thier lines and went forward at the double quick only to be broken up and come back. we were on the extreme right of the line the 10th 2nd RI and the 7th Mass and were the last to be brought into action and when the three gallant Regiments advanced the Rebels had everything thier own way and were advancing with a rush waving thier old red rag of a battle flag and yelling like demons, but there was one stump for them to run against which they had not counted upon as soon as our fugitives passed to the rear we up and opened upon them. they faultered and laid down and we advanced upon them and they Skeedadled and ran back to the woods. we advanced still further and behold along line of them jumped up from behind a brush fence and made tracks after thier flying bretheren. we kept up our fire until our ammunition was exhausted and night had come on, when we fell back to the position where we first opened fire. Col Browne of the 36th NY was seriously or rather dangerously wounded when we first opened fire, and Col Eustis took command of the Brigade. immediately after Adjt Jones of the 36th NY was wounded and next morning Col E sent for me to take his place as Acting AAG in which capacity we have acted ever since. I am very comfortably situated having a large wall tent with one other Staff Officer for a companion and much better rations and quarters than when in the Regiment how long it will last I do not know but I presume Col E will have the Brigade for some time but perhaps for good.

After we had fallen back to our first position the men were permitted to lie down and were soon fast asleep with thier dead comrades scattered all around them and the yells of the poor wounded men sounding in thier ears. I had to sit up until the supply of ammunition came up and serve 60 rounds more to every man, and I laid down and was immediately lost in sleep.

I awoke about 4 o'clock Monday morning. the Brigade was placed under arms then came the order from Col E to report to him for AAAG. We laid there all that day (Monday) in line of battle the Rebels constantly making attacks but all upon our left. at about 5 and ½ o'clock PM they made a desparate attack upon our left (Howes Division) and between us and Fburg where they had our little Corps nearly surrounded and we were cut off from retreat by the way we came and our only road now was by Banks Ford, and the chances now were that they

would completely surround us. it was now nearly dark and they commenced drawing off our regts and as we were the extreme right based upon the Banks Ford road we were left to the last, and for rear guard. I tell you it looked mighty dubious as Col E and Staff were left there with only one Regt and within 200 rods of the enemy. at last the order came and off I went across the field to order this regt to withdraw they filed past us down the road, and then we waited for the pickets quietly sitting on our horses with nothing between us and the Rebs. soon the pickets came in and then we turned our horses heads and followed the retreating Column. just at this moment the Rebels discovered what was going on and set up such a yelling as you never heard nor ever will. we expected them down upon us any moment but thank the Lord they did not come and we made good our escape to Banks Ford where we formed in line of battle and the troops commenced crossing on two Bridges very soon the Rebels opened upon us with Artillery and shelled us or rather at us as the only damage they did us was to wound one man of the 2d RI Regt about half past 2 o'clock AM word was brought to us to fall in without noise and fall back to the bridges which we did crossing at about 3 o'clock on the morning of Tuesday May 5th we laid down to catch another nap when Col E calls to know if I was very sleepy of course I said no although I had been up most of every night for 4 nights then he said he wanted someone of the Staff to keep awake as they were expecting the Rebs would follow us across the river so up I got rolled up my blankets and went back towards the bridges to watch for an alarm but immediately the order came for our whole Division to fall in and we marched back about 2 miles where we went into bivouac close to Gen Newton + Gen Sedgwicks Head Quarters here we staid 3 days when we again moved down to where we now are about 100 rods from our old winter quarters, and I can tell you after we got here I made up my lost sleep with a vengeance.

The duties of a Staff Officer are very arduous upon the battlefield and during the active operations having to ride with orders night and day but still I like it very much. Col Eustis has just informed me that he had a letter from Col Parsons to day and he is coming back tomorrow which is quite a surprise to me as I did not think he would ever come back. I had the top of my flask knocked off during the shelling Sunday morning of which I am of course very proud, and Col Eustis got a bullet through his boot but I cannot imagine how either of us escaped so well for it does seem as though we could not but get hit. this Corps has the credit of doing pretty much all the work, and this Brigade won heaps of glory.[5] the 36th NY took one brass 12 pounder, and the 37th Mass took 3. there were any quantity of Rebs taken out of the houses in Fredericksburg I saw two taken out of the cellar while we lay in the Depot. the 10th lost 10 men killed 2 Officers and 55 men wounded and 8 men missing almost 1/3 of what we took into battle while the 37th with twice as many only lost one man killed and 11

wounded. Capt Shurtleff got a very severe wound in the neck and Lieut Terry S. Noble had his thumb shot off. It is feard that Capt S will lose his voice entirely but I hope it is not so.

I never was so tired in my life as when we got back every bone in my body ached as though they would split.

We have received an order to day to supply ourselves with eight days rations again so I suppose we shall pitch into them again before long, possibly this week though what they expect to make by it I am sure I cannot tell certainly men could not fight more desparately than we did.

I received your letter of the 3rd yesterday which is the first word I have had from home since I got back I began to think you had forgotten me entirely please let me know if you receive my two letters or dispatches from the battlefield written after we started from our old camp. We have received notice of Cal Ks discharge please give my respects to him and read him this part about this fight for he can appreciate it better than you can. Tell him "Galley" is all right this time and stood up with the best of them so did "Brick Top" he will know who I mean also give my respects to Mrs K and Bill and all the neighbors. love to Mother and Mat Thomas and the baby remember me to Curtis King and May Phil, and everybody else.

I hope we shall not have to cross this river again for it is not the way to Richmond but I am afraid we shall have to try it over again and that very soon, but I must bid you good night, write often with much love

Your aff brother
Charlie.

83

Head Quarters 2nd Brigade 3rd Division 6th Corps Camp near Falmouth VA
May 12th 1863

Dear Mattie,

As I promised to write to you I take this earliest opportunity, the first chance I have had to write any more than to home since I returned as I expected when I left Northampton active operations commenced as soon as it stopped raining and as of course you will read the long letter I wrote to Mary day before yesterday it is of no use to go through all that long description again. Col Browne of the 36th NY was wounded just as our Brigade opened fire at the Battle of Salem Heights or Salem Church about 4 miles beyond Fredericksburgh, and Col Eustis took command of the Brigade. Lieut Jones of the 36th NY AAAG was

also wounded in this fight and Col E appointed me in his place which is a very pleasant one except during marches or battles when it becomes very arduous as I have often to keep my horse saddled night and day and ride around in the dark with orders +c +c, but in camp as we now are it is very pleasant. we have a large wall tent for our dining and sitting room, and I have a wall tent with one other Staff Officer for sleeping tent and another for an Office, and Col E has two wall tents and the other two Staff Officers have another wall tent so it makes quite a little village and we have surrounded it by a thick hedge of cedars and it [is] really a nice place to live in I don't know how long I shall be here but probably as long as Col Eustis commands the Brigade which I presume will be for a long time to come.

The weather has taken a sudden change and summer has come on all at once and it is hot as Tophet.[6] one can hardly stir out at all after 6 o'clock in the morning.

You will read in Marys letter of our going out of Fredericksburg that Sunday morning to draw off the Rebel horses. when we returned the windows of many of the houses were full of the heads of the Sesesh damsels and as we rode along past the houses they would open an umbrella so we could not look at them. they need not have taken so much trouble for there is not one of them that a fellow would want to look twice at, but I noticed that the latest fashion in regard to ladies hats prevailed in Fredericksburg. We were guided in our perilous march to the rear of Fredericksburg that Saturday night by a contraband who was from Missisippi and a deserter from the Reb Army. While we were lying in F I tried to hire this contraband. he was a mighty smart looking nigger or rather Mulatto but when he found I expected to go out on the heights (which he knew had not been stormed then) he would not go. I gave him my address and told him to hunt me up after the fight was over, but we went forth to battle and I have not seen him since.[7] I will enclose you a copy of a flaming order we have just received from Gen Hooker. We expect orders every day to cross again but alas we shall never get those Heights again for they will never leave them in charge of so few men as they did this time. The Col who commanded the Brigade of 6,000 men who held them considered that he had men enough to hold them against the whole Army, in fact agreed to do it, but he did not know what sort of "Yanks" he had got to deal with.

The most horrible incident I have heard of was of one of Hookers fights on the right. while in the midst of a battle the woods took fire and it is feared that a number of poor wounded fellows were burned to death.

I wish you could have seen how cool and unconcerned the glorious old 10th were in both actions. our duty in the morning when we we went to the fight was merely to draw off a portion of the enemys force and it was in other words merely to be shot at without returning a shot, and as they rained that shower of

Spherical Case upon us not a man faltered or fell out, but marched along in as good order as those going upon the parade ground, and then in the afternoon to see them advance upon the exultant Rebels who were pursuing our flying troops in all the confidence of victory, stop them, and turn thier advance into a retreat, oh it was glorious.

Col Parsons returned from Hospital in Washington, day before yesterday, and if ever you saw a sett of men glad it was the old 10th for they were necessarily under the command of Major Parker whom they hate with a holy hatred if such a thing can be, and were fast growing into such a row as they had last fall. I went over to camp to see the Col and on every side was greeted Col Parsons has come! Have you seen Col Parsons? +c +c and Col Eustis was more than glad for he had been terribly worried to have to leave the Regt under Maj Parkers command. There is none of that mean cowardly talk or feeling of Col P in the Regt for they know that he was sick and could not help it that it came just at the time we had to advance.

I wish you would write me often for I get no letters from home and had only one since I rejoined the Regiment, and suppose I shall not have another for weeks to come although I have written four since I came back over 3 weeks ago.

Give my love to Thomas + the baby, and to Mother and Mary when you see them, also my respects to my enquiring friends in Haydenville, and please write often to

Your aff brother,
Charlie.

84

Head Quarters 2nd Brigade 3rd Div 6th Corps
Camp near Falmouth VA
May 30th 1863

Dear Mother,

I received your welcome letter of the 24th inst. also Marys note by John Banks, and Marys of the 22nd enclosing the badges though I believe I have written once since I received the latter. I gave one of the badges to Col Parsons and he went into extacies over it, and sends ten thousand thanks to Mary, as I told him she made it for him. Col Eustis was also very much pleased with his I did not give any to the Officers of Co C as they have engaged some enamel ones for which they have to pay $2.50 each and they will not look half as well when they get them. I gave one to each of my companions on the "personal Staff" and they also

Members of Company C, Tenth Massachusetts Volunteers: (*seated, left to right*) Will Bishop, George Bliss, Edward Nally; (*standing, left to right*) Will Kingsley, Alvin Rust, Fred Clark. The cloth hats worn by Bliss and Nally were probably knitted by Charles Brewster's sisters, Martha and Mary. *Courtesy of Historic Northampton, Northampton, Massachusetts*

thought they were very nice so you can tell Miss Pary that in the next battle her handiwork will be in the very front on the hats of the acting General + Staff and on the hat of a Col also. I hope the Rebs will never get them, as they got the pretty cap you sent me about a year ago. I hardly knew which to choose the embroidered ones or those with braid but finally put on the latter and saved one of the others so that I could change it if I pleased the color was exactly right and the shape better than I was afraid she would get it. I have just been out to witness a grand review of the 1st (General Reynolds) Corps and I could not help thinking of Mary and how she would enjoy it to see the different Divisions

Brigades and Regts pass and how easily you can tell one of the old from one of the new regts. the old Colors are riddled with bullets and torn, many of them having not more than 6 inches of silk attached to the staff, just enough to show that it was once the stars and stripes. Tell Mary not to worry about the destruction of her letters as I always burn my letters from everybody as soon as I have answered them. I have not had a word from Matt in answer to my letter yet although you wrote that she was *probably* writing at the same time you were. I wrote to Cal K a few days ago. I suppose he has got it before this. tell him that Josiah Thayer of Co C died yesterday of the wound in his arm at the Potomac Creek Hospital his arm was amputated but he could not rally after it and died, also Sergt Hogan of Co D who was shot through both legs had one of them amputated after he got to the Hospital but he died, in fact it seems as though every one who has lost a leg or an arm dies. The number of deaths from wounds in this Brigade is almost equal to the number killed outright on the field. it seems as though they all died.[8]

I am sorry to hear that Cal does not get well any faster. I think he had better take the stimulant even if they do "go to his head". You asked me if I meant to leave the Major out in the cold in my presentation of badges. I can assure you I *most certainly did, and have.* I am surprised to hear that Mr Eels has not finished that job I had supposed from what you had written before about the great improvements +c. that it was all done. I wish you would write me just what he has done, for he told me that it would not take more than 3 or 4 days for the whole thing, and again Mary writes that you have had great trouble getting a man to clean up the rubbish. I am sure I do not understand it at all for Eels agreed to take all that matter into his own hands, and not make you any trouble about it.

I think Marys suggestion of Asparagus to send by J Banks a very good one as we have to pay 50 cts for a bunch such as I used to carry up to the old American Hotel as long ago as I can remember. And it is as long on the way as what you would have sent would have been.

It seems as though one of my letters must have been lost as you say in yours "you do not know but what I have seen" Mr Phillips I wrote about his being here one morning while we were at breakfast he told me he was certain that Edward was dead, and I put down on my memorandum when he was buried + the distances and directions +c and 2 or three days after that I received Marys letter telling of the Surgeon Warner and all that, which immediately raised my hopes again that he might be living, but still as Mr Phillips was a guest at the Hd Qrs of the 1st Cav and they ought to know all that could be known of Lieut Phillips I had not much hope.

Our camps are full of rumors these days among which is one that Gen Couch is going to relieve Gen Rosecrans and Rosecrans is coming to take command of

this Army but this must be all "stuff" as if Gen Couch is the man for Rosecrans Army he must certainly be a much better man for this Army, but I don't know as it would be strange under the present administration of Affairs. Why cannot they let "little Mac" come back. I am sure we never failed so terribly under him as we did this time but thank the Lord there is no question about the 6th Corps. they fought alone under the gallant Sedgwick and the 3rd Div gained credit for the Corps under Newton, and the 2nd Brigade saved the 3rd Div under Eustis, all this at Salem Heights Sunday May 3rd 1863. this does not read like the newspaper accts but I can assure you there is much more truth in it, for "I was there".

I have no news to write and we have no sign of any movement at present. Still I suppose we may go at any time. There are rumors that the Rebels are intending another raid into Maryland through the valley of the Shenandoah +c +c but as for us we know nothing.[9] Please give my love to Mary Matt + Thomas and my neice. My respects to Mrs Clark + family and Mrs Kingsley + family and all the neighbors Hoping to hear from you again and much oftener I am with much love

Your aff son
Charlie.

85

Hd Quarters 2nd Brig 3rd Div 6th Corps On the Bluff of the Rappahanock June 8th 1863

Dear Mary,

I recd your welcome letter of June 2nd containing Matties + my neices photograph which I think very nice. I suppose you will be wondering why I don't write which is for this reason last Friday part of our Corps crossed the river at this point which is the same way we crossed before, driving the enemy from thier rifle pits. next morning the whole Corps was in motion for the same point which we reached about 11 o'clock our whole Corps with the exception of our Brigade and the 3rd Brig are across the river and bivouacked on the other side. 1000 men of our Brigade went over last night and threw up rifle pits far out in the plain towards the fort the Rebels both on the other side. there is no part of the Army in this movement except our Corps. what it is all for I am sure I don't know but we have got in our holding 2 miles of the other bank of the river and our skirmishers are close up to the Rebels and there they stand and stare at each other.[10] the guns on this side occasionally send a shell over into the hills onto the other side but

that is all the Rebs do not reply, and so we wait and wonder, and before night may be in a desparate fight, or we may be all back again this side of the river. only the thousand men of our Brigade have yet been across and they returned at six o'clock this morning, having worked all night with pick and shovel. I have not been able to write before because I have been so busy with the preparations to move, and we have lain here two days in the sun, expecting to move every moment, so I could not write since we started. I received a letter from Mattie since we marched, which I shall answer as soon as I can. I am suffering again from my diarrhea and also have the rheumatism in my hip again, all of which is of course very pleasant under present circumstances. Col Eustis returned from 5 days in Washington yesterday. rumor says he is to be a Brigadier but I am afraid he is not politician enough to get it. I hope he will though, for the Brigade has great confidence in him, and he deserves it.

You keep writing that you do not hear anything about the badges you made for me. I do not know why you do not, for this is the third time I have written that they were splendid. I have also received the Harpers and the papers for which I am very much obliged. I am very sorry that Cal K is so poorly I hoped he would get well and thought he was getting so when I came away. I do not think any flags of Truce cross the river now as it is in kind of active operations, and I do not know where Gen Couch and staff will be when the letter comes here. you know Army movements are very uncertain now. I cannot write more now for I am sitting on the ground and my leg pains me so I must get up and stretch it, besides the sun is burning my face and I am afraid it will spoil my complexion which is very fair just now, about the color of my boots. Give my love to Mother Matt + my neice + Thomas. my respects to all the neighbors write often to

Your aff brother
Charlie.

Tuesday Morn June 9th 5 and ¹/₂ o'clock AM.

I could not send this yesterday so I add this postscript to inform you that there is no change in affairs here. we had troops out all night digging trenches. the sharp shooters are quite busy this morning cracking away at each other. cannot tell what will take place to day, but it does not seem as though the Rebels would allow us to dig much nearer to them. they have a strong force on the hills and why they do not open with thier Artillery and anihilate our Corps is more than I can tell.

I had quite an adventure just after I had finished writing yesterday. we all lay on the ground here at head quarters, gazing at the troops on the other side of the river I was reading when Col Eustis said What is that, a woman? I looked up and beheld coming up the hill an object that riveted my gaze in astonishment. it had

on a pair of dk blue military pants, and a short military cloak reaching nearly to the knees. that is the cape part of it, add to this a pair of short boots, and one of those black straw hats (which women all wear now a days) with a small black feather in it. it was small in size as yourself and shorter I should say although the peculiar dress might have deceived me as to this point. it came straight towards our tent, and as it approached I judging by the face of the object, jumped up and touched my hat, but when my looks wandered from the face to the dress I began to doubt again whether it was a woman or not. It inquired if this was Gen Newtons Hd Qrs, and I answered it was not. it then inquired the way to his Hd Qrs and I pointed out the way, forgetting all my politeness, manners and everything else. I presume I stared with open mouth. *she* started up the hill and then we all came to our senses and concluded it was a woman, and very much ashamed were we to think that none of us had politeness enough to go with her and show her the way. I forgot to mention in describing her dress that she had on a Surgeons Sash. it turned out that she was a female Surgeon and wants a situation in the Army. She was quite pretty but did not look as though she could endure the rough and tumble of a soldiers life for long but of all the surprising situations I was ever in this beat them. her dress after all was a very sensible one when we got over our panic and had time to think of it. I do not know what success she had in her application. There are a number of ladies here I saw five besides the *doctor* yesterday.[11] I have not time to write more this morning, love to all

Your aff
Charlie

86

Fairfax Station Va June 17th 1863

Dear Mother,

I seize a few moments this morning to let you know that I am alive and well. I have no time to write a letter but I know you must be anxious to know what has become of me. We came from the other side of the Rappahannock last Saturday night recrossing in the midst of a tremendous thundershower and we have been on the march night and day ever since. We arrived here last evening after marching 21 miles starting at 2 o'clock AM yesterday morning What our destination is I do not know but should not be surprised if we had another long march up into Maryland. I have been in the saddle most of the time for a week. We are having 5 days rations served and are girding up our loins for a long severe

march. I find that a staff Officers place is no sinacure in a march. As soon as I get anywhere that I can I will write you a long letter but this is all the paper I have with me and this was given me as a curiosity when I was home last spring. To show you at what a rate we are marching I will inform you that one Division of this Corps had 30 men prostrated by sunstroke day before yesterday 10 of whom died.[12] the weather is hot beyond conception and the roads are horribly dry and dusty. We have just heard that the Rebels are in Md and Penn and that the Militia has been called out +c +c. I just hope that *the Militia* will have a chance to meet the Gray Backs once they will find that it is not No Carolina fighting and that Army life in this Army is not such a nice thing as it is down there. Love to all and will write more fully as soon as possible

Yours with all love,
Charlie.

87

Hd Quarters 10th Mass Vols June 20th 1863 Fairfax Court House VA

Dear Mary,

I take pencil in hand to write you a few lines again. you see by my heading that I have returned to the Regiment having been relieved at my own request I did not like the place in the march as well as I expected to and as the pay is no more and the rank no higher than my position as Adjt and the cost of messing there is more than double owing principally to the quantities of liquor drank there I preferred to return to the Regiment. We have been marching most of the time night and day since we left the Rappahannock, but have lain here now two days, but are under orders to march at a moments notice. My health is not improved by the hardships of this march my diarrhea troubles me greatly but I shall not give up as long as I can stand up. Geo Bigelow is very sick and has to be carried in an Ambulance. when we are on the march as the orders are to send no Officers or soldiers away to Hospitals so if a man is so sick that he cannot live riding in an Ambulance he must die. We do not know anything in regard to our destination but are expecting to fight soon. we expected yesterday to take up our line of March to day, but do not see any signs of it as yet. We expect to see hard times and plenty of them when we do move, but we are used to those, but such of us as live have but one year from tomorrow to serve.

Our Division of this Corps were across the Rappahannock when this march commenced where we had been for 4 days, and most of the men had not had thier equipments off for 72 hours and had also been on picket or fatigue duty

every other night while we were over there which was not very good preparation for a forced march but soldiers must endure everything when necessity requires it. a few days ago the air was rent in all directions by cheers from the soldiers, caused by the getting up of a report that McClellan had been recalled to the command of the Army, which of course was a sell.

We are having lots of rain these days which does not add to our comforts at all, last night the water completely flooded the tent in which were sleeping Col P Maj P. and myself. I am messing with them now at Hd Quarters. I had a long letter from Uncle Henry yesterday containing the enclosed recipt for fever + ague. I will send a letter as soon as I have time to answer it.

Tell Mother I have got all the papers and am very much obliged. do you ever see Capt Sam now adays and is he getting impatient for an installment on the house. there is nearly 4 months due me now. the paymaster came down to the Rappahannock to pay us off but did not have time to pay but one Regt before we had to cross the river, he will come to us again as soon as we stop anywhere, long enough to send for him. My back aches with lying on the ground and writing so I cannot write more now. if we ever get anywhere again so that I can have writing materials I will write more fully. please write often and direct your letters to me as Adjt of the 10th again. Give my love to all

Very aff your brother
Charlie.

88

Hd Quarters 10th Mass Vols Poolesville Md June 27th 1863

Dear Mother,

Word has just been sent round to the Brigade that letters handed in before 8½ o'clock this morning will be forwarded to Washington I therefore seize the opportunity to send you another bulletin. I wrote you last I believe from Fairfax Ct House VA. we went the next day to Centreville and staid there two nights we relieved a Brigade of Heintzlemans men there and it was said that we were to remain there, but the second night word came to be ready to start at 5 o'clock AM next day, which we did and marched to Grainesville where we staid last night a distance of 17 miles. We started from there this morning at 4½ o'clock and crossed the Potomac at Edwards Ferry at about 3 this PM we are now about 2 miles this side of the ferry and near Poolesville Md. I expect we are near the rear of the whole Army but I am sure I don't know anything about where we are, and *I am afraid no one else does* however we are in good spirits and if the old 6th

Corps gets in the rear of "Johnnie Reb" he will suffer some before he gets back to Dixie. The inhabitants tell us that troops have been passing for 3 days before us. I have seen a Baltimore paper to day for the first time in 3 days that I have seen any paper. it reports Lee crossing the Potomac with his whole Army if this is true and we don't anihilate him this time, I shall believe we never can whip him. The papers are full of great reports of the calling out of Militia but I don't see as *the Militia* comes out much and I see that Gen this and Gen that in Penn keeps falling back, but they have one General that won't fall back if he can get half a dozen men to stay with him, and that is Gen Couch. We had a rumor that his old Division was going to Penn to join him and some of the men got jubilent over it, but of course it was not true. I cannot write more to night as it is getting dark and I am sitting in a clover field flat on the ground and as I sit the clover is as high as my shoulders. Col Parsons sits on one side writing to his wife and Major Parker on the other side doing ditto. We expect a fight within a day or two but do not know whether we shall get into it or not but it will be something unusual if a fight comes off and the sixth Corps does not have a hand in it. If we had as many old soldiers where the Penn Militia is we could destroy the Rebel Army but the Militia always *falls back*.

Give my love to all. I don't know as I ever shall hear from you again as we are on the march every day, and a good part of every night. If I ever get to a stopping place I shall endeavor to give you a more connected account of our operations. I will send Uncle Henrys letter although I have not answered it, but I don't know as I shall ever have a chance to do so.[13] Give my respects to all the neighbors and don't fail to write and direct as before even if you don't know where I am, as I shall get them sometime.

Very affectionately your son,
Charles.

89

Head Quarters 10th Mass Vols In the Saddle July 6th 1863

Dear Mother,

It is 4 and $1/2$ o'clock AM and we are about one mile on our days march and as we are halted I thought I would write a few lines to let you know that I am alive and well. we started from our bivouac on the Battlefield of Gettysburg PA yesterday about 1 o'clock and marched out I should think about six miles in pursuit of the retreating Rebels. our advance came up to thier rear guard about 5 o'clock yesterday and some shelling took place about half a mile from here. we

started out of bivouac at 4 o'clock this morning and are now halted on the march. I suppose to reconnoitre the pass in which the Rebels made a stand last night. As we came to the rear of the Battlefield yesterday we passed more than a dozen farmhouses where the Rebels had established Hospitals. the farm houses all without exception have great barns bigger than anything in Northampton even the Day Brothers, and these barns were crammed full of wounded Rebels and great camps of tents were pitched around them and these also were crowded with them.

there were 2,000 in one of these hospitals alone, and in all I should think there must have been as many as 8,000 besides great numbers which were within our lines before the Rebs retreated, and besides the host of dead as we came over the battlefield it was covered with parties burying the dead and our forces have been constantly at work at this for four days and it will take some time yet to finish. added to all this we have got thousands of prisoners though I do not know how many, but the lowest estimate I have heard was 15,000. I have seen as many as 5,000 myself I should think we have punished them terribly and the South will have cause to remember thier invasion of the North for years. Lee is now flying before us endeavoring to make his way back which we are trying to prevent. it is said that the fords of the Potomac are all impassable now and it rains continually. Our Regt did not get engaged but was held in reserve as was the whole Brigade, and were kept continually on the double quick, going from left to centre from centre to right, and back again. we got one terrible shelling on the afternoon of the 3rd wherein we had 4 men wounded, and the 36th had 3 killed and 18 wounded and the other two regts also lost some.

Although lying three days close to the city of Gettysburgh yet we have none of us seen it as our column passed to the left of it. I do not know where we now are, or where we are moving to, but we expect a fight with thier rear guard every moment. I have dismounted and seated myself in what was an oat field but is now a sea of mud. Col Parsons has done likewise and is writing home. he is well and sends respects. I have heard from home only once since leaving Fairfax VA and don't know as I ever shall again. I am writing in hopes that I shall have a chance to give this to some citizen to mail it or that we shall pass some Post Office, but I may never have a chance.

I thought I had seen the horror of war before, but the like of this battle is seldom seen. Men, Horses, Cannon Caissons, and all the implements of war piled up in almost inextricable confusion. Men with heads shot off, limbs shot off, Men shot in two, and men shot in pieces, and little fragments so as hardly to be recognizable as any part of a man. we passed yesterday 9 dead Rebels in one heap in the road probably killed by one shell, and dead Rebels were scattered everywhere and yet the ground was dotted with single graves and pits full of them.[14] the Rebels buried as fast as they could for two days and yet left all these

for us [to] complete the job with. All this has not been accomplished without fearful loss to us. Col Parsons gave a letter to a citizen yesterday, which I hope will arrive safely and it will tell you that I am all right for I know you must be anxious. You will be charmed with the appearance of this letter but I have written a few words and then chased my horse and got my hands all mud and wrote a few more lines and then chased my horse again. I don't know what has got into him this morning, he usually stands quiet enough but he seems to be crazy this morning. Love to all and please continue to write to

Your aff son
Charlie.

12 and $^1/_2$ o'clock PM. We have marched but about one mile all day. 3 Regts of our Brigade have just marched up onto a hill in a beautiful grove of Hickory formed line of battle with a Battery of Artillery in front of us. we have sent out three companies as a picket of observation and here we quietly wait the course of events. the Rebels are supposed to be in a gap in a range of tall mountains right in front of us.

Deserters from the enemy have been coming in in squads all day. the enemys force is supposed to be greatly demoralized. it is reported that Gen French has destroyed the enemys pontoon train but I do not know whether it is true or not. A darkie came in from the enemy this morning. he says the enemys Generals told them in the late battle that they had nothing opposed to them but 10 Militia. The enemy opened 100 pieces of Artillery on us at one time in the battle of July 3rd. I never heard such a terrific crash in my life and I have heard some noise. it seems as if the "crack of doom" had really come.[15] Among the incidents of the battle, I saw two Rebels bringing in one of our wounded men he was shot through both legs and had an arm placed lovingly around the neck of each of them. one of the Rebels was also wounded in the hand. On the morning of the 4th our Brigade was put in advance of the front line of battle, as support for the skirmishers. we were right in a part of the Battlefield where a desparate conflict had raged on the 2nd + 3rd the ground was almost literally covered with dead, and among them we found two wounded Rebels from Alabama who had lain there 2 nights and almost two days. One of them was a young + handsome youth with as handsome blue eyes as I ever saw. I had a little whiskey and I poured out a good drink and gave him. it revived him very much, but I wish you had seen those blue eyes follow me staring, with wonder I suppose that a "Yank" should do such a wonderous deed. he was wounded in the side just below his arm. the other was wounded in the leg, which was probably broken. they were afterwards taken to our hospital and cared for.[16]

I shall have no chance to send this to day I suppose as we are in the woods

away from everything. I suppose that the reason we do not advance any faster is that the rest of the Army is at work at some other point trying to get in the Rebels rear and it is not thought desirable to press them very fast on this side. I wonder where Gen Couch and the brave Militia are. the Army of the Potomac has done all the fighting so far. This is a most beautiful country but I have serious doubts as to the expediency of saving the inhabitants. we receive very few demonstrations of welcome and there are any quantity of able body men whose crops are being destroyed and houses pillaged and yet they loaf round and stare with open mouth wonder and when they ought to be asking for muskets and cartridges and seeking a place in the front line. The darkie who came in this morning said he saw more sesesh flags in Chambersburg than in any other town he ever saw this size, and he said there were not a quarter as many in Sharpsburg though the latter is in Md. in Westminster Md where the Rebels had been the night before we arrived there and stripped the inhabitants of everything. they brought us out bread and everything that the Rebels had not taken.

Littletown Pa was the next town we came to, arriving there about 5 o'clock in the morning after a march all night since 8 o'clock the evening previous. Col P and myself went into a house where we halted and requested permission to wash ourselves which was granted. while we were in there the soldiers came in inquiring for pies or bread but they had none until one of them offered half a dollar for a pie then they began to come forth and those women sold lots of pies at 50 cts a piece and bread for 2 dollars a loaf to these tired, hungry, dust begrimed soldiers from Lowell Mass who had been marching night and day for weeks through sun and rain, dust + mud to save the homes of these worthless wretches from destruction, but we thought of the noble city of Philadelphia where so many Union soldiers had been fed, and thier hearts made glad, and we forgave this state for these God forsaken people who reside within its limits.

I hope we shall be able to destroy Lee and his Army before they get back across the Potomac for I do not want to chase them down through the state of Virginia again. Do you realize the fact that our term of service is reduced 11 months and 15 days all are now counting the days and will soon begin to count the hours, and all are looking forward to the time when we shall be at home, but alas how many of us will live to realize it?

Among the curious incidents of this war is this. a soldier of the Penn Reserves who has been in all thier battles was killed in the late engagement on his own farm and within a stones throw of his own house. it seems very sad to think of it but yet it is not so bad as to be shot hundreds of miles away and to be thrown into a nameless grave with 50 others. Some of our Regts suffered terribly several of them drew rations for less than 100 men after the battle.[17]

George Bigelow is with us and his health is better. Col Parsons lies on the ground a short distance from me fast asleep. I have made a very long letter of this

and may make it longer still before I get a chance to send it. give my love to Mary Matt Thomas and the baby to Uncle Ed, Nell, and Ab. My respects to all the neighbors. with much love

Your aff son
Charlie.

90

Head Quarters 10th Mass Vols Boonesborough Md July 9th 1863

Dear Mary,

I sent you or Mother a letter from Mechanicstown two or three days ago it [was] finished at our first halt after leaving Gettysburg whether you will ever get it or not I cannot tell. We marched that night through Fairfield and by a rough dark Mountain road the worst I ever saw it seemed to me. We reached Emmitsburgh about one o'clock at night, clattering through the city and making the quiet streets resound with the footsteps of thousands of armed men, horses and cannon bringing night capped heads to the windows. it was quite a large city but it is now 3/4ths in ruins. we marched through and bivouacked in a field just outside of the city. next morning we took up our line of march about 8 o'clock and passing through Mechanicstown there I mailed your letter, and through two smaller villages whose names I could not understand. we climbed another high mountain higher and steeper than Mt Holyoke. We bivouacked upon the sides of it in a drenching rain, a perfect deluge, and so dark you could not see your hand before your face. we left men strung along all over the mountain, completely exhausted, and lying in the rain. Col Parsons and myself managed to secure the loft of a log house and passed the night very comfortably next morning about 8 o'clock we continued our march down the mountain in seas of mud and arrived at Middleton about one o'clock PM. we bivouacked for the night to wait the rations that came up in [the] afternoon and 3 days were issued this morning we started at 4½ o'clock on the same road I took from Frederick to Sharpsburg last fall with my recruits. we passed through South Mountain Pass and arrived here about noon to day where we bivouacked. we are now close to the enemy and expect a battle immediately probably tomorrow. our Division is in front since I commenced this letter a sharp firing of Cannon musketry has commenced at no great distance on, although it is 8 o'clock PM so dark that I can hardly see to write. our forces are Harrassing the enemy on every side. the Potomac is full almost to overflow, and altogether they are in a very bad way.

I send you three letters which were taken from a dead Rebels cartridge box,

written to his mother and sisters. Poor fellow he lay upon the field with his entrails scattered all about by a cannon shot, I cannot help pity him although as you see he expresses no very kindly intentions towards poor us but he reckoned without his post and the mother + sisters will look in vain in the far off Florida for his return, or even his grave among the green hills of Penn. where his body probably lies in a pit with lots of his comrades perhaps the very ones he speaks of in his letters. I am writing in darkness, kneeling upon the ground and I cannot see to write more love to all. I recd Mothers letter of June 29th to day. I should have got more than one I got a letter from Edmund asking about George. Please write and tell him he is well and with the regt as we may move from here before daylight and I shall not have a chance.

Yours with love
Charlie.

91

Hd Qrs 10th Mass Vols July 12th 1863 In line of Battle Funckstown MD

Dear Mattie,

I suppose by this time you have made up your mind that your brother does not intend to write to you any more, but such is not the case neither am I showing proper resentment at your long delay in writing to me but the fact is I have had no time for 5 weeks to write to anyone but home and that I have to do as you know as they are so anxious always about me. I have written them as often as once in two or three days, but have received but two or three letters from home since we left the Rappahannock although we have got all our back mails and get mails quite regularly now. I have left the letters I have written home in all sorts of places often times giving them into the hands of citizens as we pass through or near some town or village where there was a Post Office.

We arrived here about an hour ago, and about half an hour behind the retreating Rebels. we just passed through the town and have come up with thier rear guard and skirmishing is going on while I write. our Brigade is in the front line to day and if we have a fight we shall have our share of it. What a contrast between the occupations of peaceful New England and ours to day. you sitting quietly listening to a sermon in church, we lying in a wheat field, in a sweltering hot, sultry day, watching and harking for the foe and sound of the singing bullet and the screeching shell. We have been in line expecting a fight momentarily for 3 days and two nights but it has not come off yet. day before yesterday there was severe skirmishing all day, and the Vermont Brigade lost about 100 men but it

did not amount to a battle. I do not know what is going on but we expected to have had another desparate battle before this, but we get on mighty slow, and I am afraid [they] will get away from us though I hope something is doing on our left to get between them and the river.[18] one more such thrashing as we gave them at Gettysburg could finish up thier little excursion to the north. Day before yesterday morning when the Cavalry skirmish first commenced they brought in a prisoner from the 1st Virginia Cavalry and I took him to Hd Qrs. I have got his Carbine and shall send it home if I can get any chance.

We have had a terrible time for the last 5 weeks marching in heat + dust rain and mud, in the night and in the day time and if it were not for the hope of destroying Lees Army, we should be dragging out. What do people think now of the demoralized Army of the Potomac. If the growlers could have seen that desparate fighting on that battlefield at Gettysburg I think they would shut up thier potato traps about this Army though I don't suppose they know enough to realize what the consequences would have been if we had been defeated. I suppose the stay at homes are beginning to shake and grow weak in the knees over the draft which I see has commenced. I got the picture of baby and I think it very nice and looks just like her. A thunder shower is coming so I must close I don't know when I shall have a chance to send it perhaps never. Give my love to Tom + the baby, to Mother and Mary, and my respects to all my friends in H. With much love

Your aff brother
Charlie.

92

Head Quarters 10th Mass Vols
Williamsport Md
July 14th 1863

Dear Mother,
I sent a letter to Mary this morning but I will commence another to you this evening soon after I concluded Marys letter this word came Inform our Picket that they have advanced beyond the rifle pits and could find no enemy. we at once packed up and started in pursuit towards this place, but alas the bird had flown, not a vestige of a Reb was to be seen. they had gone in the night, the most of them crossing at Falling Waters 4 miles below on a bridge but many of them wading and swimming the river at this place. the citizens tell us that many of thier ambulances containing thier wounded, were swept down stream as owing

to thier lightness they could not withstand the torrent. Col Kilpatrick overtook thier rear guard at Falling Waters and captured 1500 more of them and a Battery of Artillery. Col Parsons and I rode all over the town after we got here this PM. the town is skinned of everything. we bivouac here to night.

Boonesboro July 15th 1863 we marched into Williamsport this morning at early daylight and took the route back over the same road we went and arrived at this place about half past one this PM. we are having rations issued and shall probably stay here over night and then we are off for Berlin early in the morning, perhaps before morning. I suppose we shall cross the river there and then for another long discouraging chase down through VA by the same route we went last fall. Its too bad we did not catch them here. we had got already and were to pitch into them yesterday morning but they escaped us. We were accompanied on our march to day by a squad of about 500 Rebels part of the force captured yesterday, our Cavalry crossed the river and gobbled up 150 more of them last night. I suppose that our aim would be to get ahead of them somehow, at any rate we are in for another terrible hard time and it is as hot as Tophet.[19]

We have just got the papers and learned of the capture of Fort Hudson, and of the attack on Charlestown, and also of the doings of that miserable sett of wretches and in the city of New York. Oh that they would send for two or three Regts from the Army of the Potomac. how I should like to go into that mob with the old 10th. we would show them something besides blank cartridges. what can the authorities there be doing that they don't put them down, and what a sight for Americans to view, the governor of a sovereign state like NY for "*imploring*" those villains to keep the peace. why don't he open with his cannon and mow them down, and then, if he wants to do any imploring let him get down on his knees and implore forgiveness of high heaven for his many sins in bringing on such state of things, and the papers also says that our imbecile governor has ordered the draft to be stopped. Oh dear what is the use of serving such a government first order a draft. New York won't submit, therefore shall have no draft. By the powers, I would force that draft in N Y City or I would bury every inhabitant under its ruins.[20] The same paper says there is also riot in progress in Hartford. What next, have they had one in Northampton yet? if not, why not? they don't want to go to war there any more than the New Yorkers do, and they have only to get up or not and the government will stop it. I shall not send this before we arrive at Berlin as it will take my last stamp to send this and I wrote yesterday, so I will close for to day.

Berlin Md July 16th

We marched from Boonesboro this morning at 4 o'clock and reached this place at 12 o'clock. we are bivouacked for to night and I suppose shall take the road into Virginia tomorrow and probably in the course of two weeks shall be

down on the Rappahannock again just where we were 6 weeks ago. I do not see how we can get any farther into thier country than we were for after the Battle of Gettysburg a field report (as it is called) was and our whole strength was 48,000 men, and Lee must have taken 70 or 75,000 men back with him, and the Militia which we had here. we met yesterday on thier way home, also the 9 mo's men who joined us from N. C. must soon return some Regts time is out now and all of them within 10 days, and they cannot be intended to go into VA with us so when we cross into VA it must be with our old Army minus our loss in the Gettysburg Battle or about 50,000 men at the largest calculation, still there may be large acessions of force that I know nothing about so you will please not take this as an official report.

I must close now as I am going down to the village with the Major where I shall mail this when I shall have another chance to send I do not know. My love to Mary Matt and Thomas + Mary Campbell. I don't know as I shall write any more until I get a letter from home.

My respects to all the neighbors with much love

Yr aff son
Charlie.

93

Head Quarters 10th Mass Vols Philemon VA July 22nd 1863

Dear Mattie,

I received a letter from Mary the night before we crossed the river containing the sad news of our little darlings death and I can find no words to express how grieved I am, nor how much I feel for your great sorrow. Words become useless on such occasions but I assure you none but you can feel the loss more deeply than I do, for none loved the little cherub better than I *unless* it was her mother and I would willingly have given my own life for hers. it did not seem as though the death of anything could ever affect me so again but I cannot get the dear little one out of my thoughts at all. I have thought so often of the time when I should come home and find her trotting round the house. I have imagined it all a thousand times and I cannot realize that she is gone forever. It seems as though it was of no use for us to look forward to any happiness, for all our hopes are doomed to disappointment.

We crossed the Potomac at Berlin Sunday forenoon and have proceeded two short days marches into VA. We arrived at the place day before yesterday about sundown and have remained here ever since. there is a report this morning that

we are going back, that the Rebels have been headed off by Gen Dix and that our troops hold the gaps in the mountains, but it does not seem as though it could be true although some of the Cavalry and Artillery are now passing on the road back the way we came. We know nothing of what is going on in the outside world but the last paper we saw said that Gen Dix was to take command in N Y City so I don't see how he can be down in VA. ahead of the Rebs. The weather has been terribly hot yesterday and to day the wind has blown and it is as cool and comfortable as possible, very different from Harrisons Landing at this time last year. I am lying in my little shelter tent flat on my back in a beautiful grove of oaks and although there are thousands of men covering every hill around, yet with the exception of a band discoursing sweet music everything is as still and peaceful as New England Sabbath.

Col Parsons is lying beside me. both he and myself have had a severe attack of diarrhea during the last twenty 24 hours. he wishes to be remembered to you.

We sent off three Officers and six men after the conscripts yesterday. Capt Weatherell is one of them. We need 370 to fill up our Regiment to the maximum standard so I suppose we shall be a big regiment once more. I long to see the list of drafted in Northampton I guess there is a shaking among the dry bones there. I almost pity the poor fellows though that have got to come out here and go into this rough life without any preparation. it will kill lots of them I think it one of the most outrageous laws ever made that allows a man to be exempted for 300 dollars for it obliges only the poor to go who have less at stake in the contest than any other class.[21] still with a very natural selfishness I am glad it is in force if Tom should be drafted, I suppose he would pay rather than come out and I hope he would, though now I think of it I don't know but he belongs in the 2nd class. Capt Newell one of the Captains of this Regt who was cashiered last fall has been drafted. I see also that Fred Baker who was a clerk in Dwights store with me is drafted. But I am running on in a heartless manner for you I know must care nothing for these matters at this time. I have got another chance to be Captain but cannot make up my mind to accept it for I am afraid I should not be able to stand it now to go on foot. Remember me with all sympathy to Thomas in his affliction. With love to Mother and Mary

Yours in love and sorrow,
Charlie.

[Ripped out page follows]

Warrenton VA July 26

Dear Mattie

I have a chance to send a letter this morning. The day I wrote the other part we packed up about noon and marched to Goose Creek and bivouacked for the

night. next day we marched to Rectorstown and after staying there three or four hours we marched to Barbers Cross Roads arriving there about mid night. it is in Chester Gap, and Rectorstown is in Manassas Gap. Next morning we marched at 4 o'clock and went back to Manassas Gap and after staying there three or four hours packed up and marched back again to Barbers Cross Roads and 4 miles beyond. Yesterday morning we started at 7 o'clock and arrived here at about 4 o'clock yesterday afternoon. we are two miles from the town. It is Sunday and there is a prospect of our lying still to day, and perhaps longer. The mail is just going. the first one for a week and I must close. I am going down to see if I can find Mr Barten the Episcopal minister who did live here last fall. Love to all from

Your aff brother
Charlie.

94

Head Quarters 10th Mass Vols near Warrenton VA
July 30th 1863

Dear Mary,

I received your most welcome letter of the 27th and as it is only four days since I received your last I have concluded that you deserve a reply, for your exceeding great favour of writing me a long letter.

We have lain here in camp ever since I wrote home last from this place, but we expected to have taken up the weary line of march to day but did not, but we cannot I think stay here many days as there is only our Corps left in sight now, and the Cavalry and the Flying Artillery have been moving through here yesterday + to day, and I understand that 2 Corps have crossed the river already. And there are rumors to day that a fight has already taken place between the Rebs and our 8th + 2nd Corps on the Heights of Fredericksburgh, whether true or not of course I cannot tell for we are some 25 miles from our battlefields of last winter plus spring at those places, but we expect to have a fight before many days, and everybody seems to expect it will be on the line of the Rapidan River.

Col Parsons and myself have been down to make Mr Barten another call to day he was very glad to see us, and gave us each a note to influential persons in Richmond, to use in case we should have to go there against our own wills, or in other words be *gobbled up*,[22] in some encounter. he says we can borrow money or anything else on them, and he will refund it, and we can pay him after the war is over, or at any other time when we are able. he is a splendid man and I find he has been in the habit of lending money (Confederate) to all Officers whom wounds

or sickness have compelled a forced stay in Dixie. he has a wonderful faith in men and things, and I hope he may never find himself a victim of misplaced confidence. he is the idol of all the region hereabout, and the umpire in all cases of dispute between the Authorities (Union) and the inveterate "sesesh" the letters he has given us are to Episcopal bishops and clergymen in Richmond. he says that my name alone would secure me everything that could be had in Richmond, for his wife has friends there, and one Col Brewster who was taken somewhere was treated with every consideration, even after disclaiming any relationship with him, but was afterwards in Warrenton and sought out Mr Barton and told him of it. his wife has a cousin a Lieut Brewster in our army. I carried him some Candles and salt. he had to pay $2.75 per pound for candles (tallow) and could get but four pounds at that.

I do not see by your account, and the accounts in the paper that we are going to get any accession of force from the draft. I thought when I read the conscription bill in the summer that it would amount to just about as much as it seems to. why cannot the cowards see that if they would only come and fill up our ranks that the battle would be half won by the very act. it is discouraging to read in the papers as I did to day, of 43 drafted men presenting themselves for examination and 39 of them exempted while Jeff Davis is forcing in every man between the ages of 18 + 45, and if he can lift a musket no power within Jeffs Dominion can exempt him. I declare it seems as though sometimes it was desireable the horrors of war should be brought to Mass firesides, merely to see if there was courage enough left in these Dolts to defend thier own hearth. I often doubt whether there is or not. What fools they are and why they cannot see that there is a future for this country even if thier paltry lives are lost, but I suppose it is much easier to stay at home and curse the Army of the Potomac, for not gaining victories, than to come and put a shoulder to the wheel and help do it.

I was full of hope a few weeks ago, and really thought that we were to have our more than decimated ranks filled up, but it looks doubtful now. meantime our Army must dwindle away, by exhaustion, battles, +c, and the next thing will be a repulse, a stop in our victorious career and another falling back, but thank the Lord there can hardly be but one more "falling back" within my term of service even if I live it out.

I am glad to hear that the Carbine arrived safe. it was taken from a member of the 1st Virginia Cavalry and a saucy one he was there was no demoralization about him, and he looked upon the Battle of Gettysburg as only another exposition of the extraordinary military genious of Gen Lee. we were in the first line not they and he was brought into our Hd Qrs and I took him over to Brigade Hd Qrs. I asked him how much force Lee had, and he answered "I reckon your fellows will find enough of them." I am only sorry he did not give "us fellows" a chance to find them.

I was very much surprised and shocked to hear of the death of Will Wells. it does not seem possible. it seems as though it was only yesterday that I left him at Poolesville Md. so full of life and enjoyment. I hope the good people and *brave* men of N Hampton will be able to find something else to talk about now. he has given his life to the cause whatever he, or his motives were. How many of the things that wear pantloons around them, have given even thier services. I see that Capt Pierce of Co G in our Regt has been restored so that cuts off my chance for Captaincy, but I had decided to remain Adjutant so it makes no difference. Col P supposed he would not be restored as it had been so long since he was dismissed, and the recommendations for a promotion would have been made three weeks ago if I had decided which to do, but it is just as well as it is. I have got another horse (a female horse) and some poor "sesesher" will morn the loss of her. she is saddled with a saddle marked "Confederate States" and Jefferson is minus herself and Equipments, but he can afford to lose her and I can afford to keep her because I am allowed forage for two horses.

I have been interrupted by Officer friends four times since I commenced this letter once each from the 37th + 18th Mass once from the 1st Mass Cavalry and once from the 2nd RI and now comes Rogers announcing that supper is ready so I shall have to finish by candle light.

I have had a very good supper of Cold Mutton, Blackberries, Hardtack soaked and fried, the mutton was foraged from our sesesh friends. our men go out most every day and bring in Sheep cattle or hogs and the Regt has been well off for fresh meat. It seems to me that the Army was never so lawless as now, but Mr Barten says that the Army never behaved so well in this part of the country, and by his accounts Popes Army when here must have acted like fiends he has had his house searched, even his wifes bed room almost before she could leave it, and I think that would make me "sesesh" if anything could but, after all it is war, and much as this people have felt it they have never experienced war as war is realized in other countries. Mr Barten even says that they don't know what war is as it is carried on in the old country he said that when war breaks out there they expect to lose house lands and everything. it is what our Rebel friends chose and I suppose it is weak to feel any pity for them but my sense of justice and my feelings are sadly at varience on this subject.[23]

We have just received a new sett of colors from the State House and have packed up our old sett of worn and tattered and battle stained sett to return there. Col Parsons ordered them while I was at Brigade Hd Qrs, the new ones are very bright and showy, but why anyone should prefer them to the old battle stained banners is more than I can see. I had a love for those ragged old fellows, but I spurn these bright new ones. They savor of bounty Volunteers, or drafted conscripts, and I cannot get rid of the feeling. however I am not the command-ing Officer so I must put up with my feelings. in fact I have no right to any

feelings, but still as the colors and thier guard are the Adjutants especial charge I may be excused from having some feeling on the subject and I cannot take such pride in these new fellows as I did in the old rusty ones, until they have waved over such fields as thier predecessors have, and (it is possible they never will).

I see by to days papers there is a probability that New York will escape the draft altogether. I should not wonder it would be in keeping with everything else it seems to me that the powers that be are almost demented. You did not write what Abel Kimball was down to Gettysburg for nor when he was there. I was probably within at least fifteen or 20 miles of him if he was there within 4 or 5 days after the battle. I should like to see him very much I found a Corporal of the 12th New Hampshire, with letters upon him +c. I also found the Corporals warrant close to him. I laid it upon his breast so that the burial parties could identify him and put up a head board if they wished. I wish I had language to give you a realizing sense of a battlefield like that men dead in all sorts of positions and horses almost without number, all saddled, many of them kneeling on all fours, with saddles on, precisely as though they had kneeled down for a lady to mount, heads bowed down, and necks beautifully curved, but stone dead. it was terrible and I saw plenty of horses and men with legs entirely shot away and lying just where they fell and bled to death.

You say you sent a list of the drafted but I did not get it, but it makes no difference as I had already seen it both in the Gazzette + in the Republican and also in the Free Press.

Please give my respects to the young lady at Mrs Clarkes. (or my love! which?) I admire her sentiments in regard to the rioters and I regret we could not have had a chance at them. we all boil over with wrath when we think how the miserable rabble, intimidated the whole of a great city like N Y. I am sorry that Bill K was drafted for I do not think it his duty to go except in the last extremity, and I hope he will get out of it, as for Cal he cannot go, if his discharge papers are in proper form. I am sorry to hear that Julia Clarke is so unwell. I hope it is nothing serious. I presume it is the effect of being shut up in that close office. it would kill me now, I believe to be confined to an office or a store. Give my respects to them all I have never seen General Meade, and of course I like him if he can whip these Rebs, thats the main point, I don't think Lee can make a very sudden dash on Washington, as long as our Cavalry sticks as close to him as they do, and there is as much force of infantry and Artillery between him and that place.

I was very much pained to hear of Mothers sickness don't fail to let me know just how she is when you write. I do hope it is nothing serious it seems to me you had better let the boarders go, and not try to keep any. after the next payment I can furnish you money enough to live on, and I am afraid that the keeping of boarders worrys Mother to much, and it certainly cannot pay. I have heard that

Fred Clarke was just gone with consumption, is it so? I have seen the names of 5 or 6 of the discharged men of Co C who have been drafted, and three of the dismissed Officers. Capt Lombard + Capt Newell of Springfield and Lieut Moore of Greenfield.

You wrote me a good long letter and I think I have repaid it. Where my next one will be from I cannot tell. I expect we shall tramp tomorrow but still we may not.

Give my love to Thomas + Matt, with lots to Mother. My respects to all the neighbors tell Cal if we stay here tomorrow I shall write to him. With much love

Your aff brother
Charlie.

95

Head Quarters 10th Mass Vols near Warrenton VA
Aug 2nd 1863

Dear Mother,

It is Sunday night and the Tattoo is just beating and although I do not owe any letters home I thought I would just write a few lines to let you know that I am still at this place with no immediate prospect of moving as I can see. to day has been a tremendous hot day and it does not cool off any although it is 9 o'clock at night. every rag of my clothes are wet through with persperation and I have to keep continually wiping my face to keep it from wetting the paper I am writing. it is very much like our Harrisons Landing weather of last year, but not quite so hot but it seems as if this was hotter than I can bear.

Last Friday night we were all aroused by a great commotion in the camp of the 37th and finally I got up and went over to see what the row was, and found them all up getting breakfast, and chattering like a flock of black birds, over an order for them to start for Warrenton Junction at 3 o'clock to take the cars for NY City, in pursuance of which order disappeared the next morning. they were almost crazy with joy at the idea of going. they think that they are going to be stationed there to guard conscripts, but "I cannot see it" in that light. 3 other regts from the Corps went at the same time, and they were ordered to be the largest regts so it looks to me as though they were destined for some expedition, perhaps Charleston, at any rate it does not look like work for us for we need reinforcements for all sending men off.

Col Parsons and myself rode into town last night and through the streets. it looks very gloomy in the evening, for none of the houses are lighted for the very

good reason that they have nothing to light with or so little that they do not light up except on very important occasions.

The Guerrillas are all around us and many men straggling from camp have been gobbled up, some 6 or 7 sutlers also were captured day before yesterday within three miles of here. this is done by the citizens who put on the "Cornfed" uniform and arm themselves for such purposes and when pursued become peaceable citizens again. I wish the authorities would drive every man over the lines as we go in.

We have had no mail to day, and I don't know as I should have got a letter if we had as it is, not a *week* since I received one, however I continue to expect until they come. we are always as much disappointed when the mail does not come as though it was full of letters for each one of us. We have been hoping to see the Paymaster but I don't know as we ever shall again. it is now almost six months since we have been paid and every body is out of money and has been for a long time. it is always so. we never get our pay when we ought to.

We have moved our camp to day from down in a miserable low ravine up to a high hill, and hope to get more and purer air than we had before.

Our Regiment has got clothed and shod again, so that they make quite a presentable appearance again. Oh Oh dear the miserable black bugs come flying into the tent banged against the tent, desk, my head, or anything that comes in thier way. for all the world like the minnies at Fairoaks. they are so thick I cannot write.

It is Sunday night and I had not intended to write but sat so long after sundown in the tent door, gazing on the distant town, and hearing the whistle of the Locomotive, and the striking of the town clock that I grew homesick, and thought I must write although I owed you none, and had nothing to write about either, most 11 long months more even if we live to come home at all. it seems longer to look forward to than 3 years when we came out, for alas we know what trials and tribulations those eleven months must bring as they roll slowly over our heads, that many of us must yet lay down our lives before the rest turn their joyful faces homeward.[24]

I saw a notice in Saturdays Herald that the 52nd had arrived at Cairo Ill on thier way home I suppose they will be there before this reaches you. they have seen much more of the world in thier short nine months than we have in over two years. if we could only be sent out of this miserable state of Virginia, even to worse hardships it seems as if it would be a relief, but worse hardships are not to be found than we have endured since March 1862 but you do not hear so much of them now, for it has got to be so much a matter of course that we do not write of them so much as we used to but I suppose you'll hear enough of them, when the conscripts get here, if they ever do which I very much doubt, as near as I can make out from the papers about $9/10$ or $11/12$ of those drafted are

exempted, and I guess poor Uncle Sam will turn up minus men but with pockets full of money.

The bugs have gained the victory and I must close and surrender. Please remember me with respects to Mrs Shannon, and to Miss Hawes, also to all the neighbors. with love to Mary Mattie + Thomas, I am with much love

Your aff son
Charlie

Tuesday Aug 4th 1863

I did not finish this letter yesterday as I did not know but I should get a letter, or have something to write about, but neither is the case. I see one of the papers doubts the fact of pontoon bridges, but it is true our Army has two at least at Rappahannock Station and is also rebuilding the Orange and Alexandria R R bridge across the Rappahannock. Col P and myself are going down to make Mr Barten another call. please write oftener to

Your aff son
C

96

Head Quarters 10th Mass Vols Aug 11th 1863

Dear Mary,

Your welcome letter of the 7th inst came duly to hand last night which with one received from Mother on Friday makes two received from home since I have written, a most unheard of occurrence so I hasten to answer, although it is hotter than Tophet and I have been running round all the morning about a report I have to make out, about as long as our old family Bible.

I was much interested in your account of the 52nd arrival, but I wish it had been the 10th instead but we have got longer yet to serve than they have been in the service. however I suppose the time will come though it seems awful slow, and how many of us will live to see it no one can tell. Give my respects to Elbridge and congratulations that he got safely through. I know he feels much better and prouder than when he went than if he had followed the example of others and staid at home with the cowards to be drafted and have to pay 300.00 to get off. I am sorry to hear that Ned Hamlin fared so hardly It was very sad that young Phelps must die just as they got ready to come home.

I am very much worried about Mothers health, and I do hope to hear that she is better you must take good care of her. You did well about Sarah and I will be

glad to pay the price of her wages if I ever get any pay myself. it is almost six months since we have seen the paymaster, or rather since we have been paid for he did come to pay us off while we were across the river last time, just before we commenced in pursuit of Lee but he was not allowed to come across and we could not come across to him, and when we came back he had been obliged to "skeedadle" and we started for Pennsylvania on the jump. I don't know why he does not come now but he is a slow coach anyway. it is reported that his clerk is sick, and so all these soldiers have to wait until he gets well, for his clerk is his own son and his wages are 75 dollars a month, which I suppose he does not want to go out of the family by getting a new clerk. You can get anything you want at Kelloggs and I will pay for it.

I should like very much to see Abel Kimball you did not say how long after the battle he was there or what he thought of it.

I have already named my horse "Mollie" so Cora or Bess will have to wait until I get another of the female persuasion, and I am afraid that your calculations about my keeping one of them will come to naught I fancy you have not much idea how much it costs to keep a horse, to say nothing of building a barn to keep him in My lady horse is not a remarkable horse in any respect, a very good saddle horse but not fast like Tommie. She is intended to carry my saddle bags, blankets +c on the march. As to how I got her you should not be inquisitive, perhaps Jeff Davis presented her to me, and perhaps he did not. at any rate she is a native of the sunny south, and has arrived at the age of about 7 years. As for beauty she is not near as handsome as my Tom, but of course being a lady horse she could not expect to be but she is very amiable, which you know makes up for any lack of beauty. I am sorry to hear that Mr Henry Strong is so sick remember me to him and Mrs Strong.

I cannot write more than three words without stopping to drive away the flies. they are as thick as thick can be and torment the lives out of man and beast, and the sweat just rolls off me in great drops as I sit here and write.

We have got a new Gen (Brig Gen Terry) in command of our Division. Gen Newton took command of the 1st Corps after Gen Reynolds death. he is a Michigander, and what they sent him here for I do not know. I have not seen him yet. Brig Gen Bartlett of this Corps has been in command since Gen Newton left until now.

I have just got up and had a grand battle with the flies and drove them all out of the tent but they all got back again before I got seated. it is mighty hard work to fight flies and write too. I do not see any signs of our moving and hope I shall not until the weather gets cooler. Our Brigade sends out a patrol of 100 men every day and Sunday 4 men of the 7th Regt were taken prisoners. they gave thier parole which they had no right to do, consequently when they came in they had to take a Court Martial.

This is the greatest country for black berries I ever saw and there is an old nigger who lives close by here who has a cow that gives fabulous quantities of milk, so we have berries and milk morning and night. some rascals from another Regiment stole the poor Nig's cow and calf one night, and he came rushing over to us in a peck of trouble, so I started out a Sergeant and 2 men and they succeeded in overhauling them and bringing them back which was more than we expected, as it was very dark and they got into the woods.

Col Parsons and myself rode down to Warrenton last evening to call upon Mr Barten but he was not at home. the streets were full of ladies and four out of five I should think were dressed in mourning but they are desparate Rebels, and glory in thier treason and shame. I have no doubt but that it is the Southern women keep this rebellion up and I don't know but what we shall have to kill off all the men before they will come to terms.[25]

I see by Mothers letter that she thought I gave the articles I mentioned to Mr Barten. I only bought them for him of our Commissary, which he cannot do. he offerred to pay me for them in gold, greenbacks were just as good. I was not possessed of money enough to buy them. I was very much surprised at Eels bill. he told me before I gave him the job that it would not cost more than 30 or 40 dollars, and his bill is over 70. I shall write him about it and if he don't come down some, he never will get any more jobs from me.

I am very glad to hear that Mattie is better, give my love to her and Thomas I wonder if she has forgotten that she owes me a letter. Mrs Parker received the copies of those letters and sent her thanks to me, so you can have them and welcome.

I do not think of anything more of interest to write in fact it is hard work to get enough incident out of this dull life in camp to make a letter of. when on the march there is enough but then one cannot get any chance to write it. Give my best love to Mother, and my respects to all the neighbors. I wrote to Cal K last week. With much love

Your aff brother
Charlie.

97

Head Quarters 10th Mass Vols near Warrenton VA Sept 7th 1863

Dear Mary,

I received your *little note* last Saturday night and I had begun to think you did not know you had a brother in the army. I have just returned from the Picket line. Lieut Munyan and I rode out to see if we could not get some tomatoes as

the Picket line crosses the Winchester Road about one and one half miles from here and the country people bring in produce to the line to sell, but we did not see only one dowdy looking female with 2 or 3 dozen eggs to sell. the Yankee Army is a perfect god send to these people notwithstanding they hate us so, for our Commissaries sell them salt sugar tea and coffee at government prices whereas if we were not here they could not get them at any price. We went to the nearest post to where Capt Ives of our regiment was captured last Thursday night. there is a house a little ways outside the lines where lives the wife of one of Mosbys guerillas,[26] whom report says is no better than she should be. Capt Ives was Field Officer of the Day, and he went out there and while quietly chatting and displaying his pretty airs and graces seven guerillas came down upon him and he is on his way to Richmond where he can reflect at liesure upon the uncertainty of human events and the reliability of Sesesh grass widows. The house is within 1/4 of a mile of our Picket post where I went this morning, and Lieut Munyan was in command of the post at this time and hearing almost immediately of it, he started four men and a Corporal to the assistance of Capt I. but he surrendered at discretion and they had galloped him off before the boys could get there. if he had made any resistance he need not have been captured, but he is not one of the resisting kind, and he will have to serve the rest of his time in Libby prison.[27] however he was not worth anything as an officer and nobody cares for him. he had when captured a borrowed sash, and pistol and horse, which the Rebs got. he had not 25 cts in his pocket and I reckon will not have a very pleasant time. We have received a note from him on the road telling what he wants done with his affects and saying he was well treated I am very sorry for his wife as she has a baby about a week old, but still I should think she would be glad for he was a scamp and never treated her well at all. they were married you remember while the Regiment was in Hampden Park.

That is the only incident of any interest that has happened since I wrote last I believe. The guerillas take somebody prisoner of our men most every week, but as they are generally privates, they do not keep them but generally let them go, but Capt Ives having a horse they took him along. The Court Martial of which Col Parsons is president are still in session, and they have one or two Conscripts to try for desertion so I presume we shall have some shooting to do before a great while.

The 2nd RI Vols is the only one which has received any Conscripts in our Brigade and these deserters are of them. I hope they will be shot but I hate to have to go and see it done as we shall have to if they are shot and I have no doubt they will be though the sentence has not transpired yet.

I am sorry you did not go to Goshen if you wanted to go what anybody could want to go to Goshen for passes my comprehension but I suppose it is all right. Deerfield is a much better place to go to. I suppose Mrs Fowles Party must have

been a very grand affair, but I am glad I was not obliged to endure anything of that kind. I should rather do a three days tour of Picket any time.

The weather here is very warm in the day time but quite cool nights so that three blankets are very comfortable. I don't know but what we are going to stay here all winter I do not see much signs of moving, although we have orders to be ready at a moments notice every little while. I suppose the Rebs are busy conscripting and will be down upon us in great force before long. meantime we get no conscripts, nor anything else, and I hope we shall not for our term is so short now only a little more than 9 months that it seems too bad we should have to spend the rest of our term drilling thieves plus robbers but however we shall have to stand it so there is no use grumbling.

You speak of going out to Matties I wonder if she remembers she has got a brother in the army, I guess not. have not heard anything from her for a long time.

Mr Barten + wife are as lively and entertaining as ever and always overjoyed to see us when we go there. she plays on the piano and sings splendidly.

I have lost my horse Molly. Gen Sedgwick sent one of his aids de camp down a few days ago and invited me to deliver him up to an ill looking old Sesesh who accompanied him. the aid was not about it and so was I but could not help it. however, the Confederacy owes me a horse now and I hope to get it before the war is over.

The Sesessionists think there never was a Gen like Sedgwick he allows them to buy of the Commissaries, which no other Gen would ever do, and people come in from a long distance beyond the lines and buy of them. I presume the stolen green backs from the guerillas, there is much feeling on the subject but I suppose nothing will be done about it, but one thing is certain I shall confiscate another horse at the first opportunity.

I cannot think of anything more to write, and so I must close please write oftener, for it is terribly dull here and if I do not get letters it makes me homesick.

Give my love to Mother Matt + Thomas and respects to all the neighbors, particularly Mrs Clarke + family and Mrs Kingsley + Mrs Cooks.

Very aff your brother
Charlie.

SIX

If My Life Is Only Spared

October 1863–February 1864

By the autumn of 1863 a veteran of the Army of the Potomac could rightly view the war as interminable. Back in Virginia, in slow pursuit of Lee's army once again, Brewster participated in the Bristow campaign in October and the battle of Rappahannock Station in November. He began to worry seriously about his ability to make a living in civilian society, if he survived the war. He relished his officer's status, grieved for his slain horse, and endured his third winter at war, this time at Brandy Station. Mercifully, a furlough sent Brewster home for thirty-five days in February and March. The worst was yet to come.

98

Head Quarters 10th Mass Vols Bristow Station VA Oct 7th 1863

Dear Mother,

You will no doubt be surprised when you observe the heading of this letter. Last Wednesday night just at dusk came an order for the Third Division to pack up and be ready to march at once which was done and after waiting until 11 o'clock we finally got started and marched to Culpeper C H and then turned off onto the Orange and Alexandria R R towards the latter place. We marched with very little rest until 9 o'clock next morning when we arrived at Rappahannock Station our way having been enlivened by several smart showers during the night. here we halted to make a cup of Coffee and eat a hardtack, and the 3rd Brigade went into camp as they had arrived at thier destination after resting an hour and a half, we (the 1st + 2nd Brigades) resumed our line of march and just as we started it commenced to rain and I never saw it rain harder it really beat through everything and we could hardly make our horses face it. Every little gully became a roaring torrent and the soldiers had to wade continually. we kept on in this way until about 3 o'clock PM. and the rain never held up at all, when

Capt. James H. Wetherell (*left*), Lt. Col. Joseph B. Parsons (*center*), Capt. Flavel Shurtleff (*right*) of the Tenth Massachusetts. This photograph was probably taken at the regiment's camp in Warrenton, Virginia, in 1863. A year later, on May 12, 1864, Wetherell was fatally wounded in the battle of Spotsylvania. Parsons commanded the regiment from July 1862 until June 1864, when the Tenth completed its term of service. *Courtesy of Jonathan Allured*

we were halted and told to camp for the night. When it immediately cleared off and the sun came out beautifully. this was near Bealton Station, next morning we started again and marched to Catlets Station where we halted for dinner and left the 1st Brigade and 2 sections of a Battery. after an hours halt we took up our line of march and arrived at this place just before dark 44 miles from the front which we had left. we went into camp, and everything indicates that we are to stay here

for some time. our business is guarding the rail road and the Bridge at this point, which is one of those that the Rebels destroyed in Popes retreat, in the rear of his train and the road for miles is strewn with the remains of the trains of cars which he destroyed. the houses here have all been destroyed and the soldiers use the lumber to make thier bunks more comfortable. I rode down yesterday to an old camp at Manassas Junction, with two wagons and loaded them with old boards. it was right in the midst of the old Rebel fortifications which are now all covered over with grass and weeds and the whole country looks desolate enough. It seems quite like civilized life here as a train of cars goes by on the rail road not 6 rods from where I am writing, about once in 15 minutes one train follows another in the number of 6 or 7 then after a little while, a lot of them going the other way.[1] they are loaded with supplies for the Army and Conscripts one long train has just gone by with nothing but Conscripts, and I should think the Army was being somewhat recruited but not enough to do any good. Capt Weatherill arrived yesterday and reports that we shall not get any recruits unless we have another draft.

The principal subject of conversation in the Regiment now is the circular from Head Qrs of the Army announcing that those Regiments whose term of service expires this spring and summer can (if they will reinlist for three years or the war) go home to recruit and reorganize. I hardly think this Regiment could do so, but I wish they would because then we could come home and stay this winter. I do not know however as we could get any volunteers if we should come. patriotism seems to be at a very low ebb just now. Many of the Officers of the Regiment will undoubtedly agree to come out again but the men are convinced that they never will try soldiering again though I presume that after they got home and had been at home a month or so they would be glad to come back.

I am hardly able to write this morning. I am afraid I am going to be troubled as I was last winter. last night I was taken with terrible griping pains in the bowels and after groaning and tumbling around I sent the doctor who gave me something which quieted them, but I am very weak this morning. I was also taken vomiting and thought I should throw up my boots. however I hope I shall not be sick, but shall get over it all right.

Every one is wondering of course what we are going to do, and whether we shall stay here all winter or not. the rest of our Corps has gone still further to the front than where we left them. we are going to building earthworks here but some think we shall be relieved and sent to Tennessee, but I cannot see any indications of it. the 11th + 12th Corps have gone however and it is reported that more are to go. we are only about 30 miles from Alexandria but cannot get down there any more than if we were 300 miles off.

George Bigelow is quite well, and desires to be remembered to you all. he had his valise stole night before last containing every rag of clothes except what he

had on his back. he has been mighty unfortunate in this respect for he lost everything in the same way about a year ago at White Plains when we were on the march down to Falmouth. Col Parsons is also well and sends respects. I suppose he would be made a Col if the Regiment had been filled up but under existing orders no regt that has less than a minimum of men can have a Col and neither can it have any new 2nd Lieuts so I am afraid there will be no promotions in this regiment.

I cannot think of anything more to write and besides I am sick at the stomach and very sleepy from the effects of the opium I took last night. Give my love to Mary Matt and Thomas. Uncle Ed + family, and my respects to all enquiring friends particularly Mrs Clarkes Mrs Cooks, and Kingsley's families. how is Mr Henry Strong. you wrote a while ago that he was very sick. please write and let me know about him, and please write often to with much love

Your aff son Charlie.

99

Head Quarters 10th Mass Vols Warrenton VA Oct 30th 1863

Dear Mother,

I have seated myself to write you a short letter although I am and have been for the past week quite sick with a violent cold cough chills accompanied by diarrhea and have been lying on my back most of the time. I wrote to Mary about a week ago, just after we came to this camp. I then intended to write to Mattie next day but have written to no one since that time. I am somewhat better to day but do not feel like sitting up a great while at a time as the medicine I am taking makes me quite sick at the stomach.

There is nothing of interest to write about. we have heard some quite heavy firing of Artillery occasionally during the week and have had orders twice to be ready to move at a moments notice but nothing comes of either and we go on and fix up our quarters little by little every day just as though we are going to stay all winter. to day there has been a rumor that this Corps was going to Tennessee but nobody believes it and there is also a report that work is suspended upon the Rail Road, but I do not know whether it is true or not. things operate very curiously in this army now a days and we are as ignorant as anybody as to what is going on, for indicated by our movements or rather no movements.

You spoke in your letter of Oct 12th about Eels bill I have not been able to send him anything yet but expect to next pay day which we suppose will be in about 10 day's or two weeks, when I shall send him part and the rest the next pay day he

made the bill double what he said it would cost and I thought he could afford to wait a while especially as I told him when I got him to do the job that it might be two pay days before I could pay him. he described everything that would need to be done and then I pressed him to say how much it would cost. he said between 30 + 40 dollars not more than the latter, and then his bill comes in for $72.00 I have no doubt he has overcharged on the time, but as of course you kept no account of it I shall have to pay it, then as soon as it was done he wrote me quite a sharp letter about not hearing from me. I thought I would not worry myself though I shall send him a part this pay day. You need not worry yourself about it and if he comes dunning around you you can tell him he must talk to me and not bother you for you did not order the job and knew nothing about it. he will have his pay all right and more than is his right in my opinion, but I do not [want] you to worry about it for there is no need of it, and it is not your concern and I can take care of the business myself. I am sorry you have lost King from your family for I liked him very much but you have got Elbridge back so that makes it up. I was quite alarmed at hearing in one of Col P-s letters that you have sprained your ancle. I expected to get a letter from home last night but as usual when I expect one most, was disappointed. Mary wrote in her last that you were getting better but I want to hear again, just how you are. I am glad Tom and Mattie are coming to be with you this winter for I know it will be very pleasant for you all. Do you realize that our term of service is reduced to 7 months 22 days, and if my life is only spared I shall be a free man again in that time I wonder how it would seem to be ones own man once more, and have nobody with a bigger pair of shoulder straps than ones own to tell him when to lie down and when to get up, and to be able to go 10 Rods without asking permission like a school boy but after all I presume I shall be anxious to get back again after a short period of liberty, but I never shall enlist to carry a musket again but what is the use of talking, I may not live to see the time but when I think how short the time is it seems as though it was almost here.[2]

We have had a very pressing invitation to reenlist and go home for six weeks to recruit up but this regiment "can't see it" they are bound to be free once more anyhow, and think it would be time enough to reenlist when they get ready I do not blame them much. But I must close. this is not a very interesting letter but there is nothing to write about to make it so. Give my love to Mary, Matt + Thomas. Uncle Ed + family My respects to all the neighbors and friends, particularly to Elbridge, Mary Fil and Mrs Kingsleys Clarkes and Cooks. Tell Mrs K I had a letter from Bob the other night. I cannot think of anything more to write. With much love

Your aff son
Charlie

100

Head Quarters 10th Mass Vols Rappahannock Station VA Nov 9th 1863

Dear Mary,

I had but just sealed and put into the mail bag my last letter to Mother last Friday when orders came that we should march the next morning so last Saturday morning we started for this place 15 miles distant from Warrenton we reached the rail road at Bealton Station about noon and halted and had lunch and then started up the rail road. we soon came across the 5th Corps and turned to the right and immediately saw that we were in for a battle by the long lines of soldiers in battle array. Gen Shalers Brigade was to have the advance. it is the 1st Brigade of our Division and as he needed two more Regts he requested that he might have the 7th + 10th Mass so we were immediately ordered to report to him, and of course as is our usual luck got a front seat in the fight. we immediately took our places on the line, and directly the whole line started, and it was a glorious sight, you may well believe. the line was fully a mile long and as it moved forward it looked like a thick hedge moving over the fields, but I am not master of language suitable to describe it.

The Rebels were in earthworks and rifle pits on top of a hill close on the bank of the Rappahannock and between us and them was another hill our skirmishers drove the Rebel skirmishers off this last hill and we advanced up to it our Batteries immediately took possession of the top, and we lay down and the ball commenced. it was then about 3 o'clock, and the Artillery firing was kept up until dark when the left of our line swept round and charged upon the Rebels, and routed them utterly, capturing 1600 prisoners, 2000 muskets, 4 Cannon 7 Limbers, plus 9 stands of colors and we had only 1500 men engaged on our side. it is the most glorious victories of the war for its size. the charge was made by the 6th Maine + 5th Wisconsin Regts. We lay and supported the Batteries, our Regt lost 1 man killed and one wounded, the latter lost both his hands and was wounded in the leg besides, and I have lost my beautiful, my pet, my almost brother Tommie. I can hardly write it without crying. I rode up to the front, and when the shelling commenced I dismounted and my man took him by the bridle and we both lay down right at his feet. I will never forget how proud he looked, merely pricking up his ears a little as the shells burst all round and over him. all at once he gave a jump and my man got up but could not keep him still. he finally got him quiet, and called to me to see how he trembled. we both supposed he was afraid, and wondered at it but the Regt was immediately ordered to another part of the field to support another Battery and I told the man to take the horse off behind a hill some distance off. About sundown he came up to the Regt and said Tommie was wounded and could not go hardly at all. I told him to bring him up and sure enough he was wounded right in the breast a little hole about as

big as my finger, but I hoped he could be cured, but we were ordered the next morning to march about 3 o'clock and the man tried to lead the poor fellow, but he fell down every few steps and he had to leave him.[3]

This I learned from others, as I have not seen the man since we started yesterday morning but as the rest of our Brigade went to Kelleys Ford I suppose he followed them, thinking that we should rejoin them, but instead of that we are left here to guard the bridge and wagon trains which are all parked just the other side of the river crossing many acres. The rest of the army has gone on they had a skirmish with the Rebels at Brandy Station four miles from here last night but drove them, and the 3rd Corps is now three miles beyond Brandy Station and consequently about four miles from Culpepper CH. At the same time that the 5th + 6th Corps came to this place, the 1st + 2nd + 3rd went to Kelley's Ford and effected a crossing there and we hear that Birney's Div captured a whole Regt of North Carolina Rebels there. the Rebels were just commencing to build winter quarters here and had no idea of being disturbed We are on the south bank of the river. there is a short range of hills that crosses the river at this point and they are covered with earthworks of all descriptions, which have been made over two or three times as the Rebs or our forces have held them at different times. this is the same place where we left the 3rd Brigade of our Division when we went down to Bristoe Station. I don't know what all this move amounts to but the orders were to advance, and pitch into the enemy wherever we found him and these orders have been obeyed to the letter so far. The guns we captured here belong to the famous Washington Artillery from New Orleans, the same we took the guns from Marye's Heigts last may, and they begin to think that the 6th Corps is after them with a sharp stick.

One Reb officer, a prisoner wanted to know what Corps it was that fought them. he was told it was the 6th "I knew it" said he. "I would have bet my bottom dollar on it" they have a wholesome dread of the 6th Corps.

They all say I can get pay for my horse, but there is so much red tape about the operation that I have my doubts but money can never make his loss good to me, but it is a wonder I was not hit myself for it came just where I used to stand and hug him when he was standing still but as it was it did not go a great ways from me. I am writing this letter, not knowing whether I shall have a chance to send it for a week or not. I do not think of anything more to write Give my love to Mother Matt + Tom and respects to all the friends and neighbors. With much love

Your aff brother,
Charlie.

101

Head Quarters 10th Mass Vols Camp Sedgwick Nov 21st 1863

Dear Mother,

Your welcome letter of the 16th came safely to hand last night, and I hasten to reply although I wrote to Mattie day before yesterday, but I want to encourage you to write oftener if I can. I have not much to write about we have been expecting to march every morning since last Tuesday but the word has not come yet, and last night a northeast rain storm set in which may put in a veto upon our moving at all. we have several rumors that our forces are tearing up the rail road from Culpepper C H to Brandys Station I do not know whether it is true or not but if true I cannot see what they are doing it for. Yesterday we had a grand review of the Corps by General Sedgwick[4] and some English Officers. it was a grand sight and I wish you could have seen it, as our Regiment passed the General I saw him point to us almost all the Regiment saw it and saw him turn and say something to one of the Englishmen. One of the staff Officers it is reported, overheard what he said, it was "if all the Regiments in my Corps were like the 10th Mass I could go to Richmond and back again." So of course we are jubilent there at. I must tell you a little of Brig Gen David Russell.[5] he used to be the Colonel of the 7th Mass Regt in our Brigade. he was the General who stormed the works at Rappahannock Station. he rode his old black horse right up to the intrenchments and jumped the rifle pits, and rolled into the Fort at the head of his men. he was wounded in the foot but never said anything about it until days after the battle. he also had a number of bullet holes in his clothes, but when asked about them he said he tore it on the saddle. he was designated as the man to take the captured colors to Washington and present them to the president. it is considered about as high an honor as could be given to a man, but he did not want to go, and requested that Col Upton might go instead, but Sedgwick plus Wright insisted upon his going, so he went, but when he got there, instead of going himself, and making the most of it as most Generals would do, he sat down and did them up in paper, and addressed them to the President, and sent them by another person.

I am slightly acquainted with him and Col Parsons is intimately acquainted. he is one of the most perfect of Gentlemen, but makes no show at all. he wears an old slouched hat, and a common soldiers blouse but he has courage and judgement enough for a dozen common Brigadiers.

Well I don't know as this will interest you at all. Our pay master has been here three days but has not paid our Regt yet. our turn comes tomorrow. I shall send Eels part of his money when we are paid. I am sorry if I have offended in writing that his bill is none of your concern. I meant his bill not the work he did and that he was not to come bothering you with it, and you need not be afraid because

even if I do get killed there will be enough to pay him. I do not think much of your house full of boarders for I know it must cost more to feed them than you get pr week for thier board, I am afraid that the more you have the worse off you are. however I suppose if you do not run in debt you must at least make both ends meet, but I do not see how, for our mess buys everything at cost, and we cannot get along less than $5.50 per week, and we don't have any of the luxuries that you have to buy either, but we have to pay the government $16.50 per month for our cook (Rogers) he being an enlisted man. I notice you have been reading Army Regulations, but you have made a great mistake when you say that, they say that the Adjutant gets more pay than a Captain for they don't say any such thing. the difference is just $10 in favor of the Captain, but a Captain can get along without a servant, but the Adjutant having one or two horses cannot. and as there are no opportunities to hire any others, we have to take enlisted men and I have to pay $24.50 per month for mine, the difference between him and Rogers is that mine draws his rations from the government while Rogers eats our own fodder. it is a little singular that only the night before your letter came I was talking with the new Chaplain about Madame Dwight. he wanted to know if she was living, and I could not tell him, neither could I tell him whether Prest Allen was living or not, in fact when I think it over that I know hardly anything of Northampton.

Lieut Bridgman got back yesterday, but I have not seen him to speak with yet. I saw him at Review yesterday.

As to my horse I have not heard anything yet. I sent my papers to Washington to the proper Department but I do not much expect to get anything for it would be my luck you know. any body else would probably get paid for him, but I have been so cursed with ill luck all my life I do not expect any favors, nor fear any frowns of fortune now.

I have nothing to look forward to, and I don't know as I care much therefore. I am well acquainted with Capt Wilcox of the 27th. he used to be Sergt Major of our Regt. he is a good fellow, and no doubt a brave and competent Officer, notwithstanding he got tight, and I suppose that is all he had to do. now soldiers are looked upon with such loathing by all stay at homes, it is the general feeling among the old regiments, the real *Volunteers,* that the generality of the citizens loathe and hate them. this has arisen from the great anxiety, always (when a soldier gets a short respite and goes home) of the stay at home cowards to find out when he is going back, and what he came home for.[6]

You make a great fuss at home if an Officer gets set up, but nine tenths of your stay at homes spend thier time in getting drunk and getting over it, and yet not doubt, if you could be present you would see these same Officers, perfectly sober rushing up to the Cannons mouth amid a storm of lead and iron, and amid such sights and sounds as would alone kill the race of disabled men who have crept out of the draft on the strength of a corn on the toes, or a scratch on the finger.

I am very sorry to hear that John Cook has left his place in Boston, and I was very sorry he did not go to Oscar Edwards instead when he went to Boston, but no one however much older, could tell him anything, but I suppose all boys are the same. he will know 10 or 15 years hence that he knew nothing at the present period of his life, but I suppose experience must teach all, and generally when it is too late. I talked with him when I saw him last in Boston, and gave him earnest and good advice. (Perhaps you will laugh at the idea of my giving good advice) but I talked with him as I would a brother, and until he cried like a child and as I told him I talked of what I knew, and as one who knew of what he talked, in fact I plead with him, as I would with but very very few, for I am not an advice giver, and I do not like to meddle in other peoples affairs, any more than I like others to meddle in mine, but after all there was my own example you know and I felt all the time that it would amount to nothing.

The occasion of it all was his coming to see me one night at the American House when he was tight. it was the first time I had ever seen him so, and I felt badly enough, although you may not think that such a hardy sinner as every body considers me but it is true never the less, and I was fool enough to labor with him as tell you, however let it pass, it is only the experience of millions, and God you say is all powerful and could prevent it but He does not, and nothing and nobody else can, for each must fulfil his own destiny. Well, that is quite a new strain for me I don't know what I wrote it for, don't for worlds tell anyone that I ever wrote such a thing of Johnnie. I was questioned about him quite often and stoutly but I stoutly denied any knowledge of any thing of the kind of him.

Your gossiping letter as you call it is just what I like, for although I don't like gossiping at home, it is quite a different matter when it comes to letters. at home one hears the same thing over + over again, until you get sick of it, but out hear he has to depend upon letters entirely, you would be astonished to know what unimportant items become of great interest when one is away from home so long. Do you know whether Cal K has received my letter or not. Give my respects to him, Bill and Mrs K and all the family.

I should like to be able to inform you what we are going to do and when we are going to do it but I cannot nobody can make so little calculation ahead as the soldier. I think the experience must be good for us all, and learn us to take things as they come without fretting about the future, for when one quietly eats his breakfast in the morning and in the afternoon finds himself 15 miles away, engaged in deadly battle, it makes things generally look very uncertain.

I see the Gazzette gives our loss in the battle as 2 or 3 killed and eight or 10 wounded. we lost only one killed + 1 wounded it also says Adjt Brewster's horse was shot under him, whereas it was shot over him, but the missle came near to me than it would if had I been on his back.

Well you see in the letter what a long letter your letter has produced so I hope you will be encouraged to continue in well doing, writing both oftener + longer.

Give my love to Mary, Mattie + Thomas, and respects to all the neighbors. Give my love to Uncle Ed and family, and Aunt Lu when you write. Please write me again what regts Brown + Stuart Campbell[7] are in. if we should have a fight and gobble any prisoners I should want to look for them. We have got your storm that you wrote about I guess. It rains in torrents and is cold. Guess you will get tired of reading this long scribble, but if you do you can stop. With much love

Your aff son
Charlie.

102

Head Quarters 10 Mass Vols near Brandy Station VA Dec 9th 1863

Dear Mary,

It is one week tomorrow since we came back to this camp and since I wrote home last next day after writing we had four mails, and I got yours of Nov 22 plus 29th but have had nothing since. I suppose you are waiting until you hear that the Army has settled down again but I wish you would write just the same whether the army is on the move or not.

I have nothing to write about, it is very dull here. We are now engaged logging up and making a chimney and winter quarters, for the third time this fall. We are not permitted to know whether we are to stay here any time or not, but all the orders we had last year was "halt", and "rest", and we staid there five months. The weather is very cold, much colder than it was last year at this time I think. Everybody seems to think that we have done campaigning for this season, but I see that papers at the north are making a great fuss about our not fighting when we went over the Rapidan so I suppose they will blow about it until we shall have to start upon another grand splurge such as we made under Burnside last year. I wish some of the grumblers had been with us over there and had to stand in line of battle in drenching rain storms, and bitter cold nights possibly they would not be as anxious to fight as they are in thier comfortable houses at home.

I am glad to hear you had such a good time on Thanksgiving. you can easily imagine what our Thanksgiving was, marching through the mud, and not stopping to get anything to eat until 11 o'clock at night. it was the greatest wilderness over the other side of the river that I ever saw.[8] we were in the woods all the time we were over there. the houses were mostly mere huts in the woods, and most of the inhabitants fled at our approach, and many of them lost thier houses by the means which they would have saved if they had staid in them and minded thier own business. We found arms plus amunition in some of the houses, which was proof that they were the haunts of guerillas, and such got but

little mercy. we found one such just as we got across the river. the house was quite a small hut but the barns and outbuildings were large. The Army tore down all the buildings but the house and would have served that the same but there was a woman and child in it, but they carried of everything there was to eat in it, and all the furniture and crockery.

One of the turkies I told you we brought back with us has gone where good turkies go and other is fattening for the same fate. I reckon we enjoyed him full as well as you did, even if we did not have all the surroundings as you did. I don't think there is any hope of many reenlisting in this Regt. we have not got but one man yet we will count on Northampton's quota, as that is his residence. his name is C H Bigelow. he was painter and came out in Co C. he is very anxious to reenlist.

It is mighty hard to find enough to write about to fill up a letter, and probably will before 4 months to come, as nothing happens while we are in camp. We have an order for 2 Brigade Drills a week, aside from that I do not go out of camp once a week. The Major of the 37th Regt has left the service, and Mark Moody is to be Major in his place. he was a private in Co C. he has got along pretty fast and he is a good soldier and deserves it and has had the best of luck. I suppose there is no invitation to Officers to reenlist, and so we shall all come home when our time expires. has Northampton filled her quota yet, and is she going to escape the draft. the last I heard there were thirty enlisted from Northampton.

If Sue Mins, or Butler is with you give my respects to her and tell her she can come down and visit me and I will build a log hut for her, in magnificent style. thats the advantage of living in the Army when you have company you can build an addition on to your house.

I received notice from Washington they received my papers relating to my horse but they did not say when they would pay for him, or whether they would at all or not, so I am in just as much suspence as ever.

I received a letter from Cal Kingsley at the same time I received yours. tell him I will answer it soon, and also give my respects to him and all the family.

I have not bought me another horse yet and don't mean to if I can help it but I suppose I shall have to if I remain Adjutant. if I had known I was to lose him so soon I should have taken the last Captaincy that was offered me when Bishop was promoted.

Tell Matt I don't know but she considers the little addenda she made to your letter was to be considered as her letter. she owes me but it is not, won't pass as such at all. Give my love to her + Thomas to Mother, and to all Uncle Ed's family. give my respects to all the neighbors + friends. How does Johnnie Cook get along recruiting. Write very often to

Your aff brother Charlie.

103

Head Quarters 10th Mass Vols Dec 13th 1863

Dear Mother,

It is Sunday morning and as beautiful and bright a morning as sunshine can make it but it rained most all night as if the very windows of Heaven were opened but the Col and I are in snug winter quarters and we laugh at the howling of the tempest. we have our tent all logged up and a nice fire place and plenty of wood, and are as comfortable as it is possible to be while serving in the field, and our only fear now is that we shall have to get up some fine morning and depart leaving our good quarters and taking in exchange the cold ground and no tent at all.

There is nothing new to write about in this Army. I see the stay at home lawyers are terribly indignent we did not have a lot of men killed in our last campaign and are drawing comparisons between us and Grant's Army, not at all flattering to us, but still perhaps if this Army could be reenforced at the rate the other has been, instead of being depleated, we might make more of a show, and besides they got defeat out in Tennessee and until they got two Corps from this Army who won the first victory after the disgraceful defeat [at] Chicamauga, so I don't think it becomes them to plume themselves as quite much as they do about thier great victory for they had all the troops that could be spared from any other spot in the United States, and if they could not whip the Rebels then, I don't know when they could.

The reenlistment fever has broken out slightly in the Regiment and nine men have reenlisted two of which are Northampton men so two of the tremblers at home can take courage. the Regt is full of rumors that we are to be sent home this winter to recruit, but I don't see it but I have no doubt if we were to go home a good many of the men would enlist again, and perhaps nearly the whole Regiment, but they do not like to trust to any promises of a furlough and they all can move about that than they do about the bounties, though those are very acceptable.

If the Army stays here they will clean out the country as it did the country round Falmouth. there was plenty of wood when we came here within a mile of camp and now we have to go 3 miles for it. I am writing on a very nice mahogany table which was foraged out of a house out side the picket lines. a party went out the other day and brought in all the furniture of a large stone mansion and pretty much all the boards in the house and out buildings, some of the men have got a nice rose wood door made out of a piano top. such proceedings are rather rough, but such is war, and war is what this people wanted, especially the women, so I have not much pity for them. the owners had deserted this house or it would not have been molested.[9]

They are granting furloughs again, and this Army on the plan of Hookers last winter, and one Officer has gone from this regiment, but I shall not come home for it does not pay to come for 10 days, and our time is so near out. I think it is just as well to stick it out and [be] done with it.

I received your letter of Dec 6th and was much amused at your thinking you had got a photograph of my Tommy. the one you have is a picture of another Tommy and he belongs to Major Parker. it was taken before I bought this one, he is not to be mentioned the same day with my beauty.

The weather here has been awfully cold but to day it is uncomfortably warm which I do not like at this time of the year. it makes a fellow feel so lazy.

George Bigelow is just the same as ever. we are all lotting upon coming home next June but many of us may not live to see that time for there is plenty of time for a campaign next spring before our time is out, and I presume we shall have several battles before that time but I hope not I never want to see another, I do not wonder that the 27th Regt is going to reenlist for they have never had any hard soldiering to do and don't know anything about it. I wish they could have one of our campaigns to go through with.

Tell Mattie she must not think she can get rid of writing me a letter by tacking little notes on to yours or Marys for "I don't see it."

I wish you could see what a nice cozy place we have got for our quarters, but I suppose you would not think it as good as our old hog pen and no it is not. but it still is a palace for a soldier, this soldier experience has been a great thing for us for now we can go to housekeeping anywhere and at any time, after we get out of the service. We find that none of the things that were once considered necessary for comfort are really so and that a fellow can live just as well without a house as with one.

I cannot think of anything more to write, in fact there is just nothing at all to write about, and I cannot make a letter if I try. Give my love to Mary, Matt + Thomas and respects to all the neighbors and friends. I have ordered a new coat from D Kingsley, which will be sent on soon I suppose. Please write oftener to

Your aff son,
Charlie.

104

Head Quarters 10th Mass Vols Jany 7th 1864

Dear Mother,

It is some ten days since I have written home, and for the reason that before this I expected to have been with you. You know that I have been enlisting Veteran Volunteers and the business grew upon my hands, and in fact increased

greatly in the whole Army making more work necessary and more orders kept coming from Washington until they got the whole thing into such a mess that nobody could understand what was wanted and what was not. but one of the orders said that Officers rendered supernumerary (by the operations of volunteering) might be ordered home with the Veterans for 35 days, provided said Officers signifyed thier willingness to reenter the Military Service of the U S after the expiration of thier present term. well I signifyed and expected to come home with 118 men I had enlisted, but all at once came orders to be ready to move with 8 days rations and 60 rounds of ammunition and everything stopped then came a terrible storm of rain and it turned into snow, and that movement was stopped then came orders for our Division to be ready to move by rail immediately, and the 3rd Brigade went off in the night, and two or three days after the 1st Brigade followed it and we expected our turn would be next, but we have not gone. we hear that the 1st Brig is at Sandusky Ohio and the 3rd is at Frederick City Md. and now we expect to stay here. meantime all furloughs to Veterans are stopped and neither the Officers or men of this Regt can go at present and no one knows when they can, and everything appears to be in a hub bub. our Division Hd Quarters are not here and our mails do not come we have not had a sign of any mail for three days. I am much disappointed for I had calculated to come home for 35 days and as we were not on leave of absence but ordered home it would cost nothing to go. but now no one can tell whether we shall go at all or not.

The weather here is intensely cold and the ground is covered with snow. We had nothing like it at Falmouth last winter. there was a rumor day before yesterday that 15 men were frozen to death on picket but I do not know whether it is true or not. I hope not and I presume that the number is exaggerated if any were frozen.

I am very sorry for the men who enlisted, for they did it simply to get the furloughs, and no bounties would have tempted them without that, and now they are mad as hornets and are afraid they will not be furloughed at all. I worked night and day on the business, for there was an immense amount of writing to do and now to find it amounts to nothing, but just getting so many men to enlist and fooling them in this kind of way. I say it is a disgrace to the government, and there ought to be some way to compel them to keep thier promises however it is no use growling over it, for we cannot help it.

We have had pretty much all the select men or thier agents of all the towns in Mass who have any men in this Regt. and they might just as well have staid at home for all the extra men they got to reenlist, but they got some pretty pointed expressions of opinion from some of the men. one man told a couple of them that he had served 2 and ½ years but said he "I'd go in for another three years if you will" it shut the fellow up completely he could not say another word.

The Army is much weakened by the furloughing of Veterans so much so that

it has been contemplated moving back to Centreville but I guess they have concluded to remain here. there is a rumor that the 8th Corps and the troops around Washington are coming out but I do not know whether it is true or not. It makes the duties of those that are left much harder as the picket line of this Army is 72 miles long. Our Brigade is temporarily attached to the 2nd Division and I hope they will get the mails regulated so that we can get letters I don't know as letters go from here any better but I can see no reason why they should not.

Col Parsons has just left for Court Martial but does not expect to find any Court as many of the Officers composing it belonged to the Brigades which have gone. He has invited me to write a letter to his wife after I get this finished but I do not think I shall do it.

I heard yesterday that Dr Chamberlin is coming back as Medical Director of this Corps. if it is so it will rather interfere with his little arrangements for spending the winter in Philadelphia.

I do not think of anything more of interest to write this morning. Give my respects to all the neighbors, and my love to Mary, Mattie + Thomas reserving a large share for yourself from

Your aff son
Charlie.

105

Head Quarters 10th Mass Vols Brandy Station Va Jany 31st 1864

Dear Mary,

Your Welcome letter of the 23rd by Col Parsons came safely to hand on Wednesday and I have seated myself to night to answer it. I am all alone as Col Parsons has gone to Brigade Head Quarters. The weather up to yesterday has been terrible hot so much so as to render the meaning of a thick coat uncomfortable and coming right upon such very cold weather as we had just been having it prostrated us very much. we have had much colder weather and also much hotter weather this winter than last and I do not like such great changes.

The Chaplain has got a new Chapel and has held services in it all day and there is a meeting in progress now and at this moment they are singing and I think the noise of so many men singing together would astonish you if you could hear it.[10]

I perfectly agree with Mother as to writing on large sheets of paper and wish you to keep up the practice. Col Parsons had a very nice time at home and only

complains that the time was so short. I notice what you say in regard to his staying in the Army I don't know but I may as well tell you that he signifyed his willingness before he went home the same as I have done, but the matter is yet in doubt whether they are going to allow the Officers who did to go home with the men or not. there are 11 Officers of this Regiment who have signified thier willingness to remain and I hope they will order us home they may not and if they do not why then the signifying will amount to nothing and they cannot keep us. our number of Veteran Volunteers now amount to 133 and I presume there will be more of them when they see these go home as the furlough is the great object with them though the bounties help.

I am glad you had such a pleasant time in Springfield and also at the sleigh ride I see they are having gay times at home and I wish some of us could be there to participate. I am very sorry that Elbridge is going to leave you for he has been so kind to you all and I thank him very much for it. I agree with Mother that it is much pleasanter to sit in the old dining room. By the way if I should come home shall I not have to bring my camp bedstead and blankets you are so full I don't see where you are going to put me but I might build a little hut in the yard I am much amused at your leap year Ball and shall be happy to furnish the funds when you require them and if it is not coming off to soon shall perhaps be there to go. if you can get some very handsome young lady to invite me. I am very much obliged for the books. I had read East Lyme and have been reading Sylvias Lovers all day and have got about half through.

Probably if our Veterans come home we shall not come with our arms as the 27th did as these men are furloughed individually and will turn in thier arms and equipments to the Ordnance Officer and receive them again when they return as no Regiments go home as an Organization unless 3/4 of them reenlist which they probably will not do.

The camp has been full of rumors for 2 or 3 days of great squads of Rebels deserting and coming into our lines. It was reported that 150 of them came in day before yesterday and 130 yesterday but I do not know whether it is true or not. It is also reported that two Mississippi Regts tried to fight thier way in but did not succeed. I hope the reports are true but think that they should be taken with a great deal of allowance. We have had such warm weather the ground has dried up so that we began to think they would set up to campaigning again. It commenced to rain yesterday and there is every appearance that it is going to keep on so for some time so I guess there is no danger of that.

We had a Brigade Dress Parade night before last and in that performance the Adjutants of the several Regiments have to gallop down to the centre of the line, present arms and report. Well my horse took it into his head to be contrary and baulked and kicked up behind and before. the parade was got up for the edification of the Generals wife and the ladies at Head Quarters and you can

imagine how nice I felt at such a performance at such a time but I finally by a diligent application of my sabre and spurs brought him to a sense of his duty in the premises and he concluded to go on and mind his business, but I was mad enough to kill him on the spot.

Major Parker is sick and in the Hospital has been sick a week. I had a feast of butternuts to day. they were given me by one of the men who had them sent to him from home. I have not tasted anything so good for a long time not since Nellie Cooke sent me out some a year ago.

Capt Bishops wife is here in camp in a little 7 x 9 tent just big enough to turn round in. they were up here to dinner day before yesterday, but it does not seem to me that I should want my wife out here if I had one but there are a great many ladies out here at this time. There was a small fight somewhere yesterday we heard the firing but have not heard where it was. Give my love to Mother Matt + Thomas and my respects to Mr Clarkes Cookes and Mrs. Kingsleys families and all the rest of the neighbors. With lots of love

Your aff brother
Charlie.

106

Head Quarters 10th Mass Vols February 3rd 1864

Dear Mattie,

I have been considering for some minutes which to write at the commence-ment what I have for Dear Mother or Mary, but you are so uppish if one of the letters that comes into the house is not once in so often not directed to you that I concluded that I would address this to you. I have been very busy all evening folding and Endorsing, Muster In, Muster Out, + Description Rolls and Enlistment Papers for Veteran Volunteers, who still come dropping in and enlisting slowly. I have been quite busy for the past three days with them but not nearly as much so as with the first lot as there is not nearly so many, and I now understand the business and can get along better with it. If Northampton's quota is not full you can rejoice thier hearts with the information that one more man has reenlisted on thier quota. his name is Eben M Johnson. you can tell Tom and he can tell the selectman or he need not just as you and he please. I don't care I am sure. I had a letter from H K Starkweather during the time I was enlisting the first lot *anxiously* enquiring about the number that had enlisted on North-amptons quota, and when I got ready I wrote him. it was a curious letter and I almost wish I had kept it, as I should have liked to have shown it to you at home.

I burnt it as I do all my letters. I might I suppose have secured a large number of our floating no residence fellows to count on Northamptons quota, but I do not love the people of that delightful village as a whole, and as I owe them ooo I would not lift my little finger to get a man for them. I saw a list of the towns in Western Mass that had filled thier quotas, a few days ago and N Hampton was not among the number. I had supposed thier quota was full. I suppose the President's new call for 500,000 makes thier knees weak, did it not? I have not much faith in our Armys getting many men though, and I do not believe in *drafted patriotism* after the specimens we had last summer.

The Chaplain has been dedicating his new Chapel to night. Gen Eustis + wife and one of his aids and his wife, and Capt Bishop + wife were there and I suppose it was a great affair in a nutshell. I did not go, but they all say it was quite creditable for a camp demonstration. I saw a Reb the other day who had just come in and delivered himself up. he belonged to the 2nd Virginia Cavalry and was from near Lynchburg, but as usual I had forgotten what Regiment Brown Campbell belonged to and this fellow of course did not know him, nor anything about Highland County or in fact much of anything else. the Rebels come in quite freely lately I guess but we do not see many of them. this one and another came in the night before and had got permission of Provost Marshal Genl Patrick to try and sell thier horses. they said that the horses were allowed only four ears of corn per day in thier Army, but I think they must have stretched that story a little though the horses looked as though they had not had anything to eat for a month. We had Capt Bishop and wife up here to tea last night and in the evening we had quite a jolly time cracking walnuts + c. meantime up came a heavy thunder shower, and she had to borrow my great Military Overcoat to wear down to thier tent. she made quite a comical appearance with it on. she likes living in camp very much she says. she is quite lively, and quite intelligent and witty but not very handsome.

We have a rumor to day that the 5th Vt (Will Robinsons) Regt has gone to Tennessee but do not credit it, as the rest of the Vermont Brigade is here, and they would not be likely to send that Regt away from it.

The Veteran Volunteers who were furloughed a month ago to day are beginning to return in great numbers, some 2 or 300 have passed our camp to day. it is also reported that our 3rd Brigade (the one that went up into Maryland about a month ago) has gone to join the Army of the Cumberland. I was much amused at reading in the Republican a few days ago that the 1st + 2nd Divisions of the 6th Corps had gone to Tenn and that the balance of the Corps would soon follow under the command of Gen Sedgwick. I don't know but it is so but at sundown to night we were all quietly lying in camp here except the 1st + 3rd Brigades of our Division which as you know are gone, one to Johnsons Island and one up into Maryland somewhere. Col Joe had two letters from his wife in

one day, fearing they would not reach him before he was gone. Why did not some of you get scared and write me two or three letters, or did not any of you care if I had gone. if it was summer I should like the idea very much in fact I would like to go anywhere out of Virginia. we do not hear anything of the furloughs for the Veterans of our Regt yet, which is a burning shame as they ought to have gone home three weeks ago.

It is Wednesday night and I fully expected a letter from home but as usual when I want one most (for I am a little homesick to day) I got none. I hope I shall get one tomorrow night.

How are all the people in Haydenville I never hear anything about them now you and Tom are not there. please remember me to any of them you may happen to see also to Warner Smith when you see him. I suppose they still board at the Warner House. I almost wrote Mansion House. I am beginning to forget even the names of places in Northampton. Do you ever see Aunt Hannah or Mrs Josiah Hayden if so please give my love to them.

I am still hoping to come home with the Veterans but do not know any more about it than when I wrote last.[11]

I am afraid you will not think this a very interesting letter but I have been writing all day and a good part of the night for it is now past 12 o'clock and I wrote until 1 o'clock last night, so you must excuse it.

I have got a Photograph a group of Officers of our Brigade which I intend for you if I ever get a chance to send or carry it. it is not very good but I thought perhaps you would like it. Give my love to Mother Mary + Thomas, respects to all the neighbors and friends and imagine me curling up in my blankets in just 3 minutes from this time. Write soon and often to

Your aff brother
Charlie.

SEVEN

Terrible, Terrible Business

March–June 1864
The Wilderness, Spotsylvania, Cold Harbor Campaign

After a series of intrabrigade baseball games in April, Brewster's regiment crossed the
Rapidan River with Grant's army in early May. Awaiting them was a deadly fate:
the cruelest sustained fighting of the war. Brewster emerged unhurt from the slaughter
at the battles of the Wilderness, Spotsylvania Court House, and Cold Harbor, where
the Army of the Potomac suffered some sixty-five thousand casualties in seven weeks.
These letters take the Tenth Massachusetts to the end of its three year enlistment and
provide a revealing chronicle of individual survival in the face of modern war.

107

Head Quarters 10th Mass Vols Brandy Station VA March 18th 1864

Dear Mother,

We arrived safely here in our old camp about 3 o'clock this PM and I hasten to
acquaint you with the fact. We arrived in NY Wednesday Evening about 6
o'clock and hastened to the Jersey City Ferry where we were met with the
pleasing announcement that we could not go on the 7:30 train as no Military
tickets were received on that train and so we had to wait until 12 o'clock at night
and did not get into Washington until 11 o'clock yesterday consequently we had
to stay in Washington last night. I was provoked enough for if I had known of it I
might have staid in Northampton until 5 o'clock PM or have stopped over
Springfield with the girls but there is no help for it.

We had not been back an hour when there came an order to be ready to march
with three days rations at a moments notice. Don't know whether we shall go
anywhere or not, it is reported that Stewart is across the Rapidan with 6000
Cavalry for a raid so you can see they commence immediately with us and it is so
natural that it does not seem as if we had been gone at all.

I see by this mornings papers that the Head Quarters of the U S Army are to be with the Army of the Potomac for the present so you can see we are going to have Gen Grant himself for a commander. he had better look out or he may lose his Military reputation for he has got a different style of Rebels and a different General to fight but I hope he will succeed in taking Richmond but if he don't "what a fall my countrymen."[1]

It is said that the first Corps has gone on a reconnaisance with 5 days rations, also that they are to be consolidated with our Corps but I don't know anything about the truth of it. I have no news to write of course, as I have not been here long enough to collect any but just send you this short note to let you know that we arrived safely. Give my love to Mary Matt + Thomas reserving a large share for yourself, from

Your aff son
Charlie.

PS I send on a couple of Photographs which please put away for me.

108

Head Quarters 10th Mass Vols April 3rd 1864

Dear Mary,

I received your very welcome letter March 28th and am very glad to get it but was surprised to hear that my letter to you was the first you had received at home from me as I wrote to Mother first the day after I got back, then to you and then to Mat.

I have received only two from home since I got back. There is no news at all here. it seems to me it is forty times more dull than ever before. it has rained or snowed almost constantly since we returned and the Blue Ridge has been covered with snow for 10 days and is now, so you can imagine what the mud is. We have not seen the great General yet and the wonderful review did not come off but will I suppose as soon as the weather will permit. The detached men of our Regiment are being returned in quite "respectable numbers." I believe I wrote you that P W Kingsley had returned. it is only 2 months + 18 days now to the expiration to the Regiments term of service, but we do not know anything about what is to be done with the Officers who went home with the Veterans. The 3rd Brigade of our old Division has returned and the first Brigade is expected every day but the old Division is no more, and I suppose we must give up the old blue cross and mount a white one as we belong to the 2nd Division

now and a Division of the old 3rd Corps is coming to be our 3rd Division but I suppose this does not interest you much and you cannot sympathize with any preference for a blue cross over a white one.

Tell Mrs. Matt that I congratulate her upon her promotion into the ranks of the old married ladies, and her invitations to thier tea drinkings, and tell her moreover not to forget to answer my letter.

I am glad you have heard from Aunt Lu again and have a prospect of communicating with her. I think I shall write to her. I was thinking of writing to Charlie Howes formerly of Co C. who is now Major of the 12th West VA Cavalry and stationed at Weston but I do not know as he is any nearer Highland than I am but thought perhaps he might be, or might have to go there some time as he belongs to a Cavalry Regt but I guess his Regt does not get much active service.

I hope Tom did not tell Brown what I wrote in his letter as it might make unpleasant feelings yet I don't know as I care any great about it.

I don't know whether we are to have a dreadful battle as you expect or not I should not wonder if we did though, but I do not think anything very serious will happen before the 1st of May, as I think these heavy rains are likely to continue until about that time. I saw by the paper yesterday that General Grant is at Fortress Munroe I wonder what that is for can it be that he is going to try Peninsular route? somebody told me the other day that there are 70,000 troops on the Peninsular but I cannot believe it for that must be more than we have here, but all we can do is wait and see what we shall see. I do not like to have you go to teaching. I wish I knew what is to become of me after the term of the Regt is out if I am to stay in the service I can take care of you after I get the house paid for. it is dreadful to be so poor but I see no help for it.

This Military is a hard worrying and at the same time lazy miserable business but it pays better than anything else so I think I had better stick to it as long as I can. if I could only get some Military situation out of active service where I could reasonably expect when I went to bed to be allowed to stay in bed until morning I should like it but it seems as though I have done my share of campaigning but someday must campaign and somebody else must have all the easy money making places and as the harder lot was always mine in civil life I suppose I must expect the same in Military. Well! "So mote it be" "What can't be cured must be endured".[2]

To day is Sunday and I think you would be surprised to see how quiet the different camps are to be sure you would hear the sound of an ax occasionally, but that is no more than I remember hearing in NHampton when I was home and when you consider there is nothing to hinder these men from playing ball or performing any other week day operations you will agree with me that it is quite wonderful. Col has gone over to the Brig Hd Quarters, and the Major has gone

out to see some Sesesh women particular friends of his and I am supporting the dignity of Head Quarters. If you were here now it would be a nice morning to visit or cut lamp shades. the Hickory fire burns cheerily on the hearth, and the wind howls around the tent snapping the canvass and doing its utmost to tear it away, occasionally rushing down the chimney and puffing out the smoke, I suppose to testify its wrath at its inability to [do] anything more serious. Well I cannot think of anything interesting to write so I will wind up, with my love to Mother, Mat + Tom + Charlie, and my respects to all the neighbors. I forgot to mention that it is reported that Col Edwards of the 37th has resigned. Col Joe was afraid that they put our Veterans into that Regt and perhaps want to keep him for Col. it would be nothing strange he is much the more able Commander in the Brigade. Don't speak of this to anyone, for I do not want my tattling to get out and so damage the reputation as a staff Officer of

Your loving brother,
Charlie.

109

Head Quarters 10th Mass Vols April 8th 1864

Dear Mother,

I received your welcome letter of Mch 31st in due season, but have not recd anything from home since and 8 days seemed a very long time to wait. I fully expected one last night and to night but not a word. I should have written sooner this week but the fact is I have not a thing to write about. it is so confounded dull here. until to night I have not been out of camp since I came back but I walked over to the camp of the 37th about sun down to night. I suppose we shall have stirring times enough to make up for it though before a great while as an order has come to night for all surplus baggage to be sent to the rear, and for all suttlers + civilians to clear out by the 16th inst. although I do not think we can by any means move as soon as that for the roads are in very bad condition yet. but yesterday and to day have been very pleasant and warm though the Blue Ridge is still covered with its white mantle.

I could not suppress a pang when I read that the old Apple tree was gone but it was better to have it cut down before it all decayed and fell upon somebody but I hate to think that I shall eat no more baked apples and milk from it (the apples, I mean as I believe the tree did not furnish the milk.) It makes me very retched to think how hard it is for you to get along but I do not know what to do, or what I shall do if I have to leave the service when the time the Regiment is out. if I should not get knocked over before the curse of poverty has always clung to us

and I suppose always will. if it were not for you all at home I sometimes think it would be better to receive a bullet and [be] done with it for life is little less than one long misery.[3]

I saw that piece in the paper about Gen Grant and our luxurious living and all that nonsense created in the brain of some line scribbler I only wish he could come out and share the luxury with us for the next six months, and then have his teeth knocked down his lying throat, then his head made to follow it. I wonder if the lightening does not strike some of these scoundrels who sit in their easy chairs and do nothing but concoct such dastardly tales as that you saw in the Republican. I am glad you liked the papers I send. I think the Army and Navy Journal is a very interesting paper it takes such sensitive views of things, and it is edited by one who has been through the mill and knows what he writes about.

Will Robinson has gone home on a 10 days furlough again. 40 days was not enough so he had to put off home again. George B thinks it very foolish and so do I but I do not suppose that makes any difference for he has got a right which is another mighty foolish thing. How strange it is that every fellow who cannot take care of himself must go and get married at the first opportunity so as to have to have two to take care of or to increase the chances of making more widows. I wonder the women do not have more sense if the men have not. We have a new Brigade Band as you probably have heard, and it is to take turns at a Dress Parade with the different Regiments of the Brigade, tomorrow is our turn, and to day they were at the 7th. it seemed very much like Brightwood times although the band now looks almost as long as the Regiments and in those times it used to be quite a tramp for them from one end of the Regt to the other and back again.

It is nearly 12 o'clock PM Col has been abed and asleep for an hour and a half and there is no sign in camp save the distant rumbling of the cars and the chirping of frogs in a neighboring swamp combined with the snoring of the Quartermaster in the next tent. I see by todays paper (or rather the one that came to day) which is last Wednesday's that the 57th Regiment is under orders to march next week for Ananapolis. I wonder when that expedition is going and I wonder what they want to send off any more little fiddling expeditions for anyway.

I shall no doubt have sufficient notice before we march to let you know, and if so I certainly shall. Do you realize that in two months + 13 days it will be 3 years since our old Regiment came out, and that it will be coming home all except the Veterans. we do not learn anything about what is to be done with the Officers yet but I have seen a copy of an Order from Army Hd Qrs to Corps Commanders to forward the names of those who signified the willingness to reenter the service so I suppose our case is being agitated somewhere, and we shall know sometime I suppose. But I am getting sleepy and I must close. give my love to Mary Matt + Thomas + Charlie, to Uncle Eds Family, and my regards to all the neighbors.

One thing more an order has just come cautioning all not to let the order I spoke of about the baggage suttler etc get into the newspapers so be careful about talking about it, as you have Maj Gen Meades orders to the contrary. With much love

Your aff son,
Charlie.

110

Head Quarters 10th Mass Vols April 18th 1864

Dear Mattie,

I received your welcome letter of Apr 10th and was glad that your arduous duties had finally permitted you to write. I can sympathize with you in your dread of spring snow storms for we get a little squall and yesterday we could see every little while a snow storm passing over the Blue Ridge almost hiding them from our view. in addition to the occasional snow storms we have terrible rains almost every other day. one storm raised the streams so that the Potomac [is] now over Long Bridge, and Bull Run comes off the bridge over that stream and one or two other streams did likewise so that we had no communication with the outer world for three days. the mud is awful in the roads, and I suppose it will be some time before we can move.

It is reported that Culpepper is to be fortified and 40 days rations are to be stored there for the whole army so that the troops who are now guarding the Rail Road can be withdrawn and if the Rebs want to pull it up they can have priviledge. it takes now the whole of the 5th Corps to guard the Rail Road. All civilians except the newspaper men and the sanitary + Christian Commission folks have gone. Sutlers and all and what we are to do for Tobacco I do not know. I don't think anything would demoralize this army so easy as to deprive them of Tobacco again. they can go it without much to eat or drink but Tobacco they must have. We are ordered this morning to be ready for review in marching order which means with knapsacks and all the paphernalia of the march put on, but we do not know whether the review will take place or not. we have got ready several times but the wonderful General G has not made his appearance yet. All the Pioneers of the army are ordered off with 2 days rations to day whether to prepare the roads leading to the river or to commence on the aforesaid fortifications is not known. Our Regt and the 2nd RI are to have a grand match of Base Ball to day. a few days ago they played a game of Wicket with the 37th and our boys beat them handsomely. Dr Chamberlain was here and spent the day yesterday. Erastus Harris is under close arrest over in the 37th he has been cutting

up shines after his style among other things drawing his pay for two months twice which is a thing perfectly easy to do but sure to be found out in a week or two. Will Kingsley is back with the Regt as are lots of men who have been gone a long time. a great many men are leaving the army to join the Navy but only one has gone from our Regt.

I have a nice boquet of Daffies Hyacinths + Narcissus I believe is what we used to call it. Rogers got it out to some house I don't know where. it is not very handsome being all yellow purple + white but it is very fragrant. The boys are impatiently looking forward to the expiration of thier term of service 60 days from day after tomorrow. if Gen Grant don't hurry up his cakes they won't get a chance to help him take Richmond. We are all wondering where Burnside is going, on some wild goose chase I suppose, as usual, where they can land on some deserted shore and get glory without loss of life or limb. I suppose that the Rebs have got from forty to fifty thousand more men than we have in thier Army of the Potomac, but all we can do is wait and see what we shall see.

I notice what you say about having Mother shut up the house and go out to live with you, but I cannot bear the idea any more than Mother can I want some home to go to you know, and then what could she do with all the traps about the house. they would all have to be sold and would not bring anything either, whereas they many of them are just as good to use. I think it will be very pleasant indeed for you if Nell Hayden comes to Haydenville to spend the summer. I am sorry you do not like that place any better than you do. I don't know how it is now but I used to think it was the nicest place I ever lived in.

It is awful dull here this spring it seems to me I never was so sick of this kind of life, and yet I dread the spring. I suppose one reason is that I may have to stay three years longer and yet I should not go out of the service at the end of the Regts term, if I can stay in it. that is not until I get the old house paid for. If I had anything to do where I could make anything at home I should come home, but never mind the time will pass fast enough when we get started on the campaign and if we can only get these Johnnys once started we shall go into a comparatively new country.

I received a letter from Mary night before last which I shall answer soon if I can find anything to write about which is doubtful for every day is just alike here.

I should think by the accounts of the speculation in the north and the price of gold +c that our currency was in a fair way to become as worthless as the Rebels before long. I cannot think of anything more to write. Give my love to Thomas + Charlie, Mother + Mary and my respects to all my friends in Haydenville and please write soon to

Your affectionate brother
Charlie.

Evening.

Well the great Review has come off and it was quite an affair. I have seen the General and he don't look as though he would set the great river on fire. The matched game of ball came off also, and our boys beat the 2nd RI so that is all satisfactory.[4]

Yours +c
Charlie

III

Head Quarters 10th Mass Vols April 21st 1864

Dear Mary,

Your letter of April 13th is before me and the lecture received for which I shall cuff your ears when they come within reach. I cannot yet see much for you to be thankful for in the fact that I have been spared, nor can I see much ground for hope or much encouragement in the fact that Mother is not discouraged after sixty years of trial and suffering and disappointments in fact it strikes just contrary, for you nor I will never see nearly sixty years, it is no use talking about it.

Sixty days from to day the three year term of this Regiment expires does it seem to you so long, and yet coming sixty days looks longer looking forward than the whole two years and 10 months looking backward though I don't know as it should interest me at all as I do not know as I shall come home.[5]

We had a grand review of our Corps by Gen Grant a few days ago and I wish you could have seen it. it would have made your eyes open wider than they ever did yet. our Corps has 26,000 men in it now and the whole thing was reviewed Wagons, Artillery Ambulances and troops. after it was over Gen Grant and a host of other Generals rode right through our camp among them were Gen Meade Gen Sedgwick Gen Wright Gen Neil Gen Eustis and others. I did not see them until after they had passed as we were at dinner and I have not yet had a good look at Gen Grant.

A new Regiment or rather one that has been in the coal districts of Pennsylvania, went by our camp the other day on thier way to join the Jersey Brigade of our Corps. they had been serving up there and consequently every body I suppose thought they were always going to, and so joined them until the Regiment is said to be 1500 strong. it was a sight good for the eyes to see a full Regiment once more but they will find they have come to a different kind of service now. it was the 10th New Jersey and the road was lined with old soldiers on both sides to see the trainers, and you would have died laughing to hear the remarks complimentary and quite otherwise that were poured out upon them without measure. it brought quite forcibly to mind the time when our Regt was almost as long but

alas now our whole Brigade is not much longer when on the march than this one Regiment.

I don't understand why you should think Abel Kimball was provoked and would not write but you seem to take it for granted that I do. I suppose, *you do* but you know I was not let into any mysteries, if mysteries there are.

Things begin to look a little more like moving though the smart ones, or those that pretend to be, say that we shall not move for a month. I don't know anything about it and it is no use to speculate about it.

Endicott was down here the other day and said the 11th + 12th Corps were just across the Rappahannock but I don't believe it simply because he said it.

I wrote to Mrs. Parthy a few days ago so I am expecting a letter from her in six or eight weeks, and I am very glad you did not write that Sunday night. it would be so distressing to have two letters come near together. it is much pleasanter to have a week or two intervene so be sure and not write to often. you know you are so apt to all of you. I meant to have spoken to you about it before but it slipped my mind.

I have read two very nice books lately The Initials + Deep Waters. I borrowed them at Brigade Hd Qrs. Col gets a letter from his wife almost every day so I sometimes hear from you it must be very nice to have a letter every day. we are still wondering what they are going to do with the Veteran Officers, but do not hear anything. I wish we might know something about it. That is the misery of this Military business you cannot count upon anything as probable. in civil life although there are no certainties there are probabilities but here there are none. When you lie down at night you do not know but you will be 20 miles away before morning. I shall send some Photographs in this if I do not forget it which I want put away with the others that I have sent home. While we were at home some of our men got drunk on picket, and kicked up a row and have been sentenced one of them to 12 months of hard labor and loss of pay and another to three months plus loss of pay. it is pretty tough for the 12 months man and he feels mighty bad over it now he has got sober.

The second Corps is to be reviewed to day and Col Parsons has gone to see it.

When the campaign comes in I expect it will be very tedius as the troops are ordered to carry nothing in thier knapsacks except what is actually necessary as they will have to carry subsistence in them. Subsistence I suppose you know means rations and rations means hard tack and salt pork.

I do not think of anything more to write. Give my love to Mother Matt Thomas + Charlie and my respects to all the neighbors. By the way what is the matter with Mrs Clarke? you said she was failing every day.

Don't write any oftener than you can possibly help to

Your affectionate brother,
Charlie.

112

Head Quarters 10th Mass Vols Brandy Station April 26th 1864

Dear Mother,

Your welcome letter of the 20th came safely to hand last night although I cannot conceive why it was so long time in coming. I had almost despaired of ever hearing from home again and had written to the neighbors to know if you were still living in Northampton. We have just got over another delightful rain storm, but the sun when it does shine is very hot and dries the ground up rapidly. we are expecting the forward march every moment now.

the Express Agent is ordered to leave tomorrow, and an order came down to day ordering all visitors to leave immediately though who has got any visitors is beyond my comprehension entirely. I am sure there are none about here, among other conveniences which have been ordered for our benefit are 10 rounds extra of ammunition. We have just got news of the capture of and horrible butchery at Plymouth N C, and if our government does not call out 6 or 8 hundred of the Rebel prisoners now and shoot them, then they had better acknowledge that they are unable to protect thier soldiers, and end the war in my opinion it is the only way to put a stop to such performances and I would advocate it if I was a prisoner in thier hands. it will save life in the end, and there is no other way to bring them to thier senses. I fancy the Rebels will suffer for that and Fort Pillow[6] if we get the best of them in the coming fight. The papers to day tell us that Burnside has gone up the Rappahannock but I don't suppose they know anything about it.

Our Regiment played another match game of Base Ball with the 2nd RI to day and beat them as usual. they played a second game of Wicket with the 37th last Saturday and beat them again worse than the first time.

I was out with the Officers of our Regt and the 7th this morning playing Wicket when I got a hit in the eye with the ball which has blacked it most beautifully. my eye is ornamented with a black spot as big as a silver dollar, if you can remember the size of one of those, I had almost forgotten it.[7]

Col Edwards of the 37th wrote to the State House applying for the Veterans of our and the 7th Mass Regts, and got a reply that those Regiments are to be filled up. it does not say how but I understand that Mass is 8000 behind on her quota and I suppose they will have to stand thier little draft but I do not see how they are going to accomplish it before the 21st of June unless they operate faster than they ever did yet with thier drafts. One story has it that Gov Andrew is going to try to have these two Regts and the 15th sent home Veterans and all and so is try to fill them up by volunteering, but I don't hardly see it. however we cannot tell anything about it and can only possess our souls impatience until the time comes.

Meantime the balance of the Regiment are very impatient at the slowness of time and cannot hardly wait to have the 21st of June come. the Mass Regts will begin to come home very soon now the 11th goes about the middle of May and the 1st must go even before that ditto the 2nd if there are any left of them. I have not heard of either of them for a long time.

The country here is beginning to look as well as it can. the fruit trees where there are any left are all in blossom and the grass where it is permitted to grow at all is quite green and at last the snow has gone off the Blue Ridge. Everybody is wondering what next and where we are going to move to and when but everything is unknown to our own Army although I presume the Rebels know all about it as usual.

A great many men who have been serving away from the Regiment and loafing round the cities and some deserters have been returned to the Regiment and our ranks are fuller than they have been for a long time.

I was very much surprised to hear of Mr Banks death. I heard also that A W Thayer was dead but Cols wife says nothing about it so I concluded it is not so.

Well I can't think of anything more of interest to write. I owe you all a good lecture for not writing oftner but lecturing does no good. you won't write and I cannot help it. I have said all I could say on the subject, and despair of ever getting you to mend your ways.

Please give my love to Mary Matt Thomas + Charlie and to Uncle Edward + family. I suppose they must be quite anxious to hear from John. I think they are much to blame for not writing to Abner oftener. Give my respects to all the neighbors and all enquiring friends, and do please write oftener to

Your aff son
Charlie.

113

Head Quarters 10th Mass Vols April 30th 1864

Dear Mary,

We are expecting every moment the order to move and I thought I would have a letter in preparation so I could send it at short notice. The great mystery of the Burnside Expedition is solved and he has come to guard our railroad while we advance. The mountain has brought forth a mouse. We almost expected when we went to bed last night, that we should go before morning as we received secret instructions +c but we found ourselves still here this morning and have been mustered and now all we have to do is wait for the word go.

It is said that the mails from this Army are stopped but I don't hardly believe it yet. I fully expect we shall be on the move by Monday if not tomorrow. I wonder very much where we are going to pitch at them but of course nobody knows. it was currently reported that Burnside had gone to Fredericksburg but it seems that is not so.

I wrote to Mattie yesterday having received a letter from her two or three nights ago. I have not received one from you for a long time. I received one from Mother a few days ago which I have answered.

We are expecting a mighty hard time when the campaign opens and shall probably see a great many tired and hungry days but we shall think nothing of that if we can only whip these Rebs. I think I could go a month without anything to eat if I knew that was to be the result. I suppose we have a larger Army than ever before and so no doubt has Lee and the shock of battle will be terrible when the two armies meet. old Sheldon of Haydenville, Emmelines father would say that it was the Armageddon prophesied in Scripture and that the end of the world was certainly coming immediately. I imagine that if he could be there he would think it had come sure.[8]

The sick have all been sent to the rear this morning and everything is in trim now I expect we shall move in the night when we do move, and everybody thinks that it will be tomorrow night. I am hoping to have a letter from you to night as I hear you have written one, but it has not got along yet. some of my letters are twice as long in coming as others, I do not know the reason why. I see by the papers that Judge Hodges was drowned at Plymouth N C I was very sorry for I always liked him and he never lost an opportunity of saying a word for me. he put that piece in the Springfield Republican about me, and he was a much better patriot than many I know even if he did go for a Quartermaster. There is but one more Muster Day for this Regiment now and that is the MUSTER OUT of service in about seven weeks. we do not know anything certain as to what is to be done with the Veteran Officers but it is certain that Gov Andrew means to fill up the Regiment but whether he will be able to or not is another question. there are 8,000 men still due from Mass which he says will be enough to fill up all the organizations to minimum strength, but I don't suppose he will draft until he is ordered to and if that does not take place pretty soon there won't be time to get the men here before the Regts time is out.

If the Regiment is mustered out in the field the Regiment will not come home as an organization, and I presume it will be if the Veterans are to keep the organization I only wish we might know something about it.

I suppose John Cooke is somewhere out this way but I do not know where. I wish I did for if it is not to far off I might ride there and see him, but he may be in Alexandria for all I know as the Corps is probably scattered all along the railroad.

It is said that our Corps is to be in Reserve again which I hope is true although

I suppose you will call that a cowardly wish but although we see a great many in print, we see very few in reality, of such desparate heroes that they had rather go into the heat of battle than not, when they can do thier duty just as well by staying out, and when the reserves are called in they always get the toughest fighting.

Your letter of the 26th has just come to hand. Now Mary Brewster I know perfectly well that you don't write me quite often. on the contrary never oftener than once a week and not always as often as that. moreover you know perfectly well that it is your duty to write to me every day, and that you are very guilty when you do not give me a letter as often as every other day. I heard from Mattie that you were out there when you ought to have been at home writing to me I think with you that if a bad beginning makes a good ending we ought to have a glorious ending to the Campaigns this summer for the beginning has been bad enough in all conscience.

We have additional proof that it was intended to commence our campaign soon for it has begun to rain like guns as it always does when we move so I feel very sure of it now. We could not move without a rain possibly.

Lieut Eaton who was blown up at the explosion of the Cartridge Factory in Springfield returned to the Regt to day he is looking finely and is not marked or scarred though he has not much hair on his head. it was all burnt off and has not grown out yet.

I presume this is the last letter you will have from this place and where the next will be from is more than I know, or anybody else, and perhaps I shall have a great battle to write about next time. I have got to close now for the pay rolls have come back from the mustering Officer and I have got to do them up and send them off.

Give my love to Mother Matt Thomas + Charlie, all of Uncle Edwards folks and my respects to all the neighbors. Tell Julia I am very much obliged to her and shall rely upon her in the future for news of my family that is unless you intend to mend your ways. Remember now we are going on campaign letters will be all we shall have to look forward to. the rest of the time will be all misery so you will write often to

Your aff brother,
Charlie

114

Head Quarters 10th Mass Vols May 11th 1864

Dear Mother,

I have squatted on the ground in the hot sun to commence a letter to you although whether I shall ever finish it or ever have a chance to send it is more than I can tell. We started from our camp at Brandy Station at 4 o'clock on the morning of May 4th and crossed the Rapidan before night and bivouacked on the heights on this side that night. The next day we moved a short distance into the wilderness where we saw the usual signs of a pending fight. we went into line of battle and waited, or rather moved round from place to place, until about 4 o'clock PM It was thick woods and a man could hardly make his way through. At 4 o'clock we moved forward in line of battle and soon came upon the enemy who opened fire upon us. We fought them in our usual style, and in a very short time the old 10th lost one Officer killed + 4 wounded and 15 men killed + 86 wounded. The names of the Officers are Lt Ashley Co I killed Lt Graves (K) Lt Midgely (H) Lt Eaton (F) Lt Eldridge (E) we were relieved and the fight went on and our forces drove the scamps about half a mile and it then became dark. we went back to the road and replenished our ammunition and went back again. We lay down without blanket and shivered through the night and were aroused about 4 o'clock by the roar of musketry and had to fall in without any breakfast. The battle soon became general and lasted all day neither side gaining much advantage but both losing thousands of men. This day we did not get into the front line and lost but 3 or 4 men and Capt Shurtleff wounded in the arm. Night came on and we lay down and we thought to have a nights rest, but I had only just lain down when an order came to fall in and away we went to join the 1st + 3rd Divisions of our Corps. We had been detached as usual to do some fighting with other Corps. The next day we started at 4 o'clock AM and spent the day maneuvering round and marching in the hot sun but did not get any fighting.

At 8 o'clock PM we started and marched all night, arriving at Chancellorsville in the morning shortly after sunrise. Our Corps had lost up to this time 8000 men. After a halt of about 5 minutes we were started on the Spottsylvania C H road and marched until about 2 o'clock PM when [we] were halted and expected to sleep all night, but very soon we were ordered to fall in and marched off on to a range of hills where we saw the usual signs of battle in mangled men brought to the rear on stretchers and the woods each side of the road filled with the mingled bodies of dead Rebels and Union soldiers.

We were halted and lay down in the woods a short time when we were assigned our position, first to support a battery and then to form part of a storming party and to take some hills on our front. Our Regt and the 2nd RI formed the left of the line and had to cross a swamp of tangled briers and mud

knee deep and before we could reach our position, the first line advanced and we took our places in the 2nd and advanced as well as we could through a dense thicket, but we could not keep up our connection with the rest of the line, and as the attempt failed we being on lower swampy ground did not see when the rest fell back, and consequently were left far in advance of the rest of the Division. We did not hear the orders to fall back and we would not fall back without, and soon found out that we had no communication with the rest of the Army.

It was almost dark and we knew not which way to go, so we concluded to make the best of it and stay where we were all night. It soon became so dark that we could not see a thing and the enemy advanced came down the hill into this hole. We kept quiet until they were under our very noses and then poured a volley into them, when they broke and disapeared like the work of Magic.

We soon became aware of a line of battle approaching in our rear and now the question was whether they were friends or enemies and none could answer. So I went back towards them and as I approached they cocked thier pieces and I began to think it was all over with me and my poor Regiment.

I hailed them, "What troops are those?" "Who be you?" was the reply. I replied United States thinking it best to settle the question at once. Come into the lines then said they. I went it as I knew it was of no use to run as I should bring thier whole fire upon my Regiment if I did. Judge how glad I was to find they were the 77th New York! but I had hard work to convince them that I was not a terrible Rebel in disguise, but I finally succeed and now I saw more trouble, for I knew that if the Rebels advanced again they would open fire and our Regt would catch it both ways. Time was precious, as the Rebs might come again at any moment and we must get our Regiment into the same line with them. When do you think the cowards would not allow it. That is when we proposed the arrangement they insinuated that we were afraid to stay in the front line.

Well it was finally agreed upon that they should uncap thier pieces and we would hold the front. Pretty soon the Rebs did advance again and sure enough a lot of the cowardly devils did blaze away, and there we were between two fires, but we succeeded in stopping them and they probably held thier pieces so high that they did not do us or anybody else any damage, but if we had not got them to uncap thier pieces we should have been destroyed.

As it was we lost 1 killed and 8 wounded, but I cannot tell you the half or tenth part of the terrors of that horrid night. How I got again taken prisoner by the 61st Penn Regt in the same line and lots of other things which I cannot write about that you cannot understand when I tell you.

About six o'clock that morning we were ordered out of that place and came back and joined the rest of the Brigades when the Army began to build breast works, and here we lie in the same place we came to that morning. we are well fortified and the Rebels are all along our front also fortified and fighting is going

on all the time. Our losses are enormous and so are the Rebels. We captured in our first fight May 5th we captured 2500 prisoners and yesterday 3400 and every day between more or less. we have been without communication with the rest of the world since we started but I understand that our wounded have finally been carried to Fredericksburg, and communication opened with Washington but we have received no mail nor sent any since we started. Our Division General (Getty) was wounded in the fight May 5th. Gen Hayes + Gen Wadsworth were killed Gen Shaler was captured. And Oh greatest of all losses our beloved Sedgwick was killed by a sharpshooter day before yesterday. His Corps weeps. He was our Uncle John and we shall never see his equal his loss to the country at this time is irreparable. Gen Eustis has gone to command a Brigade in the 1st Division and Col Edwards is commanding ours which is another misery as he does not know anything and we have another fool somebody Neil to command the Division [nearly two lines erased and illegible] before we get to Richmond. As an offset to all this we hear that Longstreet is seriously wounded. he was to the Rebel Army what Sedgwick was to ours. It is reported this morning that Gen Augur has arrived with the 8th Corps 27000 strong to reinforce us and I hope it is true.

[All but the last sentence of the following paragraph was crossed out, but it can be read] At the 2nd days fight Burnsides Corps came up and the 57th Veterans of Mass who broke and ran at the very first fire as might be expected the 56th + 58th did not do much better and thier performances together with part of the 2nd Corps came very near finishing the business for the Army. Our Regiment was out all day yesterday and all last night as support for the picket line of our Brigade.

The fighting was terrible all day long on different parts of the line, and thousands must have been killed and wounded on both sides but in our immediate front nothing was done but heavy skirmishing which we had 5 wounded.

I am lying just inside the Breadworks [breastworks] and every little while a sharpshooters bullet from the other side of the line goes humming past my head and smack into a tree or the ground out while out on the skirmish line is the continual popping of the opposing lines which may at any moment break out into the terrible war of the line of battle and the thunder of Artillery but the day is given up to rest on our side if the enemy does not attack and if he attacks us in our fortifications Lord have mercy on him.

It is said that the loss of this Corps is greater than any in the Army and greatest in our Division of the Corps. Our Brigade has lost up to this morning 541 in killed and wounded, the Vt Brigade is almost all used up it is reported this morning that there are but 900 left of it fit for duty. Bill Robinson was wounded twice but not seriously. Our wounded after the 1st + 2nd days battle were brought along in ambulances except such as could walk and there were not

enough ambulances + empty wagons for all of them so some had to be left at Chancellorsville which consists of one or two houses and no inhabitants.

It was mighty hard to have to come away and leave them. there were from our Regt and there were lots of wounded Rebels left at the same time many of the Ambulances had wounded Rebels in them and it created great indignation that they were not put out and ours brought off on as many as could be after we got back of Fredericksburg and communication was established the wounded who could walk were started off on foot ahead of the Ambulances and escort of cavalry, and in arriving at Fredericksburg it is reported the citizens armed a lot of boys and marched them off to Richmond as prisoners and yet I do not suppose this blessed government will ever retaliate upon them for it. we are so excessively merciful I have moved about ³/₄ of a mile since I commenced this letter, and am now sitting under a tree that much farther to the right in the line of battle. the reason is that the Brigade on our right has gone to support another Division which is about to make an assault and we have to extend our front so as to occupy thiers and our own. Just at this moment everything is perfectly still and in a few moments I presume the very air will be rent with the roar of musketry and Artillery.

At Chancellorsville we passed over the battle ground of last year there were lots of human skulls and bones lying top of the ground and we left plenty more dead bodies there to decay and bleach to keep thier grim company. the woods we have fought over both there and here are strewn with the dead bodies of both parties who lay as they fell unburied, but I cannot give you an idea of half the horrors I have witnessed and yet so common have they become that they do not excite a feeling of horror.[9]

Word has just come that letters sent in 5 minutes will go to night so I wind up abruptly. Love to all

Your aff son
Charlie

PS Col P is well.

115

Head Quarters 10th Mass Vols May 13th 1864

Dear Mary,

I wrote to Mother day before yesterday since which time we had fought another terrible battle. We went in at six o'clock yesterday morning and came

out about the same time this morning. I am writing this seated in the mud covered with blood + dirt and powder I have not time to give you the particulars much but yesterday morning some of our troops charged the enemys works in the rain before or at daylight and captured 20 guns and any quantity of prisoners including Maj Gen Johnson + 2 Brig Generals. we went up to hold the enemys rifle pits and redoubts and had not been there long before the enemy charged them. our Regiment was the right of our Brigade and on the right of us was the 2nd Brig of the 1st Div who broke and ran like sheep without firing a gun. the Rebels came into the same rifle pit with us and commenced an enfilading fire before we knew they were there and we had any quantity of men killed and wounded in much less time than it takes to tell of it. Capt Weatherill was hit as were Capt Knight Capt Johnson Capt Gilmore + Geo Bigelow also Major Parker and his horse was riddled with bullets + killed.

Lieut Munyan was also wounded but I think not seriously. Geo Bigelow's wound did not disable him and he is still on duty, a bullet grazed his throat I do not know how many men we have lost yet as we have not got but about 30 muskets with us this morning and some of the Officers are missing yet. both flagstaffs were hit three times and the state flag was cut short off.

We staid there what part of us did not break when the Rebels flanked us and fought until 4 o'clock PM and staid there in the mud without sleep in the mud until about 6 o'clock this morning. I cannot begin to tell you the horrors I have seen, but I must wait to tell you about this campaign when I get home there is to much of it, the incidence crowd upon me so and I have but a little time and it is commencing to rain our men fought the Rebels close to the other side of the breast works and knocked thier guns aside, and jumped up on the work and shot them down. I saw this morning the other side of the pit and the Rebels are piled up in heaps 3 or 4 deep and the pit is filled with them piled up dead and wounded together I saw one completely trodded in the mud so as to look like part of it and yet he was breathing and gasping. it was bad enough on our side of the breast work but on thiers it was awful. some of the wounded were groaning and some praying but I cannot write more this morning.[10] I just wrote a line to let you know that I am safe so far. So is Col P. Have not heard from home yet since the campaign commenced we have had no mails. Love to all

Yours
Charlie.

116

Head Quarters 10th Mass Vols May 15th 1864

Dear Mother

I wrote to Mary day before yesterday the day after our last battle but when I got it done I directed it to you and as I had but that one envelope I had to let it go so. It is Sunday to day and as we are waiting here in line of battle and throwing up rifle pits, I thought I would commence a letter to you although I do not know that we shall remain here ten minutes. We started yesterday morning about 2 o'c from near our last battle field and marched to the Bowling Green Turnpike striking at some 12 miles from Fredericksburg marching there until about 4 or 5 o'clock PM and then started on and came out into the fields and formed on the left of the 5th Corps preparatory to a grand charge upon the enemy. we have got into a comparatively open country and it was a grand sight to see six lines of battle stretching across the hills and through the vales. we are right upon the banks of the river Po and the men were cautioned to hold up thier cartridge boxes when they crossed the river. some batteries were brought up and threw about 150 shells over onto the opposite hills but got no reply. the Johnies had skeedadled so we were spared one great fight and in the night two which was a great relief to us I can tell you.

But previous to all this in the afternoon a Brigade of the 1st Div of our Corps had crossed alone and the Rebels charged upon them putting them to flight and capturing a large proportion of them. After the performance, we lay down here and had a good nights sleep. it was the most quiet night we have had since we started upon this campaign. Our Regiment suffered terribly in the fight the other day losing 6 Officers wounded and 8 men killed + 34 wounded that we know of besides probably a good many that [we] do not know of and from 12 to 20 taken prisoners. this makes a grand total of 13 Officers killed + wounded and 24 men killed 135 wounded + 46 missing making 218 Officers + men in 12 days the Regiment is reduced to 150 muskets and at this rate there will be none of us left to see Richmond. Sidney Williams[11] 1st Sergt of Co C is missing since the battle and his company all think he is taken prisoner, although it is possible that he might have been hit and wandered off into the woods. if you tell his people any thing about it you must say that he is taken prisoner without doubt I think he is. Lieut Munyans wound is quite serious and it is feared he will lose his leg. Major Parker also they say will have to lose his right fore arm. Capt Knight was shot in the side, and is in a very critical condition.

We had plenty of rumors yesterday that Richmond was taken but do not place any confidence in them. we have not seen a paper nor recieved any mail since we started. we have had a general order announcing Gen Shermans victories at Tunnell Hill and Dalton[12] and that Gen Butler had captured Petersburgh, also a

communication from Gen Sheridan commanding the cavalry, that he has turned the enemys right and got into thier rear, destroyed 10 or 12 miles of the Orange Railroad and expects to fight the enemys cavalry of the South Anna River. They have destroyed a large Depot of supplies of the enemys at Beaver Dam, and recaptured 500 of our men who were taken prisoner by the enemy.

We are being largely reenforced by fresh troops and there is need enough of it, as we should not have any army left by the time we should get to Richmond at the present rate. Our Division started with nearly 9000 men and we have lost about $^2/_3$ of them we seem to get into every fight that takes place. We are tired sleepy and worn out but if we could believe that everything was working out all right we should be satisfied.

We took in the fight of Wednesday 8000 prisoners, 18 guns, 22 colors + 2 General Officers. the field hospitals are full all the time and the Ambulances and empty wagons are kept constantly going with the wounded to Fredericksburgh. I wish it might end soon for it is dreadful to be kept in a constant state of excitement like this. you must remember that we have been 11 days under fire more or less every day and almost every night.

I wish the cowards at home who snear at the noble Army of the Potomac, might be forced out here to take thier share of the luxuries of the Officers Confound them. it is outrageous and abominable that the Army must be slandered and abused by the cowards that stay at home and cannot be coaxed or forced out here at any event. Now that the business seems almost winding up it seems almost as though a government that could not draft its own subjects to fight its battles, is hardly worth volunteering to fight for. I get enraged every time I think of it.

We are encamped on a splendid plantation and the corn and wheat is growing finely or rather was before we came but I am afraid the crops will be very small this year. [scratched out line here] We have not seen our Wagons since we started, and I am getting sadly delapidated. my rear is entirely unprotected I having worn the seat of my pants and drawers entirely off.

The most terrible sight I ever saw was the Rebel side of the breast work we fought over the other day. there was one point on a ridge where the storm of bullets never ceased for 24 hours and the dead were piled in heaps upon heaps and the wounded men were intermixed with them, held fast by thier dead companions who fell upon them continually adding to the ghastly pile. The breast works were on the edge of a heavy oak woods and large trees 18 inches or more in diameter were worn and cut completely off by the storm of bullets and fell upon the dead and wounded Rebels. those that lay upon our side in the night when the trees fell said that thier howlings were awful when these trees came down upon them. when I looked over in the morning there was one Rebel sat up praying at the top of his voice and others were gibbering in insanity others were

Confederate soldiers killed at Spotsylvania, May 20, 1864. The Tenth Massachusetts experienced its fiercest fighting and suffered devastating casualties during the Wilderness-Spotsylvania campaign. During the seven-week period beginning May 5, the Army of the Potomac alone lost some 65,000 troops *Library of Congress*

groaning and whining at the greatest rate while during the whole of it I did not hear one of our wounded make any fuss other than once in a while one would sing out Oh! when he was hit. but it is a terrible terrible business to make the best of it.[13]

Some of our cavalry the other day took a squad of Rebel prisoners a few days ago and among them was a deserter from our ranks. he was shot without ceremony. that is not much ceremony. I don't know whether he was tried or not but a square was formed and he was to be hung but we were all marching for battle and there was no time to hang him so he was shot. I don't know what Regt he belonged to. we were marching by at the time.[14]

I shall enclose in this a list of names and wounded which you have better have published if there has been none. you can hand it to the Gazzette and they can do

as they have a mind to.[15] I don't know when you will get this however as I do not know as any mail is going to day. this is the third letter I have written since I started from camp you must be sure and let me know if you get them. There is a tremendous mail for the Army but nobody can stop to assort consequently we are kept without it I don't know where it is but I suppose at Fredericksburg. Give my respects to all the neighbors, and love to Mary Matt + Thomas reserving a large share for yourself from

Your aff son
Charlie.

117

Head Quarters 10th Mass Vols Caroline Co VA May 23rd 1864

Dear Mary,

I had just sent my last letter to Mother when we received a mail from home and I got 4 letters and I cannot find words to express the joy it gave me and all the Regiment and you can little imagine the amount of happiness one such mail brings to even one Regt of this great Army. We had two large grain bags full, and I assorted it but alas there was terrible sorrow connected with it which was the many letters for our dead and wounded comrades. I think I found as many as a dozen letters for poor Lt Bartlett who was killed only the day before. We started from near Spottsylvania C H last Saturday night and marched all night long and all day yesterday arriving at this place about 8 o'clock last night. I don't know where we are except that we are some miles south west of Gurneys Station on the Richmond + F'ks'brg R R and in Caroline Co and not a great distance from Bowling Green. We were roused this morning at half past 3 o'clock with orders to get breakfast and be ready to resume the march at 5 o'clock but it is now 8 o'clock and we have not budged an inch.

there is every prospect of a heavy rain storm to day, which will of course add very much to our comfort. The men are entirely out of rations and we know of no chance to get any.

We are travelling through a beautiful country, with lots of splendid plantations but there is nothing growing but corn except an occassional field of wheat.

Just in front of where I am sitting in a sandy cornfield on a side hill is a small swamp full of magnolias in full bloom and thier perfume is very refreshing after the continual stench of the dead bodies of men and horses which we have endured for the last 19 days. One of Co C has just brought in a great boquet of the Magnolias and he has given me two and I will perhaps put one of them in

BREWSTER'S CASUALTY LIST

Killed

Lt W. A. Ashley

Co A
?Frank Cudney

Co B
R. F. Hunt
Stephen Hicox
O. S. Harwood

Co C
Sgt James Abbott

Co D
Guy Bardwell
R. Ryan
Jas. Cassidy
A. Brewer
Sergt Geo Consius
Corpl C. L. Roth

Co E
Sgt C. W. Thompson
Corpl Jonas Chase
Corpl Geo Ellis

Co G
Gaius T. Wright

Co H
Corp W. F. Cone
Corp L. Fogg
J.R. Campbell
J. S. Emerson
M. Gorman
Chas. W. Russell
Jas. Connors

Co K
J. Jones
Geo. Robinson
E.T. Moore
S. Sprague
Jas. Dineen

Wounded

Capt. W. I. Bishop

Co A
Sgt. M. B. Buck
Corpl C. P. French
Lee Cummings
R. L. Chadwick
S. D. Newton
G. R. Pendleton
Hugh Magee
C. B. Scudder
Rufus Pervere
Davis Hart

Co B
Sgt Wm E. Briggs
Corp H. H. Fuller
Corp C. C. Wiley
Thos. Carl
Levi Green
Peter Galligan
John Riley
C. G. Houghteling
John Walker
J. Sheldon
J. W. Wallace

Co C
Capt. Jas. H.
  Weatherill
Corp J. C. Clarke
N. S. Cornwall
J. W. Harris
J. E. Hartwell
Sgt. J. Colburn
Geo Reynolds
Robt. Sheehey
M. Kennedy
S. Erving

Co D
Capt H. G. Gilmore
1st Sgt O. W. Pierce
Sgt. S. B. Cook
Corp Geo Kellogg
Corp D. Hamill
Corp J. Fanucane ?
P. Murphy
H. Nobles

Co E
Capt E. L. Knight
Lt. S. N. Eldridge
Sergt J. S. Paddock
1st Sgt Jesse Prickett
Corp John Day
Corp L. T. Black
Corp Levi Black
Corp Geo Talbot
Chas. E. Adams
H. B. Barton
D. M. Barton
Edgar Clough
Chas. H. Day
Edmund Dunphy
Luther Hitchcock
Chas. Hickey
Thos. Shannon
W. J. Skidmore
Jas. Londergan
J. W. Templeman
Wm. Thompson
Wm. Warcillow
H. A. Wiggins
Saml. Crawford
Jas. Walsh

Co F
Lt. L. O. Eaton
Corpl. L. Averell
Corp J. C. Hunt
B. F. Wickersham
M. H. Moffat
W. D. Keyes
E. P. Coombs

Co G
1st Sgt. John Cooley
Sgt. M. A. Potter
Corp H. N. Dodge
Corp M. Waite
D. R. Scott
D. M. Wilcox
F. Ripley
Albert Smith
O. J. Gilligan
Geo Garland
F. Williams
A. A. Jewett
F. Nixon

Co H
Sgt J. F. Bartlett
J. E. Austin
F. D. Bardwell
E. P. Conant
C. F. Drake
J. Herman
J. W. Hersey
W. F. Lamb
Chas. Russell

Co I
1st Sgt H. N.
  Converse
Corp Martin Card
Corp Jas. Baldwin
Corp F. Cahill
Corp S. W. Reed
D. O. Judd
Enoch Clark
J. E. Casey
M. Cochrane
D. Riley
C. H. Hartwell
W. R. Worthington
C. H. Decie
J. Kelley
H. P. Smith
E. P. Smith
Sgt John Walker

Co K
Capt E. T. Johnson
Lt E. H. Grays
Sgt J. Gaddes
Corpl Noble
H. H. Gorham
Thos. Moore
A. Marsells
J. Neff
T. Sargent
J. Solomon
J. Trainor
Geo. Furron
Geo Thompson
Thos. Wallace
Wm. G. Lay

this letter but when it gets to you its white waxen beauty will be all gone though perhaps it may retain some of its fragrance. We are in a country that the Yanks have never been in before and it is not so utterly devastated as the country north of the Rapidan + Rappahannock but it looks good enough here with most of its vast fields, bare and uncultivated, and its want of inhabitants hardly any white men are seen nothing but ragged negroes, and the women of the plantations though many of the latter abandoned everything at our approach and leave thier homes at our disposal. at others they set upon the Portico's and Piazzas of thier homes and stare at the long columns of Cavalry Infantry Artillery Wagons and Ambulances that cross thier fields and tear down thier fences and hedges, in stupid wonder and despair. A report has just come from Division Hd Quarters that the Rebs are all back across the North Anna River so I suppose then we shall have to repeat the desparate fighting of the Wilderness and Spottsylvania C H if so, by the time we get them out of thier strongholds there and on the South Anna we shall have very few men to take the works around Richmond.

We heard heavy firing yesterday which is said to have been Hancock thrashing Gen Ewells Corps at Bowling Green. The 2nd + 5th Corps are in advance of us I find our delay is occasioned by waiting for rations which are expected here every moment. This country is much more open than where we have been, and if it continues so and we come up with them they will get a taste of our Artillery in larger doses than they have had heretofore, as we have not been able to use it but very little as yet. it has succeeded however in killing and wounding of our own men as it is always in the rear and undertakes to throw shell over us and generally manage to burst them right in our own ranks.

There goes the Bugle so I must stop and finish some other time. our Regt leads the Brigade and our Brigade leads the Division, and our Division leads the Corps this morning.

Noon.

We started and our Regiment was immediately ordered out as advanced guard + skirmishers, at which we were greatly elated as it gives us the priviledge of the fields + c and relieves us from the march in the crowded column besides the Artillery + trains. to be sure there is always the prospect of coming upon the enemy or being met by a volley of thier bullets, but to counteract this is the coming first upon the houses before all the chickens are carried off + c. but this morning our hopes soon fell to the ground for after marching a little ways we came upon the rear of the 5th Corps so of course everything eatable was cleaned out from all the houses.

We continued the march to this place where our teams came up and we are now stopping to receive rations. they also brought a mail and in it a letter from Mattie for me dated the 16th by which it appears that you have not got any of my letters of which this makes the sixth I have sent since the campaign commenced.

it is most discouraging and it almost seems no use to write. Tell Mattie our Division is the 2nd Division and our Brigade the 4th Brigade. our General was Getty but he was wounded and we are now commanded by Brig Gen Neil who is next thing to a fool if not the thing itself Oh, how hot it is I am seated by the roadside under a rail fence and covered with the dust of the Wagons + Artillery with the hot rays of the sun presssing upon me, and the sweat and dust rolling down my face hurrying to finish this to send back by the Wagons, you must excuse any mistakes Tell Mattie I will write to her as soon as possible meantime she must claim her share in your letters.

The inhabitants inform us that Lee was here yesterday morning 10,000 men and skeedadled out of this [place] in a hurry. I meant to have made this letter longer but have to seize every chance to send so good by. Love to all. Don't fail to write often, more so than if I recd them regularly for the mail comes through all sorts of channels and some of them will get here if all don't. I was much disappointed in not getting one from home to day. Matt says you have no boarders anything you want at the stores you can have chgd to me and I will pay for it when I come home. don't fail once of writing to

Your aff brother,
Charlie.

[Letter is stained on the inside so he probably did send the magnolia.]

118

Head Quarters 10th Mass Vols South Bank North Anna River May 24th 1864

Dear Mother,

I sent a letter yesterday while we were on the march to this place to Mary and as we are informed that we are to remain here to day I thought I would commence another although I do not know as the other one has gone any further than the wagon trains which are some where in our rear. I don't know where. You will know by the other letter that we were on the march. about 6 o'clock we began to hear heavy firing and they began to hurry us up and we came about 4 miles almost on a run arriving on the north bank of the river just after dark. We met the stream of wounded coming to the rear, and found that the 5th Corps which was in advance on this road were across the river.

we also met a large squad of Reb prisoners. the firing ceased and we went into line of battle on the other side of the river in the night the Rebels left our front and this morning there have been several hundred Rebel prisoners by us as we lie in line of battle. they are most all North Carolinians and they give themselves up one whole company came in Officers, Non-Commsd Officers and all. they

acknowledged themselves whipped. we crossed the river early this morning. another squad of 15 Johnies had just gone by, and they look mighty glad to get in and I don't blame them. I expect they are even more tired and hungry than we are.

Gen Hancock with the 2nd Corps is engaged down the river on our left and it is reported he has not effected a crossing yet. we can hear the thundering of his Cannon and have all day long though it seems a little more distant this afternoon. it was reported by some of the prisoners that he had cut Ewells Corps all to pieces. poor Stewart Campbell I believe you said was in that Corps. I am afraid he may be killed or wounded for they have fared hard.

It is said that poor Munyan is going to die. he is in Fredericksburg. Major Parker has had his arm taken off Lieut Graves is very low also. I see the papers report his name as E. H. Sprague and Munyans as Munger. that is what Artemas Ward calls military glory getting killed and having your name spelled wrong in the newspapers.[16]

We received another mail this morning and I got your letter of the 17th and am glad to hear you have finally received one of my letters. I began to think you never would. I also received Springfield Republicans as late as the 19th. You must not fail to write very often. I do not feel very well to day. I got poisoned in my face yesterday in coming through the woods and my eyes are almost shut up and they are all laughing at me.

There goes another Reb he looks about 7 feet high. he is almost as tall as the Cavalry man on horseback who is guarding him. And there goes some guns in our front so we may get a battle yet to day. Our time begins to look very short only 27 days. I wish we might be spared another battle, but I know we shall not be. the 2nd RI Regts time is out in 12 days and it is reported that they are going Saturday. Regts and parts of Regts are leaving every day now. the 7th Mass has 21 days more to serve.[17] The Rebels are throwing an occasional shell at us but they do not reach the 2nd line where we are yet.

The prisoners who came in report that there are lots of others who want to come but our boys fire at them so they cannot. our men are much opposed to taking prisoners since the Fort Pillow affair, that has cost the Rebels many a life that would otherwise have been spared. I see that the papers are full of the terrible fighting that Burnsides negroes have done, but a few days ago they had not been into a fight at all and I don't believe they have now. I wish I could see them in a battle once, and know for certain whether they would fight or not.[18]

May 25th, 5 o'clock AM.

We moved forward about a quarter of a mile last night and occupied some breast works which the 5th Corps had thrown up and the 5th moved farther to the right.

We had a report last night that the 2nd Corps had captured 15,000 prisoners but we do not know that there is any truth in it.

We heard thier firing all day and up to a late hour last night and it did not seem to move much. We are under marching orders and were ordered to be ready at 5 o'clock. it is now nearly half past but we do not move. I understand that our wagon trains are ordered to the white house. we cannot be far from the VA Central R R and Sextons Junction.

I have thought 50 times of what you spoke of in regard to the Mat Ta Po + the Ny, since we have been on those rivers. There was a house right on the battle line of the 5th Corps when they fought here night before last and the occupants went into the Rebel lines. next morning they came back 2 white women and about 20 Negro women. the soldiers had killed every chicken + pig about the premises and taken all the beds out of the house and slept in them and the chairs were scattered all along the line for the convenience of Uncle Sams nephews.[19] They said when they came back that they thought that the Rebs were going to drive the Yanks all into the river. no doubt thier will was good enough but they found the Yanks a hard party to drive.

We hear no firing anywhere along the line this morning and I presume we shall take up our line of march southward pretty soon but I do not know.

Half past 2 o'clock PM

We finally marched about 8 o'clock this morning and after marching about a mile we came upon the VA Central RR and the pioneers immediately commenced to tear up the track and burn the ties and bend the rails. we struck the RR at Niels Station according to the sign. we very soon came upon the Rebels and went into line of battle and have been expecting a fight every moment all day. there has been continual skirmishing all day. I suppose we are now near Little River. We have been gradually and carefully crawling along all day. We are protecting the flank to day. Our Corps received 7000 reenforcements yesterday.

Poor Munyan is dead. He died Saturday night he was occasionally out of his head and his brother says he would keep asking for me and inquiring if Adjutant was there. Poor fellow I did not know he was wounded until he was carried from the field and I never saw him afterwards. We have just heard that Capt Weatherells leg has been taken off above the knee. I sat down to finish this as the Q M 2nd RI has come up and offers to take back a mail, so this is right from a prospective battle field which may be one in five minutes from this time. Love to all write often to

Your aff son
Charlie

119

Hd Quarters 10th Mass Vols 4th Brig 2nd Division 6th Corps Near Sextons
Junction VA May 26th 1864
PS I shall have to stop writing letters pretty soon for want of paper + pencils.
We have not seen our baggage wagon since we started.

Dear Mattie,

I received your welcome letter of the 15th and was very glad to get it for you
cannot in the least imagine what a comfort letters from home are in these trying
times. The mail takes rank even before rations with the soldiers, when our first
mail came, it came on the same wagons with the supplies and although the men
were all out of rations and hungry, and we might have to leave at any moment
even before the rations could be issued, yet nobody would pay any attention to
the rations until the mail was all distributed and there were two great grain bags
full of it, but alas a large proportion of it could be claimed by no owners now with
the Regt. as we did not get any mail until over 200 Officer + men were killed,
wounded and missing our Lieut who was killed only the day before had as many
as a dozen letters. it is very sad.

I sent a letter to Mother yesterday by the Quartermaster of the 2nd RI who
took a mail back to the wagon trains.

We crossed the North Anna River day before yesterday morning and remained on the south bank all day and night. yesterday morning we started about
8 o'clock and crossed the VA Central RR and the pioneers immediately commenced tearing it up. they have utterly destroyed several miles of it. immediately
after we came upon the pickets of the enemy, and pursued them to the Little
River where the enemy were found in force and fortified on the south bank. we
formed our lines and threw up breastworks which we have gradually extended
nearer and nearer. the pickets are constantly firing at each other and as I write an
occasional bullet goes hissing over my head. The enemy have got fourteen pieces
of Artillery in front of us which can be seen, but our batteries have banged away
at them at intervals ever since we arrived but do not succeed in getting any reply.
We have been expecting to attack or be attacked every moment since we got here
but have not as yet.

Word just came that the enemy were pressing Gen Griffins front, and we must
hold ourselves ready to go to his assistance at a moments notice if required. Gen
Griffin commands a Division of the 5th Corps who are on our left.

I have headed my letter so that you can see the number of our Brigade +
Division + Corps. The lamented Sedgwick you know was our Corps Commander when we started, and the Corps is now commanded by Gen Wright.

Gen Getty was our Division Commander when we started but he was
wounded in the Battle of the Wilderness and Gen Neil now commands the Div.

Gen Wright formerly commanded the 1st Division of this Corps, and is an able commander and was much relied on by Gen Sedgwick. Gen Neil is the worst commander it was ever our misfortune to serve under, and I don't think he is fit to command a company. Gen Getty was a most able and gallant General. he had taken command of the Division but a short time before we left Brandy Station and I never saw him to know him. You will think this strange when I tell you that he was wounded not far from where our Regiment was at the time. I saw Gen Wadsworth not ten minutes before he was killed. we were right on the plank road and he told us to pull up the planks and make a breast work. he was an elderly gray headed man and rode his horse on up the road, while the enemy were making a furious attack and forcing our lines back. our Regt was almost the only one left in reserve, and it was just before Burnside came up. The enemies sharp shooters were firing down the road and his fate was certain. Capt Shurtleff was wounded on the same road, and several men.

Our Regt was also close to where Gen Sedgwick was killed and the same party of sharp shooters succeeded in wounding 5 of our men at a very long distance as we lay resting on the edge of a piece of woods. The men where he was cautioned him that there were sharp shooters who commanded that place but he laughed and said they could not hit an elephant at that distance and had hardly said so when he was hit and killed almost instantly.

In the Battle over the Rebel Breastworks (the one I wrote home about where the Rebels were piled up so) I was standing talking to a Capt Shaw of the 2nd RI. I stood partly turned towards him and my elbow just touching his, when a bullet came and struck square in the breast, tearing it open and making an awful sound, but one only too familiar to my ears. He turned round, fell on his face and was dead.[20]

It is very sad to think of the happy party of Officers who spent the winter at Brandy Station. of 28 field line and staff Officers who were with our Regt 4 are dead and 13 wounded besides one (Capt Bishop) who was slightly wounded and returned to duty in 3 or 4 days. One of the others is very slightly wounded a bullet just scratched his face, Lt Cottrell of Pittsfield but he is not at all remarkable for courage and is making the most of it and staying round the Division Field Hospital in the rear. it [is] not the first time he has played sick to escape dangerous duties. his wound was not half as bad as Capt Bishops, or Geo Bigelows first wound in the throat, or my poisoned face. When we think that we have been on this campaign but 22 days and have got 25 men to stay and that considerably more than half our numbers are taken already, the prospect looks rather dark for the rest of us.

P W K is doing very well for him and keeps up tolerably well now he was in the Battle of the Wilderness, and part of the time at the next battle he disappeared for two or three days but has kept up since.

You are mistaken about thier being nothing cowardly about me. I am scared most to death every battle we have, but I don't think you need be afraid of my sneaking away unhurt. Capt Haydens leg was not shot away nor do I understand that it is taken off although it may have to be. I hear Mr Joel Hayden is in Fredericksburg also Joe + Sid Bridgeman. they say our wounded get but little care, there is but one surgeon for all the wounded Officers in the 6th Corps so you can judge what the enlisted mens chances are. it is a singular fact that two thirds of the killed and wounded in our Regt are Veteran Volunteers.

We get no intimation yet whether the Officers who recd the 35 five days furlough are to go home with the Regt or what is to be done with them. Our line of our breastworks here runs right through a farmers garden and close to his back door through peas in blossom and radishes + tomatoes +c +c I imagine how Mother and Mrs Clarke would look to have 100 blue jackets with musket + bayonette rush into thier gardens stack arms and seize the spade + shovel and go to throwing up a ridge of Earth five foot high. it makes ones prospect for garden sarse [sauce] very poor indeed.

I have written this letter as it is reported that our Commissary is coming up to night and I may have a chance to send it. You must write often. Give my love to Thomas + Charles and to Mother + Mary, and respects to all

Your affectionate brother
Charlie.

120

Head Quarters 10th Mass Vols
near Hanover Town May 28th 1864

Dear Mary,

I sent a letter to Mattie from the South bank of the No Anna River, and shortly afterwards we took up our line of march at 9 o'clock PM day before yesterday and recrossed the No Anna, and marched easterwardly across the railroad then southerly. we marched at a tremendous rate all night until about 4 o'clock in the morning. I never in all my experience was quite so sleepy. I came mighty near falling off my horse several times. at 4 o'clock we stopped and our Commissary came up and issued one days rations. I threw myself down on the ground and instantly went to sleep, and slept for two hours like a log. we started again as soon as the rations were issued and marched rapidly all day, stopping only half an hour at noon and an hour about 5 o'clock PM. at about half past eight we bivouacked for the night and at daylight this morning we resumed the

march and about 7 o'clock we came to the Pamaunkey River which we crossed as soon as the Engineers could throw a bridge across where we halted until the country for a space round about was skirmished over and examined for traces of the enemy. we then marched out about 3 or 4 miles and bivouacked and are now throwing up breastworks, and so here we are once again almost down on the Peninsula, and are to draw our supplies from the famous White House again.

I expect we have stolen quite a march on Mr Lee, as we are only about 18 miles from Richmond and we left him quietly in the night, very busy fortifying himself on the Little River and at last accounts he was still at work at it. I suppose we shall soon be upon the Chickahominey again. Is it not funny here we always come round to the same place again after leaving it once, but it has always been so.[21]

We are now near Hanover C H + Mechanicsville where Stonewall Jackson came down upon the right of our army when we were on the Peninsular before, and kicked up such a muss generally, so I do not see but McClellans route to Richmond is to be vindicated after all, and if he had had such an army as Grant has he would have taken Richmond at that time.

It is reported that Grant has said that he shall be ready to commence the seige about the last of July, but I have no idea that he ever said any such thing.

We have great difficulty in getting supplies and the Regt has eaten thier last hard tack but we expect something to night.

The 7th Regt was on Picket when we left the other position night before last and consequently they did not get a days ration on the march that we did, and they have had nothing to eat for 48 hours, which they naturally consider rather tough. (I hope we shall have another mail soon but do not know as we shall. The boys are beginning to count the number of hard tack they have got to eat before thier time is out. The 2nd RI Regt goes next week and the 7th Mass 9 days after and ours 6 days after that or 24 days after to day.)

It is the most difficult thing to keep the day of the month that you can imagine and as to the day of the week it is just impossible. Two Sundays have passed on this campaign and I did not know either of them until two days after. I suppose it [is] because we turn night into day so much that we do not note the passage of a day.

I hope this Regt will not have to go into another fight, but have not much doubt that it will have to. there will be lots of slaughter when we come to storming the enemys works round Richmond and Grant always loses $^1/_3$ his army before he takes to the shovel and begins his seige operations. I suppose if there had been no limit to his army or to the capability of reenforcing him he would have sacrificed a million men to have taken the enemys position at Spottsylvania, but after trying repeatedly to go through them, he went round them finally which I suppose he might just as well done in the first place but of all the diggers

he is the king.[22] McClellan was not a circumstance. we have to throw up breastworks if we don't stop but one night, so that between work with the spade, marching and fighting the hours of rest are few indeed.

Sunday morning May 29

I had to stop last night on account of the darkness and I had also to go and make details for working on the breastworks. The boys are mighty tired and hungry this morning. the Commissary did not come up last night and no one know when he will come. I understand we have no communication with any place. Baldy Smith is at the White House and we are here about 2 ¹/₂ miles above Hanover Town but there is no communication between us and I hear that Gen Sheridan encountered serious opposition yesterday in trying to open communication. There are two New Jersey Regiments whose time is out but they cannot get away as there is no road for them to go. To day is Sunday but there is no rest for the soldiers they have got to go on digging all day.

We had information last night that the enemy were massing in front of our Corps, that we must use the utmost vigilance, but we should act upon the defenses tomorrow to day. tomorrow I suppose we shall resume the offensive. our Division is again in the advance and I expect we shall catch it hot and heavy as soon as another advance takes place. I have not the slightest idea when I can send this letter but I hope something will turn up so that I can send it soon. I suppose our Regt will have to go out on Picket to day as it is our turn. we have seen but very little of the enemy here. the 1st Brigade on our left ran into a squad of thier cavalry yesterday when they were going into position but both parties were so surprised that we did not capture but one prisoner and should not have got him but he was so scared that he tumbled off his horse.

I cannot think of anything more of interest to write perhaps something will happen before I send this, if so I will write it. Give my love to Mother Matt Thomas + Charles, Uncle Ed + family and my respects to all the neighbors and write very often to

Your aff brother
Charlie.

[separate note enclosed]:

On Skirmish Line May 30th

Dear Mary,

We moved from where I closed the letter last night about dark and came up to near Hanover C H this morning we moved about daylight. our Regt advanced guard. our Q M has just come up and will take this back. We are at Peakes

Station on the VA Central RR and are skirmishing with the enemy, but I think they have nothing but cavalry. we are 15 miles from Richmond, I cannot write more as I expect the bullets to whistle every moment So good bye, Love to all

Charlie.

121

Head Quarters 10th Mass Vols Gaines Farm Coal Harbor VA June 2nd 1864

Dear Mother,

I have given you our locality in the above heading as well as I can get at it from all the enquiries I can make.[23] We left the place where I closed my last letter to Mary soon after I sent it and fell back to the turnpike which runs from Hanover C H to Richmond. We had merely advanced to cover the approach of our Corps and trains to the turnpike and after they had all passed our own and Wheatons Brigades fell back and then the skirmish line. I remained back with the latter the Rebels followed us up closely with cavalry and two pieces of Artillery, and we had rare fun and considerable adventure in lying in wait and blazing at the Johnnies as they followed us up. I was complimented with 20 or more shots from them at one time as I rode across an open field to give an order to the skirmish line to fall back, but although they came very close none of them hit me or the horse. after getting back to the turnpike we turned to the right and marched about a couple of miles, crossed a small creek and the Johnnies still following us up, poured in a considerable fire from a high ridge on our left but did not succeed in hitting anyone. after marching half a mile we had orders to go back retake the bridge across the creek and hold it at all hazards so back we went drove them away and tore up the bridge and then we were relieved by another Regt and we bivouacked for the night. At 12 o'clock we had orders to pack up and be ready to move at once, which we did and as usual waited until 5 o'clock next (yesterday) morning before we started.

we finally started however and marched all day and such a hot dusty march you never saw, first the sun was hot enough to bake meat, then the road and fields by the passage of troops was ground to a powder which filled the air, and got into the noses, mouths, eyes + ears and in addition the pine woods were blazing in fierce flame on both sides of the road and the thick black smoke almost choked us, so that take it altogether it was about as uncomfortable a march as I ever experienced. The men encumbered by knapsack and gun fell exhausted by the road side in scores. Well we finally got here, such as were strong enough, and went into line of battle in a plowed field with the hot sun pouring down upon us. it was about 4 o'clock. about 5 o'clock the order came to fall in and move forward

to attack the enemy who were posted on our front in a strong line of battle well fortified on a ridge behind a dense woods as usual. so the lines were formed our Brigade in the 2nd + 3rd Lines supporting the VT Brigade who were in the advance line. we moved out into an open field in front of our rifle pits and directly the enemy commenced to shell us. our Batteries opened upon them and a furious cannonade was kept up for an hour when the enemy tried to turn our flank and our Brigade was ordered off double quick to oppose this demonstration. we went into line at right angles with the main line of attack and soon afterwards the Corps moved forward and the musketry became fearful. the attack was furious, and the resistance equally so. the firing was kept up until a late hour at night the last I heard of it was about midnight when I went to sleep. the balls were occasionally whistling over us and one struck about six feet from where Col P and I lay down. The moving to the flank saved us another bad cutting up as by that we were relieved from participating in the main attack. we only lost 3 men wounded, 2 seriously and one slightly, but the 2nd Corps is now coming up to our support and we are to swing round into the front line and then we are to attack again some time to day. We are endeavoring to swing this Corps round on to the Chickahominey, and Mr Beauregard who is reported to be our opponent, objects most decidedly.

The accounts of the affair last night are most contradictory. some say our 3rd Division took one line of thier rifle pits. at any rate some of our men have seen a squad of 700 prisoners. it is reported that Gen Eustis was wounded in the attack. Welly Kingsley who fell out *exhausted* when we moved *forward to the attack* yesterday says he saw the General carried to the Hospital on a stretcher. We had a large number killed and wounded. Gen Smith (old Baldie) has joined us with 15,000 men among whom are the remnent of the 27th, the 2nd New Hampshire who are in the same Corps (18th) laughed greatly at the 27th. say they did not fight at all, and that there was no need at thier losing thier colors. I guess they find that this is a different kind of fighting from what they have seen and I imagine if they stay here long they will begin to believe the 10th has possibly been in a general engagement during thier 3 yrs term. at any rate we still keep our colors and intend to while one of us lives to hold them. the 27th has got 300 men left yet, so it is reported almost as many as we had when we left Brandy Station, and yet they lost thier colors in the engagement at the rifle pits of the Rebels up at Spottsylvania I had only 22 muskets with the colors at one time and yet we did not lose them.

The 27th has proved just what I thought it would if they ever really got into a fight all brag and no cider.

They find that this is a different kind of fighting from sustaining seiges behind strong earthworks. I mean to go up and see them if there is time before the attack takes place.

Our time is reduced to 19 days but from present appearance they will be terrible days. the 2nd RI has got but 4 days more and if they get into a fight I don't think they will stand a minute. it makes all the difference in the world with the mens courage. they do dread awfully to get hit just as thier time is out.

The time is not quite near enough yet to effect our Regt. very much but still you can see it does some. I do wish we might be spared any more fighting I think we have done our share. I received a second letter from Mattie day before yesterday. I had just written one to her. I did not get any more from home which is all the more surprising, as Matties was dated the 24th of May and the last one I had from home was dated the 17th I believe, about the 15th of this month you can stop writing until you know whether I am coming home or not. if I should live through this I am writing this as we expect the Commissary up with rations and I hope to send it back by him. I do not hear much from you and don't know as you get many of my letters. I have averaged as many as two a week since we started. Don't fail to write often before the 15th. Give my love to Mary Mattie + Tom and respects to all the neighbors. Tell Mattie I recd her last letter and that P W K is alive and well but very weak on such days as yesterday. write often to

Your aff son
Charlie.

122

Head Quarters 10th Mass Vols Coal Harbor June 9th 1864

Dear Mother,

I take this opportunity to drop you a few lines having come about a mile to the rear to get to my desk and papers for the purpose of making out a list of the number of men who are going home and the number who are to stay here. Our time is now reduced to twelve days but I do not know whether I am to go home or not. Col P and myself are all the Officers who agreed to stay if wanted, that are not either killed or wounded and of the reenlisted men there were but 51 left a week ago, and there have been several killed and wounded since.

We have received an order to make no more assaults but make advance upon the enemy by regular seige approaches and are now quite close on to them each party keeps up a constant fire and we can do but little digging in the day time. our Regt goes up to the front at 2 o'clock in the morning and comes back at 2 o'clock the next morning. The 2nd RI Regt have gone home that is all but the Veterans and the Conscripts. We are building large forts also for heavy Artillery and Mortars, and I suppose the seige of Richmond has actually commenced but

as we are yet 7 miles off I think it will take a good deal longer than the seige of
Vicksburg.

Fred Wright was wounded 3 days ago. I did not see him afterwards but our
Rogers did and said he told him to tell me to write to his father or George that
his wound was slight you will please send word to them, as soon as you get this as
this is the first Opportunity I have had to write, and I presume they will have
heard of it before this reaches you. I saw him every day while he was here. thier
Regt is pretty much used up as well as most of the other Mass Regts especially
the old ones. I do hope they won't get ours into any more assaults before they go
home for I think they have had thier share and more two. Every camp here is
fortified and there is no place but what is reached by the enemys bullets or shells
day + night the rattle of musketry plus roar of Artillery goes on. And we have
now got so used to it that we never dodge, which is a great point gained.

I do not think of anything more to write as this tells the whole story and there
is a wonderful sameness about it. I think this will be my last letter unless I find
out that I am not coming home in which case I shall continue to write as usual. I
have received your letters of May 30th. I think you made Mr B quite a visit. Give
my love to Mary Mat + Thomas and Uncle Ed and family Respects to all.
Hoping to see you all soon I remain

Your aff son in haste,
Charlie

123

Head Quarters 10th Mass Vols In a Bomb Proof
June 11th 1864

Dear Mattie,

I received yesterday your welcome letter of June 7th and am very much obliged
to you all for writing so frequently for these are miserable long dreary days for
even the bullets now fail to furnish cause for attention or a remark as they go
singing by our ears, or whack into the trees around us.

I wish I could furnish you a description that would convey to you any idea of
the place where I am now sitting to you but I do not believe I can. it is on top of a
ridge or hill and forms part of our line of battle. there is a square place dug out
about a foot deep on the sloping side away from the enemy and on the edge of
this is built up a double row of pine logs in this form. [Brewster includes criss-
crossed markings to indicate how the logs are constructed] and the space
between is filled with sand. the space between the logs is about 4 feet wide and it

is about six feet high over this are placed poles covered with branches of trees to protect us from the sun. across the corner of this runs the rifle pit over the hills and through the ravines. the rife pit is more properly the breastwork is built of logs laid one above the other to the height of about 4 feet and earth piled up against these upon the side towards the enemy in this lie the men all day and all night with equipments on and musket at hand ready to spring up at any moment and repel any attack of the enemy. in front of us is another breastwork running parallel to this and distant about 30 yards this is the front or first line of battle ours is the 2nd line in front of this about 20 or 30 yards are dug little holes in the ground with the earth thrown up towards the enemy and there lie the sharp-shooters and skirmishers. they lie in these little holes, in the sun all day long and can only be relieved after dark and continually crack away at any head they can see across the open field in front at a distance varying from 50 to 200 yards. the enemy return these compliments continually and so we eat sleep and drink with the continual cracking of all sorts of firearms day and night. the bullets come singing whistling or humming some making more, some less noise, patting against the outside of our mimic fort, or whack into the pine and oak trees, and occasionally thug into the body limbs or head of some poor blue coat for the men cannot be kept lying still but get up and move about with a most supreme indifference to these messages of death. we know when one gets hit by an occasional Oh, or a groan. he is picked up and carried off to the hospitals in the rear by stretcher bearers perhaps to die perhaps to have his arm or leg cut off or perhaps to be fixed up and lie round a few days and come back and begin the same life over again.

Along the line is occasionally a heavy fort of earth provided with one two or more guns as its position or the circumstances warrant and in these lie the Cannoniers all day long watching enemys lines and occasionally he jumps up, says fire, and another Cannonier pulls a little string and bang goes the gun followed by the rush of the shot shell or cannister and the crashing through the trees and limbs in the woods on the enemys side and if it is a shell the dull report of its bursting to the damage of numerous grey backs as we fondly hope, but probably do very little damage to anyone. these higher compliments are also returned at intervals by the enemy, and so the work and war goes on. We came up here last night about half past one o'clock taking position considerably to the left of the one we have been holding for 8 or 9 days past, in consequence of the stretching out and thinning of our line. the 6th 18th + 9th Wrights Smiths and Burnsides Corps are now holding the line which has heretofore been held by them and the 2nd + 5th Corps the two latter have been withdrawn and have gone off on some mysterious expedition probably to our left of which you will probably hear sooner than I shall.

Meantime we possess our souls with what patience we can for 10 days longer. I

wrote to Mother two or three days ago and told her it would probably be my last letter, I begin to fear that I may have to stay after the Regt goes home. I do not know what to do if I had anything to do when I came home I should try and see if I could not get away anyhow but I do not know as I can get any employment if I came home and I might have to enlist as a private soldier again for my daily bread, which I should dread to do worse than anything but *sawing wood*. But I am very much worried to hear that Mother is so ill both from you and Mary and am now sorry that I signified any willingness to reenter the service. besides if I staid I should have to give up my horse and I feel that I could not stand it a great while as a foot soldier. However, perhaps I shall not be called upon to stay at all I hope not. the 7th Mass Regt goes out in 3 days and I can judge better by what they do with thier Officers. it is impossible to get any information in advance and they keep all the Regiments on the line of battle until thier time is out to the last moment. You ask why they do not put the Negroes in the fights I imagine that they do not amount to any certain sum in a fight and in such tough battles as we have it will not do often times to put in troops which you cannot depend upon. another reason I presume is because the Rebels show them no mercy if captured and our government is too weak to protect them and compel fair usage for them, but if they do not save any lives of white men they add considerably to the strength of the army for they can do many of the duties in the rear which white soldiers once had to do. But though I have seen accounts of thier fighting in the Northern papers I do not believe they have been in any fight at all. still I may be mistaken as they are all in the Burnsides Corps and we see but little of them.[24]

Tell Mary I received her letter at the same time I did yours and will answer it soon. I have written you quite a long letter as I had plenty of time nothing to do but lie around and dodge bullets. Give my love to Mother Mary Thomas and Charlie and my respects to all enquiring friends With much love

Your aff brother
Charlie.

124

Head Quarters 10th Mass Vols near Charles City C H VA
June 15th 1864

Dear Mary,

As the 7th Regt leaves for home this morning I thought I would improve the opportunity by writing to you. You will see by my heading that the army has made another movement to the left. we started the night after I wrote to Mattie

at 11 ¹/₂ o'clock and marched all night and all next day and far into the next night. We passed on the way many familiar places that we had seen in the Peninsular campaign 2 years ago, and halted to rest once in the very place where we camped 2 or 3 days in May 1862. it was about 2 miles from Bottoms Bridge which is 6 or 7 miles from Fairoaks.

We are now about 2 miles from the James River and expect to cross to day the 2nd Corps crossed yesterday, the 18th Corps went to the White House and took transports, so here we are on McClellans old ground and about 10 miles from our elaborate fortifications at Harrisons Landing.

It is rumored that we are going to take Petersburg and commence the process of starving them out of Richmond which I think will be a long tedius process.

I received your welcome letter of June 7th and intended to have answered it the day after I answered Matties but alas things is very onsartin in War. we were ordered away our Railroad torn up and White House abandoned leaving us without communication and poss[?] I was riding along in the hot sun and blinding dust at the time I proposed to be writing to you. I don't know as this letter will reach you before I do as it is decided that the regt will start for home next Monday the 20th. I expect to come with it if nothing happens more than I know of now and provided we do not have another fight and I get killed or wounded.

The 7th Regt is over joyed and as they are right side of us and all are busy saying thier farewells +c. I cannot hardly collect my thoughts to write a letter and indeed it seems almost useless as I expect to be with you so soon. Our Veterans are going into the 37th and I possibly may have to stay with them but do not expect to now.

The 37th and a small Battallion of Veterans of the 2nd RI will be all there is left of the old Brigade when our Regt goes, and the Brigade will probably be broken up.

I don't know what I am to do for a living when I come home perhaps I shall have to come out again as a substitute. As the end of my service grows near I cannot but feel rather bad to leave it for all its hardships and horrors + dangers it is a fascinating kind of life, and much freer from slander jealousy + unkindness than civil life which I almost dread to come back to. everybody in civil life knows your business better than you do yourself, and can give you so much advice and attend to your affairs, and is so ready to give you two kicks if somebody else gives you one.[25]

The boys are happy as clams at the idea of going home so soon while the Veterans wear rather long faces. the others spend most of thier time in counting the moments left, and how many hard tack they have got to eat yet. poor fellows they do not know any of them but what they will have to fight and bleed and die yet for there is plenty of time yet in the five remaining days, and then how quick

Sgt. H. M. Converse (*left*) and Sgt. E. B. Gates (*right*), veterans of the Tenth Massachusetts Volunteers present the regiment's tattered colors at the Massachusetts State House in Boston, December 22, 1865. Inscribed around the border of the photograph are the names of the battles in which the regiment fought. *Courtesy of Jonathan Allured*

the pleasure and novelty of being at home will wear off, and how soon they will find out that those who will welcome them with such apparent joy over it, and be ready to do them any injury for the sake of a dollar, I know that many of them will come back to the army, although they laugh at the idea now and declare they would not enlist again for all the wealth of the United States.

I am very glad to hear that Capt Weatherill is getting along so well. I do not like to say anything about [erased] I am afraid he is braver in N Hampton than in Virginia I went to see him the day before we left Brandy Station and he did not look to me as if he was going to die right off but enough of that don't mention it.

I must close now as I have some papers to make in relation to our going home. this will be my last unless I have to stay. just think *my last letter from the war*[26] Give my love to Mother Matt + Thomas respects to everybody from

Your aff brother,
Charlie

EIGHT

Living among Strangers

July–November, 1864

In July 1864 Brewster reenlisted to be a recruiter of black troops in Norfolk, Virginia. Restive and anxious about future civilian life, he searched for black men who would be soldiers, lived among former secessionists and ex-slaves in a boardinghouse, and observed the many ironies of war, race relations, and southern mores. In November, three and one-half years after he joined the Union army, a matured Charlie Brewster came home from war.

125

Norfolk VA
July 30th 1864

Dear Mother,

I take pen in hand at the first opportunity to inform you of my safe arrival.[1] we got to Fortress Munroe on Thursday after missing two connections and being detained in NY one night in Baltimore one night.

We found nothing ready for us and no Rendezvous established for receiving niggers even if we got any which looks to me very doubtful. The agents are pouring in here from every state, and I presume that before a week there will be 500 or more here more than there is niggers in the whole Dept. however the AAG of the Dept is a Mass man and has done everything for us a man could and I hope if we stick by we shall eventually be able to do something. New Jerseys agents have already gone back disgusted but they did not understand Official Ropes very well and did not have proper papers.

Brig Gen Wild[2] has to day been appointed to superintend the recruiting and I hope we shall get under weigh first of the week. however I shall not stay here long unless the compensation is increased as board in private houses is $40 per month without rooms at that.

The weather here is awful hot, and keeps a person in a dripping sweat night and day. I hope we shall not have the yellow fever. the quarantine is very strict. there is a vessel below Baltimore in quarantine which is almost depopulated with yellow fever and no one can be got to go to it, and no one is allowed to go from it so I think they must be in a terrible condition.

There are rumors of a terrible fight at Bermuda Hundred but we get no certain information and shall not until we get the NY Papers to day which will reach us Monday.

We had to come to Norfolk as there is no place to stay at Ft Munroe and this is the place to find niggers if there are any to be had, but the agents of other states are authorized to pay any amount for recruits while Mass pays only $325.

Tell Elbridge he had better deposit his $125.00 for a representative recruit as I am afraid I shall not be able to arrange the matter as we talked about and then if he don't get one the money will be refunded to him.

Brig Gen Wild has been appointed to superintend the Rendezvous and it will be probably at Ft Munroe or at Sewalls Point, but our Hd Qrs will be at Norfolk and you will address all communications at present to Norfolk, VA.

This is quite a city, and about as crooked as Boston, but it looks very dilapidated. there are quite a number of nice houses deserted which are nicely furnished. I have not much to write about, and will make a longer letter next time. Give my love to Mary Matt + Thomas and my nephew, and write soon to

Your aff son
Charlie

126

Head Quarters Recruiting service for Mass Norfolk VA
Aug 4th 1864

Dear Mary,

I have been here a week tomorrow but have heard nary a word from home, except by Mrs Fannie Cook. I went down to the wharf day before yesterday when the Baltimore boat came in, and who should hail me before the boat got near the wharf but Hen Dickinson, and with him Mrs Cook. I should as soon have thought of seeing the Old Nick himself, but I immediately surmised what had brought her down here, and I am very sorry that she could not get a pass to the front, but I could have told her that it was impossible as no one is allowed to go without a pass from Gen Butler and he is up at the front. I am afraid they will think I was not very attentive but I was awful busy that day and having but just

got started and an Office opened I could not do any more than I did. besides I was full of business having 11 niggers on my hands to get mustered, and Col P [had] gone over to Portsmouth.

We are quite pleasantly situated here. our Office is at No 62 Church St and we (Col + I) board at a private family No 98 Main Street, with a Mrs Mitchell. her husband is in the Rebel army. she has three little boys. her mother lives with her, and she has one son in our Navy and another in the Rebel army. they (the ladies) have all taken the oath of alligeance. There is also a Miss Barlow boards there. she took the oath of allegiance yesterday. she calls it a Military necessity and makes rather wry faces over it but after all I don't believe she feels very bad about it. The other boarders are Mrs Caswell and a little girl wife and child of Capt Caswell of the 10th NH Regt and Mrs Irving wife of an officer on a gun boat which is here for repairs.[3]

Everything is very high here, much higher than at the north and that is useless, that is everything except fruit that is plenty and cheap of all kinds. every morning the market is stocked with Peaches, Pears, Figs, Melons, Apples, Sweet + Common Potatoes and all sorts of vegetables, and I wish you were here to partake of them.

We have secured 13 recruits so far and a black set they were I can tell you. We have been much hindered by the non arrival of our Paymaster Starkweather, who has not made his appearance yet and we lost quite a number by his not being here but finally we made an arrangement with the National Bank here and have thus been able to pay the bounties to our recruits. I don't know what Starkweather is thinking of. the paymaster for the Newbern Dept arrived here this morning on his way to join Col Richmond at Newbern. There are any quantity of agents here from all parts of New England and New York New Jersey Penn + Maryland. I expect to go over to the eastern shore tomorrow or next day to see what I can find over there, and possibly I may go out to the outpost at Suffolk next week though I do not propose to do much running myself.

The Rendezvous has just been established and Gen Wild is to command it. his asst Adjt Genl is a young fellow named Allen who was in Littlefield + Mortons store when I was in Haydenville. Tom will remember him. most of the other Staff Officers are from Mass so that we stand as good a chance as any of the agts.

Just above our Office here is an old church built in 1739 it is like the beautiful church at Hampton that was destroyed by the Rebels and like it surrounded by a church yard filled with old graves. this street is full of churches and I suppose derives its name from that fact.

To day is the Presidents fast and all the stores Bar Rooms +c are closed but open Sunday. they are all open and in full blast, but then General Orders from the Hd Quarters of the Dept this morning stated that it was expected that all

Freed black laborers in Alexandria, Virginia (date unknown). After completing his three-year term of service in the Union army, Charles Brewster reenlisted to be a recruiter of black troops. Stationed in Norfolk, he recruited among the emancipated slaves of coastal Virginia from July to November 1864. *Brady Collection, National Archives*

loyal citizens would close thier places of business and attend church, all *loyal* citizens took the hint and acted accordingly. This Military is a big thing to enforce piety. I had seen no notice of this fast until yesterday, and up to my boarding house they had got it that it was a Thanksgiving and had got up a big dinner to do it honor, when low + behold, it was fast instead of feast. Mrs Taylor, Mrs Mitchells Mother is a real Jolly old lady and does the marketing every morning. I went down with her this morning and went all through the market with her, followed by a darkie girl with a big basket to carry the purchases. I thought it was real fun. I cannot think of any more of interest to write this PM but as the mail does not go but once a day and that at 2 and $^1/_2$ o'clock tomorrow perhaps I shall have something to add.

Friday Morning Aug 5.

I have nothing new to tell. I have just walked out to the new camp for recruits it is about a mile from here and I am one complete drip with perspiration. I am now going down to the P O with this and hope to find a letter from you. Give my love to Mother Matt Thomas and the baby and respects to all the neighbors and please write to

Your aff brother
Charlie.

127

Norfolk VA August 20th 1864

Dear Mother,

I have been here now three weeks and have written home twice in that time, but since I came here I have not received a word from a living soul not a scrap of writing has come to me from anybody. I had vowed I would not write another word but I so long to hear from somebody that I thought I would try once more. if you don't any of you intend to write me any more I wish you would inform me of the fact by letter so that I may make up my mind to it.

I can not tell what to think of it. I have been over to Ft Munroe, and have sent over time and again but still the same answer, nothing for you. Col gets letters almost every day, but there is nothing in them about you, and thus I am left to conjecture. I do not know how Mattie is, or how the baby is, in fact I don't know as you are all alive. I expected to have letters in the office there to be sent to me, even if you did not any of you write, but not a thing have I received yet.

I have nothing of any interest to write about. there is no news here and

nothing going on, and recruits are very scarce. we have not got but about 40 since we came here. there are two agents to every man who will enlist. it is very tedius dull business but I suppose will not last long if the draft comes off the 5th of September.

It is said that there are several cases of yellow fever across the river in Portsmouth but I don't know whether it is true or not. it has been terribly hot here the thermometer ranging from 95 to 100 every day but for two days past we have had considerable rain, and it is cooler. everybody rejoices for the inhabitants here depend upon rain water to drink. the well water is not fit and nobody but the niggers drink it. it had got to be very scarce so that the woman where I board had to buy water to use.

Although much nearer the seat of war than you are we do not get the news as quick as we have to depend upon the northern papers which get here the day after they are published. There are but very few troops here and there are rumors of the Rebels being quite near and intending a raid, but I reckon it is all moonshine. There is a colored cavalry Regt doing Provost duty, which does not suit the sesesh at all, but they can not help themselves.

These niggers are a very pius race and hold meetings and sing and pray all night long, but I do not suppose it is very deep piety. for instance I heard a boot black bragging last Sunday that he had made two dollars and been to Sunday School, which he seemed to think quite a performance and so do I. The grown up ones are no better. they would all lie and steal, and pray and go to church, but after all they are very much like thier white bretheren in that respect. And such a shiftless set. up at the house they have got three and among them all they cannot keep the slop pail in one room. about any other day either that, or the wash bowl or something will be missing, and in setting the table they invariably leave off about one third of the things.[4]

I cannot think of anything more to write, especially as I have no letters to answer. If you should write to me direct to Box 236 Norfolk VA. Give my love to Mary Matt + Thomas + the baby, and my respects to all the neighbors and do please write to

Your aff son
Charlie.

128

Norfolk VA Aug 21st 1864

Dear Mary,

I put a letter into the P O yesterday telling how I had received nothing since I came here and immediately after I came here I found a letter from you, one from Bill Turner and one from Capt Bishop. they had been mislaid, and not put into my box. they were dated Aug 10th. The Official Document you spoke of has not arrived and is probably lost, although I am going over to the Fort in the morning to see if I can find anything there, but I do not expect to find it I suppose it was my certificate from the Ordnance Department to enable me to get my pay, and I shall be sorry to lose, I expect to go up to Washington one of these days, and hope to get another.

I notice what you say in regard to a substitute for Thomas and Elbridge. I might possibly get them, but I should have to come home with them, and run the risk of losing them on the way for the country is full of substitute runners, and they are paying $1,000.00 for them in New York and I might not be able to run them through. The state pays no bounties to substitutes, and they would have to pay that. then again Gen Butler has issued an order that no colored man shall be taken away from this Dep't but shall be put into the regiments in this Dept so I should have to get white men. however I am on the trail of some white men and if possible I will get a couple and bring them in but you must not be to sure as I may fail, nothing is certain here. you can get anything you wish promised but nobody seems to think it all necessary to fulfil promises. You did not say certainly that Tom wanted one. you must be sure and write me if they get one, so that I need not bother about it.[5]

My address is Capt Chas H Brewster. Box 236 Norfolk VA. You did not say whether you had written more than once or not, so I suppose you have not I was glad to hear from Mattie and the baby and that they are well. Major Pierson of Holyoke is here. he is the one they used to call Squire Pierson. he is a Paymaster in the army, and has been very sick with the Typhoid fever but has got most well.

I spent most of the afternoon with him to day. There is a rumor that two agents for recruiting have been killed by Guerillas, and 3 Companies of soldiers have gone out to investigate. they were out about 20 miles from the city it is said. I think some of going down to Pungo on the canal that leaves to Albemarle Sound to see what I can find down there, and I should also like to see the country. small steamers run down there 3 times a week. it is the inland route to Newbern.

It is said that they are clearing out all the Hospitals about here and over to Portsmouth, and everybody thinks that something wonderful is going to take place up at the front, and that they are preparing thier Hospitals for a reception of the wounded. it may be however only for the wounded in the operations the

other day, although I should think that enough of them have passed Fort Munroe to make up all they had.

I was very much surprised to hear that Mrs Cook had been to the front I supposed she had gone home long ago. I hope John will get well. I suppose he will not have to be talked about now he has been wounded. I saw the death of Mr Lincolns son in a paper. by the way I wish you would send me the Republican and Gazzette.

We do not know anything about how long we shall stay here. if you hear of anybody coming down I wish you would send me a couple of pairs of knit socks. there are none to be had here and I did not bring but one pair. I am wearing cotton but they make my feet sore. I had a terrible attack of Cholic a few days ago, and from half past four in the afternoon to 12 o'clock at night, I was in perfect misery. I took 25 drops of Laudanum, four opium pills, and two doses of Camphor and ginger. I was so weak next day that I had to lie abed most all day.

My address is Asst Adjt General, but you had not better put it on as there are so many Asst Adjt Generals that it might go to the front. how did you direct the official Document. please write and let me know.

I hope you will have a pleasant time at Watertown.

I think with you that Elbridge is foolish to get a substitute before he is drafted but I suppose he can get one cheaper now than after the draft. I should not want to make anything out of him, as I could dispose of them in N Y at $1,000. each if I got them. it would cost all of $500. to get one and have him agree to go to Mass that is including the bounty. I am not absolutely certain whether the state pays the bounty to substitutes or not, I think not. I wish Elbridge would find out and write me immediately. I do not want to write to the state house about it, as they discourage the procuring of substitutes and would not like it if they knew I got them. Give my love to Mother Matt Thomas and baby, and write again very soon to

Your aff brother
Charlie

129

Head Quarters Recruiting Service for Mass
Norfolk VA
August 30th 1864

Dear Mattie,

I received your welcome letter of Aug 24th this morning. Col Joe having carried it in his pocket for I don't know how long. neither does he. he would forget his own head if he could take it off. I was very glad to hear that you had got

well enough to come to Northampton and very glad that my nephew is so smart.
I have no doubt that he would know me the moment he saw me. I have not much
of interest to write, for there is nothing here to write about. recruiting goes very
slow. we have got 53 in all but it is hard work for Mass to get recruits for the
bounty is so small. other states send thier agents from the different towns and
they pay anywhere from 500. to 1000 dollars, and the recruits are credited
directly to the towns while we have only the state bounty of 325.00 and are not
allowed to recruit for towns at all, but I think if some town would send a man
down here with money to pay a town bounty I might get quite a nice little lot
into the Marine Corps by paying them a town bounty of about 400.00 but I do
not know of any state that pays so much [as] in Mass We cannot recruit sailors or
Marines for the state at large as Mass pays only 100 dollars to either class while
other states pay the same bounty as they do to soldiers, and they count on thier
quotas just the same, and so other states get all of that class of which there have
been a good many.

The reason Tom could not get my pay was that he did not have my ordnance
certificate which was sent to me from N Hampton P O directed to Fort Munroe
and I did not get it until after the Regt was paid. I suppose the rules will now be
sent to Washington and I shall go up there as soon as I hear from the Paymaster
at Boston to whom I have written to know when he is going to send them.

I went over to Portsmouth yesterday and went on board the captured Rebel
Ram Atlanta formerly when in the Rebels possession called the Fingal. she is a
monster piece of strength and bears the dents of two of our shots which hit her at
the time she was captured. you remember she was built by contributions of
jewelry by the ladies of Savannah, and was captured in the Savannah River. our
side has put on board of her 200 pounder Parrots and 2 100 pounders and she is
quite aformidable affair. she is undergoing some repairs now. the only trouble
about her is that she draws 17 feet of water and is very apt to run aground. we
were shown over every part of her.

Tell Mother I have not enquired for Pendleton although I have been over to
Portsmouth several times and have thought of him, but there are very few male
inhabitants in either Portsmouth or Norfolk who were here before the war broke
out and the railroads are run by the United States when they are run at all which
only wood trains or an occasional train for some other military purpose.

I am glad the Scotch woman proved such a valuable acquisition to your
household, and did such justice to my faith in *her honesty*. I have never received
the large package of documents you speak of and I can't imagine what they were.
I do not know why I have such trouble in getting my mail as Col gets letters
almost every day. I got a letter from Bishop which was redirected by Carlisle. I
ran across a man the other day who was 12 years postmaster at Woodstock VT
and knew Cousin Tom, and Eliza Martha + Maria, and Frank Clarke. he said
he brought up Carlisle. I did not learn his name.

I was very glad to hear that Aunt Lu found Stewart at home. I was intending to go to Point Lookout to see if I could find him. I have not been to Pingo Landing in Albemarle Sound yet, but I think I shall go next week or perhaps this.

Fred Hillman is well and safe, and had not been gobbled up yet, or had not at last accounts. he is over in Northampton Co on what is called the Eastern Shore. we had a letter from him Saturday.

I am glad to hear that John Cook is likely to live. give my respects to him when you have a chance.

My title now is Capt. you directed your letter exactly right. Box 236, but it should be Capt instead of Lieut.

Lieut Knapp has just arrived from N Hampton we wrote for him 10 days ago when it looked as though we should need him but it does not look so now.

I don't know how long we shall stay here but I expect not much longer than the 5th of Sept. when the draft takes place. if I had 500. dollars I would leave the state service and go into the substitute business where I think I could make some money as from 1000 to 1200 dollars is freely offered for substitutes, and if I was out of this and could stay here and look round I think I could get some, but as it is my business is mostly in the office and I could not very well leave to take them north.[6] I cannot think of anything more to write so I will close. please write again soon. Give my love to Mother Mary and Thomas my nephew + Charlie, and my respects to all inquiring friends. With much love

Your aff brother
Charlie.

130

Norfolk VA Sept 16th 1864

Dear Mother,

Agreably to promise I take pen in hand to inform you of my safe arrival which with her ladyship (the Asst Provost Marshals wife.) this morning about 10 o'clock, we were both much tired when we reached Baltimore but a good nights rest refreshed us both, and we procured that on board of the boat last night. Col Joe met us in Baltimore and we had from 6 o'clock in the morning until 5 ½ at night to remain there. Col hired a carriage in the afternoon and we rode out to Green Mount Cemetary which is a beautiful place. in the forenoon I ascended to the top of the Washington Monument, erected to his memory by the state of Maryland it is 180 feet high and situated on top of a hill in the heart of the city. it furnishes a beautiful view of Baltimore and its surroundings. I think Baltimore one of the most beautiful cities in the Union.

We reached Fortress Munroe about 7 o'clock this morning and visited the Fort going all around the ramparts. the famous Rebel pirate Georgia was there she had just arrived. The cars and the Boats are full of recruits going to the front. there was a rumor this morning that a heavy fight was going on yesterday up at the front but I have not heard anything about it this PM.

I hope you arrived safely at Cousin Edmunds as I presume you did. I suppose you are now engaged in taking care of your wonderful grandson and that you and Mrs B are taking solid comfort in mutually admiring him. Tell him his Uncle sends his love, and will be ready to enlist him for a soldier as soon as he gets tall enough, which is 5 feet and 3 inches. will he be ready by New Years? I have been quite homesick on my way out and to day. I don't know what to make of it, but I wish I could get a job so I could live at home. I am tired of living among strangers, where every person only looks at you with an eye as to how much can be made out of you.[7]

Col Joe and his wife are supremely happy, and give themselves considerable airs, which is all right if they can only support them, I don't take brass for gold. She has been down to the office to day, and announced that we must have the floor scoured, and get some spittoons, if she is going to visit us. Ergo, if a dirty floor +c will keep her away, it will be some time before it is scoured, for I don't want woman bothering round in my office and if she wants her darling she can take him away and keep him. I can easily run the machine without his aid.[8]

I cannot think of much interesting matter to write. Norfolk has not changed any as I can see since I went away, certainly not for the better. They have procured two recruits since I went away, and I have discovered one who I enlisted a month ago, but he slipped through my fingers, but I have got him fast now.

Give my love to Mattie + Thomas and tell Mattie to write. Tell Julia I found her letter but do not consider such short epistles as that, letters at all. Give my love to Mary when you write, and my respects to all my friends in Haydenville + N Hampton. Hoping to hear from you soon, I remain

Your affectionate son
Charlie.

131

Norfolk VA Oct 5th 1864

Dear Mother,
I have to acknowledge some negligence in not answering your letter before but I have been quite busy having been up to Washington among other things for 3

or 4 days, on business, trying to get my pay but I did not succeed and I don't know as I ever shall. there is so much red tape about it, I am almost discouraged. There is nothing here of interest to write about. our recruiting business goes on very slow and I don't think we shall get many more. I took four over to Newport News day before yesterday, they were white men. we have now got 68 in all since we have been here. I should not think they would keep us here much longer at that rate but I do not know anything about it.

All interest centres in the operations at the front now and we wait anxiously from day to day for tidings for you know we have to depend on the N Y papers and have to wait longer than you do for information of operations that are only 90 miles off. the Hospitals at Hampton are filled with wounded and new tents are going up every day, and quite a number of Surgeons have gone over from here to assist. there has also been a call for Surgeons and nurses to go to Newbern NC where the yellow fever is raging terribly. several Surgeons volunteered to go. I should think it would require some courage to do that. I don't know whether I told you that when I went to board at Mrs Mitchells there was a Capt Caswell, his wife, and little girl boarding there. he went to the front just before I went home, and his wife and child went home to New Hampshire. we have just heard to day that he was killed in a late battle on the north side of the James River. it is very sad. his little girl was about 12 years old and she and I scraped acquaintance immediately on my going there and I used to play with her continually. when he got a pass for his wife to go home he had it made so she could return on it, and jokingly said "she would want to come out and see him again or come after his body".

I had a letter from Mary Saturday. she appears to be enjoying herself finely. I answered it Sunday. I have been almost sick to day. I woke this morning with a pain in my side could hardly draw a long breath, and was very sick at my stomach and vomited up all my breakfast, but I feel better this afternoon. The weather here is quite warm an sultry, with considerable rain.

I suppose you are all Cattle Show up there this week, and I should like very much to be there, and also at election perhaps I may at the latter.

The sesesh here looked blue enough over the late victories and amuse themselves by starting absurd rumors every night after the Old Point boat comes in. the other night they had it all round town that Gen's Grant + Birney were killed and all our cavalry captured. the near approach of the fall of Richmond don't suit them a bit.

I am glad you had so pleasant a time in Springfield, and I would have staid longer if I were you and enjoyed it. It was to bad to lose the pears.

I agree with you that Sheridans victories were splendid, and I expect to hear of more of them. I don't think they will ever send our army kiting down that valley again.[9] I see the remnant of the old 10th got a front seat as usual, of course they

would, but they get no mention, as I suppose they are now a part of the 37th. I saw a Sergeant in Washington going to the front, who was wounded in the Wilderness and has been in Hospital ever since. he was 1st Sergt of Co D. he still walks with a cane and I don't know what use he will be when he gets there. They wanted him to go into the Invalid Corps but he "could not see it".

Well it is almost Supper time and I can think of nothing more to write. I meant to have written by this mornings mail but I had some reports to make out so I could not get to it in time. I forgot to tell you I saw Gen Devens here a few days ago. he was riding by in a carriage as I was coming up Main St. and bowed very low to me as I touched my hat. Gen Shepley was with him. Give my love to Mattie Thomas and my nephew who I suppose grows more wonderful every day. Also my love to Mary when you write, and my respects to my enquiring friends. With much love

Your aff son
Charlie.

132

Norfolk VA
Oct 12th 1864

Dear Mother,

Your welcome letter of the 9th inst came safely to hand this morning, and one from Mary at the same time. You probably received a letter from me about the time you wrote, but you should have received it before.

One reason I do not write oftener is that there is positively nothing to write about here it is the dullest hole I ever saw as far as anything of interest to write about is concerned. The recruiting business is very dull. we have not even had a nibble for the last two weeks and it does not seem possible that they will keep us here much longer if we do not get any recruits.[10]

There is an occasional murder here but it creates no excitement and is merely passed off by a short paragraph in the paper. for instance, 3 nights ago some sailors were confined in the guard house of the Provost which is in the 3rd Story of a brick building on Main Street, and a colored barber was confined with them. in the night they got into a quarrel and the sailors very cooly opened the window and pitched the colored man head foremost out on to the pavement and smashed his head all to pieces. every little while the night guard shoots a man, but nobody but those immediately concerned ever hears of it and pays no attention to it when they do but it is just the difference between a state of war and of peace. you

know what a commotion it makes if a person loses an arm or a leg, or even gets badly bruised in NHampton. it furnishes talk for a month while here nobody would give it a second thought.[11]

Praises of the negroes and the late operations at the front are in everybodys mouth, and they all agreed that they fought nobly. the Hospitals at Portsmouth and over to Hampton are full of thier wounded and mangled bodies, which I suppose is one reason for the scarcity of recruits. I suppose the arrival of so many of them has a tendency to scare the negroes.[12]

I was very sorry to hear of your being all alone in the house as you are, and I would stay with Mattie until some of us get home, or else get Annie or Julia to come and stay with you which I am sure they would be willing to do. it is not right for you to stay there all alone, in your poor health.

Major Starkweather returned to day and reports a very successful Cattle Show. we had a letter from him before he returned telling of Mr Wells death, which must have been very sad. last time I spoke to him he was telling me that we were just the men to go back to the army as we had been there and knew all about it. I wrote a long letter to Aunt Lu a few days ago and directed it to Milton Hart as you told me when I was at home last. how do the late operations in the valley affect her?

I have no idea when we are coming home any more than I had when we came here, but it does not seem as though they would keep us here a great while longer. I should like very much to go to work for Tom, if he wanted me but he never intimated anything of the kind to me. I should like to get something to do in N so that I could live at home, but I see no way for me when this job is over but to go into the army again if I can get a position. I presume Col Edwards will be made a Brigadier and have not much doubt but that I could get a position on his staff if he does, as he wanted to keep me when I came home last summer, but I dread to go back to the wild and roaming life of a soldier again.

I remembered that Wednesday [Monday] was my birth day but I don't hardly remember whether I am 31 or 32 I incline to the latter number however.

Mrs Parsons packed her trunk to start for home to day but changed her mind. I don't know when the next appointed day is.

I see Sheridan has just had another splendid victory in the Valley, but I do not understand what he is falling back for but I have no doubt but that it is all right. he knows what he is about and that is enough. I am very anxious to hear from the Pennsylvania Election. I hope it has gone Union, for if we elect Lincoln I believe the days of rebellion are short.[13] An Officer of Gen Wilds staff from Newport News was just in here. he said they heard very rapid firing last night at the front. they can hear the guns quite plain over there although it is over 60 miles off.

There is a great Naval Expedition fitting out here for some place, probably Wilmington, and it is probably almost ready to sail. There is no end to the ships,

and no end to the sailors and naval officers the streets are crowded with them, and I hope soon to hear that Rebel post is shut up. A Lieutenant of the Osceola one of the ships boards where I do. he thinks they are going there, and he expected to sail this week but thinks they shall not now.

Give my love to Mattie Thomas and my nephew. You did not say much about him in your last. Also my respects to all enquiring friends and accept much love from

Your aff son
Charlie.

133

Norfolk VA
October 27th 1864

Dear Mother,

It seems such a long time since I have heard from you I hardly know what has become of you, or whether you are in the land of the living or not. I certainly wrote you and Mary last, and have not heard from you since the early part of week before last. I have been up to the front and fully expected to find letters from you both when I got back, but there was nothing neither has there been any thing since. I presume Mrs. Parsons told you I had gone and so you thought you would not write which was a very foolish conclusion to come to.

I have been wanting to go to the front ever since I have been here, but could not get a pass, but week before last Major Pearson paymaster, formerly of Holyoke, told me he was going up to pay off several Regts and Batteries, and I asked him to take me along as an extra clerk which he agreed to, and so on Sunday before last we started at 1 o'clock on a Bread boat and arrived at City Point next morning about 7 o'clock. we immediately changed boats and started for Bermuda Hundred three miles distant arriving there we procured an Ambulance and started for the 10th Army Corps, 12 miles, arriving there about 3 o'clock PM, on the very ground where Kauty Cavalry was driven back a few days before. we were close to the Rebel lines and it seemed quite natural to be peering over breastworks again in the old style. they were very quiet, and the pickets on both lines were walking around in plain sight of each other and not farther apart than from our house to Mrs Fannie Cooks. we slept 5 nights close under the breast works, one of which was in a house of which the corner and one chimney had been knocked down by a Rebel shell, and there were eight heavy guns trained upon it all the while from a Rebel fort about a quarter of a mile off. We

were at the Hd Qrs of the 3rd Division 10th Corps, which is commanded by a Col Fairchild who is a very nice man, and very vigilant. he was up all night until 2 o'clock in the morning, going round his lines. We paid one Battery in the famous Fort Harrison, which was so gallantly taken by our boys, and which the Rebels have so vainly assaulted since. the slope of the hill on which it stands is covered with the graves of our men, and the other, with graves of the Rebels. On the picket line of the 10th Corps is a tall pine tree, and from it you can look into the streets of Richmond with a glass, and can see the Capitol and churches and other buildings very plainly with the naked eye. it is distant but 4 and $^1/_2$ miles. I do not climb the tree as it is too hard work but the other clerk did.

We went all along the lines north of the Appomatox, from the right of the 10th Corps, to the left of the eighteenth, and paid Battery B, 1st Artillery, at the foot of Butlers famous look out tower. this was one of the Batteries which lost its guns, when Kauty was driven back.

From the last place we proceeded again to Bermuda Hundred on horseback, and got a tug and came down to Wilson Landing, Friday night from which place, after paying another Battery, we hailed the gunboat Wilderness, and got aboard and started for Norfolk where we arrived about half past eight Saturday night. After a very pleasant trip, which as you may imagine I enjoyed very much indeed. We were up there when the salute of shotted guns was fired in honor of Sheridans great victory, and thought a battle was going to take place until we learned what it was. What a glorious old fellow Sheridan is and how he does keep the poor Johnnies hopping up in the valley.

There is nothing of interest in Norfolk to write about. it is about the dullest place in the world. recruiting is as slow as ever, we know no more how long we are to stay than we did when we came, nor can we find out anything about it. we are all coming home Thanksgiving if we live, if we do not come before, for good. Mary I suppose has arrived home before this but I do not know anything about it nor whether you are all alive or not. I wish you would write and let me know something about it. it [is] a long time, two weeks to be without a letter.

We have moved our office from Church Street down on to Main Street, and have got a much better place. it has been a recruiting office for colored Regts for a long time though its former occupants have gone to the front, but the darkies know no difference and we have to read thier letters from and write letters to thier husbands and friends at the front daily, so that I expect I shall be adept in writing love letters,[14] when I have occasion to do so on my own account. they invariably commence (the married ones) with "my dear loving husband", and end with "your ever loving wife until death" One fellow writes from the front in a letter I read yesterday that he determined to fight the devil. I hope he will recognize the devil in those devils in butternut color in front of him.

Please give my love to Mary, Mattie + Thomas and my nephew. I have got so

far when Maj Starkweather came in and handed me your letter of the 23rd. I think Miss Mary has made quite a visit. I am very sorry that your Asthma troubles you so much, but am glad that Thomas and Mattie are coming in to live with you and are going to bring Kate. I was thinking of bringing in a contraband when I come.[15] Please write again to

Your aff son
Charlie.

EPILOGUE

Like Everything Else in This World War Is "Kinder Mixed"

*Letters from Mary Kate Brewster's "Journals,"
transcribed in 1893*

When Mary Kate Brewster took her father's letters with her on an around-the-world voyage in 1893, she transcribed them into journals. What follows are four examples of letters for which no originals exist; only these versions of the copies are available. Major portions of these letters are, no doubt, faithful to the originals, but there is sufficient internal evidence to suggest that Mary Kate Brewster occasionally wrote in a different voice and refashioned her father's accounts into her own narratives. These letters still tell us much about Brewster's experience. But they also exhibit the historical imagination of the 1890s, an era when idealized Civil War reminiscing became a family pastime. The reminiscences themselves became a major aspect of American popular and literary culture and a sentimentalized memory of soldiers' experience emerged as a staple of national reunion. Such letters are both documents and reconstructions. Some of the descriptive reality of Brewster's writing survives here; but these letters also represent war as rugged adventure, full of danger and loneliness, but also of comradeship, spectacle, incomparable exhilaration, and "great glory." The longest letter in the collection (probably written on July 4, 1862), labeled simply "On James River, Don't know where nor why," provides a classic example of how a soldier (perhaps in collaboration with his twenty-two-year-old daughter) had helped forge what Oliver Wendell Holmes, Jr, called in 1884 the soldier's "faith . . . true and adorable which sends a soldier to throw away his life in obedience to a blindly accepted duty, in a cause which he little understands, in a plan of campaign of which he has no notion, under tactics of which he does not see the use."[1] As much as any second lieutenant, Brewster did understand his and the Union's "cause," but the experience of battle is something that he tried very hard to record for its own sake. He was both proud and stunned at how "curious" and "mixed" the emotions of battle could be; and he yearned, as in the famous song he quotes, for when the "cruel war" would be over. Making war did forge a certain kind of soldier's "faith." Brewster testified to such a faith and his daughter both preserved and sanitized it in memory.

On James River Don't know where *nor why*
[undated, but probably written on July 4, 1862]
I have taken my pencil in hand to commence a letter to you, though whether I can finish or if I finish whether I can send it, or when I can, is more than I can tell.

I wrote last from my old camp near Seven Pines. That night we slept there, and the very air was feverish with apprehensions and rumors, the roar of musketry and artillery was tremendous. We were under arms and ready all day but it was not until 3 o'clock that orders came to pack up and fall in which we

Mary Katherine Brewster, youngest daughter of Charles Harvey Brewster, aboard the clipper ship *The Great Admiral,* en route to Australia, 1893. During the voyage, Mary Kate began transcribing her father's letters into journals that became a family heirloom. *Courtesy of Jonathan Allured*

did, and when the line was formed we were surprised and nonplussed to find ourselves out in front of the rifle pits, from behind which we had expected someday to pour death and destruction upon quaking Rebels, and facing to the rear towards Savages Station. Soon we took up our line of march to the rear, about half a mile, and formed line facing to the front, after half an hour we again started to the rear and marched to Savages Station and formed line facing to the front. We staid here until 6 o'clock I should think. When we went we marched again to the front almost up to our camp. When we took a road to the right and marched some 4 or 5 miles up to reinforce somebody. I don't know who but our business when there was to gather stragglers and guard them, men who had run away from the battle that day. We staid here until 12 o'clock at night when "fall in" was the word, fall in we did and took up our line of march again, and such a march![2]

At top speed we went, past our old camp, off to the rear, past Savages Station and on past our old camp of weeks ago, and turning to the right kept on, without rest and with no water and hardly anything to eat. I had been up all night 3 nights out of 5 this week and about half past 4 that morning I was obliged to give up and sit down. I could not struggle on another step. After resting a little I started on so, resting a little and pushing on a little further. I managed to keep along, all the while brigade after brigade of infantry and battery after battery of artillery passed, intersperced with long wagon trains, ambulances and varied traps, vehicles and appertainances of an Army. We kept on in this way until about ten o'clock when we came to a crossroads and halted, throwing out skirmishers in every direction and posting artillery to command all the roads. At night Co C had to go on Picket making 5 nights out of 6 this week that I and most of the Company had been up. We came in at 5 o'clock Sunday morning and I laid down to snatch a little rest, when close in front, a little to the left, came the familiar sound of the cracking muskets of the Pickets, first scattering then growing closer and finally breaking into the right rear row of the battle. We sprang to arms and formed in line, and now the Artillery opened, and gun after gun from the battery just in front awaits the echoes in the surrounding swamp. The occasion of all this was a body of Rebel Cavalry, scouting through here. (not expecting any body but our scattered Cavalry Videttes, which is all we have had here before this) but right on thier way was the 7th Mass Regt, and as they came dashing on, in all the pride of Southern Chivalry when they supposed themselves to be out of danger they got closed on the aforesaid *mudsills* from Mass, when, at a distance of a few roads, uprises that line of shining rifle barrels and gleaming bayonettes and forth from the muzzle bursts a storm of whistling, stinging, humming minniballs. Saddles are emptied and the noble sons of the sunny South bite the dust, and are rolled in thier own sacred souls. And now the deadly artillery of the mudsills opens on them, and before they can take themselves away, the terrible grape and

cannister is among them, and following them as they make thier best effort to put distance between us. The result is that they leave a large number of dead and wounded and from 20–25 prisoners, including thier Major, in our hands.[3]

Well after this pleasant commencement of our Sabbath services the rest of the day has passed quietly, with the exception of large bodies of troops constantly arriving.

Just before sunset we would then take up our line of march, taking a short road to the southeast, and after marching about half an hour we reached a high ground and a refreshing breeze coming over hills, much like our own New England, brings new life to us and the brightening eye and quickening step tell better than any words what it is to the almost exhausted soldier. We arrived at a magnificent plantation, turn into a field of bright green clover and lie down. This is just at dark. In front of us is a dense woods to the right of that an open field. While we lie here thousands of troops pass us, Infantry, Cavalry, and Artillery, and pass into the right of the woods just on the edge of which is a narrow country road, the branches of the trees meet and close over head.

Finally our turn comes and we follow on. The brush beats against our faces on both sides, but the road is dry and hard and we made good speed. I wish I had the power of the poet to describe that nights march.[4] As we march along, now across a level country where the woods are more open now down, down in the deep ravines, where darkness is to be felt, and across small streamlets, where candles will be stuck on the trees to guide the Artillery in crossing, and then up steep hills on the other side, wherever and anon the artillery gets stuck in some mud hole caused by a mountain spring, and the Infantry has to come to thier rescue and taking hold lift them by Main Strength, and on they go, still pressing on.

Now the dawning day begins to show in the East, and we reach a level road upon high land, but still in the woods. the road begins to descend, and just before sunrise we cross a stream and emerge upon a vast field almost entirely covered with Wheat, ripe and suffering for the harvest. And here, to our surprise, we discover thousands of our wagons. The fields like these and the hills around are covered with thier white tops, but we have no time to spend in wondering. We stack arms and in 5 minutes every tired soldier has thrown himself on the ground and is oblivious to all surroundings, but alas, they cannot sleep long for now the burning, scorching, blistering sun pours down his way, hotter and hotter, he must get up or be broiled, and now we find we are on the very banks of the James River where we lie all day wondering, what next? And far off over the woods come the booming of Artillery, now hotter and faster, now slower, and again rivaling the most terrible thunder. And still we stay there and wonder. About 3 o'clock we hear cheering which runs like wild fire from one part of the woods to the other. It is taken up in one spot and rends the air, it passes through another

and rends the air, and now the news comes, the Rebels have attacked our rear guard and have been repelled with terrible horrible slaughter and a loss of ten guns, and 4,000 prisoners left in our hands. Hardly had the news reached us when on comes a calm cool but fierce and determined Gen Couch with his staff and are now almost idolized Gen Palmer (commanding Brigadere) spurring on as though life depended on thier efforts.

And now we are wanted. We fall in in less time by half than it takes to tell it, and take up our line of march back toward where we came from. On we hurried to the edge of the woods and form in line of battle. The order comes "off with your knapsacks" it is done. Each co piles its own in a heap, one man left to guard them. There is common to the soldiers, no mistaking with proceedings. It means work.

We right face and in we go, not by the road we came, but across the country, through woods, across fields of grass and fields of corn and everything else. All the time the roar of battle grows near, but now it seems close at hand. We stopped behind a hill and our generals ride to the top to reconnoiter. We start on and form in line of battle on the top of the hill. And now we see what we did not know before, that our whole division is behind us. They come pouring over the brow of the hill and form line after line behind us. And now the battle recedes, and we hear occasionally the yell and cheer of our invincible "mudsills" as they take the bayonet and drive back the foe. Back and fall back, and now the sun sets and an occasional volley that breaks the quiet of a summers evening. We are in a vast field of wheat partly reaped and put up in shocks. We are disposed for the night and immediately fall upon the straw and make ourselves oh so comfortable for the night. Sergent B + M are my bedfellows and as we lie down I remarked, "Boys, this is too comfortable for us. We shall not be allowed to spend the night here." Sure enough we hardly had laid down before "fall in", "fall in" and we fall in "Take arms" "right face" "forward march". On the march across the country until we strike a wide road, and on that we marched weary mile after mile and somewhere between 9 and 11 o'clock we arrived in another field, form our line of battle again and lie down, but oh, what a contrast! the ground is bare, damp and hard as a Negher Millstone. Our blankets are ten miles behind us. We lie down and I just get into a doze and I find I am freezing, and I must get up. I walk until I can stand on my feet or keep my eyes open no longer, I lie down and get into another doze, covered with dreams of icebergs and all the cold things I have ever seen or read about, but it is not for long, even this kind of rest. Just before 5 o'clock comes the order to fall in again, and almost before we can get our eyes open the order is "right face, forward march"! and we take the way back, marching by the flank, four regiments abreast, and at a rate that would indicate that the whole southern army is at our heels. We keep this up until we had made, I should think 4 miles, and then turn off and form the line of battle again. It is in

a whirlwind and the dust is 6 inches deep but down we go and in a few minutes are all asleep. There we are allowed to stay until daylight, about 3 hours. When it is fall in again, and now we are assigned positions in line of battle, we are told we have posted and everything indicates that we soon are to have a battle.

Skirmishers are called out, and our regiment and the 36th NY are filed out at right angles with the regular line of battle. About 10 o'clock, I should think, the skirmishers commenced firing and soon the Rebels come on, yelling and hoot-ing, but our Artillery opened on them with grape and cannister and drove them back. But one man of our regiment was wounded in this skirmish, although fragments of shells and minnie bullets were flying thick over our heads.

The battle now subsided into an Artillery battle and was quite lively for some time, finally down the way drew almost perfect silence, except occasional firing by the skirmishers. About noon our regiment was moved around by file right into a ravine and lay there a long time under the firing of our own and the Rebel Artillery, but in a perfectly safe position as far as that was concerned.

We lay just behind the edge of the woods at about 15 feet in front of a field of oats. About 3 o'clock the Rebels came round to our right in a ravine, and in fact a continuation of the same we were in. The 55th NY (French) was on our right, and with them our regiment advanced in line, into the oat field which was a hill and immediately after we came into the field the battle became hot and furious on our right and almost in our rear. The 55th gave way at first, but the Artillery got the range of the ravine and raked the Rebels most horribly, and the 55th rallied and drove them back and took thier colors. It was said that of the Rebel regiment which came up this ravine not fifty men came out unhurt.

Meantime we are in a precarious position where the struggle between the 55th and the Rebels took place almost directly in our rear. Thier bullets struck close to us in our rear while the Rebel bullets came over the brow of the hill in our front. But the contest in our rear was soon over and now our time was coming and after a few minutes our skirmishers in front commenced firing.

We were lying down in the oaks and kept still until they got within 2 or 3 rods of us. They did not come parallel to our lines consequently only our left became engaged, but as I said before when they were within 2 or 3 rods, our boys jumped up and gave it to them hot and tight full in thier faces. It lasted but a few minutes, but we laid them out. It was in many instances a hand to hand fight. Our men shot the color bearer of the Rebels and one of the 36th NY ran out and seized thier colors and brought them in, and they sent the rest aflying in hot haste.

After this we lay down quietly and all was silent for some time. Pretty soon our skirmishers sent word that the Rebels were bringing up Artillery directly in front of us (the 10th). We lay still until all at once on our left the Rebels came down in hords, yelling like demons. Immediately by an aid came down the orders for us.

We jumped up, faced to the left and went round at the double quick about 40 rods, when "halt! front!" and there we were, facing the Rebels, who were advancing in line of battle in countless numbers, and not more than 150 yards from us. We immediately lay down and commenced firing, and the way we put bullets into them was a caution to Rebs, and it would have done your heart good to see those Rebels "skeedaddle". They broke and ran like sheep. Our Artillery was all the time plying them with persuasive arguments in the shape of shells of all sizes and kinds, sent into thier ranks over our heads. We drove them back but they rallied, or rather brought on fresh ones, and again we poured it into them and again they broke and ran, and still another line came on behind these, came and did likewise. Came up boldly, and you would have thought they were going to walk on the handfulls of mudsills, but they could not stand the perfect storm of bullets we sent into them together with the storm of shells from the Artillery. Oh it was glorious! Glorious!! Glorious!!! to see these, who have boasted themselves for bravery and chivalry and the cream of everything in the United States, to see them break and run like sheep before the Mudsills, we see Mechanics and small fisted farmers of the glorious north, and in numbers they were like as a drove of cattle to the drivers.

Co C had 36 men here, all the fighting men left of the once large company, who left thier homes one year ago. It would do thier friends good to see how they gave it to the Rebels, and the whole regiment has gained great glory.

Gen Palmer can not say enough about us, calls us his regiment of Sharpshooters, and says we fought as though we were behind breastworks, and so they did. Not a man flinched or ran, they fired all thier cartridges, 60 rounds, and then waited with fixed bayonets and would have waited until this time, if they had not been ordered away, as it was then long after dark, and reinforcements had come up. We had 3 men wounded in this battle and among them is our C. he is not seriously hurt, a bruise on the temple. No one could go off the field with him but he went alone and after the battle was over and we had marched off Lieut W and I went to try to find him through the woods and over the fields, into every group of wounded men and into every house we could find, calling his name as we went. Although I was almost ready to drop, I searched for two and a half or three hours but could not find him. This would seem improbable to you, and there are no words that can give you any realizing sense of what a field is after a battle. We could not find where our surgeons were.

We returned to the regiment long after all but ourselves were asleep, and turned in supposing that we should stay there that night and could resume our search in the morning, but we had hardly got asleep when it was fall in again. It was near 12 o'clock at night when we marched until 8 o'clock the next morning. When we found ourselves way off here on the James River, and all the army with us. Our sick and wounded who were unable to travel were left in the hands of the

enemy, with a surgeon and nurse to take care of them. C was able to walk and get over here and I presume is now on his way home and will get there before this letter does.

I do not know what is to become of us. Our Officers who were not killed or wounded are many of them sick. I am in command of Co C as Lieut W is sick, and so am I.

Tell Cals people that he was as cool and brave as any general in the grand army, and I have incidents [that will?] prove it. When I can see them to tell them about it but my head is now so filled that I can write no more.

I will write no complaint of our suffering for I cannot begin to give you an idea of it. Suffice it to say that until night before last I had not had my boots off, nor my sword or belt, since last Friday morning. Nor slept more than two hours at any one time, nor have the boys except when it was necessary to take them off for a few minutes, and all the time we have been on the go. We have had no rations sent out to us since we left the rifle pits when we took three days rations. I am yet unhurt and have cause for unceasing gratitude that I have been able to endure what I have for the last ten days.

July 5th 1862

We are now in a dense wood engaged in filling it and building rifle pits, and when we get them done probably we shall leave them if the Rebels want us to. We have built entrenchments all the time since we have been on the peninsula and never have fought behind them yet. At Seven Pines and on that line the army built entrenchments as strong as the defenses of Washington. We work day after day there, and built great forts. With platforms for guns, and every other kind of entrenchments and yet if we fought the enemy we had to go out a mile beyond them and fight without any sign of a breastwork. From the fort we built there never has been a gun fired and now they are in the hands of the enemy. We have got about sick of this kind of business.

The express Mattie sent has never reached me, nor do I care much for I have become used to going without anything to eat drink or wear without sleep which is very economical way of getting along in the world.

The 36th NY came out of the battle the other day before us, and as they passed Gen Palmer he asked where the 10th was. They told him we were on our position yet but almost out of ammunition, and when we came marching out in regular order as good as though we were at a regimental drill it is said he fairly jumped up and down and clapped his hands.

Capt B, being in command, sent to Gen Couch for more ammunition but he said "tell Capt B to come out. He has done enough, the 10th regiment has done enough". Is it not all glorious to belong to such a noble regiment? The actual

fighting force of the regiment was not more than 400. The nobleness of these men it would seem is enough to redeem a nation, and as I saw them the other day stand there and view that line of Rebels, which could be seen for more than a mile coming down on them again and yet again, and see them hold the leaden hail upon them and drive them back in utter confusion, not a waiver nor a look to the rear among our brave boys, it seemed as though my heart would fly out of my mouth in exultation, and I could have hugged every one of them, and laughed or cried or danced or turned somersaults or done any other very unbecoming thing. Instead of which I merely said, "Now boys, the best thing is to go off the field in perfect order so close up". And they did and I think there is not one who did not regret coming away. I know I did not and during that terrible 4 or 5 hours that we were there I had not a thought of fear nor anything like fear, on the contrary I wanted to rush on them and have them hand to hand, and I know that was just what the boys wanted, so it was hard to restrain them from it, but orders were positive not to advance beyond the first line and yet will you believe it? all day before the battle began I dreaded it like the veriest power in existence, and actually prayed for courage, and yet it seemed as the moment came all fear and all excitement passed away and I cared no more than I would in a common hail storm. How curious it is, is it not?[5]

January 14th 1863

Yes Co C got thier New Years dinner, and a splendid one it was, but I was about divided between joy for them and sorrow for the rest of the Regiment who had no feast.

I wish you could see the soldiers flock around a big box like that from home, and hear the remarks and exclamations and see the eyes sparkle and the curiosity as each package is unrolled. These great blue coated fellows then become like a pack of little children opening thier stockings on Christmas Morning, and you could hardly realize that these blue coats would march with unfaltering step into a very tempest of bullets, or up to the cannons mouth and never flinch. Oh, it is a glorious thing to be a soldier after all. Ahem! that is to night, and after the fights are all over so far and one can sit and talk them over. But then on the long and weary marches, in rain mud and cold, in sunshine heat and dust, often during the weary hours of night, it does not *seem quite so glorious*. Then again when the lines of battle are formed and the raging foe rushes upon them again and again (as at Malvern Hill) only to be broken crushed and driven back, or as we saw at Rappahanock Station, the long line crossing the fields, up the slopes and over the earthworks, and heard the shout and roar of battle and saw the guns that had been hurling the crashing shell at us, turned upon the foe, then heard the cheers of ten thousand men as they rend the air. Oh! then war is glorious.

Now all is still again presently come the stretcher bearers, bringing the mangled forms of the wounded minus legs, minus arms, one or both, gun shot wounds and mangled in every way, and to look upon the dead bodies scattered here and there and everywhere, with heads blown off, bodies torn open and men killed in every conceivable way why then war does not seem quite so glorious. Well, I think that is enough in that strain. Like everything else in this world War is "kinder mixed". I do not know what I have written all that stuff for unless because I have no need to write, for certainly there is nothing very glorious in being cooped up in a little 7 x 5 tent with nobody to see and nothing to do but open the door look out upon a sea of red mud, then shut it again sit down and look into the fire.[6] Well, the Colonel has gone to bed and is sleeping soundly and I suppose I must follow suit as I have got to the end of both ideas and paper.

You are right in supposing that the evenings in camp are very long. We have to go to bed in sheer desperation then roll and toss all night. I often get up and smoke and read a little when I cannot get to sleep.

Funkstown Md July 13th 1863

We advanced our Pickets yesterday and drove back the Rebel line about half a mile taking some 200 prisoners.

The Militia has begun to arrive, also some 9 months men from No Carolina and Yorktown. We expect to have a desparate battle tomorrow and so we did to day. We have thrown up a long line of rifle pits. The Rebels favored us with five shells to day but as we did not answer them they desisted. Col P and I have just returned from a ride of a mile and a half up the lines to see Gen Briggs who has just arrived with a Brigade from Maryland Heights, and joined the 1st Corps.

It is reported that we have taken 500 prisoners since we came to this place, or rather that they have come in and given themselves up. I had written so far when the newspapers came and of course I had to stop to read them then an order came for a report of the number of muskets we could take into action and by the time I had that finished it was dark and I sat down on the ground by the few glimmering coals that constitute our campfire and ate my supper and before I finished that it commenced to rain and I beat a retreat and crawled into my little shelter tent and here I lie flat on my back, holding the paper before me and endeavoring to write intellibibly by the light of a flaring candle. So you can judge under what difficulties I carry on my correspondence.[7]

I expect by the report I was ordered to make out to night that the great battle will take place tomorrow, as we always have to make out that kind of report before an engagement. It is a glorious sight, and a glorious subject to contemplate these two lines of battle stretching across the country for miles, silent and

dark. With the exception of an occasional glimmering light. Where the rain has not entirely extinguished the little campfire by which the enemys cup of coffee has boiled, or where some soldier, like myself is writing a few lines to the loved ones at home which perchance may be his last. It is as dark as dark can be and as silent as the city of the dead, except an occasional crack of the rifle in front, where the watchful Picket peers through the darkness and imagines a lurking foe, with a distant rumbling of Artillery as it moves into position and makes ready to belch forth its fire and smoke and storm of iron hail. Tomorrow or whenever the one man whose word can change this silence into the noise and tumult that will shake the earth, shall speak.[8]

But I must close for my arms ache with trying to write in this cramped position and my eyes also ache, and seem to plead to be allowed to close for the night. Tuesday AM July 14th. The Reb Pickets are gone this morning and we are all under arms and expect to follow them. One Division and two Batteries from each of ours (3rd 5th and 12th Corps) have gone on a reconnaisance to find their line of battle if they have any. As I write squads of prisoners are coming in continually I am afraid their main force has got over the river and we shall have another long chase down through Virginia. There go the cannons. So it seems the reconnoitering force has caught up with them.

Head Quarters 10th Mass Vols Camp Sedgewick Nov 25 1863

Well tomorrow is Thanksgiving Day and the last that I shall spend in the Army. You I suppose, are expecting a good time and I can imagine you all seated around the loaded table tomorrow. I can see the big brown turkey the chicken pie and the pudding with Mince pies, pumpkin pies, and cranberry sauce ect ect "deployed as skirmishers" all around the table, Oh yes I can see it all.

Well while you are at it, just let your eye wander off to this red clay desert hundreds of miles away, and let them rest upon the edge of a little pine grove, facing to the south and looking out upon miles and miles of little white tents each the size and shape of an old three cornered hen coop. Upon the edge of the pine wood aforesaid, you can see three walled tents with a big fire of hickory log burning in front; just back of them behold a square piece of canvas spread over some rails, and under it a board set upon pine stakes driven into the ground. On this table set with pewter plates and cups tomorrow at noon we can see (unless we march before that time) the Lieut Col the Major and the Adjt taking thier Thanksgiving dinner of beefsteak and potatoes each one, probably thinking of the far off New England home and the circle of friends and relations gathered round the festive board. Oh Well! "when this cruel war—7 months I mean—is over."[9]

We are much better off though than we were last Thanksgiving for there we had only pork and hard tack, wormy and not enough of it at that so that we ought to give thanks in abundance this year.

There is the greatest mystery as to where we are going when we move. The wagons are loaded with an unusual quantity of supplies and the greatest pains have been taken to have the shoes in perfect condition and the arms and ammunition in perfect order. So it all points to a long march. The wildest rumors prevail and our destination is staked at all points of the compass. We are expecting a hard time and plenty of fighting. We are not at all eager for the "fray" but we are already which is much better. Where ever you find a soldier "eager for the fray" the newspapers have it, you may be sure that he has never been in any fray, for being in one takes away all eagerness for it, I assure you.[10]

PS 7 PM

We have again received orders to be ready in the morning but it is clouding again and we may not march but if we do go you can imagine me marching along instead of enjoying the dinner I spoke of.

NOTES

Introduction

1. Paul Fussell, *The Great War in Modern Memory* (New York, 1975), 6.

2. Maris A. Vinovskis, "Have Social Historians Lost the Civil War?: Some Preliminary Demographic Speculations," *Journal of American History* 76 (June 1989): 57. For the new social history of the common soldier, also see Maris A. Vinovskis, ed., *Toward a Social History of the American Civil War* (New York, 1990); Joseph T. Glatthaar, *The March to the Sea and Beyond: Sherman's Troops in the Savannah and Carolinas Campaigns* (New York, 1985); Joseph T. Glatthaar, *Forged in Battle: The Civil War Alliance of Black Soldiers and White Officers* (New York, 1990); Reid Mitchell, *Civil War Soldiers: Their Expectations and Their Experiences* (New York, 1988); Phillip Shaw Paludan, *A People's Contest: The Union and Civil War, 1861–65* (New York, 1988), 316–38; Randall C. Jimerson, *The Private Civil War: Popular Thought during the Sectional Conflict* (Baton Rouge, 1988); James I. Robertson, Jr., *Soldiers Blue and Gray* (Columbia, S.C., 1988); Michael Fellman, *Inside War: The Guerrilla Conflict in Missouri during the American Civil War* (New York, 1989); Warren Wilkinson, *Mother, May You Never See the Sights I Have Seen: The Fifty-seventh Massachusetts Veteran Volunteers in the Army of the Potomac, 1864–65* (New York, 1990); Michael Barton, *Goodmen: The Character of Civil War Soldiers* (University Park, Pa., 1981); Earl J. Hess, *Liberty, Virtue, and Progress: Northerners and Their War for the Union* (New York, 1988); and Marvin R. Cain, "A 'Face of Battle' Needed: An Assessment of Motives and Men in Civil War Historiography," *Civil War History* 28 (March 1982): 5–27.

3. Bell I. Wiley, *The Life of Billy Yank: The Common Soldier of the Union* (Baton Rouge, 1952), 15; Bell I. Wiley, *The Life of Johnny Reb: The Common Soldier of the Confederacy* (Baton Rouge, 1943).

4. *Hampshire Gazette and Courier* [Northampton, Mass.], April 23, 30; May 7, 14; June 11, 1861, Forbes Library, Northampton; Alfred S. Roe, *The Tenth Regiment Massachusetts Volunteer Infantry, 1861–64* (Springfield, Mass., 1909), 378–84.

5. Roe, *Tenth Regiment*, 18–28.

6. Robert Hunt Rhodes, ed., *All for the Union: The Civil War Diary and Letters of Elisha Hunt Rhodes* (New York, 1991); Geoffrey C. Ward, with Ric Burns and Ken Burns, *The Civil War: An Illustrated History* (New York, 1990). For the creation of the brigade in which the Tenth served, see Frank J. Welcher, *The Union Army, 1861–1865: Organization and Operations* vol. 1, *The Eastern Theater* (Bloomington, Ind., 1989), 8. On March 13, 1862, Brewster's brigade became part of the Fourth Corps of the Army of the Potomac,

and from September 1862 until the end of its service in June 1864, it was part of the Sixth Corps (Roe, *Tenth Regiment*, 318–19).

7. Roe, *Tenth Regiment*, 295.

8. *The Brewster Geneology, 1566–1907: A Record of the Descendants of William Brewster of the Mayflower, Ruling Elder of the Pilgrim Church Which Founded Plymouth Colony in 1620*, vol. 2, comp. Emma C. Brewster Jones (New York, 1908), 868–69. On the ordinary soldier escaping from ordinary life, see Philip Caputo, *A Rumor of War* (New York, 1977).

9. Brewster letter, June 15, 1862, Historic Northampton (all letters published in this volume are hereafter cited simply as "letter"). On the importance of letters and connections to "home," see Reid Mitchell, "The Northern Soldier and His Community," in Vinovskis, *Toward a Social History*, 78–92.

10. Letters, July 12; June 21, 1862.

11. Letters, July 9, 1863; May 23, 1864. Brewster refers to the death of Edwin B. Bartlett, who was killed at Spotsylvania on May 18 (Roe, *The Tenth Regiment*, 271).

12. Letter, November 24, 1861.

13. Letters, November 10; September 22; November 6, 10, 17, 24; December 14, 1861. Also see letter, November 21, 1863, where he describes himself as "cursed with ill luck all my life."

14. Letter, January 9, 1862. Brewster was subsequently promoted to first lieutenant, September 29, 1862, and as adjutant of the regiment, December 1862. He was technically a staff officer and not a field officer.

15. Letter, January 15, 1862.

16. Henry W. Parsons to Aunt Julia, September 1861. Parsons Family Papers, Historic Northampton, Northampton, Mass. Both Parsons's quotations come from a single letter.

17. Mitchell, "The Northern Soldier," 89; Eric J. Leed, *No Man's Land: Combat and Identity in World War I* (New York, 1979), 213.

18. Letters, November 25, 1862; February 23, November 21, 1863.

19. Letters, February 3; April 3, 1864.

20. Letter, June 15, 1864. See Leed, *No Man's Land*, 12–33.

21. Gerald F. Linderman, *Embattled Courage: The Experience of Combat in the Civil War* (New York, 1987), 284, 266–97.

22. Ibid., 7–110; quotation is from 34.

23. William Manchester, *Goodbye Darkness: A Memoir of the Pacific War* (New York, 1979), 46–47. A growing literature exists on the questions of manhood, male tradition, and war making. Helpful to me have been Linderman, *Embattled Courage;* Kim Townsend, "Francis Parkman and the Male Tradition," *American Quarterly* 38 (Spring 1986): 97–112; Peter G. Filene, *Him/Herself: Sex Roles in Modern America* (New York, 1975), 69–112; and Edward O. Wilson, *On Human Nature* (Cambridge, 1978), 99–120. An important critique of Fussell's *Great War in Modern Memory*, which is useful to understanding what may be peculiarly male about the experience of war, is Lynne Hanley, *Writing War: Fiction, Gender, and Memory* (Amherst, 1991), 18–37.

24. Letters, May 24, 25, 27, 28, 29, 31; July 27, 1862.

25. Stephen Crane, *The Red Badge of Courage*, Avon Edition (New York, 1979), 39–40; Letters, December 15, 23, 1862.

26. Letters, April 30; May 26, 1864. From May 5 to May 12, the Army of the Potomac suffered thirty-two thousand casualties: killed, wounded, or missing. During the first seven weeks of Grant's campaign against Lee in Virginia, northern casualties reached the appalling figure of sixty-five thousand, a daily cost in life and limb that Brewster's letters

help document. These seven weeks also constitute almost exactly the final days of the enlistment of the Tenth Massachusetts, which was mustered out on June 22. These casualty figures were horrifying to Northerners because of the devastation they represented for so many families in towns like Northampton, but also because in spite of them, there was no clear sign of an end to the war; Lee's lines in Virginia had not been broken as the siege of Petersburg began, though his casualties had been proportionately as high as Grant's. See James McPherson, *The Battle Cry of Freedom* (New York, 1988), 732, 741–42.

27. Letter, April 3, 1862. This very date was actually a "fast day" in Massachusetts. See also letters, February 21; March 16, 1862. Brewster missed the battle of Antietam while on furlough. Some of Brewster's letters were printed in the *Daily Hampshire Gazette,* though he protested about their publication to his mother and others. See letter, July 13, 1862.

28. Letter, May 7, 1862; Aitken is quoted in Fussell, *Great War,* 174.

29. Letters, June 2, 5, 12, 15, 21; May 10, 1862. Some readers will wish to follow the theme of Brewster's many physical maladies and the variety of medical treatments and drugs he endured.

30. John Keegan, *The Face of Battle: A Study of Agincourt, Waterloo, and the Somme* (New York, 1976), 35–45, 320–43.

31. Letters, July 30, 1863; May 11, 13, 15, 1864. Many of Bierce's stories would serve as comparisons, but see for example "A Horseman in the Sky" and "The Mocking-Bird," in *The Civil War Short Stories of Ambrose Bierce,* compiled by Ernest J. Hopkins (Lincoln, Nebr., 1970), 97–108.

32. Letters, October 23; September 25, 1861; May 21, 1862; May 23, 26, 1864. "The Death of Charles H. Brewster" (obituary), *Daily Hampshire Gazette,* October 9, 1893.

33. See Wiley, *Life of Billy Yank,* 109–15; Glatthaar, *Forged in Battle,* 11–12.

34. See Dudley T. Cornish, *The Sable Arm: Black Troops in the Union Army, 1861–65* (Lawrence, Kans., 1956), 24–25; Ira Berlin et al. eds., *Freedom: A Documentary History of Emancipation, 1861–67,* ser. 2, *The Black Military Experience* (New York, 1982), 1–7.

35. Letters, November 24, 17, 1861.

36. Letter, December 4, 1861.

37. Letters, January 2, 15, 1862.

38. Letters, March 5, 8, 12, 4, 1862.

39. Letters, January 15, 23; February 9, 1862. Ralph Ellison, "What America Would Be Like without Blacks," in *Going to the Territory* (New York, 1986), 109; Mark Twain, *The Adventures of Huckleberry Finn* (1884; New York, 1966), 282–83; "Annual Message to Congress," December 1, 1862, in *The Collected Works of Abraham Lincoln,* ed. Roy P. Basler (New Brunswick, N.J., 1953), 5:537.

40. Roe, *Tenth Regiment,* 291, 342; Rhodes, *All for the Union,* 164.

41. Letters, August 20; October 12, 1864. On recruiting black troops, see Glatthaar, *Forged in Battle,* 61–80; Berlin, *Freedom,* 6–15. Brewster's appointment as a recruiter, signed by Governor John A. Andrew, July 23, 1864, as in Brewster Family Papers, Sophia Smith Collection, Smith College. Brewster was appointed assistant adjutant general on the staff of Col. J. B. Parsons.

42. Letters, August 30; September 16, 1864.

43. Letters, August 4; October 5, 12, 1864. One of the murders Brewster describes is that of a "colored barber," who, while jailed with three white sailors, was thrown to his death from a third-story window. A year earlier in July 1863, as a newly organized company of the United States Colored Troops (USCT) marched through the streets of Norfolk, led by their lieutenant Anson L. Sanborn, Sanborn was publicly assassinated by

a prominent physician and secessionist. The physician was later executed, but the incident and others like it diminished recruiting efforts in the area for many months to come. On this incident, see Glatthaar, *Forged in Battle,* 69. As Brewster described these "occasional murders" that few paid any attention to, he concluded that "it is just the difference between a state of war and a state of peace" (letter, October 12, 1864).

44. Letter, October 27, 1864. The two examples from a freedman's letters that I quote here were not written by Brewster, but they were sent from the Norfolk recruiting area in 1864. See letters by black soldier Rufus Wright, February 2, May 25, 1864, in Berlin, *Freedom,* 661–63. Wright uses the phrase "give my love to" eight times in these two short letters, forming the very kind of example that Brewster found so memorable and educative.

45. "The Death of Charles H. Brewster" (obituary), *Daily Hampshire Gazette,* October 9, 1893; letter, Aunt Mary to Mary Kate Brewster, November 9, 1893, Brewster Family Papers, Sophia Smith Collection, Smith College. Brewster's real and personal estate was valued at approximately $15,000 at his death in 1893. Administrator's Estate Inventory, filed October 26, 1893, Probate Court, Hampshire County, Northampton, Mass. Brewster's more than twenty land transactions are recorded in Register of Deeds, Hampshire County, Northampton, Mass.

46. Brewster to "My Dear Children," October 7, 10, 11, 1886, Historic Northampton. Linderman, *Embattled Courage,* 297. On the G.A.R. also see Stuart McConnell, "Who Joined the Grand Army? Three Case Studies in the Construction of Union Veteranhood, 1866–1900," in Vinovskis, *Toward a Social History,* 139–70.

47. Mary Kate Brewster, "Log Book" (diary, 1893–94), 3–7, 19, 21, 26–27; letter Mary Kate Brewster to Gertrude, January 9, 1894, Sydney, Australia, Brewster Family Papers, Sophia Smith Collection, Smith College; "The Death of Charles H. Brewster," *Daily Hampshire Gazette,* October 9, 1893; Mary K. Brewster obituary, ibid., January 7, 1951.

1. My Commission

1. "Mat" is Brewster's sister Martha.

2. Camp Brightwood was located in the northeast corner of the District of Columbia. Tom is Tom Boland, who was soon to marry Brewster's sister Martha.

3. Gen. George B. McClellan was commander of the Army of the Potomac through most of 1861–62.

4. Brewster often referred to his sisters Martha and Mary as Parthy and Pary.

5. Aunt Lu and Mr. Campbell are Brewster's aunt and uncle on his mother's side. They lived in western Virginia; Campbell and his two sons, Stuart and Brown (Brewster's first cousins), served in the Confederate army in Virginia. As subsequent letters will indicate, Aunt Lu would move between the lines during the course of the war, writing to and visiting Northampton, as well as her nephew at the front. This subplot in the letters is an interesting illustration of how American families had become divided by this war.

6. This offers an early example of Brewster's views on such topics as religious piety and women; it also demonstrates how camp life afforded him the time and opportunity to explore his own values in relation to new experience and compelled him to write.

7. Col. Henry S. Briggs, a lawyer from Pittsfield, was promoted to brigadier general in July 1862. He was wounded three times during the war. William R. Marsh, a hotel keeper from Northampton, commanded Company C until after the battle of Fair Oaks in June 1862.

8. This letter demonstrates not only Brewster's ambitions for a commission, but also the *local* nature of the organization of Civil War regiments.

9. Brewster refers to the Union invasion of Cape Hatteras, N. C., August 26 to 28, 1861. The successful establishment of this beachhead had propaganda effect out of proportion to its military value, as demonstrated by Brewster's rhetoric (E. B. Long, *The Civil War Day by Day: An Almanac* [New York, 1971], 111–12).

10. This is Jefferson Davis, president of the Confederacy and P.G.T. Beauregard, the Confederate general commanding in northern Virginia.

11. Cyrus N. Chamberlain was the regimental surgeon from Northampton.

12. This gives an early illustration of Brewster's views on duty, honor, and courage. Dying properly on the field of battle and in the eyes of one's *mother* made it honorable. See Linderman, *Embattled Courage*, 11–15, 25–27.

13. Here is another illustration of the local, community-based nature of regiments. This practice of pooling funds to send home the dead would change, of course, as casualties mounted.

14. Brig. Gen. Don Carlos Buell helped organize troops around Washington in late summer of 1861 before moving west to become commander of the Department of the Ohio (Mark M. Boatner, *The Civil War Dictionary* [New York, 1959], 96).

15. Brewster demonstrates a healthy suspicion of military and political propaganda.

16. Here Brewster expresses the first of many perceptions of a "savage" South, an enemy completely set apart. On soldiers' perceptions of their enemies, see Jimerson, *Private Civil War*, 124–79; Mitchell, *Civil War Soldiers*, 24–55.

17. Juba was a black man from Northampton who served as a cook in the Tenth Massachusetts and who may have worked with or for the Brewsters.

18. In the complete absence of censorship, the contents of Civil War soldiers' letters became very much part of community discussion. Brewster desperately wanted to see the local newspapers but feared reading about himself in their pages.

19. Hampden Park, Springfield, Mass., was where the Tenth camped in late June 1861.

20. This was President's Fast Day.

21. Henry W. Parsons, a farmer from Northampton, died of disease at Camp Brightwood, October 7, 1861. On soldiers' reactions to death see Mitchell, *Civil War Soldiers*, 60–64.

22. Kingsley and Cook are two of Brewster's neighbors and closest friends (at least at the outset) from Northampton. Calvin B. Kingsley, was wounded at Malvern Hill, July 1, 1862; John H. Cook was disabled from disease in July 1862 and later wounded at Petersburg, July 1864.

23. The deaf tailor-artist was John Donovan. One of his engravings is published in this volume. He died in Northampton in 1864 (Roe, *Tenth Regiment*, 355).

24. Brewster's reaction to this death is an interesting illustration of grief, maturity, and disillusionment. It may also reflect a certain yearning for a father he never knew.

25. The successful Union occupation of Beaufort, S.C., took place on November 9, 1861.

26. This marks the beginning of Brewster's lengthy discussion of the "contraband" issue—the protection, liberation, and sometimes exploitation of fugitive slaves by Union forces.

27. As slaveholder families fled the Port Royal area ahead of advancing Union forces, their thousands of ex-slaves stayed on at the old places. Brewster's observation about the

lack of blacks' loyalty to their masters would be borne out. See Willie Lee Rose, *Rehearsal for Reconstruction: The Port Royal Experiment* (Indianapolis, 1964).

28. This gives evidence of Brewster's image of himself as a have-not. He seems to reverse a variety of biblical doctrines here. See 1 Samuel 2:8; Matthew 5–7.

29. William H. Seward was secretary of state. Brewster's Aunt Lu was trying to get a pass through the lines from Seward.

30. Brewster thought of the army as a place for demarcation between men and women. He resented his married comrades bringing their wives to camp.

31. Brig. Gen. Erasmus Darwin Keyes was commander of the division in which the Tenth served from November 1861 to March 1862. He was later Fourth Corps commander (Boatner, *Civil War Dictionary*, 458).

32. Union soldiers frequently commented on the physical characteristics and former property values of the slaves they encountered. See Wiley, *Billy Yank*, 109–23; Glatthaar, *Forged in Battle*, 11–33.

33. On Union soldiers' drinking, see Wiley, *Billy Yank*, 252–54.

34. President Lincoln's Annual Message to Congress, December 1, 1861.

35. This detailed list of instructions is a striking example of just how much Brewster desired the commission and its requisite symbols.

36. See Stephen W. Sears, *George B. McClellan: The Young Napoleon* (New York, 1988), 79–81.

37. Such simple moments of irony—comic life next to tragic death—are common in war letters, and Brewster's are full of such experiences.

38. Brewster refers here to the "Trent Affair," which began on November 8, 1861, with the seizure of Confederate agents James Mason and John Slidell aboard the British steamer *Trent* in Havana harbor. Captain Charles Wilkes of the federal *San Jacinto* achieved a short-lived fame for his daring feat. The bravado toward England expressed by Brewster was also short-lived as the Lincoln administration eventually apologized to England and released Mason and Slidell.

39. This flourish of joy over the commission and his comrades' admiration marks just how important these elements of status and accomplishment were to Brewster.

2. My Contraband

1. Brewster's contraband was from Montgomery, Md. On Union officers taking blacks as servants or otherwise employing them, see Jimerson, *Private Civil War*, 77; Glatthaar, *Forged in Battle*, 4–6.

2. Lord Lyons was Great Britain's ambassador to the United States. Brewster's insinuation here is that the United States had "bowed" to the British during the recent "Trent Affair" (see chap. 1, n. 38).

3. The Union sea-borne expedition, under command of Brig. Gen. Ambrose Burnside, landed at Hatteras Inlet, N.C., January 13, 1862. In Kentucky a Union victory at Mill Springs on January 19 had cleared eastern Kentucky of Confederate forces (Long, *Day by Day*, 162).

4. The reference to Tennessee is to the surrender of Fort Henry, on the Tennessee River, to Ulysses S. Grant, February 6, 1862.

5. Brewster's is an exemplary statement by a soldier, yet to see real war, yearning for any kind of action to break the boredom of camp life.

6. On February 8, Burnside's forces won an important victory at Roanoke Island,

gaining control of Pamlico Sound, N. C. The surrender at Fort Donelson on the Cumberland River in Tennessee occurred on February 16. The successes of Roanoke Island and Forts Henry and Donelson were part of a much needed wave of good military news for the northern people during this winter (Long, *Day by Day*, 168–69, 171–72).

7. Such rejoicing was about the Union capture of Fort Donelson in the west.

8. Levi Elmer was an eighteen-year-old farmboy from Ashfield, Mass. This brief episode illustrates the vicious contradiction the soldiers encountered between their conception of courage and the ravages of disease. See Linderman, *Embattled Courage*, 115–17.

9. Brewster renamed his black servant. The significance of the name Harry Hastings is unclear. A Henry Hastings of Greenfield, Mass., served in Company E of the Tenth, but there is no reason to assume a connection. Freedmen changed their names as a means of asserting a new identity during the process of emancipation. That Brewster would do the same *for* his contraband is an indication both of the soldier's possessiveness and of his awareness that he was now part of great changes in the southern labor and racial system.

10. Blacks were commonly the brunt of humor and abuse in Union camps. See Mitchell, *Civil War Soldiers*, 118–19; Wiley, *Billy Yank*, 112–15. Such racist humor was practiced by abolitionist and nonabolitionist soldiers alike. A curious mix of bigotry and abolitionism, though odd to some modern readers, was quite typical of the time. On nineteenth-century racialist thought, see George M. Fredrickson, *The Black Image in the White Mind: The Debate on Afro-American Character and Destiny, 1817–1914* (New York, 1971).

11. Brewster's Aunt Lu received her "pass" from Secretary of State Seward and was attempting to make her way through the lines of both armies to reach her home in western Virginia.

12. This letter contains some of Brewster's most potent abolitionist rhetoric.

13. Here Brewster makes a clear statement of his seriousness and bitterness about the fugitive slave issue.

14. This is a soldier's statement on the nearly universal problem of confusion in war reporting.

15. Brewster gives here a harsh judgment on the freedpeople's abilities to fend for themselves. Brewster had lost "my contraband"; his attitude here is not unlike that of southern slaveholders who lost their slaves during the war.

3. Oh It Was a Fearful, Fearful Sight

1. Lt. Catesby Roger Jones was commander of the ironclad *Virginia* (*Merrimac*). The regiment was camped on Jones's estate (Boatner, *Dictionary*, 561; Roe, *Tenth Regiment*, 61).

2. Brewster's unit made a long march in the rain into northern Virginia. This maneuver was necessary because Confederate forces had begun to withdraw southward from Manassas (Roe, *Tenth Regiment*, 61–63).

3. The Tenth had embarked from Washington, March 27, 1862, aboard three boats; Hampton had been completely burned by Confederate forces under Gen. John B. Magruder.

4. McClellan would soon have more than 100,000 troops on the Peninsula, between the James and the Rappahannock rivers.

5. Brewster's comments about the *Monitor*, the Union ironclad, were indicative of the

widespread amazement at the new, strange looking vessels that had revolutionized naval warfare and caused considerable fear up and down the coast. See McPherson, *Battle Cry of Freedom,* 373–78.

6. Two days after Brewster wrote this letter the siege of Yorktown began. McClellan's massive army was opposed by only fifteen thousand Confederate troops; but rather than attack he built siege lines.

7. Brewster overestimated the Union army's numbers, but the sheer size of the operation would continue to amaze him.

8. Brewster used several spellings for "picket."

9. This is an order to check the barrels of guns for mud and water.

10. In this long letter we see Brewster's attention to detail. It is almost as though he wrote as a journalist for hometown consumption.

11. This is a reference to Comdr. Charles McCauley, the sixty-eight-year-old commander of the Norfolk navy yard at the outbreak of the war. On April 18, 1861, McCauley ordered the yard abandoned, its facilities burned, the cannon spiked, and the ships scuttled. These actions proved tragic and unnecessary, as Confederates captured the *Merrimac* and converted it to the C.S.S. *Virginia* (McPherson, *Battle Cry of Freedom,* 279–80).

12. Slaves and free blacks were widely employed as laborers on fortifications by the Confederacy—at this early stage and throughout the war. It is not likely that they were used as soldiers on picket. See James H. Brewer, *The Confederate Negro: Virginia's Craftsmen and Military Laborers, 1861–65* (Durham, N.C., 1969), 131–64.

13. These are the First U.S. Sharpshooters, a group of expert marksmen organized by Hiram Berdan, a mechanical engineer from New York City (Boatner, *Dictionary,* 61).

14. This is the first of Brewster's frequent statements of his resentment of civilian criticism of the Army of the Potomac from the North.

15. Gen. Irwin McDowell commanded the First Corps held in reserve in northern Virginia to protect Washington, D.C.

16. Blacks were not organized into Confederate regiments. Thousands worked on fortifications. Brewster's knowledge of this incident may have resulted from rumor or second-hand accounts.

17. Thaddeus Lowe founded balloon observation for the Union forces. Gen. Fitz-John Porter, who directed the Yorktown siege, was nearly carried away in one of Lowe's balloon experiments when the holding lines broke.

18. Brewster gives a New Englander's criticism of the southern landscape and lack of orderly development. Blaming the "curse of slavery" for alleged southern backwardness was common among Yankee troops.

19. The siege of Yorktown ended on April 3; Confederate forces eventually numbering nearly fifty-five thousand troops had stymied McClellan's army of twice that number for almost one month, buying time for the fortification of Richmond.

20. New Orleans fell to Union admiral David Farragut on April 25. On the same day Fort Macon, N.C., fell to Union forces (Long, *Day By Day,* 203–4).

21. This description of the battle of Williamsburg, which occurred on May 5, is an example of Brewster's attempts to write narratives of battle experience.

22. Soldiers have often found it useful or necessary to sustain a conception of their enemy as "savage" and wholly different from themselves.

23. Confederates evacuated Norfolk on May 9 and burned the *Merrimac.*

24. From daily experience, Brewster equates physical hardship with combat.

25. From this point, Brewster draws frequent contrasts between the romantic, home-front conception of war and the "hideous" reality he now understood.

26. Such a harsh attitude toward the South perhaps made it easier for Brewster to do his job. It also provides an interesting reflection on future northern attitudes toward Reconstruction policy.

27. From such passages one can begin to imagine what the moments and process of emancipation must have been like for the freedpeople. For blacks' own feelings during these encounters, see Leon F. Litwack, *Been in the Storm So Long: The Aftermath of Slavery* (New York, 1979), 64–291.

28. Brewster's occasional literary flair in describing spring mornings and in providing other striking contrasts of natural beauty and images of war gives evidence of his intelligence and sensitivity.

29. The Army of the Potomac's slow march up the Peninsula toward Richmond was underway. On May 25, the day of this letter, Stonewall Jackson scored one of the major victories of his Shenandoah Valley campaign at Winchester, Va.

30. It seems unlikely that they were actually "enjoined to depend" upon the bayonet, since Civil War soldiers only rarely actually fought with their bayonets.

31. Gen. Nathaniel P. Banks, commander of the Fifth Crops in the Shenandoah Valley, was out maneuvered and became the victim of most of Jackson's victories in May 1862.

32. Brewster offers an interesting perspective on McClellan's infamous caution and preparedness.

33. Brewster copes with chronic and debilitating diarrhea, worries about his "courage," and tries every remedy he can find.

34. Brewster refers to the allotment system whereby a designated amount of money was sent home on each pay day.

35. The battle of Fair Oaks (Seven Pines), May 31, 1862, was the first full-scale engagement between the Army of the Potomac and the Army of Northern Virginia. The Tenth suffered 124 casualties (27 dead) which represented one-fourth of those engaged (Roe, *Tenth Regiment*, 87–106). This letter was published in the *Hampshire Gazette.*

36. Gen. Samuel P. Heintzelman was commander of Third Corps and Gen. Charles Devens was commander of First Division, Fourth Corps. Devens was wounded three times during the war. He later served on the Massachusetts Supreme Court and as U.S. attorney general under President Rutherford B. Hayes (Boatner, *Dictionary*, 392, 238).

37. Brewster has begun to romanticize his own role in the battle.

38. Brewster accused Marsh of "cowardice before the enemy." Rather than allow Marsh to face court-martial, members of the Tenth (Brewster included) signed a petition allowing him to resign, which he did on June 14. Marsh is also the man Brewster blamed for preventing him from receiving a commission earlier, and for forcing the contraband issue to a proslavery conclusion (March 4, 5, 1862).

39. The guerrilla attack Brewster refers to is Gen. J. E. B. Stuart's "first ride around McClellan," June 12–15, 1862. Stuart's cavalry rode nearly 150 miles and destroyed considerable Union supplies.

40. Brewster was not among the vast majority of the Union soldiers who admired McClellan.

41. Some of these officer resignations were due to illness, and some to accusations of cowardice or improper discharge of duty (Roe, *Tenth Regiment*, 109).

42. This is probably another reference to J. E. B. Stuart's raids and is a further example of Brewster's growing contempt for southern civilians.

43. Brewster gives here an especially good example of his occasional flair for writing narrative and provides evidence that he knew some of his letters would be published.

44. Hiram A. Keith was acting adjutant during the Peninsula campaign (Roe, *Tenth Regiment*, 336).

45. One can only imagine how Brewster's mother managed to quiet her "nerves" while reading such passages.

46. Brewster describes here the battle of Oak Grove, the opening engagement of the Seven Days campaign, McClellan's decisive and unsuccessful attempt to capture Richmond.

47. The battle of Mechanicsville, June 26, 1862, was the first full-scale engagement of the Seven Days. Brewster's high spirits at the "good news" would soon be dashed as the Army of the Potomac retreated slowly southward toward the James River at great cost.

48. The fight was severe indeed. During the Seven Days, casualties were sixteen thousand Federals and nearly twenty thousand Confederates. Richmond did not fall, and a much longer war was in store for the country (Long, *Day By Day*, 235).

49. Lt. Col. Nelson Viall of the Second Rhode Island was temporary commander of the Tenth. Brewster's opinion of Viall was inconsistent with the rest of the regiment, as several officers petitioned Gov. John Andrew urging Viall's appointment as permanent commander (Roe, *Tenth Regiment*, 124).

50. Brewster refers to the battle of Malvern Hill, July 1, 1862. The Tenth was heavily engaged and suffered sixty-three casualties.

51. Brewster's startling lack of interest in seeing Lincoln is perhaps symptomatic of the level of his discouragement.

52. Brewster must have had the kind of relationship with his mother that allowed him to write her with a sense of humor and fatalism about his own death.

53. Brewster's attempt at narrative style presents a veteran's realism.

54. Frederick W. Clark was a twenty-year-old paper maker from Northampton. This kind of communication about soldiers' behavior was common in Civil War letters and could become deadly gossip in local communities.

55. The northern civilian imagination would be riveted to these letters; one day they were about the horror of battle and sickness, the next they depicted scenes of "all quiet" along the James.

56. This is an example of the pervasive value of "courage" and the need to pass its tests in battle. Such comments reflect how cruel and unforgiving this standard of courage was, especially early in the war.

57. Brewster gives a sarcastic characterization of McClellan's "strategic withdrawal" during the Seven Days.

58. Mr. Trumbull was editor of the *Hampshire Gazette*. Brewster was upset that some of his letters had been published in the newspaper, yet he probably had written some of them with publication in mind, and was, in this case, the victim of his own gossip.

59. The army and the war had become Brewster's community and vocation. Jealousies about rank and old ideological scores were constant issues, especially in the wake of major battles when due to casualties officers and ranks had to be reshuffled. As Brewster and his comrades were preoccupied with rivalry, sickness, and frustration, President Lincoln, on this day, read a preliminary draft of his Emancipation Proclamation to his cabinet.

60. Edward H. Stanley, a twenty-three-year-old baggage master from Northampton, died of typhoid, July 27, 1862. The scale of death he now observed evoked a spiritual response even from Brewster.

61. Dyspepsia is a common term for indigestion and sour disposition. Brewster seems to have been serious about his resignation. He did, however, actually receive a furlough and this letter was his last before he left for home.

62. Gen. John Pope commanded the newly created Union Army of Virginia, which occupied northern Virginia and tried to draw the Confederates away from the Peninsula.

63. Brewster may not have been fully accurate in his portrayal of Sherman's politics, but his contempt for McClellan's strategy and proslavery leanings was unusual in the Army of the Potomac.

64. This particular death seems to have had a profound impact on Brewster. The sermon that so impressed him was based on the lines from Luke that end with the verse: "Be ye therefore ready also: for the son of man cometh at an hour when ye think not."

4. I Don't Know Where It Is All to End

1. Brewster's anti-Irish prejudices come through clearly here. He was temporarily stationed in Cambridge, Mass., on detached recruiting service. The Tenth, meanwhile, was back in the Washington, D.C., area, in Alexandria, Va.

2. Brewster would later change his tune about conscription. On the Union draft, see James W. Geary, "Civil War Conscription in the North: A Historiographical Review," *Civil War History* 32, no. 3 (1986): 208–28.

3. Brewster refers to the battle of Antietam, September 17, 1862, near Sharpsburg, Md. That battle was the costliest single day of the Civil War. Antietam nevertheless proved less decisive than it might have been; Lee's forces were driven back into Virginia but were not destroyed. The Tenth was ordered to Harpers Ferry, Va., on September 17, only to be ordered back to the Sharpsburg area by the next day. Mercifully, they missed Antietam's worst hours (Roe, *Tenth Regiment,* 136–38).

4. This remarkable journey with new recruits took Brewster on a whirlwind trip throughout the eastern war zone in the aftermath of the battle of Antietam.

5. Eleven officers in the Tenth resigned in bitter protest of the appointment of Maj. Dexter F. Parker as commander of the regiment. All eleven were tried and cashiered in November 1862 (Roe, *Tenth Regiment,* 139–41).

6. The discouragement evident here indicates why a new vision of the war's purpose—emancipation—was so necessary for northern morale in the autumn of 1862. The previous day, November 4, the Democratic party made important gains in state and congressional elections. Also on November 5, Lincoln once and for all removed McClellan from command of the Army of the Potomac. Brewster and his regiment did not participate in the emotional farewell to McClellan.

7. Gen. Darius Nash Couch took command of Second Corps, October 7, 1862.

8. This letter is remarkable for its account of the winter sufferings of soldiers, as well as of the low state of morale among Union troops in late 1862.

9. Brewster's physical sufferings were probably typical, but he was so sick during this December campaign that his service in the war almost ended.

10. Brewster worried constantly about the imputation of cowardice, which probably only aggravated his physical suffering.

11. Psychologically and physically, Brewster was perhaps at the lowest point in his service.

12. Federal forces occupied Fredericksburg on December 11 and the disastrous battle of Fredericksburg took place on December 13. These were the "sounds" that tortured

Brewster's conscience. There were 12,653 Union and 5,309 Confederate casualties. As Brewster wrote this letter on the fifteenth, the humiliated Army of the Potomac withdrew across the Rappahannock River, defeated once again by Lee.

13. It is likely that Brewster's condition was made worse by these drugs. On disease and the inadequacy of medical care for Civil War soldiers, see Robertson, *Soldiers Blue and Gray,* 145–69.

14. This is the remarkable lament of a man driven by the tradition of manliness, but who was physically and emotionally beaten by its demands.

15. Brewster was appointed adjutant on December 21, 1862 (Roe, *Tenth Regiment,* 338).

16. Henry L. Eustis, forty-three years old at this time, was a graduate of West Point and professor of science at Harvard. He was eventually promoted to brigadier general in September 1863. Eustis seems to have been Brewster's ideal of the gentleman-scholar-soldier, and his reputation was not unlike the modern reputation of Joshua Lawrence Chamberlain of the Twentieth Maine, who has gained fame through Michael Shaara's novel, *The Killer Angels,* and Ken Burns's PBS film series, "The Civil War."

17. Brewster's estimate of Burnside would become a generally accepted attitude.

18. Such disdain for politicians was common among soldiers at this point in the war, when there was no end in sight. Brewster's estimate of his own political activity may have been a bit embellished.

19. Brewster justifiably worried that his gossip about regimental intrigue would become altogether too public. This also contains an honest expression of a soldier's combination of devotion and despair.

20. Brewster demonstrates his lack of compassion for deserters and the bounty system.

21. The Army of the Potomac was in winter quarters at Falmouth, Va.

22. This was Brewster's last letter before, indeed, receiving a furlough to go home.

23. This is a mention of one of many attempts by U. S. Grant's forces to surround and take Vicksburg, Miss.

5. We Gained Great Glory

1. Brewster appears to have returned to Virginia and his regiment in the third week of April.

2. This letter describes the Tenth's role in the disastrous battle of Chancellorsville, May 1–3, 1863.

3. Brewster was never wounded in battle, despite his many experiences under fire. This simple statement of pride indicates that there were many ways soldiers claimed a badge of courage.

4. Brewster describes the phase of the battle of Chancellorsville on May 3, fought near Salem Church, Va.

5. Chancellorsville was another humiliating defeat for the Army of the Potomac. Yet, Brewster's letter is remarkable because its focus is almost entirely upon individual honor, pride, and "glory." The war had become as much a personal test as it was a matter of victories or defeats. After four horrible days of battle, Brewster could now declare: "I like it very much." The Tenth suffered ten killed and fifty-six wounded at Chancellorsville (Roe, *Tenth Regiment,* 188–89).

6. "Tophet" refers to an ancient shrine south of Jerusalem where human sacrifices were performed (Jer. 7:31). It is used as a synonym for hell.

7. Union troops—both before battle and as wounded after battle—were often guided by southern blacks. See Jimerson, *Private Civil War,* 80–81.

8. Brewster's comments about death from wounds and amputations roughly bear out official casualty statistics. Of the 110,100 Union soldiers killed in battle, 67,088 died in battle, and 43,012 died later of their wounds. See Frederick H. Dyer, *A Compendium of the War of the Rebellion* (Des Moines, Ia., 1908), 12, 18; Long, *Day by Day,* 710.

9. This rumor was true. Lee's army would begin its northern invasion on June 3 through the Shenandoah Valley.

10. This reconnaissance action took place on June 5. The bulk of Lee's army had begun its invasion northward.

11. We get here an interesting look at Brewster's views on women. In all likelihood, this woman was Dr. Mary Edwards Walker, a graduate of Syracuse Medical College and one of America's first female surgeons. Walker abandoned her Cincinnati medical practice and served three years as a nurse in the Union army. In 1864 she received a commission as a surgeon in an Ohio regiment. She was later captured, spent four months in southern prisons, and received the Congressional Medal of Honor. Walker was famous for wearing men's clothing and for her women's rights activism after the war. See *Notable American Women, 1607–1950: A Biographical Dictionary,* ed. Edward T. James, Janet Wilson James, Paul S. Boyer, 3 vols. (Cambridge, Mass., 1971), 3:532–33.

12. The Tenth left its camps on the south side of the Rappahannock on June 12. This forced march was in pursuit of Lee, who had invaded Maryland and Pennsylvania. It would culminate at Gettysburg (Roe, *Tenth Regiment,* 198–99).

13. Fatalism or faith was about all a soldier could rely upon while enduring the anxiety of the forced march to Gettysburg. Brewster's unit marched one hundred miles in four days to reach southern Pennsylvania by July 1. They marched thirty-four miles in twenty-four hours to reach Gettysburg on the afternoon of July 2. They were held in reserve on July 3 (Roe, *Tenth Regiment,* 205–11). The detail and narrative qualities of Brewster's letters make it clear that Roe's regimental history, *Tenth Regiment,* was based, in part, upon Brewster's accounts of events.

14. Brewster is attempting to describe the aftermath of the three-day battle of Gettysburg, July 1–3, 1863. Lee's army retreated toward Maryland, as every available dwelling in the Gettysburg area was used as a hospital for the twenty-three thousand Union and twenty-eight thousand Confederate casualties.

15. Brewster describes the famous artillery bombardment that preceded "Pickett's charge," the disastrous Confederate infantry assault on July 3.

16. This is an occasion when Brewster wrote with compassion for his enemy. "Those blue eyes" made a lasting impression.

17. Brewster reacts to the staggering losses at Gettysburg. The First Minnesota lost, dead or wounded, 224 of the 262 men engaged; the Twenty-sixth North Carolina lost, dead or wounded, 708 of the 880 men engaged.

18. The bulk of Lee's army would escape across the Potomac on the night of July 13 (the day following this letter). The decisive battle Union general George G. Meade was planning in Maryland never took place.

19. This lament about the escape of Lee's army into Virginia was one also heard in the Lincoln administration and across the North.

20. This is a veteran volunteer's anger and bravado about the New York City draft riots, which occurred July 13–15, 1863. The federal draft began in New York on July 11. See

Iver Bernstein, *The New York City Draft Riots: Their Significance for American Society and Politics in the Age of the Civil War* (New York, 1988).

21. Some 46,347 men were drafted by federal conscription, and another 116,188 furnished substitutes or paid the $300 exemption. The federal draft provided only about 6 percent of all Union forces (Long, *Day by Day,* 707–8).

22. Frederick A. Barton, a minister from Springfield, was the chaplain of the Tenth Regiment. "Gobbled up" was Brewster's term for capture, and his is language that fit the realities of modern war.

23. Here Brewster struggles to justify the pillaging of civilian property.

24. Here is a remarkable lament about the sheer duration of the war from a veteran's more than two-year perspective.

25. Brewster offers an example of his half-real, half-forced contempt for southern women.

26. John Singleton Mosby was the guerrilla commander of the Confederate "Partisan Rangers" in Virginia, 1863–65.

27. Libby was a Confederate prison in Richmond; Ralph O. Ives, the captured captain, spent a full year in prison.

6. If My Life Is Only Spared

1. Here is an interesting juxtaposition of desolation and civilization in Brewster's imagination.

2. Brewster frequently demonstrated this mixture of emotions: longing for and fear of civilian life. On this future question of veteran reconciliation to civilian society, see McConnell, "Who Joined the Grand Army?" 139–40.

3. This was the battle of Rappahannock Station, November 7, 1863. Brewster describes the death of his horse Tommy with as much compassion as that of the death of any of his comrades.

4. This was Gen. John Sedgwick, commander of Sixth Corps. He was killed by a sharpshooter, May 9, 1864, at Spotsylvania.

5. Gen. David Allen Russell was commander of the third brigade, first division, Sixth Corps. He was eventually killed in the Shenandoah Valley, September 19, 1864. In Russell, Brewster seems to have found an ideal of blind, honorable bravery. Like most "heroes" of this war Sedgwick and Russell were dead by the end of 1864.

6. Brewster's statement is an especially harsh example of the sense of distance between soldiers and civilians.

7. These are Brewster's Confederate cousins.

8. The region west of Fredericksburg and south of the Rapidan was known as the "Wilderness." Brewster seemed ever ready to justify the pillaging of southern property.

9. Some of Brewster's letters during this stage of the war are a chronicle of the destruction of the property and landscape of Virginia. On the destruction and looting of southern property as a function of "total war," see Mitchell, *Civil War Soldiers,* 132–47.

10. This chaplain was Francis B. Perkins, a graduate of Williams College and Andover Theological Seminary. In a matter of a few days, Perkins managed to build a seventeen by twenty-three-foot walled edifice in which to conduct services. Unfortunately, an impious Major Parker forced the chaplain, temporarily, to allow the chapel to be used for bayonet drill (Roe, *Tenth Regiment,* 243–44).

11. Brewster left on February 11 for a thirty-five-day furlough at home in Northampton.

7. Terrible, Terrible Business

1. By the spring of 1864 Brewster had a fully developed veteran's mentality. Nothing could surprise him, and he felt more at home at the front than anywhere else. His guarded suspicion of Grant was typical of members of the Army of the Potomac.

2. Brewster exhibits his anxiety about what he would do in civilian life after the war. This passage demonstrates how much social class determined his attitudes.

3. As Brewster contemplated the financial circumstances of his family and his postwar employment prospects he seems to have fallen into despair and self-pity.

4. Then as now, April meant baseball. From April 13 to 30, the Tenth played at least six baseball games against the Second Rhode Island or the Thirty-seventh Massachusetts. The only game the Tenth lost was one played exclusively by officers on April 28 (Roe, *Tenth Regiment*, 251–53).

5. The volatile emotions of this and other letters written during spring 1864 were due, no doubt, to an awareness of two facts: that only two months remained in his service; and that a desperate new campaign was about to be launched.

6. Brewster refers to the Confederate capture of Plymouth, N.C., April 18–20, 1864, and the capture or killing of some twenty-eight hundred Union troops. The Fort Pillow (Tenn.) massacre occurred on April 12, 1864. Confederate troops under Gen. Nathan Bedford Forrest forced a surrender of Union forces. Two hundred and sixty-two of the 557 federals were black troops. After the surrender, scores of Union soldiers, especially blacks, were, according to considerable testimony, "massacred." See Albert Castel, "The Fort Pillow Massacre: A Fresh Look at the Evidence," *Civil War History* 4, no. 1 (March 1958); and Glatthaar, *Forged in Battle*, 156–58.

7. Although he escaped without serious wounds from three years of war, Brewster received a black eye playing baseball on the eve of the Wilderness-Spotsylvania campaign.

8. Such great expectation was fully justified, given what was ahead. The massive Army of the Potomac (122,000 men) crossed the Rapidan River on May 4 and the bloody summer campaign began.

9. Situated now near Spotsylvania Court House, Brewster had just survived the battle of the Wilderness, May 5–6, and the beginning of the Spotsylvania campaign. May 11 afforded a brief lull in the constant offensive by Grant's army, which was moving relentlessly to the left and south toward Richmond. The next dawn brought the worst day of the war.

10. Brewster describes with remarkable accuracy the battle known as the "Bloody Angle of Spotsylvania," May 12, 1864, where twenty-four Union brigades attacked approximately three hundred yards of Confederate entrenchments. Some of the bloodiest combat of the war occurred at Spotsylvania that day. Union casualties on May 12 alone were sixty-eight hundred men (Long, *Day By Day*, 499–500).

11. Sidney S. Williams from Northampton was captured at Spotsylvania on May 12. He was imprisoned, first at Andersonville, Ga., and then at Florence, S.C., escaped twice, and, after some harrowing weeks in the southern countryside, finally found safety with Sherman's army, February 22, 1865 (Roe, *Tenth Regiment*, 399). Brewster and Williams became brothers-in-law in 1868 when Brewster married Anna B. Williams.

12. Brewster is speaking of Gen. William Tecumseh Sherman's campaign in northern Georgia, during May 1864.

13. Brewster describes the aftermath of the "Bloody Angle" at Spotsylvania. For the best historical accounts of the fighting at Spotsylvania, see Bruce Catton, *A Stillness at Appomattox* (Garden City, N.Y., 1954), 126–30; and William D. Matter, *If It Takes All Summer: The Battle of Spotsylvania* (Chapel Hill, 1988). Brewster's description of the scene confirms many other accounts of that horrifying day and place. As Catton wrote: "it was precisely here that the war came down to its darkest cockpit. It could never be any worse than this because men could not possibly imagine or do anything worse" (p. 126).

14. Official War Department records show 141 Union executions for desertion. It cannot be determined whether this episode is one of those recorded. Brewster describes this ugly drama as if it had become commonplace. See Wiley, *Billy Yank*, 205–7.

15. Brewster sent this casualty list for publication in the *Hampshire Gazette*. To understand the local impact of the war on communities like Northampton and other towns in western Massachusetts, one need only look at such a list from a single week of battle.

16. Artemus Ward (pen name of Charles Farrar Browne, 1834–67), popular journalist and humorist, wrote for *Cleveland Plain Dealer, Vanity Fair,* and *Punch.*

17. The three-year enlistments of many regiments were about to expire.

18. Here Brewster expresses the bigotry, suspicion, and curiosity that was representative of many white soldiers toward the fighting capacities of black troops. See Glatthaar, *Forged in Battle*, 169–206.

19. This is a remarkable image, full of symbolism, for the destruction that Yankee troops were wreaking upon so many southern plantations and farms.

20. Surrounded by so much death, Brewster seems to have felt compelled to describe it as best he could.

21. This is an apt short history of the Army of the Potomac.

22. Here is a telling description of Grant's tactics and of his willingness to sustain enormous casualties, given from a veteran's perspective on the trench warfare of the summer of 1864.

23. The location was more commonly known as Cold Harbor. The disastrous battle of Cold Harbor, where the Union army suffered approximately thirteen thousand casualties, occurred from June 1 to 3.

24. This illustrates Brewster's mixed assessment of the capabilities of black troops, as well as the dangers they faced. He expresses his prejudices, but at the same time admits his ignorance. The all-black fourth division of the Ninth Corps guarded the rear of the Union army until their first action at Petersburg on July 30, 1864.

25. Rarely has a veteran soldier's acute fear of civilian life been better expressed.

26. What remained of the Tenth Massachusetts departed from City Point, on the James River, on June 21, for their return home to Springfield and Northampton.

8. Living among Strangers

1. Brewster was officially discharged on July 1 in Springfield, Mass. He reenlisted to be a recruiter of black troops and was appointed a captain by Massachusetts governor John A. Andrew on July 23, 1864. Photocopies of the discharge and reappointment are in the possession of James Parsons of Northampton, Mass., obtained from Jonathan Allured, Brewster's grandson.

2. Gen. Edward A. Wild, a graduate of Harvard Medical College, had served with the Turks in the Crimean War. He helped recruit black troops for Massachusetts in 1863 and commanded the "African Brigade," Tenth and Eighteenth Corps, a unit of black infantry (Boatner, *Dictionary*, 919).

3. Brewster had reenlisted, in part, out of a sense of diminished alternatives; he needed a job. But his living arrangements in Norfolk make a remarkable contrast to the bomb shelters and trenches he had left near Cold Harbor and Petersburg.

4. Many of Brewster's prejudices remained intact, in spite of the transformations he was helping to bring about.

5. Brewster contemplated getting a "substitute" for his brother-in-law, Thomas Boland.

6. Brewster's motives as a recruiter seemed to become more and more mercenary.

7. Brewster's soldiering was over; but he was uneasy about his ability as a civilian to make a living.

8. This is a demonstration of either Brewster's loneliness or a certain contempt for women at this stage of his life, or of both.

9. Brewster refers to Gen. Philip Sheridan's campaign in the Shenandoah Valley, which ran from Aug. 7, 1864 to March 1865.

10. The recruiting of black troops, by whatever means, had run its course in the Norfolk region by late 1864. A considerable degree of impressment (varying levels of forced enlistment) had been practiced in eastern Virginia. See Berlin et al., *Freedom*, ser. 2, 138–40.

11. Among the many ironies Brewster observed in these final letters was this difference in attitudes toward killing in wartime and in peace.

12. Brewster echoed the widespread praise that existed for black troops by the fall of 1864, as they had now participated in many battles. Nearly one of every eight Union soldiers in the siege of Petersburg was black (Glatthaar, *Forged in Battle*, 167).

13. Brewster anticipates Lincoln's reelection. This was the first time in history that a republic conducted a national election in the midst of civil war. Lincoln won large majorities in the Union armies in spite of the popularity of his opponent, the former general George McClellan.

14. Sardonic to the end, Brewster nevertheless performed his duty. The store clerk turned soldier now turned clerk of another kind again, writing love letters for freed slaves. The last months of the Civil War produced countless such ironies.

15. There is no evidence that Brewster actually brought a black servant back to Northampton.

Epilogue

1. Mark De Wolfe Howe, ed., *The Occasional Speeches of Justice Oliver Wendell Holmes, Jr.* (Cambridge, Mass., 1962), 76. In his collection of documents and memoirs of the Civil War, Henry Steele Commager cautions about the reliability of war reminiscences and letters, which were often revised by families, especially, in his judgment, by the *daughters* of veterans. See Henry Steele Commager, ed., *The Blue and the Gray: The Story of the Civil War as Told by Participants* (1950; New York, 1982), xlii–xliv.

2. This longest of Brewster's letters records his experiences in the Seven Days battles near Richmond, especially the role of his regiment in the battles of Savage's Station on June 29 and Malvern Hill on July 1. I have dated the first portion of this letter July 4,

because that appears to be the first day Brewster could have found a sufficient lull in activity in order to write between Malvern Hill on July 1 and the next portion of the letter, July 5.

3. Such prose, especially the use of present tense and such a romantic narrative style, may be an example of Mary Kate Brewster's re-creations.

4. Brewster and his daughter, one on the battlefield in Virginia in 1862 and the other on a ship at sea in 1893, were both struggling for the "power of the poet."

5. This offers a striking commentary of a young man's discovery of the "curious" combination of fear and thrill in battle.

6. Writing from winter quarters in Falmouth, Va., Brewster offers a romantic characterization of what may seem "glorious" to distant observers back home. His rapid shift from purple prose to the reality of mud and loneliness demonstrates perhaps that only by mixing playfulness and anguish could he confront his experience of war.

7. The Army of the Potomac was on a long march in pursuit of Lee's army as it invaded Pennsylvania.

8. This passage represents some of Brewster's most romantic prose. He may have written it himself, but it is likely that this is a case of his daughter's embellishments. By the 1890s it was in images such as these that thousands of Americans chose to remember the "glorious subject" of the Civil War.

9. Brewster writes a New Englander's lament about Thanksgiving dinner. One can imagine Brewster's family reading aloud a letter like this one sometime after the holiday. In the diary she kept on her voyage to Australia, Mary Kate Brewster made the following entry for November 30, 1893: "Thanksgiving. a.m. Read, wrote, Looked over Papa's letters of Nov. '61, '62, '63 for an article for our paper on three Thanksgivings in the army." Whatever she did to the letters in her journals, she clearly found great stimulation for her imagination. Mary Kate Brewster, "Log Book" (diary, 1893–94), 21, Brewster Family Papers, Sophia Smith Collection, Smith College.

10. We have here a veteran's mature editorial about the "eagerness" of men for battle.

DATE DUE

BRODART, CO.   Cat. No. 23-221-003